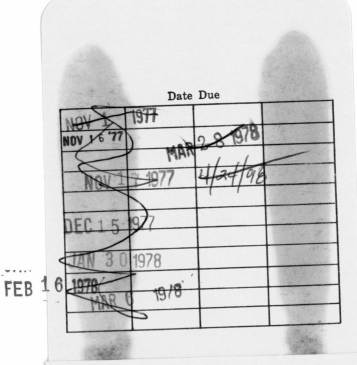

NASA SP-345

Evolution of the Solar System

Hannes Alfvén

University of California, San Diego
and
Royal Institute of Technology
Stockholm, Sweden

Gustaf Arrhenius

Scripps Institution of Oceanography
University of California, San Diego

Scientific and Technical Information Office   1976
NATIONAL AERONAUTICS AND SPACE ADMINISTRATION
Washington, D.C.

Alfvén, Hannes, 1908–
    Evolution of the solar system.

    (NASA SP ; 345)
    Includes bibliographical references and index.
    1. Solar   system.   I. Arrhenius,   Gustaf.   II. Title.   III. Series: United   States.
National Aeronautics and Space Administration. NASA SP ; 345.
QB501.A528   521'.54   76–20779

For sale by the Superintendent of Documents,
U.S. Government Printing Office, Washington, D.C. 20402
Price $11.00   Stock Number 033-000-06613-6

PREFACE

The present analysis of the origin and evolution of the solar system represents a fusion of two initially independent approaches to the problem. One of us (Alfvén) started from a study of the physical processes (1942, 1943a, 1946; summarized in a monograph in 1954), and the other (Arrhenius) from experimental studies of plasma-solid reactions and from chemical and mineralogical analyses of meteorites and lunar and terrestrial samples. Joined by the common belief that the complicated events leading to the present structure of the solar system can be understood only by an integrated chemical-physical approach, we have established a collaboration at the University of California, San Diego (UCSD), in La Jolla, during the last seven years. Our work, together with that of many colleagues in La Jolla, Stockholm, and elsewhere, has resulted in a series of papers describing the general principles of our joint approach, experimental results, and model approximations for some of the most important processes.

The present volume is a summary of our results, which we have tried to present in such a form as to make the physics understandable to chemists and the chemistry understandable to physicists. Our primary concern has been to establish general constraints on applicable models. Hence we have avoided complex mathematical treatment in cases where approximations are sufficient to clarify the general character of the processes.

The work was made possible by grants from the Planetology Program Office and the Lunar and Planetary Program Division, Office of Space Science, National Aeronautics and Space Administration Headquarters. Their longstanding help and encouragement—particularly that of Steven E. Dwornik and Robert P. Bryson—have been of crucial importance, and we are grateful also to Maurice Dubin for support. Our thanks are also extended to Homer E. Newell, John Pomeroy, Ernst Stuhlinger, and Dan M. Herman for their continuing active interest in this undertaking. In view of NASA's association through the years with the preparation of this study, we are particularly gratified to have it published (at the initiative of Steven E. Dwornik) as a NASA Special Publication.

The molding of the material into an organized and critically edited form is due to the dedicated and competent effort of Dawn S. Rawls. We also owe much gratitude to a number of our colleagues who have contributed in many ways to this work, particularly Bibhas R. De, Wing-Huen Ip, and Asoka Mendis at UCSD in La Jolla, and Nicolai Herlofson, Bo Lehnert, Carl-Gunne Fälthammar, Lars Danielsson, and Lennart Lindberg at the Royal Institute of Technology in Stockholm. Continual encouragement and advice from Professors Henry G. Booker, James R. Arnold, and William B. Thompson at UCSD have also been of importance in our work.

CONTENTS

PART B
THE ACCRETION OF CELESTIAL BODIES

PART C
PLASMA AND CONDENSATION

PART D
PHYSICAL AND CHEMICAL STRUCTURE OF THE SOLAR SYSTEM

PART E
SPECIAL PROBLEMS

1

INTRODUCTION

1.1 FUNDAMENTAL APPROACHES TO THE PROBLEM

How our solar system was formed is a question that today attracts as much interest as the problem of the Creation did in the past. In many theories advocated today, the basic approach to this problem remains remarkably similar to what it was in ancient times: The author hypothetically assumes some specific primordial configuration of matter and then deduces a process from which some significant features of the present state emerge. When the basic assumption is unrelated to actually observed phenomena, chances are that the result will be the same as over thousands of years: a model which, by definition, is a myth, although it may be adorned with differential equations in accordance with the requirements of modern times.

A realistic attempt to reconstruct the early history of the solar system must necessarily be of a different character. It is essential to choose a procedure which reduces speculation as much as possible and connects the evolutionary models as closely as possible to experiment and observation. Because no one can know a priori what happened four to five billion years ago, we must start from the present state of the solar system and, step by step, reconstruct increasingly older periods. This *actualistic principle,* which emphasizes reliance on observed phenomena, is the basis for the modern approach to the geological evolution of the Earth; "the present is the key to the past." This principle should also be used in the study of the solar system. The purpose of this monograph is to show how this can be done.

We proceed by establishing which experimentally verified laws are of controlling significance in the space environment. To achieve this, we must rely on the rapidly increasing information on extraterrestrial processes that modern space research is providing, and on laboratory studies of these processes under controlled conditions. If the large body of available empirical knowledge is interpreted strictly in terms of these laws, the speculative ingredient of cosmogonic theories can be significantly reduced.

When analyzing the origin and evolution of the solar system, we should recognize that its present structure is a result of a long series of complicated processes. The final aim is to construct theoretical partial models of all these processes. However, there is often a choice between different partial models which a priori may appear equally acceptable. Before the correct choice can be made, it is necessary to define a framework of boundary conditions which these models must satisfy. We consider this to be a main task of this monograph.

1.2 PLANETARY SYSTEM—SATELLITE SYSTEMS

Theories of the formation of the solar system must also account for the satellite systems in a manner consistent with the way in which the planetary system is treated. In certain respects the satellite systems provide even more significant information about evolutionary processes than does the planetary system, partly because of the uncertainty about the state of the early Sun.

Observing that the highly regular systems of Jupiter, Saturn, and Uranus are in essential respects similar to the planetary system, we aim at a *general theory of the formation of secondary bodies around a primary body*. This approach contrasts with that of the Laplacian-type theories in which the postulated processes for planetary formation fail to explain the structure of the satellite systems. Although it is desirable to avoid excessive terminology, we will frequently make brief reference to this specific aspect of our analytical method by using the term *hetegony* (from the Greek ἑταῖρος, companion, and γεννάω, generate).

The theoretical framework we try to construct should, consequently, be applicable both to the formation of satellite systems around a planet and to the formation of planets around the Sun. Through this requirement, we introduce the postulate that these processes are essentially analogous. Our analysis supports this postulate as reasonable. Indeed, we find evidence that the formation of the regular systems of secondary bodies around a primary body—either the Sun or a planet—depends in a unique way on only two parameters of the primary body, its mass and spin. It is also necessary to assume that the central bodies were magnetized, but the strength of the magnetic field does not appear explicitly; it must only surpass a certain limit.

1.3 FIVE STAGES IN THE EVOLUTION

Applying the actualistic and hetegonic principles, we find that the evolutionary history of the solar system can be understood in terms of five stages, in part overlapping in time:

(1) Most recently—during the last three to four billion years—a *slow evolution* of the primeval planets, satellites, and asteroids which produced

the present state of the bodies in the solar system. By studying this latest phase of the evolution (post-accretional evolution), we prepare a basis for reconstructing the state established by earlier processes.

(2) Preceding this stage, an *accretional evolution* of condensed grains, moving in Kepler orbits to form planetesimals which, by continuing accretion, grow in size. These planetesimals are the embryonic precursors of the bodies found today in the solar system. By clarifying the accretional processes, we attempt to reconstruct the chemical and dynamic properties of the early population of grains.

(3) To account for grains moving in Kepler orbits around the Sun and the protoplanets, *transfer of angular momentum* from these primary bodies to the surrounding medium must have occurred in the stage of evolution preceding accretion.

(4) *Emplacement of gas and dust* to form a medium around the magnetized central bodies in the regions where the planet and satellite groups later accreted.

(5) *Formation of the Sun* as the first primary body to accrete from the source cloud of the solar system.

1.4 PROCESSES GOVERNING THE EVOLUTIONARY STAGES

Each of the five main stages in the sequence discussed above was governed by physical and chemical processes which may be characterized in the following way:

1.4.1 Post-Accretional Evolution; Effects of Tides and Resonances

The most striking result of the analysis of this stage, which has lasted for about four billion years, is that there has been very little change. The Earth-Moon system and the Neptune-Triton system have evolved due to tidal effects, but otherwise the primary-secondary systems exhibit a high degree of stability. This high degree of stability is shown not only by the dynamic state of planets and satellites, but also by certain structures in the asteroidal belt and the Saturnian rings. The complicated pattern of resonances between the bodies in the solar system is probably a major cause of this stability.

Comets and meteoroids are exceptions; they are in a state of rapid change. Information on the changes in these populations can be derived from studies of their orbital characteristics and to some extent can be inferred from the structure and irradiation history of meteorites and lunar materials.

An evolution, although much slower, has also taken place in the asteroid belt, resulting in changes in asteroidal jet streams and families.

1.4.2 Accretional Evolution; Viscosity-Perturbed Kepler Motion and the Evolution of Protosatellites and Protoplanets From Jet Streams

Since the planets and, even more so, the satellites are too small to have formed by gravitational collapse, planetesimal accretion is the only feasible theory of formation; that is, the planets and satellites have been formed by accretion of small bodies (planetesimals and, initially, single grains). The conditions in those regions of space where planets or satellites formed must, at a certain stage in development, have borne similarities to the present state in the asteroidal region. Studies of the present asteroidal region consequently provide information on the processes governing planet and satellite accretion. The isochronism of asteroidal and planetary spin periods gives strong support to the planetesimal model which leads to a promising theory of spin.

The phenomenon basic to a study of accretion of planets and satellites is the Kepler motion perturbed by viscosity (mutual collisions between bodies). It is surprising that in all earlier cosmogonic theories the basic properties of such a state of motion have been misunderstood. It has been believed that a population of mutually colliding grains necessarily diffuse out into a larger volume. This is not correct. Because the collisions are essentially inelastic and the collision frequency less than the orbital frequency, the diffusion of a population in Kepler motion is *negative,* meaning that the orbits become increasingly similar.

This negative diffusion leads to formation of *jet streams,* self-focusing streams of bodies orbiting around a gravitating central body. Such jet streams are likely to constitute an intermediate stage in the accretion of celestial bodies.

Focused streams observed today in the asteroidal region and meteor streams may be held together by the same effect. If this is confirmed, studies of the essential properties of jet streams under present-day conditions could reduce the speculative element of hetegonic theories.

1.4.3 Processes Relating to the Angular Momentum Transfer and Emplacement

The motion of a dispersed medium under space conditions can obviously not be treated without hydromagnetics and plasma physics as a basis. The criterion for justified neglect of electromagnetic effects in the treatment of a problem in gas dynamics is that the characteristic hydromagnetic parameter L (defined in eq. (15.1.1)) is much less than unity. In cosmic problems involving interplanetary and interstellar phenomena, L is usually of the order 10^{15}–10^{20}. In planetary ionospheres it reaches unity in the E layer. Planetary atmospheres and hydrospheres are the only domains in the universe where a nonhydromagnetic treatment of fluid dynamic problems is justified.

Nonetheless, the misconception is still common that if only a cosmic cloud is "cold" enough, and stellar radiation is absorbed in its outer layer, a nonhydromagnetic treatment is legitimate. In the interior of cold, dark clouds, the factor L is certainly *much smaller* than in most other regions in space, but ionization by cosmic radiation, by natural radioactivity, and especially by currents associated with magnetic fields which are not curl-free is still sufficient to make it *much larger* than unity. L may possibly reach values as low as 10^6 in such environments, but this still means that by ignoring hydromagnetic processes one neglects effects which are many orders of magnitude larger than those considered.

If we assume that the formation of the solar system took place in a cloud of the same general character as the dark clouds observed today, we can get observational indications of the minimum possible effects of hydromagnetic and plasma processes in the hetegonic nebulae. Recent observations of strong magnetic fields and of radio emission from complex molecules in certain dark clouds give clues to the state of matter in these clouds.

In an early nebula where, according to all theories, dispersed matter was dissipating large amounts of energy, the inevitable hydromagnetic effects must have been still more pronounced. A theory of the formation of the solar system is obviously meaningless unless it is based on modern plasma physics and magnetohydrodynamics.

Our analysis shows the controlling phenomena during the emplacement of matter and transfer of angular momentum in the circumsolar region to be as follows:

(1) *Critical velocity,* a plasma phenomenon which has been studied extensively in the laboratory and also analyzed theoretically. It defines the conditions under which neutral gas falling toward a magnetized central body becomes ionized and stopped. The phenomenon is sufficiently well understood for its importance in cosmic processes to be recognized.

The application of the critical velocity phenomenon suggests an explanation of the mass distribution in the planetary system as well as in the satellite systems. It further accounts for some of the processes of chemical differentiation indicated by bulk properties of planets and satellites and by the interstellar medium.

(2) *Partial corotation,* a state of revolution of a plasma surrounding a rotating magnetized body. Evidence for the basic role of partial corotation

in transfer of angular momentum in the primordial planetary and solar nebular processes is found in the detailed structure of the Saturnian rings and the asteroidal belt.

Transfer of angular momentum from a central body to a surrounding medium is a process which is fundamental in the formation of secondary bodies revolving around their primary. This process can be studied by extrapolation of present-day conditions in the magnetosphere and in the solar atmosphere. In fact, the electric current system in the auroral region is now known to be of the same type as is necessary for the transfer of angular momentum from a central magnetized body to a surrounding plasma. Hence, this primordial process can be derived from processes now studied by space probes.

(3) *Formation and plasma capture of grains.* The solid grains in the solar system may have formed by condensation from the nebular plasma emplaced in the circumsolar region. But it is also possible that much of the solid material is interstellar dust condensed in other regions.

Infall of such preexisting grains may have been an important process contributing material to the early solar system. This is suggested by the present-day distribution of dust in dark clouds in interstellar space and possibly by some of the chemical features of the material preserved in meteorites. Since grains in space are necessarily electrostatically charged, small dust particles of transplanetary origin now found in bodies in near-circular Kepler orbits are likely to have been brought into corotation with the revolving magnetized plasma in the circumsolar and circumplanetary regions.

1.4.4 Origin of the Sun

Theories concerning the origin of the Sun and other stars clearly also must have a foundation in hydromagnetics and plasma physics. Even if appropriately constructed, such theories are by necessity speculative and uncertain. For this reason, in the present study of the formation of the solar system, we do not rely on any initial assumptions concerning the primeval Sun or its history except that during the hetegonic era it existed and was surrounded by a plasma. From our analysis of the solar system, however, we can draw specific conclusions about the primeval Sun: Its mass was approximately the same as today, but its spin and magnetization were much larger.

1.5 MODEL REQUIREMENTS AND LIMITATIONS

The completion of a set of quantitative, mutually consistent, and experimentally supported models for the evolution of the solar system is obviously still in the remote future. We need much more information from space data and from laboratory investigation to be able to reduce to a manageable level the speculative element which such models necessarily still contain.

As a first step, we have tried to identify those physical and chemical laws that, at our present state of knowledge, emerge as most important in controlling the processes in the solar system now and in early times. Within the constraints obtained in this way, we have attempted to develop a series of partial models which both satisfy the general principles outlined above and also, when taken together, define what we regard as an acceptable framework for theories of the evolution of the solar system (ch. 23). We construct a matrix (table 23.8.1) complete in the sense that it comprises all the groups of planets and satellites (with the exception of the tiny Martian satellites). The general framework also includes asteroids, comets, and meteoroids.

PART A

Present State and Basic Laws

2

THE PRESENT STRUCTURE OF THE PLANETARY AND SATELLITE SYSTEMS

2.1 ORBITAL PROPERTIES OF PLANETS AND SATELLITES

The most important invariants of the motion of a celestial body are the absolute values of the spin angular momentum and the orbital angular momentum. Although the space orientation of these vectors is not constant with time, but changes with a period ranging from a few years to 10^6 years (the first figure referring to close satellites and the latter to the outer planets), there are reasons to believe that, with noteworthy exceptions, the absolute values of these vectors have remained essentially constant since the formation of the bodies (see chs. 10, 17, and 21).

There are exceptions to this general rule. Tidal effects have changed the orbital momentum and spin of the Moon and the spin of the Earth in a drastic way (see ch. 24) and have produced a somewhat similar change in the Neptune-Triton system (see ch. 9). It is possible that the spin of Mercury was slowed by solar tides until a spin-orbit resonance stabilized the system, but it is also possible that Mercury was produced with its present spin. The spins of all satellites have been braked to synchronism with the orbital motion. To what extent the orbits of satellites other than the Moon and Triton have been changed by tides remains a controversial question. As we shall see in ch. 9, the changes have probably been very small.

In tables 2.1.1, 2.1.2, and 2.1.3, we list for planets and satellites the physical properties and orbital elements that are relevant to our discussion. Of particular importance is the *specific orbital angular momentum* **C** (that is, the angular momentum per unit mass) of the orbiting body, defined by

$$\mathbf{C} = \mathbf{r}_{orb} \times \mathbf{v}_{orb} \tag{2.1.1}$$

where $\mathbf{r}_{orb}$ is the radius vector from the central body (ideally from the common center of gravity) and $\mathbf{v}_{orb}$ is the orbital velocity. The absolute

TABLE 2.1.1

Orbital and Physical Parameters for the Planets

	Semimajor axis, a (10^{13} cm)	Eccentricity of orbit, e (°)	Inclination of orbit, i (°)	Inclination of orbit, i (′)	Average orbital velocity, $v_{orb} = \dfrac{2\pi a}{T}$ (10^5 cm/sec)	Sidereal period of revolution, $T = \dfrac{2\pi a^{3/2}}{(GM_s)^{1/2}}$ (10^8 sec)	Specific angular momentum, $C = [GM_s a(1-e^2)]^{1/2}$ (10^{19} cm^2/sec)	Total angular momentum, $C_M = CM$ (10^{46} gcm^2/sec)
Grazing planet [a]	0.00696				437	0.0001	0.304	
Synchronous planet [b]	0.253				72.5	0.0219	1.83	
Mercury ☿	[c] 0.579	0.2056	7	00	47.9	0.0759	2.72	0.906
Venus ♀	[c] 1.08	0.0068	3	24	35.1	0.194	3.79	18.5
Earth ⊕	[c] 1.50	0.0168	0	00	29.8	0.317	4.47	26.7
Mars ♂	[d] 2.28	0.0933	1	51	24.2	0.595	5.48	3.52
Jupiter ♃	[d] 7.78	0.0483	1	19	13.1	3.75	10.2	19 400
Saturn ♄	[d] 14.3	0.0559	2	30	9.64	9.34	13.8	7 840
Uranus ♅	[d] 28.7	0.0471	0	46	6.81	26.5	19.5	1 700
Neptune ♆	[d] 45.0	0.0085	1	47	5.44	52.1	24.5	2 500
Pluto ♇	[d] 59.0	0.2494	17	10	4.75	78.1	27.1	17.9

$\Sigma \approx 31\ 507$

Solar spin momentum[c] 170.

Planet	Sidereal spin period, τ 10^5 sec (e)	Inclination of equator to orbital plane, i_{eq} (° ')		Mass, M 10^{27} g	Equatorial radius, R 10^9 cm	Average density, θ g/cm³	Normalized moment of inertia, $\alpha\xi^2 = R\xi^2/R^2$ (e)	Escape velocity, $v_{es} = \left(\dfrac{2GM}{R}\right)^{1/2}$ 10^6 cm/sec (e)	Ratio of semimajor axes, $q_n = \dfrac{a_{n+1}}{a_n}$ (e)	Distributed density, $\dfrac{M}{a^3} = \rho_{dst}$ 10^{-13} g/cm³ (e)
Grazing planet [a]										
Synchronous planet [b]										
Mercury ☿	76.0			[f] 0.333	[f] 0.243	[f] 5.46		4.27	1.87	17.2
Venus ♀	210	~180		[f,g] 4.87	[f] 0.605	[f] 5.23		10.3	1.39	38.7
Earth ⊕	0.862	23	27	[c] 5.97	[c] 0.638	[f] 5.52	0.3335	11.2	1.52	17.7
Mars ♂	0.886	23	59	[f] 0.642	[f] 0.340	[f] 3.92	0.389	5.01	(3.41)	0.539
Jupiter ♃	0.354	3	5	[d] 1899.	[d] 7.16	[d] 1.31	0.25	59.4	1.84	46.5
Saturn ♄	0.368	26	44	[d] 568.	[d] 6.00	[d] 0.70	0.22	35.5	2.01	1.95
Uranus ♅	0.389	97	55	[d] 87.2	[d] 2.54	[d] 1.3	0.23	21.4	1.57	0.0369
Neptune ♆	0.540	28	48	[d] 102.	[d] 2.47	[d] 1.66	0.29	23.4	1.31	0.0112
Pluto ♇	5.52			[h] 0.66	[d] 0.320	[d] 4.9		5.24		0.0000322

[a] A grazing planet orbits just above the surface of the central body.
[b] A synchronous planet orbits with an orbital period equal to the spin period of the central body.
[c] Allen, 1963.
[d] Newburn and Gulkis, 1973.
[e] Calculated from equation given.
[f] Lyttleton, 1969.
[g] Howard et al., 1974.
[h] Seidelmann et al., 1971.

17

TABLE 2.1.2
Orbital and Physical Parameters for the Satellite Systems

	Semimajor axis, a 10^{10} cm (d)	Eccentricity of orbit, e (d)	Inclination of orbit, i ° (d)	Sidereal period of revolution, T 10^5 sec (d)	Average orbital velocity, $v_{orb}=\frac{2\pi a}{T}$ 10^5 cm/sec (°)	Specific angular momentum, $C=[GM_c a(1-e^2)]^{1/2}$ 10^{16} cm²/sec (°)	Total angular momentum, $C_M=CM$ 10^{40} gcm²/sec (°)	Mass, M 10^{24} g	Equatorial radius, R 10^7 cm	Ratio of semimajor axes, $q_n=\frac{a_{n+1}}{a_n}$ (°)	Distributed density, $\rho_{dst}=\frac{M}{a^3}$ 10^{-9} g/cm³ (°)
Jupiter											
Grazing satellite [a]	0.716			0.107	42.1	3.01					
Synchronous satellite [b]	1.59			0.354	28.2	4.49				(2.33)	
5 Amalthea	1.81	0.0028	0.5	0.432	26.5	4.79			[e] 0.70	1.59	
1 Io	4.22	0.0000	0.0	1.53	17.3	7.31	652	[f] 89.2	[f] 18.3	1.59	1190
2 Europa	6.71	0.0003	0.5	3.07	13.7	9.22	449	[f] 48.7	[f] 15.0	1.76	161
3 Ganymede	10.7	0.0015	0.2	6.18	10.9	11.6	1730	[f] 149	[f] 26.4	(6.12)	121
4 Callisto	18.8	0.0075	0.3	14.4	8.21	15.4	1630	[f] 106	[f] 25.0	1.02	16
6	115	0.158	27.6	216	3.32	37.6				1.02	
7	117	0.207	24.8	224	3.29	37.7					
10	119	0.130	29.0	228	3.26	38.4					

Σ ~ 4 461

Spin momentum of Jupiter[i] ~672 000

Saturn											
Grazing satellite [a]	0.604			0.150	25.1	1.51					
Synchronous satellite [b]	1.10			0.368	18.6	2.04					
10 Janus	1.69	0.000	0.0	0.700	15.0	2.53					
1 Mimas	1.86	0.0201	1.52	0.812	14.3	2.66	0.106	[c] 0.04	[c] 3.0	1.10	6.22
2 Enceladus	2.38	0.0044	0.03	1.18	12.6	3.00	0.255	[d] 0.085	[d] 2.7	1.28	6.30
3 Tethys	2.94	0.0000	1.10	1.63	11.4	3.34	2.16	[d] 0.648	[d] 6.0	1.24	25.5
4 Dione	3.77	0.0022	0.03	2.37	10.0	3.78	3.97	[d] 1.05	[h] 5.8	1.28	19.6
5 Rhea	5.27	0.0010	0.34	3.91	8.48	4.47	8.05	[g] 1.8	[h] 8.0	1.40	12.3
6 Titan	12.2	0.029	0.33	13.8	5.57	6.80	932	[d] 137	[d] 24.2	(2.31)	75.3
7 Hyperion	14.8	0.104	0.3–0.9	18.4	5.06	7.45	2.31	[c] 0.31	[c] 2.0	1.21	0.0957
8 Iapetus	35.6	0.0283	14.7	68.5	3.26	11.6	26.0	[g] 2.24	[g] 8.5	2.41	0.0497
							Σ∼974				
				Spin momentum of Saturn[i] ∼87 200							
Uranus											
Grazing satellite [a]	0.254			0.135	15.1	0.384					
Synchronous satellite [b]	0.607			0.389	9.79	0.594					
5 Miranda	1.29	≪0.01	0.0	1.22	6.72	0.866	0.0866	0.1	1.0		46.5
1 Ariel	1.91	0.0028	0.0	2.18	5.52	1.05	1.26	1.2	3.0	1.48	172.2
2 Umbriel	2.66	0.0035	0.0	3.58	4.68	1.24	0.620	0.5	2.0	1.39	26.6
3 Titania	4.36	0.0024	0.0	7.06	3.65	1.59	6.36	4.0	5.0	1.64	48.3
4 Oberon	5.83	0.0007	0.0	11.6	3.15	1.84	4.78	2.6	4.0	1.34	13.1
							Σ∼17				
				Spin momentum of Uranus[i] ∼1998							
Neptune											
Grazing satellite [a]	0.254			0.0974	16.4	0.416					
Synchronous satellite [b]	0.796			0.540	10.4	0.736					
2 Nereid	55.6	0.7493	27.7	311	1.11	4.08	0.122	0.03	1.0		0.000174

TABLE 2.1.2 (Continued)
Orbital and Physical Parameters for the Satellite Systems

	Semimajor axis, a	Eccentricity of orbit, e	Inclination of orbit, i	Sidereal period of revolution, T	Average orbital velocity, $v_{orb} = \frac{2\pi a}{T}$	Specific angular momentum, $C = [GM_c a(1-e^2)]^{1/2}$	Total angular momentum, $C_M = CM$	Mass, M	Equatorial radius, R	Ratio of semimajor axes, $q_n = \frac{a_{n+1}}{a_n}$	Distributed density, $\rho_{dst} = \frac{M}{a^3}$
	10^{10} cm		°	10^5 sec	10^5 cm/sec	10^{16} cm²/sec	10^{40} gcm²/sec	10^{24} g	10^7 cm		10^{-9} g/cm³
	(d)	(d)	(d)	(d)	(e)	(e)	(e)			(e)	(e)
Mars											
Grazing satellite [a]	0.0340			0.0602	3.55	0.0121					
Synchronous satellite [b]	0.204			0.886	1.45	0.0295					
1 Phobos	[c] 0.09	[c] 0.021	[c] 1.1	[c] 0.276	2.18	0.0196			0.06	2.56	
2 Deimos	[c] 0.23	[c] 0.0028	[c] 1.6	[c] 1.09	1.36	0.0314			0.03		

[a] A grazing satellite orbits just above the surface of the central body.
[b] A synchronous satellite orbits with an orbital period equal to the spin period of the central body.
[c] Allen, 1963.
[d] Newburn and Gulkis, 1973.
[e] Calculated from equation given.
[f] Anderson et al., 1974.
[g] Murphy et al., 1972.
[h] Morrison, 1974.
[i] Calculated assuming spin momentum equals $\alpha_{\Xi}^2 R^2 M 2\pi/\tau$ and using data from table 2.1.1.

TABLE 2.1.3
Orbital and Physical Parameters for the Retrograde Satellites and the Moon

Planet	Satellite	Semimajor axis, a 10^{10} cm (a)	Eccentricity of orbit, e (a)	Inclination of orbit, i ° (a)	Sidereal period of revolution, T 10^5 sec (a)	Average orbital velocity, $V_{orb} = \dfrac{2\pi a}{T}$ 10^6 cm/sec (c)	Specific angular momentum, $C = [GM_{ca}(1-e^2)]^{1/2}$ 10^{16} cm²/sec (c)	Mass, M 10^{24} g	Equatorial radius, R 10^7 cm (b)
Jupiter	12	213	0.169	147	545	0.244	51.2		0.06
	11	225	0.207	164	598	0.237	52.3		0.08
	8	235	0.378	145	638	0.232	50.6		0.10
	9	237	0.275	153	655	0.231	52.6		0.08
Saturn	9 Phoebe	130	0.1633	150	475	0.171	21.9		1.0
Neptune	1 Triton	3.55	0.0000	159.9	5.08	0.438	1.55	a 135	a 18.8
Earth	Moon	b 3.84	b 0.0549	b 5.15	b 23.6	0.102	0.391	b 73.5	17.4

a Newburn and Gulkis, 1973.
b Allen, 1963.
c Calculated from equation given.

values of C are listed, as are those of the *total angular momentum* $C_M = M_{sc}C$, where M_{sc} is the mass of the secondary body.

If M_c is the mass of the central body and G is the gravitational constant, then the *semimajor axis a* and the *eccentricity e* of the orbital ellipse are connected with C through

$$C^2 = GM_ca(1-e^2) \qquad (2.1.2)$$

All the planets and the prograde satellites, with the exception of Nereid, have $e < 0.25$. Most of them, in fact, have $e < 0.1$ (exceptions are the planets Mercury and Pluto; the satellites Jupiter 6, 7, and 10; and Saturn's satellite Hyperion). Hence

$$C \approx (GM_ca)^{1/2} \qquad (2.1.3)$$

is usually a good approximation and is correct within 3.1 percent for $e < 0.25$ and within 0.5 percent for $e < 0.1$.

The *sidereal period of revolution T* is calculated from the value of the semimajor axis:

$$T = \frac{2\pi a^{3/2}}{(GM_c)^{1/2}} = \frac{2\pi C^3}{(GM_c)^2(1-e^2)^{3/2}} \qquad (2.1.4)$$

or approximately

$$T \approx \frac{2\pi C^3}{(GM_c)^2} \qquad (2.1.5)$$

and the *average orbital velocity v_{orb}* is calculated from

$$v_{orb} \approx \frac{2\pi a}{T} = \frac{(GM_c)^{1/2}}{a^{1/2}} = \frac{GM_c}{C} \qquad (2.1.6)$$

In table 2.1.1., the *orbital inclination* of the planets *i* refers to the orbital plane of the Earth (the ecliptic plane). It would be more appropriate to reference it to the invariant plane of the solar system, the so-called Laplacian plane. However, the difference is small and will not seriously affect our treatment.

For the satellites, the orbital inclination is referred to the most relevant reference plane. For close satellites, this is the equatorial plane of the planet because the precession of the orbital plane is determined with reference to this plane. For some distant satellites, the influence from the Sun's gravitational field is more important; hence the orbital plane of the planet is more relevant.

2.2 PHYSICAL PROPERTIES OF PLANETS AND
SATELLITES

Having dealt with the orbital characteristics, we devote the remainder of each table to the secondary body itself. Given the *mass* M_{sc} and the *radius* R_{sc} of the body, its *mean density* Θ_{sc} is calculated from

$$\Theta_{sc} = \frac{3M_{sc}}{4\pi R_{sc}^{3}} \qquad (2.2.1)$$

From the observed *periods of axial rotation* (spin periods), τ, the planetary *normalized moments of inertia* $\alpha_{\bar{z}}^{2}$ are tabulated. If $R_{\bar{z}}$ is the radius of gyration and R the radius of the body, the ratio $\alpha_{\bar{z}} = R_{\bar{z}}/R$ is a measure of the mass distribution inside the body. The moment of inertia per unit mass and unit R^{2}, $\alpha_{\bar{z}}^{2}$, of a homogeneous sphere is 0.4. A smaller value indicates that the density is higher in the central region than in the outer layers of the body.

Next, the *inclination* i_{eq} *of equator to orbital plane* is tabulated for each planet in table 2.1.1.

The velocity necessary for shooting a particle from the surface of a celestial body of radius R to infinity is the *escape velocity* v_{es}. This is also the velocity at which a particle hits the body if falling from rest at infinity. We have

$$v_{es} = \left(\frac{2GM_{c}}{R}\right)^{1/2} \qquad (2.2.2)$$

If a satellite is orbiting very close to the surface of the planet, such a "grazing satellite" has $a = R$. Its orbital velocity is $v_{es}/2^{1/2}$.

A convenient scale for time is provided by the quantity

$$t_{es} = \frac{R}{v_{es}} \tag{2.2.3}$$

referred to as the "time of escape." It follows from eqs. (2.2.1–2.2.2) that

$$t_{es} = \left(\frac{3}{8\pi G\Theta}\right)^{1/2} = \frac{1340}{\Theta^{1/2}} \text{ sec } (\text{g/cm}^3)^{1/2} \tag{2.2.4}$$

It is easily shown that if a particle is shot vertically from a body of radius R with velocity v_{es}, it reaches a height

$$h = [(\tfrac{5}{2})^{2/3} - 1]R = 0.84R \tag{2.2.5}$$

after the time t_{es}. This time is related to the period T_{gz} of a "grazing satellite" in table 2.1.2 through

$$T_{gz} = 2^{3/2}\pi t_{es} = 8.9 t_{es} \tag{2.2.6}$$

For the Earth ($\Theta = 5.5$ gcm^{-3}), we have $t_{es} = 10$ min and $T_{gz} = 89$ min.

There is also a column listing the value of q_n, the *ratio of the orbital distances* of adjacent bodies, $q_n = a_{n+1}/a_n$. The quantity q_n takes the place of the number magic of Titius-Bode's "law" (see sec. 2.6).

2.3 PROGRADE AND RETROGRADE SATELLITES

All the planets and most of the satellites orbit in the same sense ("prograde") as the spin of their respective central body. This is probably the result of a transfer of angular momentum from the spin of the central body to the orbital motion of the secondary bodies at the time when the system was formed (chs. 16–17).

However, there are a few satellites which orbit in a "retrograde" direction. With the exception of Triton, their orbits differ from those of prograde satellites also in the respect that their eccentricities and inclinations are much larger. As their origin is likely to be different (they are probably captured bodies), they are listed separately (table 2.1.3). Since the Moon is likely to be a captured planet, it also is included in table 2.1.3 (see ch. 24).

The heading "grazing planet (satellite)" refers to the dynamic properties of a fictitious body moving in a Kepler orbit grazing the surface of the central body. Similarly, "synchronous planet (satellite)" refers to a fictitious body orbiting with a period equal to the spin period of the central body. The data for such bodies provide useful references for the orbital parameters of the system.

Some of the relations given in tables 2.1.1 and 2.1.2 are plotted in the diagrams of figures 2.3.1 through 2.3.4.

2.4 THE LAPLACIAN MODEL AND THE DISTRIBUTED-DENSITY FUNCTION

Discussion of the origin of the solar system has been dominated for centuries by the Laplacian model. Laplace himself presented this model only as a qualitative suggestion. In spite of many later efforts, it has not been possible to formulate theories of this type in a quantitatively satisfactory way.

According to models of this type, a primeval nebula somehow formed from interstellar matter and assumed the shape of a uniform disc of gas which contracted and, in this process, threw off a series of rings that collapsed to form planets. The model idealizes the planetary system as consisting of a uniform sequence of bodies, the orbital radii of which obey a simple exponential law (or Titius-Bode's "law").

A consequence of the Laplacian model would be that the planetary masses obey a simple function of the solar distance; however, this conclusion is so obviously in disagreement with observations that this aspect has been avoided. In a more realistic version of this approach, it is necessary to assume that the density varied in a way that reflects the mass variation of the planets. This mass distribution of the Laplacian nebula may be called the "distributed density" obtained by conceptually smearing out the mass of the present bodies.

As we shall see in the following (especially chs. 11–13, 16–18), there is yet another serious objection to the Laplacian concept. We shall find that at any given time a gas or plasma with this distributed density could not

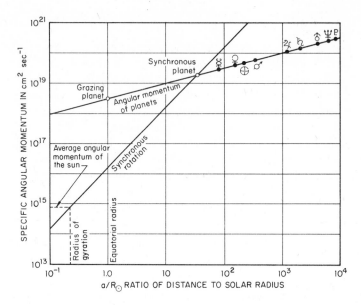

FIGURE 2.3.1.—Specific angular momentum of the Sun and planets. (From Alfvén and Arrhenius, 1970a.)

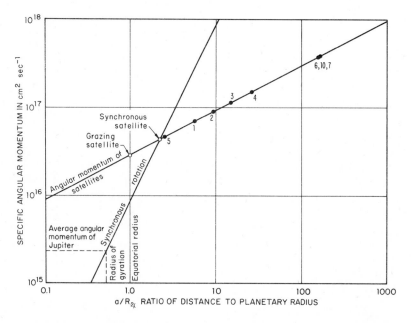

FIGURE 2.3.2.—Specific angular momentum of Jupiter and its prograde satellites.

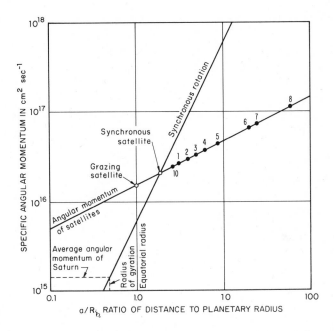

FIGURE 2.3.3.—Specific angular momentum of Saturn and its prograde satellites.

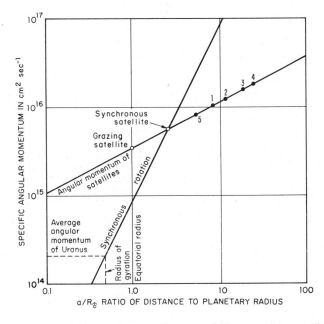

FIGURE 2.3.4.—Specific angular momentum of Uranus and its satellites.

have existed. Instead, there must have been an emplacement of plasma over a long period. However, the density distribution of this emplacement is correlated with the "distributed density," which hence is an important function, even if it should not be taken literally.

To reconstruct the distributed density in the solar system, some rather arbitrary assumptions must be made. However, as the density varies by several orders of magnitude from one region to another, a certain arbitrariness would still preserve the gross features of the distribution. For the present discussion, we assume that the mass M_n of a planet or satellite was initially distributed over a toroidal volume around the present orbit of the body. We further assume that the small diameter of the toroid is defined by the intermediate distances to adjacent orbiting bodies; that is, the diameter will be the sum of half the distance to the orbit of the adjacent body closer to the central body and half the distance to the orbit of the body farther from it. We find

$$M_n = 2\pi r_n \pi \left[\frac{r_{n+1} - r_{n-1}}{4}\right]^2 \rho_{dst}$$

$$= \frac{\pi^2}{8}\left[q_n - \frac{1}{q_{n-1}}\right]^2 r_n^3 \rho_{dst} \tag{2.4.1}$$

where r_n is the orbital distance of the nth body from the central body, ρ_{dst} is the *distributed density*, and $q_n = r_{n+1}/r_n$. Numerical values of q_n are given in tables 2.1.1 and 2.1.2, where we note that secondary bodies tend to occur in groups bordered by large expanses of empty space. The q_n value for a body on the edge of such a gap is enclosed in parentheses.

Equation (2.4.1) has no physical meaning at the inner or outer edge of a group of bodies, but in these cases we tentatively put the small radius of the torus equal to one-half the distance to the one adjacent body. Inside the groups q_n is about 1.2–1.6, which means that the square of the term in brackets varies between 0.1 and 1.0. Hence, in order to calculate an order of magnitude value, we can put

$$\rho_{dst} = \frac{M_n}{r_n^3} \tag{2.4.2}$$

which is the formula employed for the "distributed density" column in tables 2.1.1 and 2.1.2. These values are plotted in figs. 2.5.1 through 2.5.4; smooth curves are drawn to suggest a possible primeval mass density distribution.

It should be kept in mind, however, that the terrestrial planets, for example, contain mostly nonvolatile substances, presumably because volatile substances could not condense in this region of space or on bodies as small as these planets. As the primeval plasma probably contained mainly volatile substances, its density in this region may have been systematically a few orders of magnitude larger than indicated in the diagram.

2.5 DISCUSSION OF THE DISTRIBUTED-DENSITY DIAGRAMS

It is natural that there should be an outer limit to the sequence of planets, presumably determined by the outer limit of an original disc. Furthermore, it is conceivable that no matter could condense very close to the Sun if the radiation temperature were prohibitively high in this region. But unless a number of ad hoc hypotheses are introduced, theories of the Laplacian type do not predict that the distributed density should vary in a nonmonotonic way inside these limits.

As we see in fig. 2.5.1, the Laplacian model of a disc with uniform density is very far from a good description of reality. The density in the region between Mars and Jupiter is lower by five orders of magnitude than the density

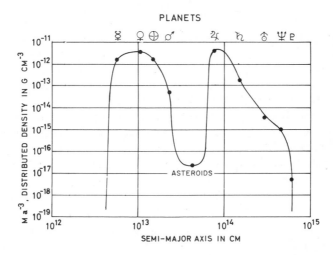

FIGURE 2.5.1.—Distributed density versus semimajor axis for the planets.

in adjacent regions. The existence of one or more broken-up planets, the fragments of which should now be the asteroids, is often postulated. Even if this assumption were correct, it could not explain the very low density of matter in this region. Within the framework of the Laplacian nebular model, this low-density region would require a systematic transport of mass outward or inward, and no plausible mechanism to achieve this has been proposed. (The difficulties inherent in this view are discussed further in sec. 11.8.)

If we try to look at fig. 2.5.1 without the prejudice of centuries of bias toward Laplacian models, we find ourselves inclined to describe the mass distribution in the planetary system in the following way.

There have been two clouds of matter, one associated with the terrestrial (or inner) planets and a second with the giant (or outer) planets. These clouds were separated by a vast, almost empty region. The inner cloud covered a radial distance ratio of $q(\sigma\!\!\!/ / \rlap{/}{\varsigma}) = 3.9$ (where q is the ratio between the orbital radii of the innermost and outermost bodies within one group). For the outer cloud, the corresponding distance ratio is $q(\Psi / \math鱼{2}\!) = 5.8$, or, if Pluto is taken into account, $q(P / \rlap{}{2}\!) = 7.6$ (see table 2.5.1). The clouds were separated by a gap with a distance ratio of $q(\rlap{}{2}\!/\sigma\!\!\!/) = 3.4$. The bodies deriving from each of the two clouds differ very much in chemical composition (ch. 20).

As always, the analysis of a single specimen like the planetary system is necessarily inconclusive; thus it is important to study the satellite system to corroborate our conclusions. We find in the Jovian system (fig. 2.5.2) that the four Galilean satellites form a group with $q = 4.5$. Similarly, the group of five Uranian satellites (fig. 2.5.3) have a q value of 4.6. These values fall within the range of those in the planetary system.

In the case of the planetary system, one could argue that there are no planets inside the orbit of Mercury because solar heat prevented condensation very close to the Sun. This argument is invalid for the inner limit of the Galilean satellites, as well as for the Uranian satellites. Neither Jupiter nor Uranus can be expected to have been so hot as to prevent a formation of satellites close to the surface. We see that Saturn, which both in solar distance and in size is intermediate between Jupiter and Uranus, has satellites (including the ring system) virtually all the way to its surface. Hence, the Saturnian system inside Rhea would be reconcilable with a Laplacian uniform disc picture, but neither the Jovian nor the Uranian systems are in agreement with such a picture.

Further, in the Saturnian system (fig. 2.5.4), the fairly homogeneous sequence of satellites out to Rhea is broken by a large void (between Rhea and Titan $q = 2.3$). Titan, Hyperion, and possibly also Iapetus may be considered as one group ($q = 2.9$). The inner satellites including the ring should be counted as a group with $q(\text{Rhea}/\text{Janus}) = 3.3$.

TABLE 2.5.1

Groups of Planets and Satellites

Central body	Group	Secondary bodies	Orbital ratio, q	Remarks
Sun	Terrestrial planets	Mercury Venus Earth Moon? Mars	$q=3.9$	Irregularity[a]: Moon-Mars problem (see ch. 23).
Sun	Giant planets	Jupiter Saturn Uranus Neptune Triton? Pluto	$q=5.8$ $q=7.6$	Doubtful whether Pluto and Triton belong to this group (see ch. 23).
Jupiter	Galilean satellites	Io Europa Ganymede Callisto	$q=4.5$	A very regular group: $e \approx 0$, $i \approx 0$. Amalthea is too small and too far away from this group to be a member.
Uranus	Uranian satellites	Miranda Ariel Umbriel Titania Oberon	$q=4.6$	Also very regular: $e \approx 0$, $i \approx 0$. The satellites move in the equatorial plane of Uranus, not in its orbital plane ($i_{eq}=98°$).
Saturn	Inner Saturnian satellites	Janus Mimas Enceladus Tethys Dione Rhea	$q=3.3$	The satellites form a very regular sequence down to the associated ring system.
Saturn	Outer Saturnian satellites	Titan Hyperion Iapetus	$q=2.9$	Irregular because of the smallness of Hyperion.
Jupiter	Outer Jovian satellites	6 10 7	$q=1.0$	Very irregular group consisting of three small bodies in eccentric and inclined orbits.

Other prograde satellites: Amalthea, Nereid, Phobos, and Deimos.

[a] We refer to a group as regular if eccentricities and inclinations are low, the mass is changing monotonically with r, and q values within the group are similar.

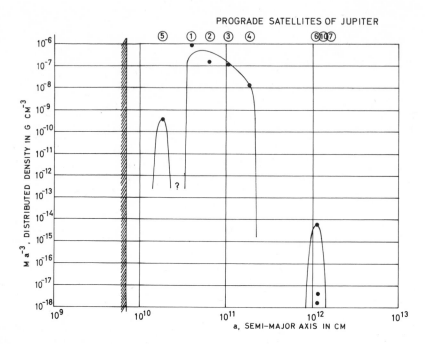

FIGURE 2.5.2.—Distributed density versus semimajor axis for the prograde satellites of Jupiter.

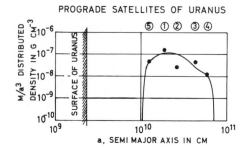

FIGURE 2.5.3.—Distributed density versus semimajor axis for the prograde satellites of Uranus.

Thus we find that the celestial bodies in the solar system occur in widely separated groups, each having three to six members. The planet and satellite groups are listed with their orbital ratios in table 2.5.1. A more thorough consideration of this grouping is undertaken in ch. 21. It is reasonable that the outer Jovian (prograde) satellites should be considered as one group consisting of closely spaced small members.

Other prograde satellites include Amalthea, Nereid, Phobos, and Deimos. The band structure, discussed in ch. 21, suggests that Amalthea is the only observed member of another less massive group of Jovian satellites. Nereid is perhaps the only remaining member of a regular group of Neptunian

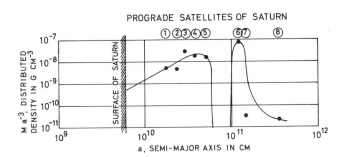

FIGURE 2.5.4—Distributed density versus semimajor axis for the prograde satellites of Saturn.

satellites that was destroyed by the retrograde giant satellite Triton during the evolution of its orbit (sec. 24.3). Phobos and Deimos form a group of extremely small Martian satellites.

2.6 TITIUS-BODE'S "LAW"

Titius-Bode's "law" has been almost as misleading as the Laplacian model. In spite of the criticism of this theory by Schmidt (1946a), it still seems to be sacrosanct in all textbooks. In its original formulation it is acceptable as a mnemonic for memorizing the inner planetary distances. It is not applicable to Neptune and Pluto, and, had they been discovered at the time, the "law" would probably never have been formulated. It is now usually interpreted as implying that the ratio q_n between consecutive orbital distances should be a constant. It is obvious from table 2.1.1 that this is usually not the case. Attempts have been made to find similar "laws" for the satellite systems. This is possible only by postulating a distressingly large number of "missing satellites."

As we shall find in chs. 11, 13, 17, 19, and 21, the orbital distances of planets and satellites are determined mainly by the capture of condensed grains by jet streams. In many cases, resonance effects are also important, as discussed in ch. 8. Both these effects give some regularity in the sequence of bodies, and, in certain limited regions, an exponential law of the Titius-Bode type may be a fairly good approximation, as shown by the fact that the value of q_n in some groups is fairly constant. But neither in its original nor in its later versions does the "law" have any deeper significance.

To try to find numerical relations between a number of observed quantities is an important scientific activity if it is regarded as a first step toward finding the physical laws connecting the quantities (Nieto, 1972). No such connection to known physical laws has emerged from the swelling Titius-Bode literature, which consequently has no demonstrated scientific value.

THE MOTION OF PLANETS AND SATELLITES

3.1 THE GUIDING-CENTER APPROXIMATION OF CELESTIAL MECHANICS

The dynamic state of a celestial body can be represented by nine quantities. Of these, three give the position of the body (e.g., its center of gravity) at a certain moment, three give its three-dimensional velocity, and three give its spin (around three orthogonal axes). These quantities vary more or less rapidly in a way which can be found from the Nautical Almanac. In our study of the origin and the long-time evolution of the dynamic state of the solar system, we are predominantly interested in those dynamic quantities which are invariant or vary very slowly.

The typical orbits of satellites and planets are circles in certain preferred planes. For the satellite systems, the preferred planes tend to coincide with the equatorial planes of the central bodies. For the planetary system, the preferred plane is essentially the orbital plane of Jupiter (because this is the biggest planet), which is close to the plane of the ecliptic. The circular motion with period T is usually modified by superimposed oscillations. Radial oscillations (in the preferred plane) with period $\approx T$ change the circular orbit into an elliptical orbit with eccentricity e. Axial oscillations (perpendicular to the preferred plane), with a period $\simeq T$, give the orbit an inclination i to this plane.

With some exaggeration one may say that the goal of the traditional presentation of celestial mechanics was utility for the preparation of the Nautical Almanac and, more recently, for calculation of spacecraft trajectories. This approach is not very suitable if we want to study the mutual interaction between orbiting grains or the interaction of orbiting grains with a plasma or any viscous medium. It is more convenient to use an approximation method that treats an elliptical orbit as a perturbation of a circular orbit. This method is applicable only for orbits with small eccentricities. From a formal point of view the method has some similarity to the guiding-center method of treating the motion of charged particles in a magnetic field (Alfvén and Fälthammar, 1963, p. 18 ff.).

3.2 CIRCULAR ORBITS

The coordinate system adopted in subsequent discussions is the modified spherical coordinate system with ϕ, λ, and r as the azimuthal angle or longitude, the meridional angle or latitude, and the radial direction, respectively. When rectangular coordinates are used the x–y plane lies in the equatorial plane and z is the axial direction.

For a body of negligible mass moving around a central body the specific angular momentum $\mathbf{C}$ (per unit mass) of the small body with reference to the central body (or, strictly speaking, to the center of gravity) is defined as

$$\mathbf{C} = \mathbf{r_{orb}} \times \mathbf{v_{orb}} \tag{3.2.1}$$

where $\mathbf{r_{orb}}$ is the orbital distance and $\mathbf{v_{orb}}$ is the orbital velocity of the small body. $\mathbf{C}$ is an invariant vector during the motion.

The body is acted upon by the specific gravitational attraction f_G (per unit mass) of the central body and by the centrifugal force f_c (per unit mass)

$$f_c = \frac{v_\phi^2}{r} = \frac{C^2}{r^3} \tag{3.2.2}$$

where v_ϕ is the tangential velocity component.

The simplest type of motion is that motion with constant orbital velocity v_0 in a circle with radius r_0. The gravitational force f_G is exactly balanced by the centrifugal force. We have

$$v_0 = \frac{C}{r_0} = (r_0\, f_G)^{1/2} = \frac{r_0^2 f_G}{C} \tag{3.2.3}$$

The orbital angular velocity is

$$\omega_K = \frac{v_0}{r_0} = \left(\frac{f_G}{r_0}\right)^{1/2} = \frac{r_0\, f_G}{C} = \frac{C}{r_0^2} \tag{3.2.4}$$

The period $T_K = 2\pi/\omega_K$ of this motion is known as the Kepler period.

3.3 OSCILLATIONS MODIFYING THE
CIRCULAR ORBIT

The circular orbit of the body can be modified by both radial and axial oscillations.

If the body is displaced radially from r_0 to $r = r_0 + \Delta r$, it is acted upon by the force

$$f_r(r) = f_c(r) - f_G(r) = \frac{C^2}{r^3} - f_G(r) \simeq f_r(r_0) + \left[\frac{df_r}{dr}\right]_0 \Delta r \qquad (3.3.1)$$

Because the force is zero for $r = r_0$ we obtain

$$f_r = -\left[\frac{3C^2}{r^4} + \frac{\partial f_G}{\partial r}\right]_0 \Delta r \qquad (3.3.2)$$

As the angular frequency of a harmonic oscillator is $\left[-\dfrac{df}{dx}\right]^{1/2}$, the body oscillates radially about the circle with

$$\omega_r = \left[-\frac{df_r}{dr}\right]_0^{1/2} = \left[\frac{3C^2}{r^4} + \frac{\partial f_G}{\partial r}\right]_0^{1/2} = \left[\frac{3f_G}{r} + \frac{\partial f_G}{\partial r}\right]_0^{1/2} \qquad (3.3.3)$$

If the body is displaced in the z direction (axial direction), it is acted upon by the force f_z which, because div $f = 0$, is given by

$$\frac{\partial f_z}{\partial z} = -\left[\frac{1}{r}\frac{\partial(rf_G)}{\partial r}\right]_0 = \left[-\frac{f_G}{r} - \frac{\partial f_G}{\partial r}\right]_0 \qquad (3.3.4)$$

The angular velocity of this axial oscillation is

$$\omega_z = \left[-\frac{\partial f_z}{\partial z}\right]^{1/2} = \left[-\frac{f_G}{r} - \frac{\partial f_G}{\partial r}\right]_0^{1/2} \qquad (3.3.5)$$

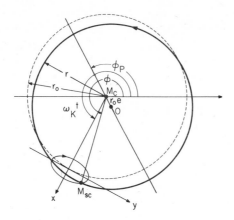

FIGURE 3.3.1.—The guiding-center method of approximating the Kepler motion. The guiding center moves
with constant velocity along the dashed circle of radius
r_0 in the center of which the gravitating mass M_c is
situated. The body M moves in an "epicycle" around the
guiding center. The epicycle is an ellipse with the axis
ratio 2/1 and semiminor axis of er_0. The epicycle motion
is retrograde. The resulting motion of M is an ellipse
which almost coincides with the undashed circle which
has its center at O. The distance from O to M_c is er_0. The
position of the pericenter is given by ϕ_P. The difference
between the undashed circle and the exact Kepler ellipse
is really less than the thickness of the line.

From eqs. (3.2.4), (3.3.3), and (3.3.5)

$$\omega_r{}^2 + \omega_z{}^2 = 2\omega_K{}^2 \tag{3.3.6}$$

We place a moving coordinate system with the origin at a point traveling
along the unperturbed (circular) orbit with the angular velocity ω_K (fig.
3.3.1). The x axis points in the radial direction and the y axis in the forward
tangential direction. The origin is called the "guiding center." We have

$$x = r \cos (\phi - \omega_K t) - r_0 \tag{3.3.7}$$

and

$$y = r \sin (\phi - \omega_K t) \tag{3.3.8}$$

where ϕ is the angle measured from a fixed direction and t is counted from the moment when the guiding center is located in this fixed direction.

A radial harmonic oscillation with amplitude er_0 ($\ll r_0$) can be written

$$r = r_0[1 - e\cos(\omega_r t - \mathrm{K}_r)] \tag{3.3.9}$$

where ω_r and K_r are constants. Because C is constant, we have

$$\frac{d\phi}{dt} = \frac{C}{r^2} \approx \frac{C}{r_0^2}[1 + 2e\cos(\omega_r t - \mathrm{K}_r)] \tag{3.3.10}$$

As $x \ll r_0$ and $y \ll r_0$ we find from eqs. (3.2.4) and (3.3.7–3.3.10):

$$x \approx r - r_0$$

$$\approx -r_0 e\cos(\omega_r t - \mathrm{K}_r)$$

$$\approx -r_0 e\cos(\omega_K t - \omega_P t - \mathrm{K}_r) \tag{3.3.11}$$

where we have introduced

$$\omega_P = \omega_K - \omega_r \tag{3.3.12}$$

We find

$$\frac{dy}{dt} \approx r_0\left(\frac{d\phi}{dt} - \omega_K\right) \approx \frac{2eC}{r_0}\cos(\omega_r t - \mathrm{K}_r) \tag{3.3.13}$$

or after integration

$$y \approx 2r_0 e\left(1 + \frac{\omega_P}{\omega_r}\right)\sin(\omega_K t - \omega_P t - \mathrm{K}_r) \tag{3.3.14}$$

The pericenter (point of nearest approach to the gravitating center) is reached when x is a minimum; that is, when

$$\omega_K t - \omega_P t - K_r = 2\pi n \quad (n = 0, 1, 2 \cdots) \qquad (3.3.15)$$

Assuming the pericenter ϕ_P to be

$$\phi_P = \omega_P t + K_r \qquad (3.3.16)$$

eq. (3.3.15) gives the expected periodicity of the pericenter, $t = (\phi_P + 2\pi n)/\omega_K$. Thus, the pericenter moves (has a "precession") with the velocity ω_P, given by eq. (3.3.12).

In a similar way, we find the axial oscillations:

$$z = r_0 i \sin (\omega_z t - K_z) = r_0 i \sin (\omega_K t - \omega_\Omega t - K_z) \qquad (3.3.17)$$

where i ($\ll 1$) is the inclination, K_z is a constant and

$$\omega_\Omega = \omega_K - \omega_z \qquad (3.3.18)$$

The angle ϕ_Ω of the "ascending node" (point where z becomes positive) is given by

$$\phi_\Omega = \omega_\Omega t + K_z \qquad (3.3.19)$$

3.4 MOTION IN AN INVERSE-SQUARE-LAW GRAVITATIONAL FIELD

If the mass of the orbiting body is taken as unity, then the specific gravitational force is

$$f_G = \frac{GM_c}{r^2} \qquad (3.4.1)$$

where M_c is the mass of the central body and G is the gravitational constant. As $f_c = f_G$ for the unperturbed motion, we have from eqs. (3.2.2) and (3.4.1)

$$C = (GM_c r_0)^{1/2} \tag{3.4.2}$$

From eq. (3.4.1) we find

$$\frac{\partial f_G}{\partial r} = - \frac{2f_G}{r} \tag{3.4.3}$$

Substituting eq. (3.4.3) into eqs. (3.3.3) and (3.3.5), eq. (3.3.6) reduces to

$$\omega_r = \omega_z = \omega_K \tag{3.4.4}$$

where the Kepler angular velocity is

$$\omega_K = \frac{GM_c}{Cr_0} = \left(\frac{GM_c}{r_0^3}\right)^{1/2} \tag{3.4.5}$$

The significance of eq. (3.4.4) is that, for the almost circular motion in an inverse-square-law field, the frequencies of radial and axial oscillation coincide with the fundamental angular velocity of circular motion. Consequently, we have $\omega_P = \omega_\Omega = 0$, and there is no precession of the pericenter or of the nodes. According to eqs. (3.3.11) and (3.3.14), the body moves in the "epicycle"

$$x = -r_0 e \cos (\omega_K t - K_r)$$

$$\tag{3.4.6}$$

$$y = 2r_0 e \sin (\omega_K t - K_r)$$

The center of the epicycle moves with constant velocity along the circle r_0. The motion in the epicycle takes place in the retrograde direction. See fig. 3.3.1.

Similarly, eq. (3.3.17) for the axial oscillation reduces to

$$z = r_0 i \sin (\omega_K t - K_z)$$

(3.4.7)

We still have an ellipse, but its plane has the inclination i with the plane of the undisturbed circular motion. The axial oscillation simply means that the plane of the orbit is changed from the initial plane, which was arbitrarily chosen because in a $1/r^2$ field there is no preferred plane.

3.5 NONHARMONIC OSCILLATION; LARGE ECCENTRICITY

If the amplitude of the oscillations becomes so large that the eccentricity is not negligible, the oscillations are no longer harmonic. This is the case for most comets and meteroids. It can be shown that instead of eq. (3.3.11) we have the more general formula

$$x \approx r - r_0$$

$$x \approx -r_0 \frac{e \cos (\phi - \phi_P)}{1 + e \cos (\phi - \phi_P)}$$

(3.5.1)

where r_0 is the radius of the unperturbed motion, defined by eq. (3.4.2) and $\phi - \phi_P$, the angle between the vector radius of the orbiting body and of the pericenter of its orbit. The relation of eq. (3.4.4) is still valid, but the period becomes

$$T' = \frac{2\pi a^{3/2}}{(GM_c)^{1/2}}$$

(3.5.2)

with

$$a = \frac{r_0}{1 - e^2}$$

(3.5.3)

It can be shown that geometrically the orbit is an ellipse, with a the semi-major axis and e the eccentricity.

3.6 MOTION IN THE FIELD OF A ROTATING CENTRAL BODY

According to eq. (3.4.4), the motion in a $1/r^2$ field is degenerate, in the sense that $\omega_r = \omega_z = \omega_K$. This is due to the fact that there is no preferred direction.

In the planetary system and in the satellite systems, the motions are *perturbed* because the gravitational fields deviate from pure $1/r^2$ fields. This is essentially due to the effects discussed in this section and in sec. 3.7.

The axial rotations (spins) produce oblateness in the planets. We can consider their gravitation to consist of a $1/r^2$ field from a sphere, on which is superimposed the field from the "equatorial bulge." The latter contains higher order terms but has the equatorial plane as the plane of symmetry. We can write the gravitational force *in the equatorial plane*

$$f_G = \frac{GM_c}{r^2}\left(1 + \frac{\Lambda}{r^2}\right) \tag{3.6.1}$$

taking acount only of the first term from the equatorial bulge. The constant Λ is always positive. From eq. (3.6.1), we find

$$\left(\frac{\partial f_G}{\partial r}\right) > \frac{2f_G}{r} \tag{3.6.2}$$

Substituting eq. (3.6.2), we have from eqs. (3.2.4), (3.3.3), and (3.3.5)

$$\omega_z > \omega_K > \omega_r \tag{3.6.3}$$

According to eqs. (3.3.12) and (3.3.18), this means that the pericenter moves with the angular velocity

$$\omega_P = \omega_K - \omega_r > 0 \tag{3.6.4}$$

in the prograde direction, and the nodes move with the angular velocity

$$\omega_{\Omega} = \omega_K - \omega_z < 0 \tag{3.6.5}$$

in the retrograde direction.

Further, we obtain from eqs. (3.3.6), (3.6.4), and (3.6.5)

$$\omega_P + \omega_{\Omega} = \frac{\omega_P{}^2 + \omega_{\Omega}{}^2}{2\omega_K} \tag{3.6.6}$$

As the right-hand term is very small, we find to a first approximation

$$\omega_P = -\omega_{\Omega} \tag{3.6.7}$$

This is a well-known result in celestial mechanics. Using this last result in eq. (3.6.6) we find, to a second approximation,

$$\omega_P = -\omega_{\Omega} + \Delta\omega \tag{3.6.8}$$

where

$$\Delta\omega = \frac{\omega_P{}^2}{\omega_K} \tag{3.6.9}$$

A comparison of eq. (3.6.9) with calculations of $\Delta\omega$ by exact methods (Alfvén and Arrhenius, 1970a, p. 349) shows a satisfactory agreement.

3.7 PLANETARY MOTION PERTURBED BY OTHER PLANETS

The motion of the body we are considering is perturbed by other bodies orbiting in the same system. Except when the motions are commensurable so that resonance effects become important, the main perturbation can be computed from the average potential produced by other bodies.

As most satellites are very small compared to their central bodies, the mutual perturbations are very small and of importance only in case of resonance. The effects due to planetary flattening described in sec. 3.6 dominate in the satellite systems. On the other hand, because the flattening of the Sun makes a negligible contribution, the perturbation of the planetary orbits is almost exclusively due to the gravitational force of the planets, among which the gravitational effect of Jupiter dominates. To calculate this to a first approximation, one smears out Jupiter's mass along its orbit and computes the gravitational potential from this massive ring. This massive ring would produce a perturbation which, both outside and inside Jupiter's orbit, would obey eq. (3.6.2). Hence eqs. (3.6.3)–(3.6.5) are also valid. The dominating term for the calculation of the perturbation of the Jovian orbit derives from a similar effect produced by Saturn. Where resonance effects occur (ch. 8), these methods are not applicable.

4

THE SMALL BODIES

4.1 SURVEY AND CLASSIFICATION

The small bodies are asteroids, comets, and meteoroids (down to the size of subvisual grains). In our analysis we shall concentrate our attention on the small bodies because they contain so much important information about the early periods of the evolution of the solar system. Furthermore, the embryonic (planetesimal) state leading to the formation of planets and satellites must necessarily have been similar, at least in some respects, to the present dynamic state of the small bodies, and we can learn much about the former by studying the latter.

In the satellite systems there may be bodies corresponding to the asteroids and meteoroids, and perhaps even to comets, but since we cannot observe such bodies we know nothing about them. The only exception is the Saturnian rings, which are known to consist of very small bodies (see sec. 18.6).

In the planetary system practically all the observed small bodies have at least part of their orbits inside the orbit of Jupiter. However, there is no reason to assume that small bodies, as yet unobserved, are not abundant in orbits beyond Jupiter.

There is a vast gap of about two orders of magnitude between the mass of the smallest planets (Mercury with $M = 33 \times 10^{25}$ g and the Moon (being a captured planet) with $M = 7.3 \times 10^{25}$ g) on the one hand and the largest "small bodies" (namely, the asteroids—Ceres with $M \simeq 12 \times 10^{23}$ g and Pallas with $M \simeq 3 \times 10^{23}$ g) on the other (Schubart, 1971). The mass distribution among *visual asteroids* is relatively continuous over 10 orders of magnitude, down to 10^{14} g for Adonis and Hermes, and probably is continued by a population of *subvisual asteroids*, down to what we may call *asteroidal grains*. We know very little about the latter groups. Neither the micrometeoroid detectors nor the optical asteroid/meteoroid detector on the Pioneer 10 flyby mission to Jupiter registered any increase in space density of particles in the range 10^{-3} to 0.15 cm while passing through the asteroid belt. A significant increase in the abundance of larger particles (0.15–1.5 cm) was, however, observed in the belt (Soberman et al., 1974; Kinard et al., 1974).

The term "meteoroid" was originally used for a body moving in space which, upon entering the Earth's atmosphere, produces a *meteor* and, in very rare cases, may be retreived on the ground as a *meteorite*. However, the term meteoroid is now used for any small piece of matter moving in space.

The comets differ in appearance from the asteroids in having a diffuse region, the coma, and, at least during some part of their orbit, dust and plasma tails. They are often, but not always, observed to have one or more nuclei. Cometary mass is not very well known but probably falls within a range similar to that for a small asteroid (10^{15}–10^{19} g).

The orbits of asteroids, comets, and meteoroids share, in part, the same region of *interplanetary space,* but they are located in vastly different regions of *velocity space.* We may describe their orbital motion by three parameters: the semimajor axis a, the eccentricity e, and the inclination i of the orbit. From ch. 3 we find that a is a measure of the average distance from the central body, e is a measure of the radial oscillation, and i is a measure of the axial oscillation about the average distance.

The orbital data for about 1800 asteroids are listed in *Ephemerides of Minor Planets.* Recently the Palomar-Leiden survey has added 2000 new asteroidal orbits (van Houten et al., 1970). Orbital data for comets are found in the *Catalogue of Cometary Orbits* (Porter, 1961).

If we classify the small bodies by their values of a, e, and i, we find that almost all of them belong to one of *six populations* (figs. 4.3.3, 4.4.1 and 4.6.1), three of which are large, and three, small. The three large populations are

(1) *Main-belt asteroids:*

$$e < 1/3, \qquad i < 20°, \qquad 2.1 < a < 3.5 \text{ AU}$$

(2) *Short-period comets and meteoroids (including Apollo-Amor asteroids):*

$$1/3 < e < 0.95, \qquad i < 30°, \qquad a < 15 \text{ AU}$$

(3) *Long-period comets and meteoroids:*

$$e > 0.95, \qquad i \text{ is random}, \qquad a > 15 \text{ AU}$$

The three small populations are

(4) *The Trojans (captured in and oscillating about the Lagrangian points behind and ahead of Jupiter):*

$$a \sim 5.2 \text{ AU}$$

(5) *The Hilda asteroids:*

$$e \sim 0.2, \qquad i \sim 10°, \qquad a \sim 3.95 \text{ AU}$$

(6) *The Hungaria asteroids:*

$$e \sim 0.1, \qquad i \sim 25°, \qquad a \sim 1.9 \text{ AU}$$

The asteroid groups (4), (5), and (6) do not lie within the main belt. The reason for choosing $e = 1/3$ as a limit will become obvious in ch. 17. The choice of the limit between short- and long-period comets and meteoroids is a question of semantics. In lists of comets the border is usually taken to be $T = 200$ yr, corresponding to $a = 34$ AU, whereas for meteors the limit is taken as $T = 12$ yr ($a = 5.2$ AU). Our choice of 15 AU is intermediate. For an orbit of eccentricity 0.95, perihelion is at 0.75 AU.

4.2 EVOLUTIONARY DIFFERENCES BETWEEN LARGE AND SMALL BODIES

The present-day evolution of the planets and satellites differs very much from that of the small bodies. As we will discuss further in ch. 10, there seems to have been very little change in the dynamic structure of the big-body population during the last few billion years. Two exceptions are known: the Moon and Triton, which are likely to have been planets. During and after their capture by the Earth and Neptune, respectively, their orbits were altered by tidal effects.

All satellites and planets have small periodic changes in their orbits due to "perturbations," but there is no certain evidence of any major systematic change in the orbits. Thus the motions of the planets and satellites are likely to have been governed exclusively by the laws of classical celestial mechanics. The large-body system probably reached a "final" state very similar to the present one as early as 4 or even 4.5 Gyr ago.

In contrast to this stability of the big-body population, the small-body populations are in a state of evolution. This evolution is very rapid for comets, which may change their appearance from one day to the next, and which have a total lifetime of the order of a few hundred years.

The asteroidal rate of evolution falls within the extreme values for come-tary and planetary evolution. If we calculate the collision probability for asteroids we find that collisions necessarily must occur, resulting in orbital changes, fragmentation, and accretion. However, these processes have never been directly observed, and as we do not know the physical properties of the asteroids, we cannot with certainty predict whether these collisions predominantly lead to accretion or to fragmentation.

As we shall see later (sec. 18.8), there are some features of the asteroidal belt which cannot have changed very much since formation. For the visual asteroids, evolutionary effects have a time constant of millions or billions of years. On the other hand, the subvisual asteroids must necessarily inter-act so much as to produce a more rapid evolution.

The mutual collisions between small bodies affect their orbits. From a theoretical point of view we are confronted with the problem of an inter-action among a large number of bodies which is similar to a basic problem in plasma physics. The treatment of celestial mechanics in ch. 3, based on the guiding-center method, is actually designed to facilitate the contact with plasma physics which is necessary for the understanding of the evolu-tion of the asteroid population and also of the precursor states of planets and satellites. The orbital evolution of the small bodies will be discussed in chs. 5, 13, 14, 18, and 19.

4.3 MAIN-BELT ASTEROIDS

The main-belt asteroids, of which more than 1700 are tabulated in *Ephe-merides of Minor Planets* and another 1800 in the Palomar-Leiden survey, move in the region between Mars and Jupiter. (The lists of asteroids also include some bodies which, according to our classification, are not main-belt asteroids.) The orbits of main-belt asteroids have, on the average, higher eccentricities and inclinations than those of the major planets. Data on asteroidal eccentricities, as given in the *Ephemerides of Minor Planets* for 1968, are shown in fig. 4.3.1. The average eccentricity is 0.14. There are few asteroids with eccentricities higher than 0.25.

Figure 4.3.2 shows the number of asteroids as a function of inclination; data are from the 1968 *Ephemerides*. The average inclination is 9.7 deg, and there are few asteroids with inclinations above 25 deg. Graphs showing statistical correlations between various orbital elements of the asteroids have been published by Brown et al. (1967).

If we plot the number N of known asteroids as a function of the semi-major axis a we obtain fig. 4.3.3 (*the N, a diagram*). We see that most of the asteroids are located between 2.1 and 3.5 AU, constituting the *main belt*. The diagram shows a series of sharp gaps where very few, if any, asteroids are found. The location of these gaps agrees well with the distances at which resonance effects from Jupiter should occur. As the period T is proportional to $a^{3/2}$, all bodies with a certain a value have the same period. The gaps correspond to $T/T_{\mathcal{U}} = \frac{1}{2}, \frac{1}{3}, \frac{2}{5}$, and $\frac{3}{7}$, the gap for $\frac{1}{2}$ being very pronounced. Gaps corresponding to $\frac{2}{7}, \frac{3}{8}, \frac{3}{10}, \frac{4}{11}, \frac{5}{12}, \frac{6}{13}$ have also been traced

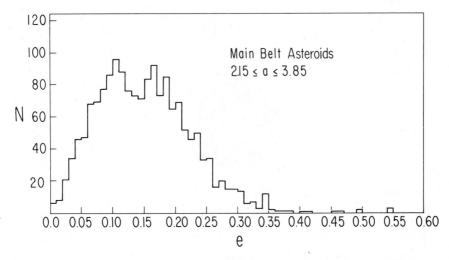

FIGURE 4.3.1.—Number of asteroids as a function of eccentricity. Data from the *Ephemerides of Minor Planets* for 1968 are shown for 1670 asteroids.

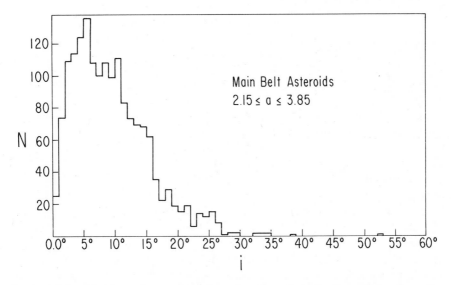

FIGURE 4.3.2.—Number of asteroids as a function of inclination. Data from the *Ephemerides of Minor Planets* for 1968 are shown for 1670 asteroids.

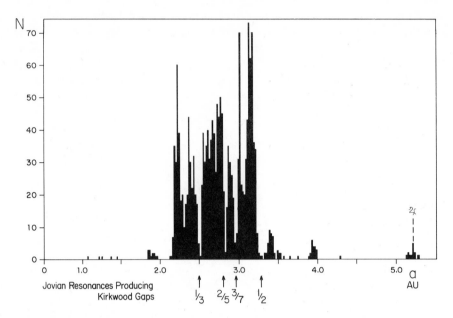

FIGURE 4.3.3.—*The (N, a) diagram* (number of asteroids as a function of semimajor axis). Most asteroids are located between 2.1 and 3.5 AU, constituting the main belt. The groups at 1.9, 3.9, and 5.2 AU are the Hungaria, Hilda, and Trojan asteroids, respectively. The sharp minima in the main belt are the Kirkwood gaps which occur at the $\frac{1}{3}$, $\frac{2}{5}$, $\frac{3}{7}$, and $\frac{1}{2}$ resonances of Jupiter.

(Hirayama, 1918). Perhaps Mars also produces a resonance at $T/T_{\sigma} = 2$ (Dermott and Lenham, 1972), but no resonance with the period of Saturn or any other planet has been found. Although the location of these gaps, which are known as the *Kirkwood gaps*,[1] at the resonance points leaves no doubt that they are due to a resonance; the mechanism producing the gaps is not understood (sec. 8.6).

As pointed out by Burkenroad (Alfvén et al., 1974), the number-density distribution (N, a) diagram does not give a very good picture of the real mass distribution (M, a) in the asteroidal belt. For example, some families contain a large number of very small bodies. As asteroid masses have not been measured directly we use eq. (4.3.3) to calculate the asteroid mass and plot the (M, a) *diagram* (fig. 4.3.4). The diagram shows that practically all mass is located in the main belt between 2.1 and 3.5 AU. Of the asteroids outside this region, only the Hildas (at 3.95 AU) have a considerable mass.

The Kirkwood gaps are more pronounced in the (M, a) diagram than

---

[1] As Kopal (1973) has noted, their existence was first pointed out by K. Hornstein.

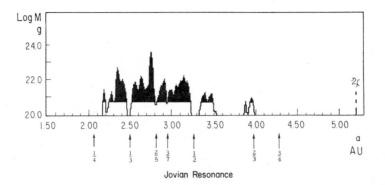

FIGURE 4.3.4.—*The (M, a) diagram* (mass of asteroids in g per 0.01 AU as a function of semimajor axis *a* in AU). To stress the logarithmic scale, the region of greatest mass density is shaded. These regions contain practically all the mass in the asteroid belt. Mass was calculated from magnitude using eq. (4.3.3). The diagram includes data for all asteroids of *a* < 5.0 AU listed in the *Ephemerides of Minor Planets* for 1968. The resonances are indicated as the ratio of the orbital period of a body at a specific value of *a* to the orbital period of Jupiter. The Kirkwood gaps correspond to the $\frac{1}{3}$, $\frac{2}{5}$, $\frac{3}{7}$, and $\frac{1}{2}$ resonances. (From Alfvén et al., 1974.)

in the (*N*, *a*) diagram, especially in the case of the 1/2 resonance gap. In contrast to the (*N*, *a*) diagram, the (*M*, *a*) plot is not likely to change very much as new asteroids are discovered since these new asteroids will necessarily be small.

The masses and radii of Ceres, Vesta, and Juno have been measured (see Schubart, 1971; Morrison, 1973), but the values are probably not definitive (table 4.3.1). The diameters of other asteroids are too small to be measured, and their masses cannot be determined directly. Therefore sizes and masses are estimated from their apparent magnitudes with reasonable assumptions about the albedo and the average density. Following Allen (1963), we use

$$\log R = 2.95 - 0.5 \log p - 0.2g \tag{4.3.1}$$

where *R* is the radius of the asteroid in km, *p* is the albedo, and *g* is the absolute visual magnitude (defined as the apparent magnitude at a distance of 1 AU). Putting *p* = 0.135 (Ceres albedo) we obtain

$$\log R = 3.385 - 0.2g \tag{4.3.2}$$

TABLE 4.3.1

Physical Properties and Orbital Parameters of Selected Asteroids

Number and name	Radius [a]	Mass [b]	Magnitude[c]	Spin Period [h]	Orbital parameters [e]			
					T	a	e	i
	km	g		hr	days	AU		°
1 Ceres	[d] 567	[f] 1.2×10^{24}	4.0	9.07	1681	2.767	0.079	10.6
2 Pallas	[e] 350	[g] 3.0×10^{23}	5.1		1684	2.767	0.235	34.8
3 Juno	[e] 98	[f] 1.4×10^{22}	6.3	7.21	1594	2.670	0.256	13.0
4 Vesta	[d] 285	[f] 2.4×10^{23}	4.2	5.34	1325	2.361	0.088	7.1
6 Hebe	116	2.4×10^{22}	6.6	7.74	1380	2.426	0.203	14.8
7 Iris	110	2.1×10^{22}	6.7		1344	2.385	0.230	5.5
10 Hygiea	127	3.1×10^{22}	6.4		2042	3.151	0.099	3.8
15 Eunomia	140	4.1×10^{22}	6.2	6.08	1569	2.645	0.185	11.8
16 Psyche	106	1.8×10^{22}	6.8	4.30	1826	2.923	0.135	3.1
51 Nemausa	46	1.5×10^{21}	8.6	7.78	1330	2.366	0.065	9.9
433 Eros	8	9.0×10^{18}	12.3	5.27	642	1.458	0.223	10.8
511 Davida	97	1.4×10^{22}	7.0	5.17	2072	3.182	0.177	15.7
1566 Icarus	0.7	5.2×10^{15}	17.7	2.27	408	1.077	0.827	23.0
1620 Geographos	1.6	6.2×10^{15}	15.9	5.22	507	1.244	0.335	13.3
1932 HA Apollo	0.5	2.0×10^{15}	18		662	1.486	0.566	6.4
1936 CA Adonis	0.15	5.0×10^{13}	21		1008	1.969	0.779	1.5
1937 UB Hermes	0.3	4.0×10^{14}	19		535	1.290	0.475	4.7

[a] Calculated as a function of magnitude g using eq. (4.3.2): $\log R = 3.85 - 0.2g$. Albedo of 0.135 has been assumed.

[b] Calculated as a function of magnitude g from eq. (4.3.3): $\log M = 26.4 - 0.6g$. Spherical shape, albedo of 0.135, and average density of 3.6 g cm^{-3} have been assumed.

[c] Allen, 1963.

[d] Morrison, 1973.

[e] Dollfus, 1971a.

[f] Schubart, 1971.

[g] Calculated using the tabulated value of the radius and assuming spherical shape.

[h] Gehrels, 1971.

With the assumption of an average density of 3.6 g/cm³, we find

$$\log M = 26.4 - 0.6g \qquad (4.3.3)$$

for M in grams (see table 4.3.1).

4.3.1 Subvisual Asteroids

There are good reasons to suppose that the asteroid population is continuous and includes very small bodies which we may call "asteroidal grains." From Earth-based observations we know nothing about the size spectra of subvisual asteroids. Extrapolations of the size spectra of visual asteroids have been made, for example, by Dohnanyi (1969), who has treated all known asteroids as one single distribution. This is a rather dangerous procedure because the (M, N) relation differs among the populations and hence varies with a (as is obvious from the difference between the (N, a) and (M, a) diagrams (figs. 4.3.3 and 4.3.4)).

The subvisual asteroids may be of decisive importance in keeping jet streams (ch. 6.) together. They may also be important for other viscosity effects in interplanetary space. The only way of getting information about them is probably from space probes sent to the asteroid belt. The micrometeoroid impact experiment (Kinard et al., 1974) on the Pioneer 10 flyby mission to Jupiter demonstrated that there is no substantial increase in the asteroid belt of particles of about 10^{-3} cm. For larger particles, which have smaller number densities, impact instrumentation does not provide statistically significant information. For the size range 10^{-2} to 15 cm, data were first obtained by the optical telescope experiment on Pioneer 10 (Soberman et al., 1974). These measurements show an increase in the largest particles (1.5 to 15 cm in size) in the asteroidal belt.

4.3.2 Hirayama Families

Hirayama (1918) discovered the grouping of some asteroids in families. The members of one family have almost the same values of a, i, and e. As Brouwer (1951) has pointed out, both i and e are subject to secular variations with periods of the order 10^4 to 10^5 yr. From a hetegonic point of view, we want to eliminate these. This can be done by introducing the "proper elements."

The eccentricity e and the longitude ϕ_P of the perihelion of a Kepler orbit are subject to secular variations. The same is the case for the inclination i and the longitude of the ascending node ϕ_Ω. Following Brouwer (1951) and Brouwer and Clemence (1961b) we write:

$$e \cos \phi_P = E \cos \Phi_P + p_0 \qquad (4.3.4)$$

$$e \sin \phi_P = E \sin \Phi_P + q_0 \qquad (4.3.5)$$

$$\sin i \cos \phi_\Omega = I \cos \Phi_\Omega + P_0 \qquad (4.3.6)$$

$$\sin i \sin \phi_\Omega = I \sin \Phi_\Omega + Q_0 \qquad (4.3.7)$$

For a given asteroid the proper eccentricity E and the proper inclination I are constants. The longitude of the proper perihelion Φ_P increases and the longitude of the proper node Φ_Ω decreases at the same uniform rate, with one cycle occurring in the period T_Φ. The quantities p_0, q_0, P_0, and Q_0 are the forced oscillations produced by planetary perturbations, p_0 and q_0 being functions of the planetary eccentricities and perihelia and P_0 and Q_0 being functions of the planetary inclinations and nodes. The period as well as the forced oscillations are all functions of the mean orbital distance a; the sample values in table 4.3.2 are taken from Brouwer (1951) and Brouwer and van Woerkom (1950). For further detail see Kiang (1966).

Figure 4.3.5 shows the relationship between the "osculating" elements (referring to the present orbits) and the "proper" elements according to Kiang (1966). The vectors E and I rotate around a center O' with periods given in table 4.3.2. The distance of the vector from origin gives the numerical value of e and i, and the angles these lines make with their respective horizontal axes give the longitudes of the perihelion and the node. The position of the center O' is essentially given by the eccentricity and inclination of Jupiter and varies with a period of 300 000 yr.

Brouwer (1951) has given the values of E, I, Φ_P, and Φ_Ω for 1537 asteroids. Based on this material, he treats the problem of Hirayama families. He demonstrates that in an (E, I) diagram the points belonging to a Hirayama family show a somewhat higher concentration than in an (e, i) diagram. This enhanced concentration made it possible for him to detect a number

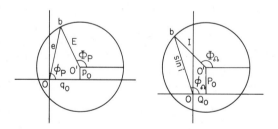

FIGURE 4.3.5.—Geometric illustration of the relationship of the
osculating elements (e, ϕ_P, i, ϕ_Ω) to the proper elements (E,
Φ_P, I, Φ_Ω) of motion for asteroids. As the representative point
b describes a circle of typical period of 20 000 yr about point
O, point O' migrates such that E and I remain constant. The
vectors give the values for e, E, $\sin i$ and I, and the angle each
vector makes with the horizontal axis gives the appropriate
longitude of perihelion or ascending node. The vector OO', a
function of the forced oscillation p_0, q_0, P_0, and Q_0, is predominately determined by the eccentricity and inclination of Jupiter.
(From Kiang, 1966.)

TABLE 4.3.2

Typical Values of the Periodic Variation in the Proper Elements of
Asteroid Orbital Motion

a (AU)	T_Φ (yr)	q_0	p_0	Q_0	P_0
2.15	41 400	+0.0567	−0.0363	+0.0108	+0.0031
2.60	26 300	+0.0302	−0.0056	−0.0006	+0.0181
3.15	14 400	+0.0374	+0.0058	−0.0029	+0.0210
4.00	4 400	+0.0421	+0.0093	−0.0038	+0.0222

Tabulated values from Brouwer (1951) and Brouwer and van Woerkom (1950).

of new families. For example, it is evident that the largest of the families, the Flora family, consists of at least two, and possibly four families, called Flora I, II, III, and IV.

For orbital motion adequately described by celestial mechanics, the sum $\Phi_P + \Phi_\Omega$ is an invariant to a first approximation (eq. (3.6.7)). Brouwer shows that for some families there is a maximum of $\Phi_P + \Phi_\Omega$ characteristic of families or groups. Subjecting all asteroid data to computer analysis, Arnold (1969) has revised Brouwer's analysis of asteroid families. He has confirmed the existence of all the Hirayama families and of some but not all the Brouwer families. Further, he has discovered a number of new families.

Lindblad and Southworth (1971) have made a similar study using another statistical method to discriminate between real families and those which are due to statistical fluctuations. They confirm Hirayama's and essential parts of Brouwer's families and also some, but not all, of Arnold's new families. They conclude that about 40 percent of all numbered asteroids belong to families. They have also subjected the new asteroids discovered by the Palomar-Leiden survey to similar tests (Lindblad and Southworth, 1971).

4.3.3 Asteroidal Jet Streams

Members of the same family generally have different values of Φ_P and Φ_Ω. This means that the space orientation of their orbits differs. In some cases, however, there are a number of orbits with the same Φ_Ω and Φ_P, so that all five orbital parameters (a, i, e, Φ_Ω, Φ_P) are similar. Hence, their orbits almost coincide, and the asteroids are said to be members of a "jet stream" (Alfvén, 1969; Arnold, 1969; Danielsson, 1969a). Using a method that has proved successful in detecting meteor streams, Lindblad and Southworth (1971) have made searches independently in the numbered asteroid population (*Ephemerides of Minor Planets*) and in Palomar-Leiden data. They find 13 jet streams with at least 7 members. The largest jet stream has 19 members. Their streams only partially overlap with those defined by Arnold.

Danielsson (1971) points out some of the limitations of the earlier work and introduces a new method to find "the profile of a jet stream." He calculates the distance between the intersections of two orbits with a heliocentric meridian plane as a function of the longitude and takes the mean quadratic value of the quantity as a measure of the "distance" between the orbits. This distance is a measure of how closely the orbits are associated. Applying this method to three of the jet streams, he concludes that the orbits of all the members of the jet stream are well collimated everywhere along the path. As an example, the profile of the Flora A jet stream is shown in fig. 4.3.6. Furthermore, two of the streams show marked focusing regions where a majority of the orbits come very close together and where the relative velocities are an order of magnitude smaller than those between randomly coinciding asteroid orbits. In fact, the relative velocities are as low as 0.2 to 1 km/sec. This should be compared to the orbital velocities of about 20 km/sec and the average collision velocity of two arbitrary asteroids, which is in the range 2 to 5 km/sec (Danielsson, 1971). As we shall see in chs. 11 and 12, this result is important for the theory of accretion.

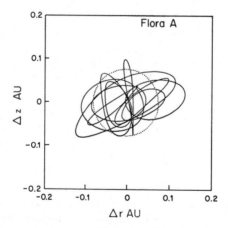

FIGURE 4.3.6.—Profile of the Flora A jet stream. Diagram shows the intersections of the individual orbits of these asteroids with a heliocentric meridional plane as this plane is rotated one cycle around the ecliptic polar axis. The positions of the orbits are shown relative to the mean orbit of the jet stream. The dotted circle shows the cross section of the jet stream as theoretically calculated in secs. 12.2 and 12.7. Most of the asteroid orbits in Flora A fall within the dotted circle. Profiles of other asteroidal jet streams show less concentration. (From Danielsson, 1971.)

4.3.4 Evolution of the Main Belt

The main-belt asteroids were earlier thought to be debris of one or more "exploded planets." As we shall find (secs. 11.8 and 18.8), there are decisive arguments against this view. Instead, we should consider them as a large number of "planetesimals," accreted from small grains that have condensed from a plasma. They are in a state of evolution that eventually may concentrate most of their mass into one or a few bodies. Even now almost 80 percent of the total mass in the asteroid belt is contained in the four biggest bodies.

The study of the main-belt asteroids is of hetegonic importance because the state in this region is likely to be similar in certain respects to a state of accretion through which all planet and satellite groups once have passed. Whereas this evolutionary period required perhaps 10^8 yr for the formation of planets and satellites (ch. 12), the time scale for a corresponding evolution in the asteroidal belt is longer than the age of the solar system. The reason is the extremely low density of matter in the asteroidal region (see ch. 2), which in fact is 10^{-5} of the distributed density in the adjacent planetary regions. The evolution of the main belt will be discussed later, especially in sec. 18.8.

4.4 THE HILDA AND HUNGARIA ASTEROIDS

Outside the main belt there is a small group, the Hilda asteroids, at $a \simeq 3.95$ AU. These are captured in resonance by Jupiter so that their periods are (averaged over a very long time) 2/3 of Jupiter's period (see sec. 8.5.4). There is a single asteroid, Thule, not very far from the Hildas which is also captured in a similar way, but its period is 3/4 of Jupiter's. These will be discussed in connection with the theory of resonances (ch. 8).

The Hungaria asteroids, at $a \simeq 1.9$ AU, are orbiting just inside the inner boundary of the main belt. They have been believed to be in 2/9 resonance with Jupiter, but this seems not to be the case (Ip, 1974b). Their inclinations are usually high ($i \simeq 25°$), but they have an eccentricity <0.2 (see fig. 4.4.1).

The existence of groups of bodies at the Jupiter resonance points 3/4 and 2/3 (perhaps 2/9) constitutes an analogy to the resonance captures in the satellite systems and also to the Neptune-Pluto resonance. At the same time, the positions of these bodies present a puzzling contrast to the absence of bodies at the Kirkwood gaps. This will be discussed in ch. 8.

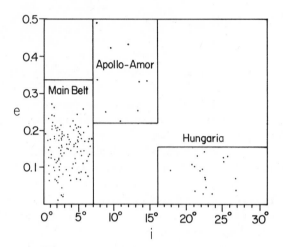

FIGURE 4.4.1.—The inner region of the asteroid belt ($a<2.2$ AU) The main-belt asteroids ($2.0<a<2.2$) have small eccentricities and inclinations; the Apollo-Amor asteroids, higher inclinations and eccentricities; and the Hungaria asteroids ($1.8<a<2.0$), high inclinations but small eccentricities. Data from the *Ephemerides of Minor Planets* for 1968.

4.5 THE TROJANS

In the orbit of Jupiter there are two points, one 60° behind and one 60° ahead of Jupiter, at which points a body can move in a fixed position with regard to Jupiter and the Sun (see fig. 8.5.3). In the neighborhood of these points—the Lagrangian points—there are a number of small bodies, the Trojans, which usually are included in tables of asteroids. They oscillate[2] about these points. Their period, averaged over a long time, is necessarily the same as Jupiter's. Their origin is probably different from that of all other groups of asteroids. In fact, they are likely to be remnants of the planetesimals from which Jupiter once accreted. It is possible that the retrograde satellites of Jupiter, which are likely to be captured, have a genetic connection with the Trojans.

It is possible that there are similar groups of small bodies in the Lagrangian points of other planetary bodies, but these have not yet been discovered.

Clouds of small bodies in the Moon's Lagrangian points (in its orbit around the Earth) were first reported by Kordylevsky. Recent observations from spacecraft in transit to the Moon are claimed to verify their existence (Roach, 1975).

---

[2] What in other branches of science is called "oscillation" is in celestial mechanics traditionally termed "libration."

4.6 THE COMETARY-METEOROID POPULATIONS

In the same region of space as the asteroids we have discussed, there is *another population of bodies*, the comets and meteoroids. Due to their high eccentricities, $(e \gtrsim 1/3)$, comets and meteoroids occupy a different region in velocity space than do the asteroids. A transition between the two regions can be achieved only by a change of the velocity vector by at least a few km/sec. This seems to be a rather unlikely process because a high-velocity impact usually results in fragmentation, melting, and vaporization, but only to a limited extent in a change in the velocity vector. In principle, a transition could be achieved by planetary perturbations of the orbits, but such processes are probably important only in special cases (Zimmerman and Wetherill, 1973) if at all. Hence there seems to be a rather clear distinction between the comet-meteoroid populations and those asteroid populations which we have discussed.

4.6.1 Comets and Apollo-Amor Asteroids

The origin of the high-eccentricity population is likely to be different from that of the asteroid population. The former will be discussed in chs. 14 and 19 and the latter in ch. 18. Most of the visible members of these populations are comets, but there are also other visible bodies in essentially similar orbits which do not have the appearance of comets but look like ordinary asteroids. They are called, after prominent members of their groups, "Amor asteroids" if their orbits cross Mars' orbit, but not the Earth's orbit, and "Apollo asteroids" if their orbits cross both. Sometimes both groups are referred to as "cometary asteroids." Figure 4.4.1 shows that these asteroids occupy a region in velocity space distinct from that occupied by the main-belt asteroids. As we shall see later, there are good reasons to suppose that the Apollo-Amor asteroids are genetically associated with the comets; they are thus sometimes (with a somewhat misleading metaphor) referred to as burned-out comets.

4.6.2 Meteor Streams

Comets are closely related to *meteor streams*. In accordance with the definition in sec. 4.1, a meteor stream in a strict sense is a stream of meteoroids in space that is observable because it is intercepted by the Earth's atmosphere where the meteoroids give rise to luminous phenomena (meteors). There must obviously be many meteoroid streams that never come sufficiently close to Earth to be called meteor streams. To simplify terminology, we will refer to all elliptic streams (table 19.8.1) as meteor streams. The orbital elements of some stream meteors are the same as those of certain comets (fig. 4.6.1), indicating a genetic relationship. We would expect that a large number of meteor streams, as yet undetected, exist in interplanetary and transplanetary space. (Micrometeoroid impact detectors on space probes are now in operation, but their cross sections are very small; optical detectors (see Soberman et al., 1974) promise improved data.)

Not all meteors belong to a meteor stream. The Earth's atmosphere is also hit by "sporadic meteors" in random orbits; however, they might belong to yet undiscovered meteor streams.

The long-period and short-period comets/meteoroids have such different dynamic properties that it is practical to divide them into two populations. The boundary between these populations is somewhat arbitrary. If we

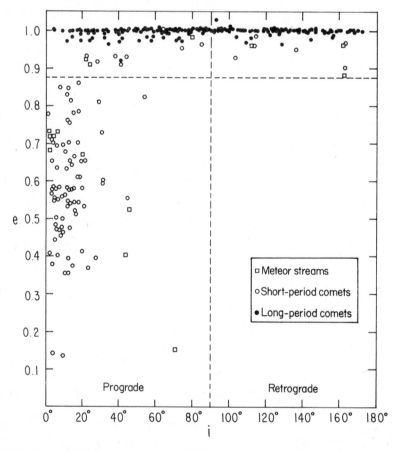

FIGURE 4.6.1.—Meteor streams, short-period comets, and long-period comets. Retrograde bodies are only found in almost parabolic orbits ($e > 0.85$). Data from Porter (1961).

classify them according to their periods, we find that for $T > T_1$ the orbital inclinations are random, varying from $+180°$ to $-180°$, and we define this population as *long-period comets/meteoroids*. On the other hand, for $T < T_2$, all the bodies have prograde orbits. We call this population *short-period comets/meteoroids*. This leaves us with a transition region of medium-period bodies $(T_2 < T < T_1)$ in which the prograde dominance becomes more marked with decreasing T. The observational values are $T_1 = 200$ and $T_2 = 15$ yr, corresponding to aphelion distances of about 70 and 10 AU.

4.6.3 Long-Period Comets

Of the 525 comets with accurately determined orbits, 199 are elliptic, 274 almost parabolic, and 52 slightly hyperbolic (Vsekhsvyatsky, 1958, p. 2; see also fig. 4.6.1). However, if the orbits of the hyperbolic comets are corrected for planetary disturbances, all of them seem to become nearly parabolic. Hence, there is no certain evidence that comets come from interstellar space. As far as we know, all comets seem to belong to the solar system. Planetary disturbances, however, change the orbits of some comets so that they are ejected from the solar system into interstellar space.

As most cometary orbits are very eccentric, the approximation methods that were developed in ch. 3 are not applicable. The following relations between semimajor axis a, specific orbital angular momentum C, perihelion r_P, aphelion r_A, and velocities v_A at r_A and v_P at r_P are useful. We have

$$C^2 = GM_c a(1 - e^2) \qquad (4.6.1)$$

$$r_A = a(1 + e) \qquad (4.6.2)$$

$$r_P = a(1 - e) \qquad (4.6.3)$$

and

$$v_A = \frac{C}{a(1+e)} = \left[\frac{GM_c(1-e)}{r_A} \right]^{1/2} = v_\oplus \left[\frac{r_\oplus(1-e)}{r_A} \right]^{1/2} \qquad (4.6.4)$$

where $v_\oplus = 3 \times 10^6$ cm/sec is the orbital velocity of the Earth and $r_\oplus$, its orbital radius. Similarly

$$v_P = \frac{C}{a(1-e)} = \left[\frac{GM_c(1+e)}{r_P}\right]^{1/2} = v_\oplus \left[\frac{r_\oplus(1+e)}{r_P}\right]^{1/2} \qquad (4.6.5)$$

As e approaches unity, we have approximately

$$v_A \sim v_\oplus \left(\frac{2r_\oplus r_P}{r_A^2}\right)^{1/2} \qquad (4.6.6)$$

It is often impossible to ascertain definitely whether the highly eccentric orbits of long-period comets are elliptical or parabolic; we shall refer to these comets as "almost parabolic." The almost-parabolic comets may in reality be elliptical but with their aphelia situated in what Oort (1963) calls the "cometary reservoir," a region extending out to at least 10^{17} cm (0.1 light-yr). Their orbital periods range from 10^3 up to perhaps 10^6 yr (see Oort, 1963). This theory has further been discussed by Lyttleton (1968). The long-period comets spend most of their lifetime near their aphelia, but at regular intervals they make a quick visit to the regions close to the Sun. It is only in the special case where the comet's perihelion is less than a few times 10^{13} cm that it can be observed. Even the order of magnitude of the total number of comets in the solar system is unknown, but one would guess that it is very large.

The space orientation of the orbits of long-period comets appears random, the number of such comets in prograde orbits being almost the same as the number in retrograde orbits. From this we tend to conclude that on the average the comets in the reservoir are at rest in relation to the Sun, or, in other words, share the solar motion in the galaxy. From eq. (4.6.6) a comet whose perihelion is at 10^{13} cm will at its aphelion have a tangential velocity of 5×10^4 cm/sec if $r_A = 10^{15}$ cm, and 5×10^2 cm/sec if $r_A = 10^{17}$ cm. As the solar velocity in relation to neighboring stars is of the order of several km/sec, these low velocities in the cometary reservoir clearly indicate that this reservoir is a part of the solar system. However, it is not quite clear whether this conclusion is valid because the comets are selected; only those which have perihelia of less than a few AU can be observed from the Earth.

If comets originate in the environment of other stars or in a random region in interstellar space, their orbits should be hyperbolas easily distinguishable from the nearly parabolic orbits observed. Hence we have confirming evidence that the comets are true members of our solar system and that the cometary reservoir is an important part of the solar system.

Oort (1963) has suggested that the comets originally were formed near Jupiter and then ejected into the cometary reservoir by encounters with

Jupiter. This seems very unlikely. As we shall see in the following it is more likely that the long-period comets were accreted out in the cometary reservoir. Objections to such a process by Öpik (1963, 1966) and others are not valid because they are based on homogeneous models of the transplanetary medium (see chs. 15 and 19).

4.6.4 Short-Period Comets

The short-period comets differ from the long-period comets in that their orbits are predominantly prograde. In fact, there is not a single retrograde comet with a period of less than 15 yr (Porter, 1963, pp. 556, 557). The short-period comets have long been thought to be long-period comets that accidentally have come very close to Jupiter, with the result that their orbits have been changed (Everhart, 1969). This process is qualitatively possible, but its probability is several orders of magnitude too small to account for the observed number of short-period comets (sec. 19.6) (unless we make the ad hoc assumption that there is a special "reservoir" supplying comets to be captured by Jupiter, an assumption that leads to other difficulties).

As we shall see in chs. 14 and 19, it is more likely that short-period comets are generated by accretion in short-period meteor streams. After a certain period of activity, the comet may end its life span as an Apollo-Amor asteroid (Öpik, 1961). Hence, the similarity in orbits between short-period stream meteors, comets, and Apollo-Amor asteroids could be due to a genetic relationship between them, which suggests that they ought to be treated as one single population (see sec. 19.6). A similar process may also account for the formation of long-period comets in long-period meteor streams.

5

FORCES ACTING ON SMALL BODIES

5.1 INTRODUCTION

Even if a hetegonic theory were restricted to explaining the origin of the planets and satellites alone, the study of the motion of smaller bodies is of basic importance because the large bodies once accreted from small bodies. A large number of small bodies—asteroids, comets, and meteoroids—move in interplanetary space. The latter category includes micrometeoroids (interplanetary dust). Although generally not included in the discussion of small bodies there are also the constituents of the interplanetary plasma: atoms, molecules, ions, and electrons. The total mass spectrum excluding the Sun covers about 57 orders of magnitude from electrons (10^{-27} g) to Jupiter (2×10^{30} g). The dynamic behavior of bodies in space depends in a decisive way on their mass. The bodies at the upper end of the mass spectrum obey the laws of *celestial mechanics*, whereas the particles at the lower end must be dealt with in the framework of *plasma physics*. See fig. 5.1.1.

5.2 GRAVITATIONAL EFFECTS

A body with a mass M is subject to the Newtonian gravitation

$$\mathbf{f_G} = -GM \sum_n \frac{M_n}{r_n^3} \mathbf{r_n} \qquad (5.2.1)$$

where G is the gravitational constant, M_n is the mass of other bodies, and $\mathbf{r_n}$ is the position vector of M_n with respect to M.

The motions of the large bodies (e.g., the planets) are exclusively dominated by $\mathbf{f_G}$ and hence obey the laws of celestial mechanics. (The tiny perturbation of the motion of Mercury, which is attributed to general relativity effects, is not significant for this discussion.)

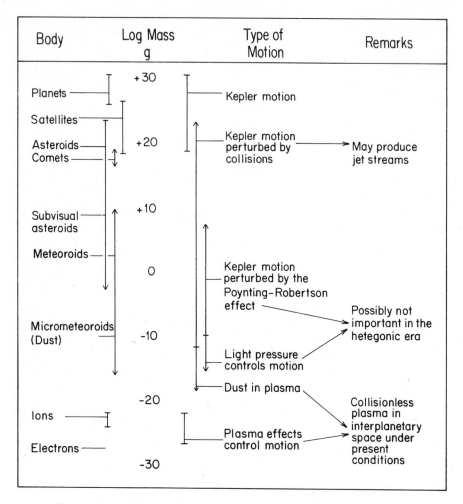

FIGURE 5.1.1.—Survey of forces governing the motion of bodies in space.

5.2.1 Kepler Motion

As we have seen in ch. 3, the motion of planets and satellites can be very accurately described by Kepler's laws. The motion of the *asteroids* follows the same laws. No exception to this rule has been observed, even for the smallest observed asteroids (of the size of one kilometer). However, because of the large number of asteroids in the main belt, we should expect that they sometimes collide, with the result that a discontinuous change in their orbits takes place. Because the collisional cross section per unit mass of all asteroids increases with decreasing size of the asteroids (see ch. 7), the influence of collisions must be greater the smaller the bodies. Thus the motion of subvisual asteroids from kilometer size down to the small particles now known to exist (Kinard et al., 1974; Soberman et al., 1974), is likely to be affected both by collisional processes and by other nongravitational forces which we discuss below.

The motion of *comets* also obeys the Kepler laws, but only to a first approximation. Deviations from Kepler motion are ascribed to nongravitational effects (Marsden, 1968), which we will discuss later.

5.2.2 Collision-Perturbed Kepler Motion

As seen from fig. 5.1.1, an important type of motion is the Kepler motion perturbed by collisions with other bodies or particles. A motion of this type is difficult to treat by celestial mechanics in its traditional formulation. In fact, celestial mechanics can handle the *two-body problem* very well, and, if sufficiently computerized, also the *few-body problem*. For example, the motion of a planet is treated as a two-body problem with perturbations caused by several other bodies. In contrast to this simplifying description of planetary motion, the mutual interaction among asteroids and among meteoroids constitutes a *many-body problem*, of the same general type as is treated in theoretical plasma physics. Indeed, the collisions among asteroids and among meteoroids are analogous to the collisions among particles in a plasma and can be treated by the same general formalism. The somewhat unconventional presentation of celestial mechanics in ch. 3 is designed to facilitate synthesis of celestial mechanics and the formalism of plasma physics.

As we shall discuss in more detail in ch. 6, the collisions between bodies in Kepler orbits lead, under certain conditions, to a focusing effect that concentrates the bodies into *jet streams*. The formation of jet streams seems to be a very important intermediate phase in the accretion of small bodies into large bodies.

5.3 ELECTROMAGNETIC EFFECTS

If a body has an electric charge q, it is subject to an electromagnetic force

$$\mathbf{f_q} = q\left(\mathbf{E} + \frac{\mathbf{v}}{c} \times \mathbf{B}\right)$$ (5.3.1)

where $\mathbf{E}$ is the electric field; $\mathbf{B}$, the magnetic field; $\mathbf{v}$, the velocity of the body; and c, the speed of light.

Let us consider the constituents of an ordinary plasma in space: atoms, molecules, ions, and electrons. The motion of charged particles in such a plasma is governed by electromagnetic forces. We will not discuss the properties of a plasma in detail until later (Part C), but we introduce plasma effects here because of their primary influence on the motion of very small particles. As will be shown in sec. 5.4, plasma effects delineate the lower limit of applicability for collision-perturbed Kepler motion.

In addition to the plasma constituents of atoms, molecules, ions, and electrons, there is likely to be a population of dust grains. These grains, if small enough, may form part of the plasma. Because, initially, they are preferentially hit by plasma electrons, they normally have a negative electric charge. This charge might change into a positive charge if, for example, an intense radiation produces a photoelectric emission. Both negative and positive grains can be considered as plasma constituents as long as their Larmor radius is small enough, which essentially means that $\mathbf{f_q}$ must be much larger than $\mathbf{f_G}$.

Dusty plasma with these general properties is likely to have been of decisive importance during the formation of a solar system, when the concentration of plasma as well as of condensed grains must have been high in the circumsolar region. Development of a detailed theory for dusty plasmas is highly desirable. When we discuss the behavior of hetegonic plasmas, we generally assume them to be dusty. A particularly important point is that the charged dust particles add to the plasma a component of nonvolatile substances (see further ch. 19).

5.4 LIMIT BETWEEN ELECTROMAGNETICALLY AND GRAVITATIONALLY CONTROLLED MOTION

We have seen that due to their electric charge very small grains may form part of a plasma, whereas for large grains gravitation rules the motion. The limit between these two types of motion can be estimated by comparing the period of gyration of a grain spiraling in a magnetized plasma,

$$T_{gy} = \frac{2\pi mc}{qB} \tag{5.4.1}$$

with the Kepler period T_K of its orbital motion. If the grain is a sphere of radius R, density Θ, and electrostatic potential V (in esu), we have $m = \frac{4}{3}\pi R^3 \Theta$, $q = RV$, and

$$T_{gy} = \frac{8\pi^2 \Theta c R^2}{3VB} \qquad (5.4.2)$$

Solving eq. (5.4.2) for R we have

$$R = \left(\frac{3VBT_{gy}}{8\pi^2 \Theta c}\right)^{1/2} \qquad (5.4.3)$$

To estimate the limiting value of the grain radius R_{Lm} at which T_{gy} becomes comparable to T_K, we set $V = 10^{-2}$ esu, $B = 3 \times 10^{-5}$ G (the present magnetic field in interplanetary space), $\Theta = 1$ g/cm^3 (a typical density for interplanetary grains), and $T_{gy} = 3 \times 10^7$ sec (1 yr) to obtain

$$R_{Lm} = 0.3 \times 10^{-5} \text{ cm} \qquad (5.4.4)$$

This limiting radius corresponds to a limiting grain mass m_{Lm} of 10^{-16} g. If $R \ll R_{Lm}$, the period of gyration is small compared to the Kepler period and the grain forms part of the plasma. If $R \gg R_{Lm}$, the grains move in a Kepler orbit only slightly perturbed by plasma effects.

In the hetegonic era B could very well have been 10^4 times larger, corresponding to an increase of R_{Lm} to 0.3×10^{-3} cm and m_{Lm} to 10^{-10} g. On the other hand, for a plasma producing particle streams around a planet we may, for example, have T_{gy} smaller by a factor of 100, and, hence, $R_{Lm} = 0.3 \times 10^{-4}$, and $m_{Lm} = 10^{-13}$ g. Hence, the transition between the dominance of electromagnetic and of gravitational forces may be anywhere in the range 10^{-10} g $\geq m_{Lm} \geq 10^{-16}$ g, depending upon what spatial environment is being discussed.

In our numerical examples, we have assumed the electrostatic potential of a grain to be a few volts. This is a normal value for a charged solid body in a laboratory plasma. However, a cosmic plasma usually contains high-energy particles such as Van Allen radiation and cosmic rays. It is known that spacecrafts often acquire a potential of some thousand volts due to the charge received at impact by high-energy particles (Fahleson, 1973). This is especially the case if some part of the surface consists of an electrically insulating material. It seems quite likely that the grains we are discussing should behave in a similar way under hetegonic conditions. This would increase the value of R_{Lm} by one order of magnitude, and the limiting mass by a factor of 1000. As the charging of the grain may take place in an erratic way, R_{Lm} may often change rapidly.

5.5 RADIATION EFFECTS

The motion of small bodies may also be affected by *radiation*. Under *present* conditions *solar radiation* has a great influence on bodies the size of a micron (10^{-4} cm) or less and may also perturb the motion of bodies as large as a meter in size. The effect is due to radiation pressure, the Poynting-Robertson effect, and the ionization and photoelectric effects produced by solar radiation.

There is no certain indication that solar radiation had a decisive influence during the formative era of the solar system. As we shall find, the solar system could very well have acquired its present structure even if the Sun had been dark during the hetegonic period. However, it is also possible that solar radiation effects, as we know them today, were important, particularly after the hetegonic era; hence they are discussed below (secs. 5.5.1–5.5.2).

Similarly, there seems to be no reason to attribute any major role to the *solar wind;* the observed irradiation of grains before their ultimate accretion (sec. 22.9.5) could as well be caused by particles accelerated in the circumsolar structures as in the Sun (sec. 16.8). A very strong solar wind, a "solar gale," is sometimes hypothesized to occur late in the hetegonic era (after accretion). This is done in order to achieve various aims such as to remove gas or excess solids, to provide additional heating of bodies, or to blow away planetary atmospheres. As we will find later, none of these effects are needed to explain the present structure of the solar system and no indication of such a postulated enhancement is found in the early irradiation record (sec. 22.9.5). Hence the "solar-gale" hypothesis appears unnecessary and counterindicated (see sec. 16.2).

5.5.1 Radiation Pressure

If a grain of mass m with the cross section σ is hit by radiation with energy flux Ψ, it will be acted upon by the force

$$f_\Psi = \frac{\sigma \Psi}{c} \qquad (5.5.1)$$

if the body is black and absorbs all the radiation. If the body is a perfect mirror reflecting all light in an antiparallel direction, the force f_Ψ is doubled. If the energy is reemitted isotropically (seen from the frame of reference of the body), this emission produces no resultant force on the body.

78

Corpuscular radiation such as the solar wind results in a force of the same kind. Under the present conditions in the solar system this is usually negligible because the energy flux is much smaller than the solar radiation, and there is no compelling reason why it ever should have produced very significant dynamic effects.

A black body moving with the radial and tangential velocity components $(v_r, v_\phi; \ll c)$ in the environment of the Sun, and reradiating isotropically, is acted upon by radiation pressure with the components

$$(f_\Psi)_r = f_\Psi \left(1 - \frac{2v_r}{c} \right) \tag{5.5.2}$$

$$(f_\Psi)_\phi = - f_\Psi \frac{v_\phi}{c} \tag{5.5.3}$$

The effect of the tangential component $(f_\Psi)_\phi$ is called the Poynting-Robertson effect; this effect is due to the motion of the body in relation to the radiation field of the Sun.

Because Ψ decreases in the same way as the gravitational force,

$$f_G = \frac{GM_c m}{r^2}$$

we put

$$f_\Psi = \gamma f_G \tag{5.5.4}$$

Solving for γ we find

$$\gamma = \frac{r^2 f_\Psi}{GM_c m} = \frac{r^2 \sigma \Psi}{GM_c mc} \tag{5.5.5}$$

At the Earth's orbital distance we have $\gamma_\oplus = 0.76 \times 10^{-4} \sigma/m$ g/cm^2 for solar radiation. As in the cases of interest to us $v_r/c \ll 1$, we have approximately

$$(f_\Psi)_r = \gamma f_G \tag{5.5.6}$$

and

$$(f_\Psi)_\phi = -\frac{v_\phi}{c}\gamma f_G \tag{5.5.7}$$

For a black sphere with density Θ and radius R we have

$$\gamma_\oplus = \frac{0.57\times10^{-4}}{\Theta R}\ \frac{g}{cm^2} \tag{5.5.8}$$

For Θ of the order of 1 g/cm³, $\gamma_\oplus = 1$ if $R = 0.6\times10^{-4}$ cm. From eq. (5.5.6) we conclude that the Sun will repel particles with $R < 0.6\times10^{-4}$ cm. (See Lovell, 1954, p. 406.) The corresponding mass is of the order of 10^{-12} g. This is one of the effects putting a limit on the dominance of gravitation. It so happens that the size of the particles at this limit is of the same order as the wavelength of maximum solar radiation. The existence of such particles today is inferred from the study of the zodiacal light and micrometeorites. From a theoretical point of view, not very much can be said with certainty about their properties.

5.5.2 The Poynting-Robertson Effect

Although comparable to gravitation effects for micron-size grains, radiation effects decrease with $1/R$ as R increases. For $\Theta = 1$ g/cm³ and $R = 1$ cm, $\gamma_\oplus$ is 0.6×10^{-4}. This is usually unimportant for the radial force, but not for the tangential component, because when applied for a long time it may change the orbital momentum C. As

$$\frac{dC}{dt} = \frac{r(f_\Psi)_\phi}{m} = \frac{GM_c}{r}\gamma\frac{v_\phi}{c} = \gamma\frac{v_\phi^2}{cr}C \tag{5.5.9}$$

we can write

$$\frac{dC}{C} = \frac{dt}{T_e} \tag{5.5.10}$$

with

$$T_e = \frac{cr}{v_\phi^2 \gamma} = \frac{cT_K}{v_\phi \gamma 2\pi} \qquad (5.5.11)$$

where T_K is the Kepler period. During a time T_e, the orbital momentum decreases by a factor of e. For a grain with $R=1$ cm and $\Theta=1$ g/cm^3 near the Earth ($v_\phi/c = 10^{-4}$, $\gamma_\oplus = 0.6 \times 10^{-4}$, and $T_K = 1$ yr) we have

$$T_e = 25 \times 10^6 \text{ yr} \qquad (5.5.12)$$

To make this e-folding time equal to the age of the solar system, the body must have $R=150$ cm ($m=10^7$ g).

It is generally concluded that the Poynting-Robertson effect causes all small bodies (as we have found, "small" means $m<10^7$ g) to spiral slowly into the Sun. This is not necessarily true. As we shall find in ch. 8, resonances are a characteristic feature of the solar system. If a body once is trapped into resonance with another body, it is very difficult to break this resonance locking. Hence, when a small grain, slowly spiraling inward due to the Poynting-Robertson effect, reaches an a value such that it is in resonance with one of the planets, it may be trapped there forever.

Consider, for example, a small body that is a member of the Hilda family and thus in 2/3 resonance with Jupiter. If the body is so small that the Poynting-Robertson effect would make it spiral inward, this has the same effect as a viscosity. Hence, the drag is compensated by a resonance transfer of angular momentum, with the result that the body remains in resonance. The only net effect is that the eccentricity of the orbit decreases.

Even high-order resonances may be efficient. For example, Jupiter may produce a series of close barricades in the asteroidal belt that prevent bodies, including grains, from changing their periods (and, hence, give them locked a values). The remarkable fact that the present structure of the asteroid belt appears to be directly related to the hetegonic processes may be due to such effects (ch. 18.8).

5.6 CONCLUSIONS

(1) Planets and satellites move in Kepler orbits determined solely by gravitation.

(2) For asteroids and all smaller bodies (including single grains), the Kepler motion is perturbed by collisions (viscosity). This type of motion has a tendency to focus the bodies into jet streams. The smaller the bodies, the more pronounced the effect becomes.

(3) Due to their electric charge, very small grains behave as ions and form part of a plasma. Such a "dusty plasma" may contain grains with molecular weights as high as 10^6 and, under certain conditions, even 10^{12} or higher.

(4) Under present conditions, solar radiation produces light pressure that completely dominates the motion of micron-size (10^{-4} cm) and smaller grains. The Kepler motion of larger grains, with sizes up to a centimeter and meter, may be perturbed by the Poynting-Robertson effect. It is doubtful whether these effects were of any importance during the formative period of the solar system, during which period solar radiation may or may not have been significant. The influence of these effects today is also uncertain.

(5) There is no certain indication that the solar wind has had any major influence on the solar system in the formative era.

6

KEPLER MOTION OF INTERACTING BODIES: JET STREAMS

6.1 INTRODUCTION

Under present conditions the motion of planets and satellites is not appreciably perturbed by collisions (viscosity). However, in the asteroidal belt and in meteor streams the interactions are in many cases large enough to perturb the motion of individual bodies. During the hetegonic era, when the matter now stored in planets and satellites was dispersed, we can expect that the interaction between grains was of decisive importance.

In ch. 5 we have seen that over a large range of mass the dominating type of motion is a Kepler motion perturbed by collisions. This chapter is devoted to a study of this type of motion, a topic that has previously received little attention. The bodies treated in this discussion are assumed to be large enough that electromagnetic effects may be neglected. In the typical examples treated in sec. 5.4 this condition is that $R \gg 10^{-4}$ cm. Radiation effects are also neglected.

It is shown that under certain conditions collision-perturbed Kepler motion results in the formation of "jet streams," self-focused streams of particle aggregates held together by means of a "dynamic attraction" or "apparent attraction." It is suggested that meteor streams and the asteroidal jet streams described in sec. 4.3.3 may be of this type. It is further argued that jet streams were of decisive importance as an intermediate stage in the accretion of planets and satellites from grains. It will be seen in ch. 22 that in jet streams characterized by collision-perturbed Kepler motion accretion of large meteoroids may take place. It is likely that the jet-stream milieu is decisive for the formation of meteoroids, and, vice versa, meteoroids may supply us with important data for the understanding of the evolution of jet streams.

6.2 THE INTERPLANETARY MEDIUM

The small grains of different sizes together with the plasma constitute what is referred to as the *interplanetary medium*. The presence of this medium means that the motions of small bodies in interplanetary space are influenced by viscous effects. For planets and satellites these effects are so small that they have not yet been discovered (sec. 4.1). For the smaller bodies we are studying in this chapter, viscosity does play a role, the importance of which increases as the mass of the body decreases. In hetegonic times viscosity effects were much more important than now.

It is generally agreed that collisions have been decisive for the evolution of the asteroidal belt. Kiang (1966) finds that a correlation between proper eccentricities and proper inclinations of asteroids suggests the existence (or former existence) of a resistive medium. However, even down to the smallest observed asteroids ($R = 10^5$ cm), gravitation is by far the main force, and viscosity only enters as a small correction.

The study of the motion of comets has revealed that forces other than gravitation are sometimes important (Marsden, 1968; Hamid et al., 1968).

It is often implicitly assumed that in interplanetary space there is a "resistive" medium that is essentially at rest. We know that in interplanetary space there is a radial outward motion of a very thin plasma (solar wind), but its density is too low to affect the motion of grains appreciably (its effect is smaller than the Poynting-Robertson effect). Hence, any such assumed resistive medium must necessarily consist of grains. However, an assembly of grains cannot possibly be at rest because the grains are attracted by the Sun. The only possibility is that they are supported by centrifugal force (i.e., they are moving in Kepler orbits).

Hence, a "resistive medium" affecting the motion of the asteroids can be "at rest" only in the sense that on the average there would in principle be an equal number of grains moving in all directions. Observations do not support the existence of such a resistive medium in interplanetary space. It seems likely that, on the average, all small bodies with short periods (i.e., asteroids, comets, and meteoroids) are *moving in the prograde sense.*

6.3 EFFECTS OF COLLISIONS

Most of the early discussion of the mutual interaction between grains in space has been based on a widespread misconception that we shall discuss in this section.

Suppose that a parallel beam of particles is shot through a particulate medium at rest. Then collisions between the beam particles and the particles at rest will scatter the moving particles. The beam will be diffused so that its particles will spread in space. Almost all treatment of the motion of bodies (grains, meteoroids, and asteroids) in interplanetary space is based on this model although it is applicable only under certain conditions, which are usually *not* found in interplanetary space.

There is a basic misconception that grain collisions, either with a "medium" or with other moving grains, will lead to an increased spread of the grain velocities and orbits. As stated above, this is true for a beam of particles that is not moving in a gravitational field. It is also true for particles in a gravitational field under the conditions that the time between collisions is smaller than the Kepler period and that the collisions are elastic. The most pertinent case for our studies, however, is that of grains making many Kepler revolutions between collisions that are essentially inelastic. In this case collisions lead to an equalization of the orbits of the colliding particles, with the result that *the spread* in both velocity and coordinate space *is reduced*.

Suppose that two particles with masses m_1 and m_2 move in orbits with specific angular momenta C_1 and C_2 ($C_2 > C_1$). According to the guiding-center picture, they perform oscillations in the radial and axial directions (sec. 3.3) with amplitudes (r_1e_1, r_1i_1) and (r_2e_2, r_2i_2), respectively, while their guiding centers move along circles of radii r_1 and r_2.

If $r_1(1+e_1) \geq r_2(1-e_2)$, the particles have a chance of colliding. If the precession rates of their nodes and perihelia are different and not commensurable, they will sooner or later collide at a point at the central distance r_3. At collision, their tangential velocities will be $v_1 = C_1/r_3$ and $v_2 = C_2/r_3$. If the collision is perfectly inelastic, their common tangential velocity v_3 after the collision will be $v_3 = (m_1v_1 + m_2v_2)/(m_1 + m_2)$. Hence, each of them will have the specific angular momentum

$$C_3 = \frac{m_1C_1 + m_2C_2}{m_1 + m_2} \qquad (6.3.1)$$

which means $C_1 < C_3 < C_2$. Collisions that are essentially inelastic will tend to equalize the specific angular momenta of colliding particles. It is easily seen that collisions also will tend to make the particles oscillate with the same amplitude and phase.

From the above discussion, one concludes that *the general result of viscosity is to make the orbits of particles more similar*. This effect is closely connected with what is termed *apparent attraction* in sec. 6.4.1.

6.4 ORBITING PARTICLES CONFINED IN A
SPACECRAFT

In spite of the fact that celestial mechanics is several centuries old, few, if any, textbooks give a clear picture of some simple cases that are of interest for the present discussion. This is because celestial mechanics is usually presented with a somewhat formidable mathematical apparatus that conceals some important physical aspects of the phenomena. The conceptual approach used here was chosen to clarify and emphasize certain fundamental characteristics of the phenomena under discussion.

Suppose that a number of particles ("apples"; see Alfvén, 1971) are enclosed in a spacecraft that is orbiting around a central point mass M_c in a circle of radius r_0 (measured from the center of gravity of the spacecraft). If the masses of the spacecraft and of the particles are so small that gravitational attraction between them is negligible, all the particles will move in Kepler orbits around the central body. At the same time, they are subject to the constraint that they must permanently remain inside the spacecraft. The confinement of particles in a physical enclosure provides an idealized model of those phenomena which cause the particles in a jet stream to keep together.

We shall study what Kepler orbits are selected by this constraint and how these orbits look, as seen from the spacecraft. We introduce an orthogonal coordinate system with the origin at the center of gravity of the spacecraft, with the x axis pointing away from the central body and the y axis pointing in the direction of motion (see fig. 3.3.1).

The condition that a particle in a Kepler orbit must remain inside the spacecraft necessitates that its Kepler period T_K be the same as that of the spacecraft (i.e., its semimajor axis is r_0). The most simple case, the particle being at rest in relation to the spacecraft, occurs when both the eccentricity and inclination are zero. In this situation the particles are located at the distance r_0 from the central body (i.e., approximately on the y axis). Hence, *the particles in the spacecraft are aligned in the direction of orbital motion along the line (or strictly the circular arc) through the center of gravity of the spacecraft.*

6.4.1 Transverse Apparent Attraction

If $e = 0$ but $i \neq 0$, the particles will move in a circular orbit inclined to the orbital plane of the spacecraft. Seen from the spacecraft, the particle will oscillate in the z direction about its equilibrium position on the y axis. The period of this oscillation is T_K. Seen from the spacecraft, the motion of the particle can be described as due to the z component of the gravitational force of the central body:

$$f_z = - \frac{GM_c}{r_0^3} z \qquad (6.4.1)$$

If $e \neq 0$ the particle will move in an ellipse. Seen from the spacecraft, its motion is an oscillation in the x direction with period T_K. It can be described as due to a force in the x direction:

$$\mathbf{f_x} = - \frac{GM_c}{r_0^3} \mathbf{x} \qquad (6.4.2)$$

However, it is coupled with an oscillation in the y direction with twice the amplitude.

If a large number of particles collide inelastically or if gas in the space-craft damps their oscillations, the eventual result will be that all the parti-cles are at rest, lined up along the y axis.

Both the oscillation in the z direction and the oscillation in the x–y plane can easily be described by the guiding-center method described in ch. 3. Using that terminology we can state: *If particles in Kepler motion are confined inside a spacecraft, their guiding centers will line up along the y axis.*

The particles will oscillate about their guiding centers as if they were acted upon by a *transverse apparent attraction:*

$$\mathbf{f_{ap}} = - \frac{GM_c}{r_0^3} \mathbf{S} \qquad (6.4.3)$$

where $\mathbf{S}$ is the vector with magnitude $(x^2+z^2)^{1/2}$ from the origin to the particle projected on a plane perpendicular to the motion. In the x–y plane, the particles move in epicycles as depicted in fig. 3.3.1.

If there is a large number of particles oscillating about their guiding centers, and if their oscillations are damped by mutual inelastic collisions or by the presence of a gas in the spacecraft, the eventual result will be that they all come to rest lined up along the y axis. (The particles may also reach equilibria when in contact with the walls of the spacecraft.)

6.4.2 Longitudinal Apparent Attraction

Suppose that a particle or grain of unit mass orbits in a circle with radius r_0 around a central point mass M_c, and the motion is perturbed by the gravitational force

$$\mathbf{f_{per}} = - \frac{Gm_{per}}{r_{per}} \mathbf{r_{per}} \qquad (6.4.4)$$

of a small body $m_{per} \ll M_c$ situated in the x–y plane at a distance r_{per} from the origin of the moving coordinate system (xyz). It is assumed that this force is applied during a short time interval Δt $(\Delta t \ll T_K)$. It causes a change in the specific angular momentum C of a particle by $r_0 \times f_{per} \Delta t$. The difference ΔC in the specific angular momenta of a particle at $(0, y_1, 0)$ and a particle at the center of gravity of the spacecraft is given by

$$\Delta C = r_0 \left(\frac{\partial f_{per}}{\partial y} \right) y_1 \Delta t = r_0 \Delta f_{per} \tag{6.4.5}$$

where

$$\Delta f_{per} = \frac{2 G m_{per} y_1}{r_{per}^3} \Delta t \tag{6.4.6}$$

The new motion of the perturbed particle can be described as a circular motion of the guiding center modulated by a motion in an epicycle (fig. 6.4.1). The new orbital radius of the guiding center is $r = r_0 + \Delta r$. Using

$$\frac{\Delta r}{r_0} = \frac{2 \Delta C}{C} = \frac{2 r_0}{C} \Delta f_{per} = \frac{T_K}{\pi r_0} \Delta f_{per} \tag{6.4.7}$$

and defining the symbol $x_0 = \Delta r$, we have

$$x_0 = \frac{T_K}{\pi} \Delta f_{per} \tag{6.4.8}$$

Since the position of the particle is changed during the short interval Δt, the x axis of the epicycle is equal to x_0, and consequently the y axis is equal to $2x_0$. The particle moves in the retrograde direction in the epicycle, and the center of the epicycle moves in a circle with the angular velocity $\omega_0 + \Delta \omega$ where, because $\omega = C/r^2 = (GM_c)^2/C^3$,

$$\Delta \omega = -\frac{3\omega_0 \Delta C}{C} = -\frac{3 \Delta f_{per}}{r_0} \tag{6.4.9}$$

Hence, after a time t the guiding center will be displaced in the y direction through a distance

$$y_t = tr_0\Delta\omega = -3\Delta f_{per}t = -\frac{3\pi x_0 t}{T_K} \qquad (6.4.10)$$

in relation to an unperturbed particle.

To return to the problem discussed in sec. 6.4.1, we want to calculate how the lined-up particles move in relation to the center of gravity of the spacecraft. Consider a particle situated at a distance y_1 from the center of gravity of the spacecraft in the forward tangential direction. The velocity of its guiding center in relation to the center of gravity of the spacecraft is $v_y = r_0\Delta\omega$. From eqs. (6.4.6) and (6.4.9), we find its displacement after a time t to be

$$y_t = 6\frac{Gm_{per}}{r_{per}^3} = ty_1\Delta t \qquad (6.4.11)$$

Since $G = 4\pi^2 T_K^{-2} r_0^3 M_c^{-1}$, we can write

$$y_t = -Ay_1 \qquad (6.4.12)$$

where

$$A = \frac{24\pi^2 m_{per} r_0^3 t\Delta t}{M_c r_{per}^3 T_K^2} = \frac{3\pi Bt}{T_K} \qquad (6.4.13)$$

and

$$B = \frac{8\pi m_{per} r_0^3 \Delta t}{M_c r_{per}^3 T_K} \qquad (6.4.14)$$

Further, we find from eq. (6.4.10),

$$x_0 = By_1 \tag{6.4.15}$$

Hence we see that the state of motion produced by the perturbation Δf_{per} is such that the y values of all the guiding centers change in proportion to the original y value of the perturbed particle (fig. 6.4.1). We obtain $A=1$ after a time $t=t_{A=1}$, which can be calculated from eq. (6.4.13). At this moment, all the guiding centers are on the same vector radius as the center of gravity of the spacecraft. The actual positions of the particles are scattered; however, all remain inside a square with its sides equal to $4x_0$ and its center at the center of gravity of the spacecraft.

A case of special interest occurs when

$$t_{A=1} = nT_K \tag{6.4.16}$$

where n is an integer. If this relation is satisfied, all the particles are back at their initial position in the epicycle. Hence, all particles are simultaneously situated at the center of gravity of the spacecraft. The condition for this result is obtained from eqs. (6.4.13) and (6.4.15):

$$B = \frac{1}{3\pi n} \tag{6.4.17}$$

or

$$\frac{24\pi^2 m_{per} r_0^3 \Delta t}{M_c r_{per}^3 T_K} = \frac{1}{n} \tag{6.4.18}$$

From the treatment of this idealized case we may conclude that, if the motion of the spacecraft is subject to perturbing gravitational fields satisfying certain conditions, the row of particles has a tendency to contract toward the center of gravity of the spacecraft. Hence, in addition to the transverse focusing discussed in sec. 6.4.1, there is also longitudinal focusing. Under certain conditions, which need to be investigated in detail, all the particles in the cabin are collected at one point (the center of gravity of the spacecraft). The condition for this to occur is expressed by eq. (6.4.18). In analogy with the transverse apparent attraction, the longitudinal focusing may be considered to be the result of a *longitudinal apparent attraction*, although the type of motion produced by this attraction is rather different. Hence, we find that under certain conditions *the center of gravity of the spacecraft "attracts" all the particles in the cabin*, in the sense that the particles have a tendency to be brought together there. (If the perturbing force is directed along the x axis, there is instead an apparent repulsion by the center of gravity of the cabin.)

Because the spacecraft is assumed to have a negligible mass, one may ask why its center of gravity has such a remarkable property. The answer is that this point merely defines the state of motion of the whole assembly. Suppose that the mass of the spacecraft is much smaller than the mass of the particles and that their original common center of gravity was situated at an r larger than that of the spacecraft's center of gravity. Then the

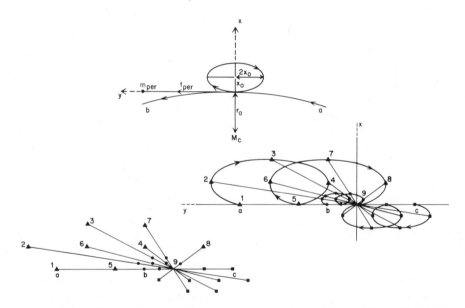

FIGURE 6.4.1.—Longitudinal apparent attraction. A particle initially moving along the arc ab with radius r_0 is suddenly perturbed by a tangential gravitational force f_{per} due to the mass m_{per}. The new motion consists of a retrograde epicycle motion in an ellipse, the center of which ("guiding center") moves in a circle with radius $r_0 + x_0$ (above). The perturbed motion of three particles, originally situated at a, b, and c, describes three epicycles (right). The numbers 1 through 9 indicate the positions of the particles at intervals of $(T_K/4)$. The unperturbed particles form the line abc (left). The perturbation makes this line turn and first lengthen and then shorten. The quantity n in eq. (6.4.16) is equal to 2 in this case and consequently after the time $2T_K$ has elapsed all particles simultaneously arrive at the point $x = 0$, $y = 0$. Hence there is a longitudinal apparent attraction of the particles to the guiding center of the unperturbed motion. (From Alfvén, 1971.)

particles would move more slowly than the spacecraft and would hit its backside wall, with the result that the spacecraft would be displaced outward so that its center of gravity would (almost) coincide with the center of gravity of the particles. (An exact statement would be possible only if the original state of motion of the particles were known.)

The apparent attraction is more important than the Newtonian attraction between two bodies of mass m_1, one of which is at the guiding center, if

$$f_{ap} \gg \frac{Gm_1}{S^2} \qquad (6.4.19)$$

which means that

$$\frac{S}{r_0} \gg \left(\frac{m_1}{M_c}\right)^{1/3} \qquad (6.4.20)$$

For a spacecraft in orbit ($r_0 = 10^9$ cm) around the Earth ($M_c = 6 \times 10^{27}$ g), particles with a mass of 6 g must be much more than 1 cm apart for the apparent attraction to be more important than the gravitational attraction between the particles.

6.5 CONCLUSIONS FROM THE SPACECRAFT MODEL

We have treated a very simple model to clarify some aspects of celestial mechanics which are of special interest for studying accretional processes. The role of the spacecraft walls in our model is to compel all the particles to orbit with the same period. We have seen (sec. 6.4.1) that if the gravitational field is unperturbed (i.e., an inverse square force) the particles will align in the direction of motion along the line through the center of gravity of the spacecraft. If the orbits of the particles have nonzero eccentricities and/or inclinations, then their guiding centers will align along the path of the center of gravity of the spacecraft. This focusing, referred to as the *transverse apparent attraction,* is a consequence of the gravitational field of the central body around which the spacecraft orbits.

If the gravitational field is perturbed (sec. 6.4.2), we have found for certain types of perturbation that the particles move toward the center of gravity of the spacecraft. We have referred to this attraction as the *longitudinal apparent attraction.*

It is important to consider to what extent similar phenomena may occur in astrophysics. Our model is based on the constraint that the particles all orbit with the same period. This effect can in reality be achieved by other means (for example, by gas friction, mutual collisions, and electromagnetic effects). The lining up of particles (due to transverse apparent attraction) is basically the same phenomenon as the focusing effects that produce jet streams in interplanetary space. The perturbation-produced attraction of the aligned particles to a common point (longitudinal apparent attraction) is related to the formation of bodies within jet streams, a process that is applicable to the formation of comets within meteor streams (ch. 14). In view of what has been said in sec. 6.1, we may look on our spacecraft as a jet-stream workshop in which meteoroids are being produced (ch. 22).

6.6 JET STREAMS AND NEGATIVE DIFFUSION

Let us consider how mutual inelastic collisions can assume the role of the spacecraft walls in the model just discussed (i.e., to compel the particles to orbit with similar periods). Baxter and Thompson (1971) have treated the interaction between particles in Kepler orbits, considering the effect of inelastic collisions on the evolution of an initially smooth distribution of particle orbits. For a two-dimensional system (all motion in a single plane), they found that inelastic collisions produced a *negative diffusion coefficient*. Hence, an initially smooth distribution will evolve and show radial density clustering (see fig. 6.6.1).

In a later paper, Baxter and Thompson (1973) generalized their results to a three-dimensional case. They further concluded that, although in order to simplify the calculations they have assumed axisymmetry, this is not essential for the clustering. A similar process is expected to occur also in an eccentric jet stream.

These investigations are essentially an application of plasma-physics formalism to the Kepler motion of grains, the grains assuming the role of interacting atoms, ions, and electrons in a plasma. This opens an interesting field of research that hopefully will lead to a better understanding of jet streams. For example, fragmentation and accretion at collision (which are not included in the simplified treatment by Baxter and Thompson) and the energy balance in a jet stream are important factors to be studied. Further, it is not yet clear what degree of inelasticity is required for jet-stream formation. Numerical simulations by Trulsen (1972b) have shown that, with elasticity exceeding a certain limit, jet-stream formation does not take place.

Meteorites can yield much information on the processes occurring in their parent jet streams. Observations in meteorites demonstrate (secs. 22.6

through 22.8) that most collisions involving their component grains were highly inelastic, leading to shock deformation, melting, and vaporization; solidified melt spray, broken rubble, and shocked metal are the most common components observed in ordinary chondrites and achondrites.

It should further be pointed out that collisions between the solid particles are not really necessary for jet-stream formation. As is evident from the model of sec. 6.3, this can be achieved by a mechanism that makes the particles exchange momentum so that their orbital parameters become similar. As an example, suppose that all particles reemit gas molecules that have previously been temporarily incorporated by occlusion, implantation, or surface adsorption. The emitted molecules hit the other particles, thereby transferring momentum. The "viscosity" caused by the gas exchange may significantly contribute to jet-stream formation. A theoretical investigation of this case is highly desirable; some discussion is given in sec. 6.8. The preservation of delicate features of condensed grains in carbonaceous meteorites provides suggestive observational evidence for equalization of orbital grain energy by means other than collision in these particular jet streams (sec. 22.6).

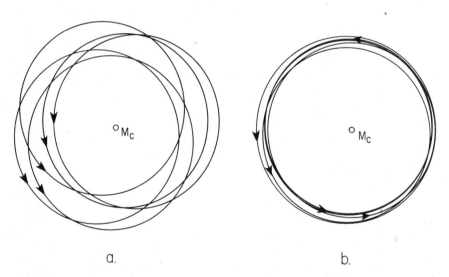

a.   b.

FIGURE 6.6.1.—Interaction of a large number of particles in Kepler orbits (a). In the discussion of collisions between particles in interplanetary space (e.g., evolution of the asteroidal belt or meteor streams) it is usually taken for granted that the state b will evolve into state a (positive diffusion). This is usually not correct. Collisions between the particles will not spread the orbits since the diffusion coefficient is negative (Baxter and Thompson, 1971, 1973). Instead, collisions will lead to equalization of the orbital elements, leading from state a to state b so that a jet stream is formed. (From Alfvén and Arrhenius, 1972.)

6.7 SIMPLE MODEL OF NEGATIVE DIFFUSION

We shall treat here a simple case that illustrates how the diffusion coefficient becomes negative. Consider a grain the guiding center of which orbits in a circle with radius r_0 around a central body. The grain itself makes radial oscillations with amplitude x_0 around the guiding center. Suppose that we have a population of such grains and divide it into two groups, one outside and one inside a certain value r'. For the first group, we define $x_1 = r_1 - r'$, and, for the second, $x_2 = r' - r_2$ (see fig. 6.7.1). We suppose that x_0, x_1, and x_2 are much smaller than r'.

Let all grains have the same mass and the same x_0, and let all collisions between be perfectly inelastic. The number of collisions per unit time between grains in the intervals x_1 to $x_1 + dx_1$ with those in the interval x_2 to $x_2 + dx_2$ is

$$\nu\, dx_1\, dx_2 = N(x_1)N(x_2)\delta(x_1 + x_2)\, dx_1\, dx_2 \qquad (6.7.1)$$

where $N(x)$ is the number density of grains and $\delta(x)$ a geometrical factor. As $\delta \neq 0$ only if

$$x_1 + x_2 < 2x_0 \qquad (6.7.2)$$

collisions take place only inside the domain within the big triangle in fig. 6.7.1.

As the r value after collision between the two particles is

$$r_3 = \frac{r_1 + r_2}{2} \qquad (6.7.3)$$

the result of a collision is a transfer of a guiding center outward through r' if $x_1 > x_2$, and inward through r' if $x_2 > x_1$. These domains of collisions are represented by the triangles a and b, respectively, in fig. 6.7.1. The net transport of guiding centers outward through r' is

$$D = \int_a \nu\, dx_1\, dx_2 - \int_b \nu\, dx_1\, dx_2 \qquad (6.7.4)$$

Suppose that the density varies linearly with r so that we may write

$$N(r) = N'[1 + \chi(r - r')]$$ (6.7.5)

where N' is the number density at r' and χ is a constant. If χ is positive, the density increases outward; if χ is negative, the density decreases outward. We now have

$$\nu = N(x_1)N(x_2)\delta(x_1 + x_2) \approx (N')^2[1 + \chi(x_1 - x_2)]\delta(x_1 + x_2)$$ (6.7.6)

Consider two equal surface elements, one in the triangle a and the other in b, situated symmetrically with respect to the border line $x_1 = x_2$. For these two elements, $x_1 + x_2$ and, hence, δ have the same value, but if $\chi > 0$, the value of ν is larger for the element in a than for the element in b (because $x_1 > x_2$). The integrals in eq. (6.7.4) can now be evaluated by summing all such symmetric pairs of elements into which triangles a and b can be divided. Consequently, if $\chi > 0$, $D > 0$. If $\chi < 0$, we find $D < 0$, so that there is a net transport of guiding centers inward through r'.

Hence, we have shown that in either case an excess of guiding centers is transmitted from the low-density region into the high-density region as a result of a collision. This means that the diffusion coefficient is negative.

6.8 CONTRACTION TIME OF A JET STREAM

Suppose that a body moves with velocity v_0 and semimajor axis r_0 in a Kepler orbit that is sufficiently close to a circle to allow us to treat it according to the guiding-center method. Suppose further that the field is that due to an unperturbed inverse square force. Hence, the orbit of the body will remain an ellipse that does not precess.

Suppose this body emits a particle with velocity v (relative to the body) in the radial direction. This particle will oscillate with an amplitude

$$x_0 = \frac{r_0 v}{v_0}$$ (6.8.1)

Similarly, particles emitted in the axial direction will oscillate with the same amplitude. Further, particles ejected in the tangential (forward) direction

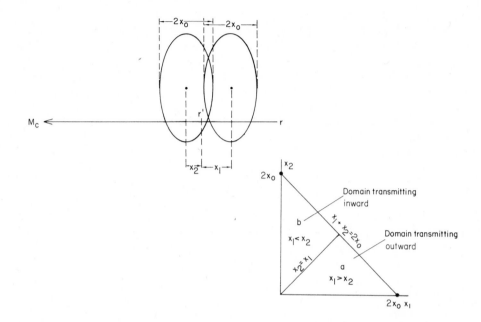

FIGURE 6.7.1.—Simple model of negative diffusion. The region of collision is shown (above) for two particles, one with guiding center at $x_1 = r - r'$ and another with guiding center at $x_2 = r' - r$. Both particles are oscillating radially with amplitude x_0. In the $x_1 x_2$ diagram (below) collisions can take place if $x_1 + x_2$ is located inside the triangle. If a perfectly inelastic collision takes place in the domain a the guiding center at x_2 is transmitted outward through r'. If the collision takes place in domain b, a similar inward transmission of the guiding center at x_1 takes place. If the density increases with r, the collision frequency is larger in domain a than in domain b, with the result that the diffusion goes outward; i.e., *toward* the higher density region. Hence the diffusion coefficient is *negative*.

will have the specific angular momentum $C = r_0 (v_0 + v)$, which, because $C = (GM_c r)^{1/2}$, is the same as that for a particle orbiting in a circle of radius

$$r' = \frac{(r_0 v_0)^2}{GM_c} \left(1 + \frac{v}{v_0}\right)^2$$

$$\approx r_0 \left(1 + \frac{2v}{v_0}\right) = r_0 + 2x_0 \qquad (6.8.2)$$

if $v \ll v_0$. Hence, it will oscillate with the amplitude $2x_0$, and its maximum distance from the orbit of the body will be $4x_0$.

The particles emitted with a velocity v will remain inside a torus with the small radius $x = \alpha x_0$ where x_0 is given by eq. (6.8.1) and α is between 1 and 4, depending on the angle of emission. This result also applies to the case when the body does not move exactly in a circle.

If a body, or a number of bodies in the same orbit, emits gas molecules with a rms thermal velocity $v = (3kT/m)^{1/2}$, the gas will be confined within a torus with the typical thickness of

$$x = \alpha \frac{vr_0}{v_0} = \alpha \left(\frac{3kTr_0^3}{GM_c m} \right)^{1/2} \tag{6.8.3}$$

We will use x as a measure of the small radius of a jet stream even if some of the particles oscillate with a greater amplitude. As a typical example, the thermal velocity of hydrogen molecules at $T = 300K$ is of the order 10^5 cm/sec. If we put $v_0 = 3.10^6$ cm/sec ($=$ the Earth's orbital velocity), we have, with $\alpha = 1$, $x/r_0 = 1/30$.

Jet streams differ from the rings in Laplacian theories in the respect that the mean free path of particles in a jet stream is long compared to the dimensions of the jet stream. Further, jet streams need not necessarily be circular. In fact, the phenomena we are discussing will take place even in jet streams with high eccentricity.

As no detailed theory of jet streams has yet been developed, we shall confine ourselves to an approximate treatment that gives at least a qualitative survey of some important phenomena. Suppose there is a jet stream consisting of a large number N of particles all confined to move inside a torus with small radius x. The average relative velocity between particles is u. If all particles have identical mass m and collisional cross section σ, each particle in the torus will collide with a frequency of the order

$$\nu = \frac{1}{t_\nu} = u\sigma N \tag{6.8.4}$$

where t_ν is the average time between two collisions and

$$N = \frac{N}{2\pi^2 r_0 x^2} \tag{6.8.5}$$

is the number density. If each particle is a sphere with radius R and average density Θ, its mass is $m = 4\pi\Theta R^3/3 = 4\Theta\sigma R/3$. The shape of the grains may deviate significantly from the spherical form (in the extreme case they may be needles), but for an order-of-magnitude estimate we assume a spherical shape. If we put the space density $\rho = mN$ we have

$$t_\nu = \frac{4\Theta R}{3\rho u} \qquad (6.8.6)$$

If we consider $u = 10^5$ cm/sec as a typical relative velocity and 3 g/cm³ as a typical grain density, we find for the respective values of grain radius R the values of $t_\nu\rho$ given in table 6.8.1.

TABLE 6.8.1

Densities in Jet Streams

R	=	10^{-3}	1	10^3	10^6	cm
$t_\nu\rho$	=	4×10^{-8}	4×10^{-5}	4×10^{-2}	$4\times10^{+1}$	sec g cm⁻³
ρ	$\geq$	1.3×10^{-20}	1.3×10^{-17}	1.3×10^{-14}	1.3×10^{-11}	g cm⁻³
N	$\geq$	1.1×10^{-12}	1.1×10^{-18}	1.1×10^{-24}	1.1×10^{-30}	cm⁻³

To keep the jet stream together, the interval between collisions for a given particle t_ν must be smaller than the time constant for the dispersive processes. Most important of these are the differential precession of the different orbits in the jet stream and the Poynting-Robertson effect. For an order of magnitude approximation we may put $t_\nu = 10^5$ yr $= 3\times10^{12}$ sec (see Whipple, 1968). This value for t_ν gives the values of ρ, and, from eq. (6.8.4), the values of N found in table 6.8.1.

The contraction of a jet stream is produced by inelastic collisions between the particles. The time constant for contraction should be a few times t_ν. This also means that a jet stream can be formed only when there is no disruptive effect with a time constant less than t_ν. For example, the differential precession of the pericenter and the nodes of an elliptic orbit will disrupt a jet stream unless t_ν is smaller than the period of the differential precession.

A more refined model of jet streams should take into account the size distribution of the particles. Since the smallest particles are usually the most numerous, their mutual collisions will be the most efficient in keeping a jet stream together.

As the relative velocities in the interior of a jet stream decrease, the accretion of grains to form larger bodies will become more and more efficient. Hence to within an order of magnitude, t_ν is the contraction time of the jet stream. However, if larger bodies are formed, the result is that t_v will increase and the contractive force will be smaller. Eventually, the jet stream may no longer keep together.

It should be remembered that a jet stream is formed only if there is enough interaction between the particles. In the Saturnian rings, this interaction between the particles is very small. They do not form a jet stream but orbit with periods proportional to $r^{3/2}$.

6.9 COLLISIONS BETWEEN A GRAIN AND A JET STREAM

Let us examine what happens if a grain collides with a jet stream. Suppose that the grain moves in an orbit which at one point a crosses the jet stream (see fig. 6.9.1). (In principle, its orbit could cross the jet stream at four points, but we confine ourselves to the simplest case.) We are considering motions in an unperturbed Newtonian field, which means that the orbits remain unchanged unless the particles collide.

In the region where the grain crosses the jet stream, it will sooner or later collide with one of the particles of the stream. The collision is likely to be partially inelastic; in other words, part of the kinetic energy due to the relative motion is dissipated. The collision may result in breakup of one of the colliding grains, or of both, into a number of fragments.

After the collision, each of these fragments will move in a new orbit that in general differs from the initial orbit of the grains. This orbit may be situated either entirely within the jet stream or partially outside it. However, all possible orbits of the fragments will necessarily bring them back again to the point at which the collision took place. Since by definition this point was situated inside the jet stream, all the fragments will repeatedly cross the jet stream. (An exception to this rule occurs when the collision has taken place near the surface of the jet stream and the latter has had time to contract so much before the next collision that the point of the first collision then lies outside the stream.) Sooner or later this orbital intersection will lead to new collisions with the particles in the jet stream.

As on the average the collisions reduce the relative velocities, the fragments will finally be captured by the jet stream. At the same time, this capture will change the shape of the jet stream so that the new orbit is a compromise between its original orbit and the orbit of the colliding grain.

Hence, a grain that collides with a jet stream will be "eaten up" by it, with or without fragmentation. In the former case, the jet stream "chews" before it "swallows." This again can be considered as a consequence of the focusing effect of a Newtonian field.

In this way new kinetic energy is transferred to the jet stream, compensating for the decrease in its internal energy. If a large number of grains

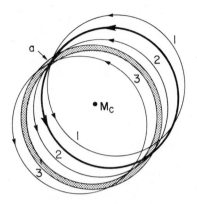

FIGURE 6.9.1.—The capture of a grain by a jet stream. The
shaded area represents the jet stream. The orbit of a grain
(thick curve) intersects the jet stream at *a*. Collisions lead to
fragmentation and fragments are ejected mainly in orbits like
2, but some fragments may move in orbits like 1 or 3. All these
orbits carry them back to the point *a*. Subsequent collision
at *a* may lead to further fragmentation, but, if the collisions
are at least partly inelastic, the final result is that all the fragments will be captured by the jet stream.

are colliding with the jet stream, a temporary state of equilibrium is attained when the energy loss due to internal collisions is balanced by the
energy brought in by the "eaten" particles. However, the new particles
increase the value of N, and, hence, the energy loss. The final destiny in
any case is a contraction of the jet stream (Ip and Mendis, 1974).

The internal structure of a jet stream depends on the size distribution
and on the velocity distribution of its particles. We have only discussed the
ideal case, in which all particles are identical. In a real jet stream, there is
likely to be an assortment of bodies of all sizes subject to the competing
processes of accretion and fragmentation. As the internal energy of the jet
stream decreases, the relative velocities will also decrease. This means that
collisions will not lead as often to fragmentation; accretion will dominate,
and larger bodies will be formed inside the jet stream.

If the Newtonian field is perturbed, the jet stream will precess, the nodes
moving in the retrograde sense and the pericenter moving in the prograde
sense. However, the rate of precession depends on the orbital elements of
the individual grains, and these are slightly different for each particle inside
the jet stream. Hence, the perturbations tend to disrupt the jet stream. The
permanence of the jet stream depends upon whether the viscosity, which
keeps the jet stream together, is strong enough to dominate. In general,
large bodies will leave the jet stream more readily than small bodies.

6.9.1 Conclusions

In accordance with what has been stated in sec. 1.1, we should not at present primarily aim at detailed theories but at a general framework in which such theories should be fitted. This describes the state of the jet-stream discussion. Even if a detailed theory of jet streams is not yet developed, it seems legitimate to conclude as follows:

(1) If a large number of grains are moving in a Newtonian field, its focusing effect (apparent attraction) may lead to the formation of jet streams. These jet streams are kept together by mutual collisions (i.e., viscosity) under the condition that the collisions are sufficiently inelastic (negative diffusion).

(2) The jet streams have a tendency to capture all grains that collide with them.

(3) The relative velocities of the particles in a jet stream decrease and the jet streams have a tendency to contract.

(4) Inside a jet stream the grains will aggregate to larger bodies.

(5) Large bodies formed in a jet stream may break loose from it.

6.10 JET STREAMS AS CELESTIAL OBJECTS

The term "celestial object" includes planets, satellites, comets, stars, nebulae, galaxies, quasars, and pulsars. It would seem that jet streams should also be counted as "celestial objects." Certainly they are transient, but so are comets and nebulae.

The jet-stream concept may be applied to several cases:

(1) *Meteor streams.* Meteor streams will be treated in detail in chs. 14 and 19. Cometary nuclei and parent bodies of meteorites are probably products of particle focusing, clustering, accretion, and compaction in such particle streams. Hence, the meteorites may give us a record of jet-stream processes (ch. 22). They provide a wealth of information on the collision processes in particle streams, including the alternating fragmentation and accretion in the course of equalization of energy of grains and embryos. A detailed discussion of the jet-stream record in meteorites is given in sec. 22.

(2) *Asteroidal jet streams.* A discussion of asteroidal jet streams has been presented in sec. 4.3.2.

(3) *Hetegonic jet streams.* Hetegonic jet streams may be important as an intermediate stage in planet/satellite formation. This will be discussed in ch. 12.

(4) Finally, there may be *galactic jet streams.* In fact, a jet stream may be formed whenever interacting bodies move in periodic orbits. This may take place, for example, in galactic nebulae, possibly leading to a "stellesimal" formation of stars (ch. 25).

7

COLLISIONS: FRAGMENTATION AND ACCRETION

7.1 PRODUCTION OF SMALL BODIES: FRAGMENTATION AND ACCRETION

There are two different ways of accounting for the existence of the small bodies:

(1) They may be produced by the *fragmentation* of larger bodies formed earlier by accretion. The asteroids have traditionally been regarded as fragments from one or more planets that have exploded or have been broken up by mutual collisions. In a similar way, the meteoroids may be fragments of comets, or possibly from other bodies like the asteroids. Although for reasons discussed in secs. 9.8, 11.8, and 18.8 the asteroids in general cannot have been derived in this manner, there is no doubt that destructive collisions occur in interplanetary space and that a number of small bodies are fragments from larger bodies.

(2) Small bodies must also necessarily be formed by *accretion* of grains, produced by condensation of the plasma that existed in the hetegonic era or later, and by accretion of fragments formed in breakup events. Accretion of such grains and fragments to larger bodies that finally become planets or satellites is a basic tenet in all "planetesimal" theories. To clarify this process, it is important to find and identify surviving primeval grains in interplanetary space. Certain types of meteorites contain particles whose structure and composition strongly suggest that they are such preserved primordial condensate grains (see fig. 7.1.1).

An important problem in our analysis is to determine the relative rates of fragmentation and accretion in the small-body populations. Even without a detailed analysis of this question, the mere existence of these bodies demonstrates that, integrated over the age of the solar system, accretion must on the average have prevailed over fragmentation.

There are three different aspects of a more detailed analysis of the small-body problem:

(1) The study of the *distribution of their orbits*. The characteristics and theory of their motions have been discussed in chs. 4 through 6, and

the observational evidence for their formation, from a partially corotating plasma, will be discussed in chs. 9, 10, and 18.

(2) The study of their *size spectra*. The theory is given in sec. 7.2 and the observations again in secs. 4.3, 18.6, and 18.8.

(3) The study of the *record in meteorites and on the Moon*. The observations relevant to accretion and fragmentation are discussed in ch. 22.

FIGURE 7.1.1.—Freely grown crystals of olivine and pyroxene forming aggregate material in the carbonaceous chondrite Allende. The delicate crystals are frequently twinned and have a thickness of the order of a few hundred Å, thinning toward the edge. The growth of the crystals and chemical composition of the material suggest that they condensed from a vapor phase and subsequently evolved into orbits with relative velocities sufficiently low to permit accretion by electrostatic adhesion. (From Alfvén and Arrhenius, 1974.)

7.2 SIZE SPECTRA

The size spectra of meteoroids, asteroids, and other bodies are of basic importance for the understanding of the origin and evolution of those bodies. A size spectrum can be expressed as a function of the radius R (assuming spherical bodies), the cross section $\sigma = \pi R^2$, or the mass $m = \frac{4}{3}\pi\Theta R^3$ (where Θ is the average density). Furthermore, it can be given as a function of the astronomical magnitude, which (as discussed in sec. 4.3) is

$$g = \text{constant} - 5 \log R \qquad (7.2.1)$$

The number of particles in the interval between R and $R+dR$ is denoted by $N(R)$, and the functions $N(\sigma)$ and $N(m)$ are defined in similar ways.
We have

$$N(R)dR = N(\sigma)d\sigma = N(m)dm \qquad (7.2.2)$$

and consequently

$$N(R) = 2\pi R N(\sigma) = 4\pi\Theta R^2 N(m) \qquad (7.2.3)$$

It is often possible to approximate the distribution functions as power laws valid between certain limits. As the variable can be either R, σ, g, or m, and as sometimes differential spectra and sometimes integrated spectra are considered, the literature is somewhat confusing. We put

$$N(R) = \chi_R R^{-\alpha} \qquad (7.2.4)$$

$$N(\sigma) = \chi_\sigma \sigma^{-\beta} \qquad (7.2.5)$$

$$N(m) = \chi_m m^{-\gamma} \qquad (7.2.6)$$

where χ_R, χ_σ, χ_m, α, β, and γ are constants. We find

$$\chi_R R^{-\alpha} = 2\pi R \chi_\sigma \sigma^{-\beta} = 4\pi \Theta R^2 \chi_m m^{-\gamma} \tag{7.2.7}$$

$$\chi_R R^{-\alpha} = 2\pi \chi_\sigma R \pi^{-\beta} R^{-2\beta} = 4\pi \Theta R^2 \chi_m (\tfrac{4}{3}\pi\Theta)^{-\gamma} R^{-3\gamma} \tag{7.2.8}$$

which gives the following relations:

$$\alpha - 1 = 2(\beta - 1) = 3(\gamma - 1) \tag{7.2.9}$$

and

$$\chi_R = 2\pi^{1-\beta}\chi_\sigma = (4\pi\Theta)^{1-\gamma} 3^\gamma \chi_m \tag{7.2.10}$$

Integrating eq. (7.2.4) between R_1 and R_2 ($> R_1$) we obtain

$$\int_{R_1}^{R_2} N(R)\, dR = \frac{\chi_R}{a} (R_1^{-a} - R_2^{-a}) \tag{7.2.11}$$

with $a = \alpha - 1$. In case $a = 0$, we obtain instead a logarithmic dependence. If $a > 0$, the smallest particles are most numerous and we can often neglect the second term.

The total cross section of particles between $\sigma_1 = \pi R_1^2$ and $\sigma^2 = \pi R_2^2 > \sigma_1$ is

$$\int_{\sigma_1}^{\sigma_2} \sigma \chi_\sigma \sigma^{-\beta}\, d\sigma = \frac{\chi_\sigma}{2-\beta} \left[\sigma_1^{-(\beta-2)} - \sigma_2^{-(\beta-2)} \right]$$

$$= \frac{\chi_\sigma}{b} (\sigma_1^{-b} - \sigma_2^{-b}) \tag{7.2.12}$$

with $b = \beta - 2$. If $b > 0$ (which often is the case), the smallest particles determine the total cross section.

The total mass between m_1 and m_2 ($> m_1$) is

$$\int_{m_1}^{m_2} m\chi_m m^{-\gamma}\,dm = \frac{\chi_m}{-c}\,(m_1^{-c} - m_2^{-c}) \qquad (7.2.13)$$

with $c = \gamma - 2$. If $c < 0$ (which often is the case), the largest particles have most of the mass.

If the magnitude g is chosen as variable, we have for the differential spectrum

$$\log N(g) = \text{constant} + 0.2(\alpha - 1)g \qquad (7.2.14)$$

Table 7.2.1 presents a summary of the mass, cross section, and size spectra for various values of α, β, γ, and g.

7.3 THREE SIMPLE MODELS

In order to get a feeling for the correlation between different physical processes and the related size spectra, we shall derive such spectra for three very simple models. The models represent the development of large bodies from small bodies through two types of accretion and the development of small bodies from large bodies through fragmentation. Our basic approach is to describe a state of accretion or fragmentation and discern the boundary conditions and size spectra indicative of each state.

7.3.1 Accretion

Given a jet stream in which a large number of embryos are accreting from small grains, we consider the growth, with respect to time, of one such embryo. A unidirectional stream of grains having a space density ρ approaches the embryo with the internal, or relative, velocity of the jet stream u. The embryo has a mass M, radius R, and density Θ. The impact cross section of the embryo is

$$\sigma = \pi R^2 \left(1 + \frac{v_{es}^2}{u^2}\right) \qquad (7.3.1)$$

where v_{es} is the escape velocity of the embryo. Assuming that the embryo remains spherical and that its mean density remains constant throughout

TABLE 7.2.1
Survey of Spectra and Models

		Non-gravitational accretion	Gravitational accretion		Fragmentation	
Differential spectra						
Number of bodies in radius interval dR	α	0	1	2	3	4
Number of bodies in surface interval $d\sigma$	β	0.5	1	1.5	2	2.5
Number of bodies in mass interval dm	γ	0.67	1	1.33	1.67	2
Number of bodies in magnitude interval dg	$0.2(\alpha-1)$	-0.2	0	$+0.2$	$+0.4$	$+0.6$
Integrated Spectra						
Number of bodies between R and 0 or ∞	a	-1	0	$+1$	$+2$	$+3$
Total cross section of bodies between σ and 0 or ∞	b	-1.5	-1	-0.5	0	$+0.5$
Total mass of bodies between m and 0 or ∞	c	-1.33	-1	-0.67	-0.33	0

	Large bodies most numerous | Small bodies most numerous
Note: Öpik's "population index" S is identical with a.	Most cross section due to large bodies | Most cross section due to small grains
	Most mass in large bodies | Most mass in small bodies

its growth period, we can adopt as a time scale the time of escape, t_{es}, of eqs. (2.2.3) and (2.2.4). The time of escape depends on the density, but is independent of the radius of the embryo. The escape velocity can now be expressed as a function of the time of escape and the radius of the embryo:

$$v_{es} = \left(\frac{2GM}{R}\right)^{1/2} = \left(\frac{8\pi G\Theta}{3}\right)^{1/2} R = \frac{R}{t_{es}} \qquad (7.3.2)$$

If all particles impacting on the embryo adhere, the embryonic mass will increase at the rate

$$\frac{dM}{dt} = \rho u \sigma \qquad (7.3.3)$$

where ρ is assumed to be time independent. Having assumed that

$$dM = 4\pi R^2 \Theta \, dR \qquad (7.3.4)$$

we can from eqs. (7.3.3) and (7.3.1) obtain

$$\frac{dR}{dt} = \frac{u\rho}{4\Theta}\left(1 + \frac{v_{es}^2}{u^2}\right) \qquad (7.3.5)$$

7.3.1.1 Nongravitational accretion. If the embryo is not massive enough to gravitationally attract particles, the number of particle impacts and consequently the growth of the embryo are not dependent upon v_{es}. We can describe this situation by specifying that $u \gg v_{es}$, which implies that the radial growth of the embryo during nongravitational accretion is governed by

$$\frac{dR}{dt} = \frac{u\rho}{4\Theta} = \text{constant} \qquad (7.3.6)$$

where we have made use of the previously assumed constancy of ρ. Under these conditions, the embryo size spectrum is given by $\alpha = 0$, $\beta = 0.5$, and $\gamma = 0.67$. As shown in table 7.2.1, for this type of spectra the mass and cross section distributed among the accreting embryos is concentrated in the more massive bodies; the size spectrum is constant for all values of R.

7.3.1.2 Gravitational accretion. Upon attaining a certain radius, an embryo has sufficient mass to gravitationally attract particles that would not, under the conditions of nongravitational accretion, impact upon the embryo. We can describe this situation by specifying that $v_{es} \gg u$, which implies that gravitational accretion is governed by

$$\frac{dR}{dt} = \frac{\rho v_{es}^2}{4\Theta u}$$

(7.3.7)

Substituting eq. (7.3.2) into eq. (7.3.7) we have

$$\frac{dR}{dt} = \frac{2\rho\pi G R^2}{3u}$$

(7.3.8)

or

$$\frac{dR}{R^2} = \frac{2\rho\pi G}{3u} dt$$

(7.3.9)

For a time-constant injection of small particles, we have

$$N(R)\, dR = \text{constant}\, dt$$

(7.3.10)

which with eq. (7.3.9) gives

$$N(R) = \text{constant}\, R^{-2}$$

(7.3.11)

which requires $\alpha = 2$.

We conclude that a state of gravitational accretion under the conditions that $\rho = $ constant and $dR/dt = $ constant R^2 indicates spectra where $\alpha = 2$, $\beta = 1.5$, and $\gamma = 1.33$. As shown in table 7.2.1, for this type of spectra small grains are most numerous and account for most of the cross section, but the mass of large bodies dominates.

7.3.2 Fragmentation

In a simple model of fragmentation, we consider a collection of bodies in a jet stream and particles with an initial random size spectrum. The collisions occurring in the jet stream will result not in accretion, as described above, but in fragmentation. We assume that whenever a body is hit it is split up into n smaller bodies that all are identical. Hence the cross section for fragmentation is proportional to σ or to $m^{2/3}$. This implies that bodies in the interval m to $m+\Delta m$ are leaving this interval at a rate proportional to $m^{2/3}$. At the same time, bodies are injected into the interval by the splitting of bodies in the interval nm to $n(m+\Delta m)$, and this occurs at a rate proportional to $(nm)^{2/3}$.

If massive bodies are continuously fed into the jet stream at a rate such that

$$N(m)m^{2/3}\Delta m = N(nm)(nm)^{2/3}n\Delta m \qquad (7.3.12)$$

applies for all mass intervals, we obtain a time-independent distribution. Introducing eq. (7.2.6), we find

$$m^{-\gamma+2/3} = (nm)^{-\gamma+2/3}n \qquad (7.3.13)$$

which is satisfied if $\gamma = 5/3$.

Thus we find that a state of fragmentation, given the conditions noted above, indicates spectra characterized by $\alpha = 3$, $\beta = 2$, and $\gamma = 5/3$. As shown in table 7.2.1, for this type of spectra small bodies are most numerous and cross section is concentrated in the small bodies, but the mass is concentrated in the large bodies.

Piotrowski (1953) has worked out a model that is essentially the same as given here. The power law with $\alpha = 3$, $a = 2$ is often referred to as Piotrowski's law.

There are a number of alternative models taking account of the fragmentation process in a more exact way. The a values are usually found to be $2 > a > 5/3$.

Dohnanyi (1969) takes account of both the fragmentation and the erosion at hypervelocity impacts and finds $\gamma = 11/6$, and, consequently, $\alpha = 3.5$ and $a = 2.5$.

All the theoretical models seem to agree that the result of fragmentation is that most of the mass remains in the largest bodies, and most of the cross section is due to the smallest particles. Hence, if the size distribution in the asteroid belt were determined mainly by fragmentation, a large amount of small particles would be expected. If collisions in the asteroid belt are mainly in the relative velocity range where accretion results, the high cross sections of the smallest particles will cause their removal into larger aggregates and truncation of the size distribution.

7.3.3 Observations Related to the Models

The particle distribution measurements made by the Pioneer 10 space probe to Jupiter are of great interest in connection with the question of relative rates of fragmentation and accretion. These measurements showed that, contrary to what would be expected if fragmentation would proceed at a higher rate than accretion, the concentration of small particles (10–1500 μm) in the asteroidal belt remained at the low background level found on either side of the belt (Kinard et al., 1974). In contrast, the larger particles (1.5–15 cm), as expected, showed an increase as the probe passed through the asteroid belt (Soberman et al., 1974). This suggests either that the fragmentation process does not produce a significant relative amount of particles in the 10–1500 μm range or that these particles are accreted as fast as they are formed. The theoretical considerations above and the observation of impact material on the Moon make the former alternative highly unlikely.

7.4 THE TRANSITION FROM FRAGMENTATION TO ACCRETION

Given a jet stream continually replenished by injected particles, one can conceptually follow the development of these particles into embryos and eventually into one secondary body.

Initially the jet stream is a composite of particles in dispersed orbits. Collisions will, as shown in ch. 6, increase the similarity of the particle orbits. Even in the first period after being focused, the jet stream is probably in a state of net fragmentation. Hence, there must be a transition from net fragmentation to net accretion before a jet stream can evolve into a secondary body.

It is reasonable to assume that the internal velocity of the jet stream is the decisive factor in the balance of fragmentation and accretion processes. At large velocities, collisions produce fragmentation. At smaller velocities, collisions result in accretion. Determining the velocity distribution in the transition region is a complex problem. It involves not only particle-particle interactions, but also the interaction of particles with clusters forming at the lower end of the velocity spectrum.

The mechanism of such cluster formation is demonstrated by the lunar surface material (Arrhenius et al., 1970, 1972; Arrhenius and Asunmaa, 1973, 1974; Asunmaa and Arrhenius, 1974). These observations show that dielectric particles exposed in space develop persistent internal electric polarization (fig. 7.4.1). The resulting electret particles adhere together by the dipole forces, forming open, loosely bonded clusters (fig. 7.4.2). The

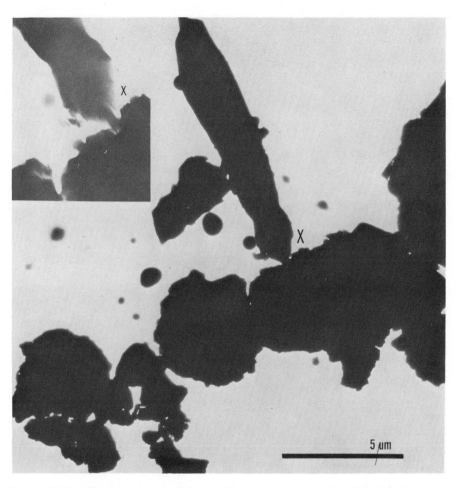

FIGURE 7.4.1.—Head-on contacts of elongated grains are characteristic of particle clustering in lunar soil caused by electrostatic field effects. Analysis of these effects indicates that they are due to persistent internal polarization of the dielectric grains, induced by irradiation. (From Arrhenius and Asunmaa, 1973.)

measured adhesion strength (10–200 dyn) and dipole moments (10^{-6} to 10^{-7} esu) indicate that such cluster formation would begin to be effective at relative particle velocities in the range 1–10 m/sec. Magnetostatic interaction between magnetized grains (which form only a small fraction of the mass), as evidenced from magnetite clustering in meteorites (sec. 22.7), would occur in a similar low relative particle velocity range (Harris and Tozer, 1967).

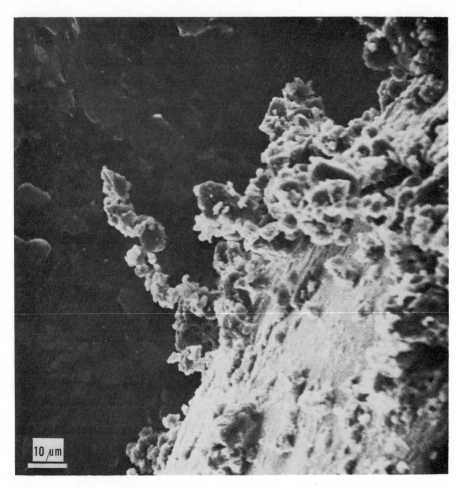

FIGURE 7.4.2.—Grains clustering to form a flexible chain extending about 40 μm from the base of the aggregate. The chain structure illustrates the electric dipole nature of the individual microparticles. (From Arrhenius and Asunmaa, 1973.)

Hence collisions in space may to a considerable extent take place between fluffy bodies, which have collisional properties substantially different from those of solid bodies, particularly in the subsonic velocity range. As we have very little experimental information about collisions between fluffy bodies, the discussion of the collisions in space necessarily must be highly speculative.

As far as single particle collisions are concerned, the investigations by Gault and Heitowit (1963) have demonstrated that such collisions in the hypervelocity range result in net mass loss rather than in accretion. Kerridge and Vedder (1972) have demonstrated that these conditions extend also into the subsonic range for hard particles impacting on a hard target. Hence, for individual hard particles accretion becomes possible only at projectile energies comparable to the energy of electrostatic (or magnetostatic) adhesion between grains; that is, at velocities of the order <10 m/sec. When relative particle velocities in a jet stream have been brought down far enough by collisions that a substantial fraction of the relative velocities is in this range, the formation of electrostatically bonded open-grain clusters, such as those formed by lunar dust, would presumably become effective.

An important process after that stage would in such a case be the collision of remaining higher velocity particles with particle clusters of low bulk density ($\sim$0.1–1 g/cm^3). Experiments modeling the hypervelocity part of this situation were carried out by Vedder (1972), who bombarded fluffy basalt dust with grain sizes in the range 0.1–10 μm with hypervelocity projectiles in the form of polystyrene spheres 2 to 5 μm in diameter. Also under these circumstances the ejected mass exceeds the projectile mass by two to three orders of magnitude. Hence, it seems unlikely that electrostatically bonded particle clusters can accumulate mass from projectiles with velocities exceeding several km/sec. Ballistic experience indicates, however, that particles in the subsonic velocity range could be captured in loosely bonded particle aggregates of sufficient size without net mass loss due to secondary ejecta. Hence, we have here, as an order-of-magnitude approximation, assumed effective accretion to begin at average relative velocities of about 500 m/sec in a population of particles constituting a jet stream.

8

RESONANCE STRUCTURE IN THE SOLAR SYSTEM

8.1 RESONANCES IN THE SOLAR SYSTEM

If we tabulate the orbital and spin periods of all the bodies in the solar system, we find that many of the periods are commensurable, indicating the existence of a number of resonance effects between mutually coupled resonators. There are resonances between the orbital periods of members of the same system and there are also resonances between the orbital and spin periods of rotating bodies.

Such resonances seem to be very important features of the solar system. As bodies once trapped in a resonance may under certain circumstances remain trapped indefinitely, resonance structures stabilize the solar system for very long periods of time.

A study of the resonance structure within a system may give us relevant information about the evolution of that system. To draw any conclusions in this respect we must clarify how the present resonance structure has been established. Two different mechanisms have been suggested:

(1) The first one, which has been proposed by Goldreich (1965), envisages that bodies were originally produced with no resonance coupling of their spin and orbital periods except those necessarily resulting from a random distribution. A later evolution of the system, mainly by tidal effects, changed the periods in a nonuniform way and resulted in the establishment of resonances.

This theory cannot in any case supply a general explanation of resonances. It is applicable only to the satellite systems and, since the tides produced on the Sun by the planets are totally negligible, another process must be invoked to explain the establishment of resonances in the planetary system. Further, the explanation of resonances as a tidal effect runs into difficulties even when applied only to satellite resonances. For example, as according to sec. 18.6 the Cassini division is genetically connected with Mimas, the orbit of Mimas cannot have changed by more than 1 or 2 percent since hetegonic times. Hence, there is not room for much tidal evolution.

(2) According to the alternative suggestion (Alfvén and Arrhenius, 1973), resonance effects were important in the hetegonic process itself, so that

TABLE 8.1.1
Types of Resonances

	Satellite orbit	Planetary orbit	Planetary spin
Satellite orbit	Jovian satellites Io-Europa-Ganymede [b] Saturnian satellites Mimas-Tethys[b,e] Enceladus-Dione [b] Titan-Hyperion [b,e]	(Sun and Jovian satellites 8, 9, 11) [a,b] (Sun and Phoebe)[a,b] (Sun and Moon)[a,b]	Tidal effects Possible effects between Earth and the Moon in the past [i]
Planetary orbit		(Jupiter-Saturn)[a,b] Neptune-Pluto [c] Jupiter-asteroids Trojans [g] Thule [f] Hildas [d] Kirkwood gaps [h] Earth-Ivar [b,e] Earth-Toro [l,m,n,o] Venus-Toro [m]	Spin-orbit of Mercury [j] Spin of Venus—orbit of the Earth? [j,k]

[a] Parentheses denote a near-commensurability, rather than a captured resonance.
[b] Roy and Ovenden (1954), Goldreich (1965).
[c] Cohen et al. (1967).
[d] Schubart (1968).
[e] Brouwer and Clemence (1961a).
[f] Takenouchi (1962).
[g] Brouwer and Clemence (1961b).
[h] Brouwer (1963).
[i] ch. 26.
[j] Goldreich and Peale (1968).
[k] Dyce and Pettengill (1967).
[l] Danielsson and Ip (1972).
[m] Ip and Mehra (1973).
[n] Williams and Wetherill (1973).
[o] Janiczek et al. (1972).

bodies were preferentially produced in states of resonance with other bodies. Hence, the resonance structure may give us direct information about the hetegonic process.

8.1.1 Different Types of Resonances

In the solar system the following types of resonances (see table 8.1.1) have been observed:

(1) *Orbit-orbit resonances.* If two planets or two satellites have orbital periods T_1 and T_2 and the ratio between them can be written

$$\frac{T_1}{T_2} = \frac{n_1}{n_2} \qquad (8.1.1)$$

where n_1 and n_2 are small integers, such periods are called commensurable. Resonance effects may be produced if the gravitational attraction between the bodies is above a certain limit. There are several pronounced examples of this in the satellite systems of Jupiter and Saturn, and the effect is also important in the planetary system, especially for the asteroids.

Resonance between the orbital motion of a planet and the orbital motion of one of its own satellites has also been discussed (Roy and Ovenden, 1954). Seen from the frame of reference of the planet, this is a resonance between the apparent motion of the satellite and the apparent motion of the Sun. Such resonances are sometimes referred to as "satellite-Sun resonances."

(2) *Spin-orbit resonances.* If the density distribution in a rotating body is asymmetric, this asymmetry produces a periodically varying gravitation field that may couple with its orbital motion. This effect generally leads to a spin-orbit resonance. The spin of Mercury seems to be locked in a resonance with its own orbital period. Whether the spin of Venus is coupled with the orbital motion of the Earth (in relation to Venus) is a matter of dispute; see sec. 8.8.

A similar asymmetry of a planet may also affect the motion of a satellite revolving around the planet. This effect is not known to be important today but it may have affected the evolution of the Earth-Moon system (ch. 24).

If a satellite produces tides on its primary, the tidal bulges corotate with the satellite. The coupling between the tidal bulges and the satellite may be considered as a spin-orbit resonance with $n_1 = n_2 = 1$.

8.2 RESONANCE AND THE OSCILLATION OF A PENDULUM

In order to study the basic properties of resonances we first treat some simple models.

As pointed out by Brown and Shook (1964), there is a certain similarity between the resonances in the solar system and the motion of a simple pendulum (see fig. 8.2.1). Consider the motion of a mass point m, which is confined to a circle with radius l, under the action of Earth's gravitational

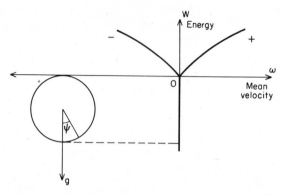

FIGURE 8.2.1.—Oscillations of a simple pendulum. If the energy is negative, the pendulum oscillates with an amplitude $\psi_1 < \pi$, and the mean velocity $d\psi/dt$ is zero. If the energy is positive the motion consists of a constant revolution modulated by an oscillation of the same period. The angular velocity ω of this revolution may be either positive or negative.

acceleration g. If the angle with the vertical is called ψ, the motion is described by the equation

$$\frac{d^2\psi}{dt^2} + A^2 \sin \psi = 0 \qquad (8.2.1)$$

where

$$A^2 = \frac{g}{l} \qquad (8.2.2)$$

Integrating eq. (8.2.1) we find

$$\left(\frac{d\psi}{dt}\right)^2 = \kappa + 2A^2 \cos \psi \qquad (8.2.3)$$

where κ is constant.

Normalizing the energy W of the system so that $W = 0$ when the pendulum is at rest at $\psi = \pi$, we have

$$W = \frac{ml^2}{2}\left(\frac{d\psi}{dt}\right)^2 - mgl(1 + \cos\psi) \qquad (8.2.4)$$

and from eq. (8.2.3) we find that

$$\kappa = \frac{2W}{ml^2} + 2A^2 \qquad (8.2.5)$$

Depending on the value κ we have three cases:

(1) $\kappa > 2A^2$; $W > 0$. In this case $\dfrac{d\psi}{dt}$ never vanishes; it could be either > 0 or < 0. We have

$$t - t_0 = \int_{\psi_0}^{\psi} \frac{d\psi}{(\kappa + 2\,A^2\,\cos\psi)^{1/2}} \qquad (8.2.6)$$

where t_0 is the value of t when $\psi = \psi_0$. The angle ψ_0 is a constant. If we put

$$\frac{1}{\omega} = \frac{1}{2\pi}\int_0^{2\pi} \frac{d\psi}{(\kappa + 2\,A^2\,\cos\psi)^{1/2}} \qquad (8.2.7)$$

we can write the solution (see Brown and Shook, p. 219)

$$\psi - \psi_0 = \omega t + \psi_0 - \frac{A^2}{\omega^2}\sin(\omega t + \psi_0) + \frac{A^4}{8\omega^4}\sin 2(\omega t + \psi_0) + \cdots \cdot \quad (8.2.8)$$

The motion consists of a constant revolution with the period $2\pi/\omega$, superimposed upon an oscillation with the same period. The motion can proceed in either direction ($\omega < 0$ or $\omega > 0$).

(2) $\kappa < 2\,A^2$; $W < 0$. In this case $\dfrac{d\psi}{dt} = 0$ when $\psi = \pm\psi_1$ with

$$\cos\psi_1 = -\frac{\kappa}{2\,A^2} = -\frac{W}{mlg} - 1 \qquad (8.2.9)$$

and the integral is

$$\left(\frac{d\psi}{dt}\right)^2 = 4\,A^2 \left(\sin^2\frac{\psi_1}{2} - \sin^2\frac{\psi}{2}\right) \qquad (8.2.10)$$

The value of ψ oscillates between $-\psi_1$ and $+\psi_1$. For small amplitudes the period is $2\pi/A$; for large amplitudes anharmonic terms make it larger.

(3) The case $\kappa = 2\,A^2$; $W=0$ means that the pendulum reaches the unstable equilibrium at the uppermost point of the circle, with zero velocity.

The lowest state of energy occurs when the pendulum is at rest at $\psi = 0$. If energy is supplied, oscillations start and their amplitude grows until ψ_1 approaches π. Then there is a discontinuous transition from case (2) to case (1).

8.3 A SIMPLE RESONANCE MODEL

In order to demonstrate a basic resonance phenomenon, let us discuss a very simple case (fig. 8.3.1). Suppose that a planet at O is encircled by two satellites, one of significant mass (M_2) moving in a circular orbit and one with negligible mass (M_1) moving in an elliptic orbit. We denote by $\omega_1 = 2\pi/T_1$ and $\omega_2 = 2\pi/T_2$ the average angular velocities of M_1 and M_2, and we treat the case where the ratio ω_1/ω_2 is close to 2. Orbital inclinations are put equal to zero.

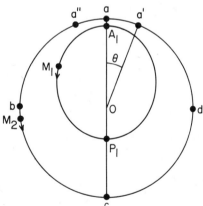

FIGURE 8.3.1.—A planet at O has two orbiting satellites, one of small mass (M_2) moving in a circular orbit and one of negligible mass (M_1) moving in an elliptic orbit. The orbital inclinations are zero and the ratio of average angular velocities ω_1/ω_2 is near 2; $\omega_1 = 2\pi/T_1$ and $\omega_2 = 2\pi/T_2$. A_1 is the apocenter of the inner satellite, and P_1 is the pericenter.

If at a certain moment the longitude angles of the satellites are ϕ_1 and ϕ_2, a "conjunction" occurs when $\phi_1 = \phi_2$. Consider the case when there is a conjunction between the satellites at the moment when the inner one is at its apocenter A_1 and the outer one is at point a. This implies that after M_2 completes 1.5 revolutions the outer satellite is at d when the inner satellite is at its pericenter P_1. When M_1 moves from P_1 to A_1 it is subject to the attraction from M_2 which works in the direction of motion, hence increasing the angular momentum. When the motion continues from A_1 to P_1, M_1 is subject to a similar force from the outer satellite, which moves from a to b, but this force will diminish the angular momentum of M_1. Because of the symmetry the net result is zero (neglecting high-order terms).

Suppose now that M_1 arrives at A_1 a certain time Δt before M_2 arrives at a. Because the orbits are closest together around $A_1 a$, the effects in this region predominate. If M_2 is at a' when M_1 is at A_1, the force between them will decrease the angular momentum C_1 of M_1. (The reciprocal effect on M_2 is negligible because of the smallness of M_1.) As the orbital period of a satellite is proportional to C^3, the period of M_1 will be shortened with the result that at the next conjunction it will arrive at A_1 when M_2 is still further away from a. The result is that the angle θ between the bodies when M_1 is at its pericenter will increase.

If on the other hand θ is negative so that M_1 arrives too late at A_1, say when M_2 already has reached a'', the angular momentum of M_1 will increase with the result that θ will become still more negative.

We can compare this result with the pendulum treated in sec. 8.2 when it is close to the upper point $\psi = \pi$. Putting $\theta = \pi - \psi$ we see that the conjunction at $\theta = 0$ represents an unstable equilibrium. We can conclude that a stable equilibrium is reached when $\theta = \pi$, corresponding to $\psi = 0$. This means that the inner satellite is at P_1 when the outer one is at a. (This implies that M_1 also is at P_1 when M_2 is at c. The interaction at this configuration is smaller than near A_1 because of the larger distance between the orbits.)

8.4 DEVIATIONS FROM EXACT RESONANCE

If we put the mean longitudes of the two bodies equal to $\phi_1(t)$ and $\phi_2(t)$, resonance implies that ϕ_1 and ϕ_2 increase such that the average value of the libration angle ξ

$$\langle \xi \rangle = n_1 \phi_1 - n_2 \phi_2 \qquad (8.4.1)$$

is zero.

The bodies can oscillate around the equilibrium position. (In celestial mechanics the word 'libration' is used for oscillations.) Libration implies that ϕ_1 and ϕ_2 increase such that ξ varies periodically with a period that may be many orders of magnitude larger than the orbital period. This corresponds to the oscillations of the simple pendulum in case (2).

In the cases we will discuss, the equilibrium position of a body (body 1) in relation to the orbital pattern of body 2 is at A_1, which is located on the apsis line (joining the apocenter and the pericenter). However, the time T_2 needed for body 2 to move one turn in relation to the apsis line is not the sidereal period T_K because of the precession of the perihelion with the angular velocity ω_P (ch. 3). According to eq. (3.3.12) we have:

$$\omega_2 = \omega_K - \omega_P \tag{8.4.2}$$

with $\omega_K = 2\pi/T_K$, and $\omega_2 = 2\pi/T_2$. Putting ω_1 we find from eq. (8.1.1)

$$\omega_1 = \frac{n_2}{n_1}\,\omega_2 = \frac{n_2}{n_1}\,(\omega_K - \omega_P) \tag{8.4.3}$$

Furthermore, in case of libration body 1 is not situated at A_1 but at an angle $\xi(t)$ from it. During one period T_1, the angle changes by $T_1 \dfrac{d\xi}{dt}$. From eq. (8.4.1) we find

$$\left\langle \frac{d\xi}{dt} \right\rangle = n_1\omega_1 - n_2(\omega_K - \omega_P) \tag{8.4.4}$$

If eq. (8.4.3) is satisfied, there is a coupling between perihelion position and the resonant orbital coupling of the bodies; the average value of the libration angle ξ is constant, and eq. (8.4.4) reduces to zero.

The amplitude of the libration is a measure of the stability of the resonance coupling. If the amplitude of the libration is increased to π the system passes discontinuously from a state of finite amplitude libration (case (2)) to a state of revolution modulated by periodic oscillation (case (1)). In the latter state, the resonance is broken but a "near-commensurability" exists, and the average value of ξ for the system will increase or decrease indefinitely with time.

8.5 ORBIT-ORBIT RESONANCES

To study the resonance phenomena in the solar system, one can start from the equations of motion of a pendulum disturbed by a periodic force (Brown and Shook, 1964). The problems usually lead to analytically complicated formulae that can be treated only by elaborate computer calculations. Very often only numerical solutions of a number of typical cases can clarify the situation. It is beyond the scope of our treatise to discuss this in detail. Instead we shall treat some simple cases that demonstrate the basic physical phenomena.

In the solar system there are a number of orbit-orbit resonances; i.e., resonances between satellites (or planets) whose motions are coupled in such a way that their orbital periods are commensurate. In this section we shall discuss some of these resonances.

In most cases of resonance the bigger of the two bodies moves in an orbit with very low eccentricity, whereas the orbit of the small body has a rather high eccentricity. We can account for essential properties of the resonance phenomena if we approximate the orbit of the more massive body as a circle. Further, we will in general only deal with the case of coplanar orbits.

8.5.1 Neptune-Pluto

One example of an orbit-orbit resonance is the Neptune-Pluto system, which has been studied by Cohen and Hubbard (1965), who have integrated the orbits over an interval of 10^6 yr. Their results were later essentially confirmed by Williams and Benson (1971), whose integrations cover 4.5×10^6 yr. The orbital periods of Neptune and Pluto are $T_\psi = 165$ yr and $T_P = 248$ yr, which from eq. (8.1.1) gives $n_1 = 2$ and $n_2 = 3$. Figure 8.5.1 shows the orbit of Pluto (as found by numerical integration) in a reference system where the Sun and Neptune are at rest. In this system it takes Pluto 500 yr $(T_\psi T_P / T_P - T_\psi)$ to complete one turn.

In relation to the Plutonian orbit, Neptune may be located at any point of the arc bac. If it is located in the middle (at a), its gravitational attraction on Pluto integrated over an entire 500-yr period is zero because of the symmetry. If Neptune is located at b, its gravitational attraction will be stronger on the left part of the Plutonian orbit, with the result that orbital angular momentum will be transferred from Neptune to Pluto. This transfer will increase the orbital period of Pluto and reduce the period of Neptune. The result is that, in relation to the orbital pattern of Pluto, Neptune will begin to move toward the right along the arc. We can express the result by saying that, if Neptune is placed at b, it will *appear to be repelled* by the closeness of the Plutonian orbit. Similarly, if Neptune is located at c, it will appear to be repelled toward the left due to the closeness of the orbit of Pluto.

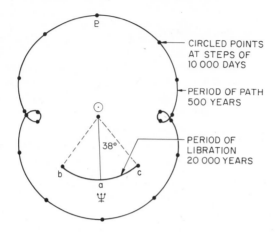

FIGURE 8.5.1.—The orbit of Pluto with respect to the Sun and to
Neptune. The orbital pattern of Pluto librates relative to Neptune,
but for clarity the Plutonian orbit is held stationary and the libration of Neptune relative to it is shown. The equilibrium position of
Neptune is at *a* and Neptune librates between extreme positions at
b and *c* with an amplitude of 38°. (From Cohen and Hubbard, 1965.)

Hence, in relation to the Plutonian orbit, Neptune will oscillate between
b and *c*, in a way similar to the pendulum in fig. 8.2.1. Cohen and Hubbard
(1965) have found the period of this libration to be about 20 000 yr. The
double amplitude of libration is 76°. The minimum distance between Pluto
and Neptune is 18 AU. Hence, because of the resonance, Neptune and Pluto
can never collide in spite of the fact that these orbits intersect.

The period covered by numerical integrations is only 10^{-3} of the age of
the solar system, so it is dangerous to extrapolate back in time to the
hetegonic era. It seems unlikely that gravitational effects alone could have
changed the amplitude of libration so much that a resonance capture will
be found to have occurred long ago. However, viscous forces from a surrounding dispersed medium could, of course, have produced such a change.
Such a process would necessarily have led to an appreciable accretion of this
medium by Pluto. This means that the establishment of the resonance is
likely to be connected with the general problem of planetary accretion.
Hence, we tentatively conclude that *the present pattern is likely to have
been established as a result of hetegonic processes.* Thus, by studying
this and other resonances we may get important information about the
hetegonic processes.

Lyttleton (1936), Kuiper (1957), and Rabe (1957a and b) have suggested
that Pluto might be a runaway satellite of Neptune. This idea was put
forward before the resonance was discovered and now seems very unlikely

because there is no obvious mechanism consistent with this idea that can account for the establishment of the resonance. In spite of that, the idea appears to still be frequently quoted.

8.5.2 Earth-Toro and Other Earth-Asteroid Resonances

As has been discovered recently (Danielsson and Ip, 1972), the Earth and Toro form an 8/5 resonance system (fig. 8.5.2). In a Sun-Earth frame of reference, Toro makes five loops similar to the two orbital loops of Pluto. The Earth oscillates on the arc *bac*, being apparently repelled whenever it comes close to Toro's orbit. In contrast to the Neptune-Pluto resonance, the resonance capture is established by two very close encounters taking place during two rapid passages in an 8-yr period. During the rest of the 8-yr period, the interaction is almost negligible.

If the encounters with the Earth were the only close encounters, the Earth-Toro pattern would have a permanent life. However, Toro's motion is complicated by the fact that its perihelion is close to Venus' orbit. The

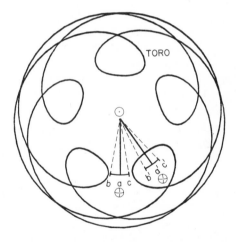

FIGURE 8.5.2.—Projection of 1685 Toro on the ecliptic plane in a coordinate system rotating with the Earth. Between 1600 AD and 1800 AD, the Earth-Sun line librates in the *b'a'c'* domain about the equilibrium position *a'*. The libration makes the transit to the *bac* domain around 1850 AD and remains there until 2200 AD. After 2200 AD the Earth-Sun equilibrium position will shift back from *a* to *a'*. The orbital pattern of Toro librates relative to the Earth, but for the sake of clarity the Earth is depicted as librating in relation to the orbital pattern of Toro. (From Ip and Mehra, 1973.)

result is that close encounters between Venus and Toro periodically shift the Earth-Toro pattern so that the Earth for a certain period oscillates along the arc $b'a'c'$. A subsequent encounter with Venus brings it back again. The crossings are possible because the orbital planes differ.

As has been shown by Danielsson and Mehra (1973), this periodic shift between two capture positions might have been permanent if only Toro, the Earth, and Venus had been involved. However, the aphelion of Toro is outside the orbit of Mars, and, as pointed out also by Williams and Wetherill (1973), it seems that close encounters with Mars are statistically probable and will make the resonance transitory with a duration much smaller than the age of the solar system. It seems at present impossible to reconstruct the orbit of Toro back to hetegonic times.

There are a number of other asteroids which are in resonance capture of a more or less permanent character. Surveys are given by Janiczek et al. (1972), Ip and Mehra (1973), and Danielsson and Mehra (1973). Ivar is trapped in a 11/28 resonance, which probably is rather stable, and Amor is trapped in a 3/8 resonance, which is unstable.

8.5.3 The Trojans

The Trojans are in a 1/1 resonance with Jupiter. They librate around the Lagrangian points of Jupiter. Figure 8.5.3. shows regions within which the librating Trojans are confined. Due to the eccentricity of Jupiter's orbit and perturbations from other planets, the three-dimensional motions of the Trojans are extremely complicated, having several different libration periods (Brouwer and Clemence, 1961b). Whether, in some cases, these librations may be so large as to throw some Trojans out of libration is still undetermined.

As the outermost Jovian satellites have a retrograde motion, they must have been gravitationally captured. It seems reasonable that there is a connection between these satellites and the Trojans, and it is possible that the satellites are captured Trojans. Whether this capture has taken place under present conditions or during the hetegonic era is still to be clarified.

8.5.4 The Hilda Asteroids

The Hilda asteroids, named after the biggest member of the group, are in 2/3 resonance with Jupiter. These asteroids have been studied by Chebotarev (1967) and Schubart (1968). Approximating Jupiter's motion as circular, and neglecting the inclinations between the orbits, the motion of a typical Hilda asteroid is shown in fig. 8.5.4.

The resonance mechanism can be explained in the same simple way as in the earlier cases: As soon as Jupiter comes close to the orbital pattern

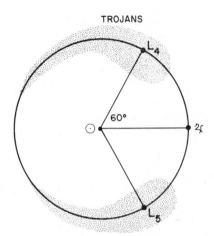

FIGURE 8.5.3.—The typical regions of libration of the Trojans around the Lagrangian
points L_4 and L_5 of Jupiter.

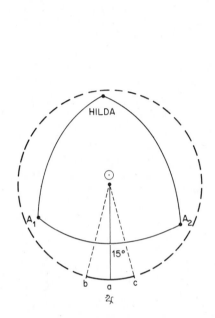

FIGURE 8.5.4.—Idealized orbit of 153 Hilda in the Jupiter-Sun
rotating coordinate system. Due to the 3/2 resonance, Hilda
describes a triangular trajectory in a time interval of 24 yr.
Due to systematic perturbations the whole orbital pattern will
oscillate with an amplitude of 15° and a period of 260 yr. Points
A_1 and A_2 are the aphelia of Hilda and also her points of closest
approach to Jupiter. The distance between Hilda and Jupiter
at close approach is never less than 4 AU. (From Ip, 1974a.)

of the asteroid, there is an apparent repulsion. Hence, the equilibrium position is at a, but normally there are librations for example between b and c.

In the cases earlier discussed, the orbits of the two bodies in resonance
crossed each other. This means that in the planar case there is no possibility
to establish or break the resonance without a close encounter between the
bodies. If the orbital planes do not coincide, the situation is more complex.

The orbits of the Hildas do not cross the orbit of Jupiter; therefore, a
continuous transition to a nonresonant case is possible. An increase in the
amplitude of the oscillations may eventually result in a transition to the
noncaptive state, such that Jupiter (fig. 8.5.4) begins to librate in relation
to the orbital pattern in the same way as the pendulum in fig. 8.2.1. does
for the case $W > 0$.

The asteroid Thule is also resonance-captured by Jupiter (ratio 3/4). Its librations have been studied by Takenouchi (1962) and by Marsden (1970). The resonances Jupiter-Hildas and Jupiter-Thule are of importance in the discussion of the Kirkwood gaps (secs. 4.3 and 8.6). It is evident that there are clusters of bodies at Jovian resonance points, and the theoretical studies show that there are good reasons for this. This indicates that the Kirkwood gaps (absence of bodies at Jovian resonance points) cannot simply be resonance phenomena but are due to other factors; e.g., collision phenomena (Jefferys, 1967; Sinclair, 1969).

8.5.5 Titan-Hyperion

In the Saturnian system the small satellite Hyperion moves in an eccentric orbit outside Titan (fig. 8.5.5). The equilibrium position is reached at conjunction when Hyperion is at its aposaturnian. For further details see Roy and Ovenden (1954), Goldreich (1965), and Brouwer and Clemence (1961a).

8.5.6 Dione-Enceladus

This resonance, also in the Saturnian system, is of the type 1/2. The pattern is shown in fig. 8.5.6; as the libration of Enceladus is only 11 sec of arc, it is not shown. The orbit of Dione is approximated by a circle, and

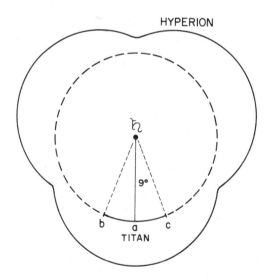

FIGURE 8.5.5.—The orbital pattern for the 4/3 resonance of Titan-Hyperion in the Saturnian satellite system. Titan librates with an amplitude of 9° about the equilibrium position at *a*. The orbit of Hyperion is strongly perturbed by Titan.

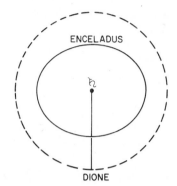

FIGURE 8.5.6.—The orbital pattern of the 2/1 resonance of Enceladus-Dione in the Saturnian system. The ellipticity of the orbit of Enceladus is exaggerated for the purpose of illustration. The perisaturnian of Enceladus precesses due to Dione.

the eccentricity of Enceladus' orbit is exaggerated for the sake of clarity. This resonance is discussed at greater length by Roy and Ovenden (1954).

8.5.7 Tethys-Mimas

It should be pointed out that if the orbits are coplanar a prerequisite for resonance is that at least one of the orbits is eccentric. If both orbits are exactly circular, no coupling between the orbits is produced.

In all the preceding cases an approximation to coplanar motion illustrated the essential character of the resonance. In contrast, the resonance between the Saturnian satellites Tethys and Mimas is dependent on the inclination of the orbits, and the resonance is related to the nodes. This is also the case for the Jupiter-Thule resonance. Detailed discussions are given by Roy and Ovenden (1954), Goldreich (1965), and Brouwer and Clemence (1961a).

8.5.8 Io-Europa-Ganymede

A more complicated case of commensurability is found in the Jovian system, where the angular velocities of Io, Europa, and Ganymede obey the relationship

$$\omega_I - 3\omega_E + 2\omega_G = 0 \qquad (8.5.1)$$

to within the observational accuracy 10^{-9}. The mechanism is rather complicated. It has been treated in detail by the exact methods of celestial mechanics; e.g., Roy and Ovenden (1954).

Table 8.5.1 gives a survey of all known orbit-orbit resonances.

TABLE 8.5.1

Orbit-Orbit Resonances in the Solar System

| Bodies | Orbital Parameters | | |
	e	i (°)	Period (da/yr)
Tethys	0.00	1.1	1.887802
Mimas	0.0201	1.5	0.942422
Dione	0.0021	0.0	2.73681
Enceladus	0.0045	0.0	1.37028
Hyperion	0.104	0.5	21.27666
Titan	0.0290	0.3	15.945452
Pluto	0.247	17.1	248.43
Neptune	0.0087	1.46	164.78
Jupiter	0.048	1.38	11.86
Hilda	0.15	7.85	7.90
Jupiter	0.048	1.38	11.86
Thule	0.03	23.	8.90
Jupiter	0.048	1.38	11.86
Trojans	~0.15	10–20	11.86
Earth	0.017	0.0	1.0
Toro	0.435	9.3	1.6
Earth	0.017	0.0	1.0
Ivar	0.397	8.3	2.545

[a] Roy and Ovenden (1954), Goldreich (1965).
[b] Brouwer and Clemence (1961a).
[c] Cohen et al. (1967).
[d] Schubart (1968).
[e] Takenouchi (1962).
[f] Ip (1974a).
[g] Brouwer and Clemence (1961b).
[h] Danielsson and Ip (1972).
[i] Ip and Mehra (1973).

TABLE 8.5.1 (Continued)
Orbit-Orbit Resonances in the Solar System

Ratio	Resonance Type	Libration Period (yr)	Amplitude (°)	References
1 2	Resonances related to the nodes	70.8	47	(ᵃ) (ᵇ)
1 2	Conjunction when Enceladus at peri-saturnian	3.89	11'24"	(ᵃ)
3 4	Conjunction when Hyperion at apo-saturnian	18.75	9	(ᵃ) (ᵇ)
2 3	See fig. 8.5.1	20 000	39	(ᶜ)
2 3	Largest body of a group of at least 20 bodies librating with different amplitudes and phases	270	40	(ᵈ)
3 4		500	∼0	(ᵉ) (ᶠ)
1 1	Two groups, one at each of the libration points of Jupiter	∼900	10–20	(ᵍ)
8 5	Resonance due to close encounter	150	10	(ʰ) (ⁱ)
28 11	Resonance due to close encounter	300	26	(ʲ)

8.6 THE KIRKWOOD GAPS

An interesting and puzzling resonance-related phenomenon is found in the main asteroidal belt (see fig. 4.3.3). If the number of asteroids is plotted as a function of orbital period, or equivalently as a function of semimajor axis, there are a number of pronounced empty zones, the so-called Kirkwood gaps, in the neighborhood of periods commensurable with Jupiter's. Gaps corresponding to resonances of 1/2, 1/3, 2/5, and 3/7 are clearly observed and some higher resonances have also been suggested (see sec. 4.3).

The Kirkwood gaps have attracted much interest, and there is a multitude of theoretical papers about the mechanism producing them (Brouwer, 1963; Schweizer, 1969; Sinclair, 1969). Some of the authors claim to have made theoretical models that adequately explain the gaps. If one tries to extract the fundamental physical principles of these models from the jungle of sophisticated mathematical formulae, one does not feel convinced of the explanations. Doubt of the adequacy of these models is aroused by the fact that, whereas both Tethys and Dione are keeping small bodies (Mimas and Enceladus) trapped at resonance 1/2, Jupiter *produces an absence* of small bodies at the corresponding period. Further, Jupiter keeps a number of Hilda asteroids trapped in a 2/3 resonance but produces gaps at a number of other resonance points in the main asteroid belt. It is essential that any theory of the Kirkwood gaps simultaneously explain both types of resonance phenomena.

In the absence of a clear answer to these questions, one must ask whether the Kirkwood gaps really are produced by the resonance effects of the type discussed by the current theories. As we have seen in ch. 5, there are reasons to believe that nongravitational effects are of importance to the motion of comets and asteroids. It is therefore possible that Jefferys (1967) is correct when he suggests that nongravitational effects (e.g., collisions) are essential for an understanding of the Kirkwood gaps. If the gaps were the result of a hetegonic process, this would make them more interesting from the point of view of the early history of the solar system. One hopes that a complete theory of the formation of the asteroid belt will afford a thorough explanation of the Kirkwood gaps.

8.7 ON THE ABSENCE OF RESONANCE EFFECTS IN THE SATURNIAN RING SYSTEM

The dark markings in the Saturnian ring system, especially Cassini's division, have long been thought to be due to resonances produced by Mimas and perhaps by other satellites as well. It has been claimed that the gaps in the Saturnian rings ought to be analogous to the Kirkwood gaps in the asteroid belt. Such an analogy is erroneous because it has been shown both observationally and theoretically (see Alfvén, 1968) that the Saturnian rings cannot be explained as a resonance phenomenon.

The accurate measurements of Dollfus (1961) are shown in fig. 18.6.1. It is obvious that there is no acceptable correlation between the observed markings and such resonance-produced gaps as would be expected in analogy to the Kirkwood gaps in the asteroid belt. Furthermore, the mass ratio of Mimas to Saturn is $1/(8 \times 10^6)$, whereas the mass ratio of Jupiter to Sun is $1/10^3$. Hence, the relative perturbation effect is 10^4 times smaller in the case of the Saturnian rings than in the case of Jupiter and the asteroid belt. Such a small gravitational perturbation is not likely to produce any appreciable resonance phenomenon.

As we shall see in sec. 18.6, the dark markings are readily explainable as hetegonic "shadow" effects.

8.8 SPIN-ORBIT RESONANCES

For all satellites with known spins the spin periods equal the orbital periods. This is likely to be due to tides, produced by their primaries, which have braked the synodic rotations of the satellites to zero. For a formal statement of such a resonance we have

$$\frac{\tau}{T} = \frac{n_\tau}{n_T} \qquad (8.8.1)$$

where T is the orbital and τ is the spin period of the body in question, and $n_\tau = n_T = 1$.

Mercury's spin period is 59 days, which is exactly 2/3 of its orbital period (Dyce and Pettengill, 1967). This means that Mercury is captured in a spin-orbit resonance. According to Goldreich and Peale (1968), this represents the final state produced by the solar tide.

The case of Venus is puzzling. It has a retrograde spin with a period of about 243 days. The spin period of Venus is supposedly in a 5/4 resonance with the orbital period of the Earth as seen from Venus (Dyce and Pettengill, 1967; Goldreich and Peale, 1968). It is surprising that the Earth can lock Venus into such a resonance (Kaula, 1968). New measurements seem to cast doubt on the reality of this resonance (Carpenter, 1970).

Another type of spin-orbit resonance is that of a spinning body such as a planet and the satellites around it. Allan (1967) has drawn attention to the fact that, if the gravitational potential of the planet depends on the longitude, a satellite will be subject to a force in the tangential direction that may transfer energy between the planetary spin and the orbiting satellite. In case the orbiting period of the satellite equals the spin period of the planet, we have a 1/1 resonance. The satellite will be locked at a certain phase angle around which it can librate. There are no examples of synchronous natural satellites, but the theory is applicable to geostationary artificial satellites.

There are also higher resonances (n_T and n_r take on larger values), but these are efficient only for satellites with high inclinations or high eccentricities. A body in a circular orbit in the *equatorial* plane is not affected. It has been suggested that such resonances were of importance during the evolution of the Earth-Moon system (see ch. 24).

8.9 NEAR-COMMENSURABILITIES

Besides the exact resonances there are a number of near-commensurabilities. In the development of celestial mechanics such near-commensurabilities have attracted much attention because the perturbations become especially large. Most noteworthy is the case of Jupiter-Saturn, whose periods have a ratio close to 2/5. The near-commensurabilities have been listed by Roy and Ovenden (1954) and further discussed by Goldreich (1965).

In the case of exact resonances, the relative positions of the bodies are locked at certain equilibrium positions around which they perform oscillations as shown in figs. 8.5.1 through 8.5.6. At near-commensurability no such locking exists. In relation to the orbital pattern of body 2, body 1 continuously revolves, just as the pendulum (fig. 8.2.1) in case (1). It is possible that some or all of these near-commensurabilities are broken captured resonances. This would be likely if the hetegonic processes had a strong preference for generating bodies in resonance. However, so far it is doubtful whether near-commensurabilities really are of hetegonic significance. If the periods of the different bodies are distributed at random, there is a certain probability that two periods should be near-commensurable. Studies by the authors cited agree that the number of observed commensurabilities is larger than expected statistically. If, however, we account for the exact resonances by a separate mechanism and subtract them, the remaining statistical excess, if any, is not very large.

Of interest from a hetegonic point of view are the near-commensurabilities of retrograde satellites and the Sun (Roy and Ovenden, 1954). The Jovian satellites 8, 9, and 11 have periods that are close to 1:6 of the orbital period of Jupiter; for 12 the ratio is close to 1:7. The same is the case for the period of Phoebe compared to the period of Saturn. There is a possibility that these commensurabilities were significant for the capture of these satellites ("resonance capture").

8.9.1 Transition From Capture to Near-Commensurability

There are two basic ways in which a capture resonance can be broken.

(1) The libration may increase. In the case of the pendulum, this corresponds to an increase in energy so that W passes from <0 to >0.

(2) A torque is applied that is stronger than the resonance can tolerate.

To take the simpler case of applied torque, suppose that the librations are zero. If we apply a torque to the pendulum, it will be deviated an angle ψ from its equilibrium. With increasing torque ψ will increase. When it reaches the value $\pi/2$, the restoring force begins to decrease. Hence, if the torque exceeds the value corresponding to $\psi = \pi/2$, the pendulum starts a continuous accelerated motion, and the capture is broken.

To apply this result to the celestial problem, suppose that two celestial bodies are captured in resonance and one of them is subject to a drag; e.g., from the Poynting-Robertson effect. The angle ψ will increase, and the drag will be compensated by the resonance force. If a certain maximum permissible drag is exceeded, the capture will be broken. In relation to the orbital period of body 2, body 1 will begin to revolve, and a near-commensurability will be established.

9

SPIN AND TIDES

9.1 TIDES

The spins of the celestial bodies contain information that is important for the study of the formation and evolutionary history of the solar system. When the celestial bodies formed by accretion this process gave them a certain spin; this will be discussed in ch. 13. There are reasons to believe that many bodies (e.g., the asteroids and the giant planets) still have essentially the same spin as they did immediately after their accretion. In many other cases the spin has been more or less drastically changed. This applies to all satellites, to the Earth and, to some extent, to Neptune also.

The main effect producing changes in the spins is likely to be tidal action by which the spinning of a body is braked. The theory of the terrestrial tides, as produced by the Moon and the Sun, has been developed especially by Jeffreys (1962) and by Munk and MacDonald (1960). The latter authors state (p. 15) that "there are few problems in geophysics in which less progress has been made." Even if this statement overestimates progress in other fields, it shows what difficult problems the tides present.

For our purpose we are interested not only in the terrestrial tides but also in the tides on other celestial bodies. The internal structure of celestial bodies is almost unknown and therefore very little about tidal effects upon these bodies can be theoretically established. We have to look for possible effects on the orbits of satellites to make any conclusions.

9.2 AMPLITUDE OF TIDES

Let us first discuss an idealized case of two homogeneous fluid bodies. Suppose that a secondary or companion body with radius R_{sc} is orbiting around a central or primary body with radius R_c. The densities of the bodies are Θ_c and Θ_{sc}, the masses are $M_c = \frac{4}{3}\pi\Theta_c R_c^3$ and $M_{sc} = \frac{4}{3}\Theta_{sc}R_{sc}^3$, and the distance between their centers of gravity is r. The gravitational attraction of M_{sc} deforms the spherical shape of M_c so that its oblateness becomes

$$\Upsilon_c = \frac{15 M_{sc} R_c^3}{4 M_c r^3} = \frac{15\Theta_{sc} R_{sc}^3}{4\Theta_c r^3} \tag{9.2.1}$$

a formula which is a good approximation for $r \gg R_c$ (far outside the Roche limit). The height h_c of the tides is

$$h_c = \frac{\Upsilon_c R_c}{2} \tag{9.2.2}$$

Similar expressions hold for M_{sc}:

$$\Upsilon_{sc} = \frac{15 M_c R_{sc}^3}{4 M_{sc} r^3} = \frac{15 \Theta_c R_c^3}{4 \Theta_{sc} r^3} \tag{9.2.3}$$

$$h_{sc} = \frac{\Upsilon_{sc} R_{sc}}{2} \tag{9.2.4}$$

Table 9.2.1 shows some typical examples. For the satellites of Jupiter and Saturn, $15\Theta_c/4\Theta_{sc}$ is put equal to 1.

TABLE 9.2.1

Tidal Effects Between Central Bodies and Their Secondary Bodies, in Terms of Oblateness Υ and Height of Tide h for Each Body (Idealized Case)

Central body	Secondary	Central body		Secondary	
		Υ_c	h_c (cm)	Υ_{sc}	h_{sc} (cm)
Earth	Moon	21×10^{-8}	67	2.8×10^{-5}	$.25 \times 10^4$
Jupiter	Io	8.0×10^{-8}	290	4.9×10^{-3}	44×10^4
	Europa	1.2×10^{-8}	47	1.2×10^{-3}	9.5×10^4
	Ganymede	1.5×10^{-8}	54	$.30 \times 10^{-3}$	4.0×10^4
	Callisto	$.23 \times 10^{-8}$	8.4	$.055 \times 10^{-3}$	$.69 \times 10^4$
Saturn	Mimas	$.20 \times 10^{-8}$	6.1	34×10^{-3}	39×10^4
	Enceladus	$.15 \times 10^{-8}$	4.3	16×10^{-3}	22×10^4
	Tethys	$.81 \times 10^{-8}$	24	8.5×10^{-3}	26×10^4
	Dione	$.13 \times 10^{-8}$	3.8	4.0×10^{-3}	8.3×10^4
	Titan	$.78 \times 10^{-8}$	23	$.12 \times 10^{-3}$	1.4×10^4
Neptune	Triton	170×10^{-8}	2100	4.2×10^{-4}	3.9×10^4
Sun	Mercury	11×10^{-13}	38×10^{-3}	$.17 \times 10^{-7}$	200
	Venus	2.4×10^{-13}	8.5×10^{-3}	$.027 \times 10^{-7}$	81
	Earth	1.1×10^{-13}	3.9×10^{-3}	$.96 \times 10^{-7}$	3.1
	Jupiter	2.6×10^{-13}	8.9×10^{-3}	$.029 \times 10^{-7}$	10

Calculations based on eqs. (9.2.1–9.2.4); data from tables 20.5.1 and 2.1.2 and Newburn and Gulkis (1973). For the satellites of Jupiter and Saturn $15\Theta_c/4\Theta_{sc}$ is set equal to one.

As shown by these examples, the tides produced by a secondary body on a primary body are very small. In fact the oblateness Υ_c never exceeds 10^{-6}. In contrast, the satellites are strongly deformed, with Υ_{sc} of the order 10^{-3}. If they are close to the Roche limit, eq. (9.2.3) does not hold. At the Roche limit, the tides become infinite.

Equations (9.2.1) and (9.2.3) can be generalized to rigid bodies by the introduction of a correction factor containing the rigidity (see, for example, Jeffreys, 1962; Munk and MacDonald, 1960).

9.3 TIDAL BRAKING OF A CENTRAL BODY'S SPIN

If a homogeneous fluid body of negligible viscosity is a spinning central body, its secondary will produce tidal bulges located on the line $M_c M_{sc}$ (fig. 9.3.1). If the viscosity of M_c is finite, the tidal bulges are displaced through an angle ϵ, due to the time lag caused by viscous effects. The internal motions in the body are associated with an energy dissipation w (ergs/sec). The energy is drawn from the spin of the body (i.e., the spin is braked). As no change is produced in the total angular momentum of the system consisting of the spinning central body and the tide-producing secondary body, spin angular momentum is transferred to the orbital angular momentum of the secondary body.

The value of w depends on the physical state of the body and on the amplitude of the tides.

Suppose that the tidal bulge is displaced at an angle ϵ in relation to the tide-producing body (see fig. 9.3.1). A quantity Q, defined by $Q^{-1} = \tan 2\epsilon$ (in analogy with what is customary in treating losses in electric circuits), is then often used. This formalism is misleading because it

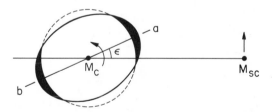

FIGURE 9.3.1.—Classical but inadequate model of momentum transfer due to tides. The force of attraction between the satellite M_{sc} and the near tidal bulge a exceeds that between M_{sc} and b; a component of the net torque retards the rotation of the planet M_c and accelerates the satellite in its orbit. The actual situation in the case of the Earth is illustrated in fig. 9.4.1. In the case of Mars, Jupiter, Saturn, and Uranus, the angle ϵ is probably negligible.

gives the impression that each body has a characteristic constant Q. In reality Q (as well as ϵ) depends both on the frequency and on the amplitude. The amplitude dependence of the tidal braking is in general very large (Jeffreys, 1962) so that Q decreases rapidly with the height of the tides. Hence, it is not correct to assign a certain Q value to each celestial body. As shown by Jeffreys (1962), the relation between the solar tides and lunar tides on the Earth is very complicated, and the Q value of the Earth is different for these two tides. This difference is even greater if the tidal amplitudes are very different.

9.3.1 Fluid Body

Seen from the coordinate system of the spinning central body, the tidal deformation corresponds to a standing wave. The fluid motion, which in a nonstructured body is associated with this wave, is of the order

$$v = 2\Omega \Upsilon_c R_c \qquad (9.3.1)$$

where Ω is the angular velocity of the central body and, for a spin period of τ, $\Omega = 2\pi/\tau$. For the case of tides produced on one of the giant planets by a satellite, we have $\tau_c = 10$ hr $= 3.6 \times 10^4$ sec; $\Upsilon_c = 10^{-7}$ and $R_c = 0.5 \times 10^{10}$ cm, and, consequently, $v \sim 0.1$ cm/sec. It seems highly unlikely that such low velocities can produce any appreciable dissipation of energy even over a very long period of time. (The order of magnitude of the energy dissipation with laminar flow is $w = \eta(v/R)^2 R^3 = \eta v^2 R$ ergs/sec where the viscosity, $\eta \sim 10^{-2}$ poise for water. With $R = 0.5 \times 10^{10}$ cm and $v = 0.1$ cm/sec we obtain $w = 5 \times 10^5$ ergs/sec.)

If instead we evaluate eq. (9.3.1) for the case of a satellite of a giant planet ($\tau_{sc} = 10$ hr, $\Upsilon_{sc} = 10^{-3}$, $R_{sc} = .5 \times 10^8$ cm), we find $v \sim 20$ cm/sec.

9.3.2 Solid Body

In a small solid body (asteroid-sized), only elastic deformations are produced with minimum of energy dissipation. In satellites which are so large that their rigidity does not prevent deformations (lunar-sized bodies) these may often be nonelastic, and, hence, associated with big energy losses.

As far as is known, all satellites have spin periods equal to their orbital periods. If a planet is a fairly homogeneous solid body, it probably experiences negligible tidal braking. The deformations are of the order $\Upsilon \sim 10^{-7}$ and may be purely elastic. In this range, deformation forces are far below the yield limit of most materials.

9.3.3 Structured Bodies

The most difficult case occurs when the body has a complicated structure involving fluid layers of different densities. The Earth is characterized by this type of layering, and in spite of all investigations we still are far from complete understanding of tidal braking of the terrestrial spin. Most of the dissipation of energy takes place in shallow seas, at beaches and regions near the shores. Hence, a knowledge of the detailed structure of a body is necessary in order to reach any conclusions about the tidal retardation of its spin velocity.

9.4 SATELLITE TIDAL BRAKING OF PLANETARY SPINS

The Earth-Moon system is the only system where we can be sure that a significant tidal braking has taken place and is still taking place. According to the elementary theory, the Moon should produce tidal bulges in the oceans (as in fig. 9.3.1); when the Earth rotates, these would remain stationary. Because of the viscosity of the water, the relative motion produces an energy release that brakes the spin of the Earth. At the same time, the tidal bulge is displaced a phase angle ϵ in relation to the radius vector to the Moon. This produces a force that acts in the direction of the lunar orbital motion. Hence, one would expect the Moon to be accelerated. However, since the force transfers angular momentum to the Moon, the lunar orbital radius increases, with the result that the lunar orbital period also increases. The paradoxical result is that the accelerating force slows down the lunar orbital velocity.

The theory of tidal bulges which is presented in all textbooks has very little to do with reality. The observed tides do not behave at all as they should according to the theory. Instead, the tidal waves one observes have the character of standing waves excited in the different oceans and seas which act somewhat like resonance cavities (fig. 9.4.1).

Even if the tidal pattern on the Earth is very far from what the simple theory predicts, there is no doubt that a momentum transfer takes place between the Earth and the Moon. The effect of this has been calculated by Gerstenkorn (1955), MacDonald (1966), and Singer (1970). According to these and other theories (Alfvén, 1942, 1954), the Moon was originally an independent planet that was captured either in a retrograde or in a prograde orbit.

There is considerable doubt as to the extent to which the models are applicable to the Earth-Moon system (see Alfvén and Arrhenius, 1969, and ch. 24). Resonance effects may invalidate many details of the models.

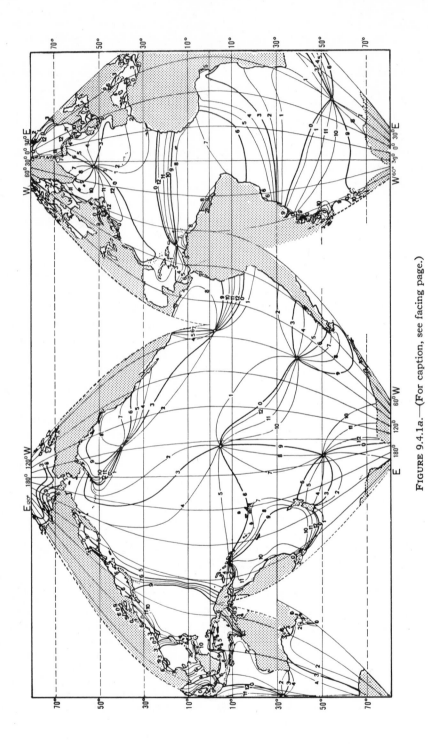

FIGURE 9.4.1a.—(For caption, see facing page.)

FIGURE 9.4.1*a*.—Phase relations of tides in the Pacific and Atlantic oceans. The map shows the cotidal lines of the semidiurnal tide referred to the culmination of the Moon in Greenwich. The tidal amplitude approaches zero where the cotidal lines run parallel (such as between Japan and New Guinea). Much of the tidal motion has the character of rotary waves. In the south and equatorial Atlantic Ocean the tide mainly takes the form of north-south oscillation on east-west lines. This complex reality should be compared to the simple concept which is the basis for existing calculations of the lunar orbital evolution and which pictures the tide as a sinusoidal wave progressing around the Earth in the easterly direction (dot-and-dashed curve in fig. 9.4.1*b*). (From Defant, 1961.)

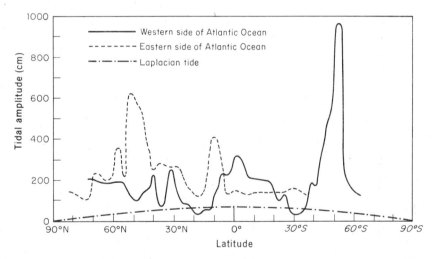

FIGURE 9.4.1*b*.—Tidal amplitude on the Atlantic coasts as an example of the actual amplitude distribution in comparison with the simple Laplacian tide concept. The curves show the average range at spring tide of the semidiurnal tide as a function of latitude. The solid curve represents the tide on the western side of the Atlantic Ocean; the dashed curve, the eastern side of the Atlantic Ocean; and the dot-and-dashed curve, the Laplacian tide. In the comparison with the (much less known) open ocean amplitudes, the coastal amplitudes are increased by cooscillation with the oceanic regions over the continental shelves. The distribution illustrates further the facts that tidal dissipation is governed by a series of complex local phenomena depending on the configuration of continents, shelves, and ocean basins, and that the theoretical Laplacian tide obviously cannot serve even as a first-order approximation. (From Defant, 1961.)

There seems, however, to be little reason to question the main result; namely, that the Moon is a captured planet, brought to its present orbit by tidal action. Whether this capture implies a very close approach to the Earth is unresolved. This problem will be discussed in more detail in ch. 24.

The Neptune-Triton system is probably an analog to the Earth-Moon system. The only explanation for Neptune's having a retrograde satellite with an unusually large mass seems to be that Triton was captured in an eccentric retrograde orbit that, due to tidal effects, has shrunk and become more circular (McCord, 1966).

As Neptune has a mass and a spin period similar to those of Uranus, it is likely to have had a satellite system similar to that of Uranus (see sec. 23.8). The capture of Triton and the later evolution of its orbit probably made Triton pass close to the small primeval satellites, either colliding with them or throwing them out of orbit. Nereid may be an example of the latter process (McCord, 1966).

The satellites of Mars, Jupiter, Saturn, and Uranus cannot possibly have braked these planets by more than a few percent of the planetary spin momenta. The total orbital angular momentum of all the satellites of Jupiter, for example, is only 1 percent of the spin momentum of Jupiter (see table 2.1.2). This is obviously an upper limit to any change the satellites can possibly have produced. As we shall find in ch. 10, the real effect is much smaller, probably completely negligible.

9.5 SOLAR TIDAL BRAKING OF PLANETARY SPINS

Again, the Earth is the only case for which we can be sure that solar tides have produced, and are producing, an appreciable change in spin. How large this change is seems to be an open question. The effect depends on the behavior of the tides on beaches and in shallow seas, as do the effects of lunar tides on Earth.

It has been suggested that tides have braked the spins of Mercury and perhaps Venus so much that they eventually have been captured in the present resonances (see sec. 8.8 and Goldreich and Peale, 1966 and 1967). This is a definite possibility and implies that initially these planets were accreted with an angular velocity that was larger than their present angular velocity, perhaps of the same order as other planets (fig. 9.7.1).

However, as discussed in ch. 8, the orbit-orbit resonances are probably not due to tidal capture, but are more likely to have been produced at the time when the bodies were accreting. In view of this, the question also arises whether the spin-orbit resonances of Mercury, and of Venus, if it is in resonance, were produced during their accretion. It seems at present impossible to decide between this possibility and the tidal alternative. The latter would be favored if there had ever been shallow seas on these planets. We have yet no way of knowing this in the case of Venus; for Mercury the apparently preserved primordial cratered surface would seem to rule this out.

It seems unlikely that solar tides have braked the spins of the asteroids or of the giant planets to an appreciable extent.

9.6 TIDAL EVOLUTION OF SATELLITE ORBITS

Goldreich and Soter (1966) have investigated the possible tidal evolutions of the satellite systems. They have pointed out that, where pairs of satellites are captured in orbit-orbit resonances, both the satellites must change their orbits in the same proportion. They have further calculated the maximum values of the tidal dissipation of energy (in their terminology the minimum Q values) that are reconcilable with the present structure of the satellite systems. There seems to be no objection to these conclusions.

Goldreich and Soter have further suggested that the maximum values of energy dissipation are not far from the real values and that tidal effects have been the reason for satellites being captured in resonances. This problem has already been discussed in ch. 8. The conclusion drawn is that small librations in some of the resonances cannot be understood as tidal effects.

Further, we observe resonances in the planetary system that certainly cannot have been produced in this way, so that it is in any case necessary to assume a hetegonic mechanism for production of some resonance captures. Finally, the structure of the Saturnian rings demonstrates that Mimas' orbit cannot have changed by more than 1 or 2 percent since the formation of the Saturnian system (sec. 18.6).

Hence, present evidence seems to speak in favor of the view that, *with the exception of the Moon and Triton, no satellite orbits have been appreciably changed by tidal action.*

9.7 ISOCHRONISM OF SPINS

Photometric registrations of asteroids show intensity variations that must be interpreted as due to rotation of a body with nonuniform albedo or nonspherical shape. Several investigators (e.g., Taylor, 1971) have measured the periods of axial rotation of some 30 to 40 asteroids and have found no systematic dependence on the magnitudes of the asteroids. In fact, as is shown in fig. 9.7.1 and table 9.7.1, almost all asteroids have periods that deviate by less than 50 percent from an average of 8 or 9 hr. It appears that this result is not due to observational selection.

Regarding the planets, we find that the giant planets as well have about the same period. It has always struck students of astronomy that the axial

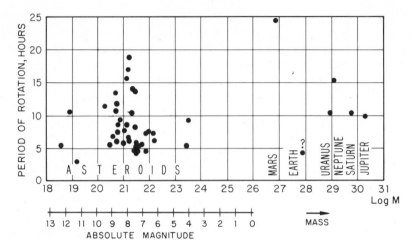

FIGURE 9.7.1.—Periods of axial rotation for some asteroids and some of the planets in relation to their masses. (From Alfvén, 1964.) The rotation period of Pluto is not well known and the rotation periods of Mercury and Venus are influenced by resonance effects; these three planets are thus not represented in the figure. The value of rotation period for the Earth is that prior to capture of the Moon. Data for asteroids is taken from table 9.7.1 and data for the planets from table 2.1.1. From the graph one concludes that spin period is not a function of mass. Indeed, most of the spin periods all fall within a factor of two of 8 hr. We refer to this similarity of periods of rotation as the law of isochronous rotation or the isochronism of spins.

rotations of Jupiter, Saturn, and Uranus are almost equal. The period of Neptune is somewhat longer (15 hr), but a correction for the tidal braking of its retrograde satellite reduces the period at least somewhat (see McCord, 1966). For the Earth we should use the period before the capture of the Moon; according to Gerstenkorn, that period was most likely 5 or 6 hr (see Alfvén, 1964).

Hence we find the very remarkable fact that the axial period is of the *same* order of magnitude for a number of bodies with *very different masses*. In fact, when the mass varies by a factor of more than 10^{11}—i.e., from less than 10^{19} g (for small asteroids) up to more than 10^{30} g (for Jupiter)—the axial period does not show any systematic variation. We may call this remarkable similarity of rotational periods *the spin isochronism*.

Obviously this law cannot be applied to bodies whose present rotation is regulated by tidal action (planetary satellites) or captured resonances (Mercury and perhaps Venus; see sec. 9.3). Excepting such bodies, the only body with a rotation known to be far from the order of 8 hr is Pluto, which rotates in 6 days. Mars ($\tau = 25$ hr) and Icarus ($\tau = 2$ hr) each deviate by a factor of three.

In ch. 13 mechanisms producing the isochronous rotation are discussed; with this as background a more detailed analysis of planetary spins will be given (sec. 13.6).

TABLE 9.7.1
Periods and Magnitudes of Asteroids

Asteroid	Name	Magnitude	Rotation period (hr)
1	Ceres	4.11	9.07
3	Juno	6.43	7.21
4	Vesta	4.31	5.34
5	Astraea	8.00	16.80
6	Hebe	6.70	7.74
7	Iris	6.84	7.13
8	Flora	7.48	13.6
9	Metis	7.27	5.06
11	Parthenope	7.78	10.67
13	Egeria	7.97	7.04
15	Eunomia	6.29	6.08
16	Psyche	6.89	4.30
17	Thetis	8.69	12.27
18	Melpomene	7.79	14
19	Fortuna	8.35	7.46
20	Massalia	7.48	8.09
21	Lutetia	8.68	6.13
22	Kalliope	7.48	4.14
23	Thalia	8.34	6.15
24	Themis	8.18	8.5
27	Euterpe	8.56	8.50
28	Bellona	8.15	15.7
29	Amphitrite	7.26	5.38
30	Urania	8.78	13.66
39	Laetitia	7.41	5.13
40	Harmonia	8.45	9.13
43	Ariadne	9.18	5.75
44	Nysa	8.02	6.41
51	Nemausa	8.66	7.78
54	Alexandra	8.82	7.05
61	Danae	8.77	11.45
110	Lydia	8.80	10.92
321	Florentina	11.38	2.87
349	Dembowska	7.29	4.70
354	Eleonora	7.56	4.27
433	Eros	12.40	5.27
511	Davida	7.13	5.17
532	Herculina	7.98	18.81
624	Hektor	8.67	6.92
1566	Icarus	17.55	2.27
1620	Geographos	15.97	5.22

(Data from Gehrels, 1971.)

9.8 CONCLUSIONS FROM THE ISOCHRONISM OF
SPINS

Concerning the mechanism that produces the similarity of spin periods in most of the tidally unmodified bodies, the following conclusions can be drawn:

(1) The similarity of the spin periods cannot be produced by any process acting today. For example, we cannot reasonably expect that the rotation of Jupiter is affected very much by any forces acting now.

(2) The equality of the spin periods cannot have anything to do with the rotational stability of the bodies. The giant planets, for example, are very far from rotational instability. It is unlikely that one could find a mechanism by which the present isochronism of spins can be connected with rotational instability during the prehistory of bodies as different as a small asteroid and a giant planet.

(3) Hence, the spin isochronism must be of hetegonic origin. All the bodies must have been accreted by a process with the characteristic feature of making their spin periods about equal, no matter how much mass is acquired. There are accretion processes that have this property (see ch. 13).

(4) The spin isochronism further shows that the asteroids cannot derive from a broken-up planet. If a planet explodes (or if it is disrupted in some other way), we should expect an equipartition of the rotational energy among the parts. This means that, on the average, the periods of axial rotation of the smallest asteroids should be much smaller than those of the larger asteroids. This is in conflict with the observed statistical distribution.

(5) The braking of the axial rotation of celestial bodies has not been very significant since their accretion. A braking produced by an ambient uniform viscous medium ought to lengthen the period of a small body much more than the period of a larger body. The fact that asteroids as small as some 10 kilometers rotate with the same period as the largest planets indicates that even such small bodies have not been braked very much since they were formed. In this essential respect, the solar system seems to be in the same state now as it was when it was formed. Thus, detailed analysis of the present state of the solar system can yield insight into hetegonic processes.

POST-ACCRETIONAL CHANGES IN THE SOLAR SYSTEM

10.1 STABILITY OF ORBITS

Celestial mechanics applied to the motion of planets and satellites shows that of the orbital parameters the longitude ϕ_P of the pericenter and the longitude ϕ_Ω of the ascending node vary monotonically, whereas the eccentricity e and the inclination i exhibit secular variations within certain limits. The most constant parameter is the semimajor axis a. There is a famous theorem by Lagrange and Poisson which states there are no secular perturbations in a to the first and second approximation. Surveys of the orbital variation and the stability of the solar system treated within the framework of celestial mechanics are given, for example, by Brouwer and Clemence (1961a) and by Hagihara (1961).

From a physical point of view, the constancy of a is connected with the constancy of the orbital angular momentum $C = [a(1-e^2)]^{1/2}$. It is difficult to change the orbital momentum of a body because momentum must then be transferred either to another body or to the interplanetary medium. As the density in interplanetary space is very low, the latter process is not very efficient. A transfer of angular momentum by tidal action seems to be the only important mechanism by which a considerable change can take place.

Angular momentum can also be exchanged through resonance effects. These may be very important, but only when bodies are locked in the resonance. In general, resonances conserve, rather than change, the structure.

A possible change in the solar rotation resulting from the solar wind flow will be discussed in ch. 25.

The authors cited above express, rather vaguely, the opinion that the solar system probably is more stable than can be proven by ordinary celestial-mechanics methods. The effects of resonances have not been included in these discussions. The study of resonance effects provides criteria for a high degree of stability.

10.2 RESONANCE AND STABILITY

Under present conditions, bodies locked in resonances are likely to remain in that state for an indefinite time. However, a breaking of a resonance capture is possible under certain conditions (sec. 8.9). The amplitude of the librations is a measure of resonance stability. If the librations increase to an amplitude of 180°, the bodies break loose from the resonance. In many cases the librations are very small (see table 8.5.1), indicating a high degree of stability.

A proportional change in the periods of all the orbiting bodies in a satellite system or in the planetary system will not alter the resonances in that system. Such a change can be produced by an increase or decrease in the mass of the central body. Consequently, little can be learned about such mass variations from a study of the resonance pattern. As discussed in sec. 10.3, we can make more definite conclusions concerning changes in the relative positions of the orbits of the secondary bodies.

10.2.1 Argument for Stability From Near-Commensurabilities

We assume with Goldreich (1965) that, if once an exact resonance is established, the bodies will remain in resonance indefinitely. Thus the existence today of near-commensurabilities establishes limits upon the amount the orbits in question could have changed since hetegonic times. As table 10.2.1 shows, the period of Jupiter is intermediate between the 2/5 resonance of Saturn and the 1/7 resonance of Uranus. Similarly, the period of Uranus is intermediate between the 3/1 resonance of Saturn and the 1/2 resonance of Neptune. Hence, if we assume that the period of Saturn $T_{\bar{b}}$ and the period of Uranus T_{δ} have been constant, we can conclude that the period of Jupiter $T_{2\!\!\!1}$ can never have been as much as 0.67 percent shorter because then it would have been trapped in 2/5 resonance with Saturn, nor can it have been as much as 1.18 percent longer, because of the 1/7 resonance with Uranus.

TABLE 10.2.1

Limits on Possible Change in Orbital Period for Jupiter and Uranus
As Indicated by Near-Commensurabilities With Adjacent Planets

	Jupiter			Uranus		
Possible resonance	$\frac{2}{3}T_{\bar{b}}$	$T_{2\!\!\!1}$	$\frac{1}{7}T_{\delta}$	$3T_{\bar{b}}$	T_{δ}	$\frac{1}{2}T_{\psi}$
Orbital period (yr)	11.783	11.862	12.003	88.373	84.018	82.39
Deviation from present period	0.67%		1.18%	5.2%		2.0%

Similarly, if T_b and T_Ψ have been constant, T_{δ} cannot have been 2.0 percent shorter because of the 1/2 resonance with Neptune, nor 5.2 percent longer because of the 3/1 resonance with Saturn. Similar arguments can be applied to the near-commensurabilities in the satellite systems.

The conclusion to be drawn from this discussion is that the orbital periods in the solar system are likely to have varied less than a few percent since hetegonic times. The only exceptions are the Earth-Moon and the Neptune-Triton systems.

However, this conclusion rests on the rather uncertain assumption that resonance locking cannot be broken. This is probably true under present conditions. It was probably not valid during the hetegonic era when viscous effects were more important. The tentative conclusion we have drawn here is not in conflict with the suggestion, also very tentative, in sec. 8.8.1 that the near-commensurabilities are broken resonances.

10.3 STABILITY OF THE SATURNIAN RINGS AND THE ASTEROIDAL BELT

Another argument for a high degree of stability of the solar system comes from the relationships between Mimas and Cassini's division. From the conclusions reached in sec. 18.6 we see that the maximum increase in Mimas' orbital distance since the formation of the rings is a few percent. Similar and even more convincing conclusions follow from the study of the asteroid belt in relation to Jupiter (sec. 18.8). Also in this case we find what is obviously a product of the hetegonic processes conserved to our time with an accuracy of better than 1 percent.

Hence, we have to accept that at least in certain respects the orbital dynamics of the solar system have a very high degree of stability.

10.4 CONSTANCY OF SPIN

As stated in chs. 8 and 9, there are also good reasons to believe that for most planets the spin has not changed much since they were formed. (As the asteroids are in a state of evolution, this does not mean that their spins have remained unchanged for 4.5 Gyr.) However, for all satellites the spin has been braked greatly by tidal effects, making the spin periods equal to the orbital periods.

Much of the primeval spin of the Earth has been transferred to the Moon, and to a smaller extent the same is true in the Neptune-Triton system. The other giant planets have probably not been braked appreciably after their satellite systems formed. Even the transfer of angular momentum during satellite formation did not change their spins by more

than a few percent. In fact, for all the giant planets the total orbital momentum of the satellites is more than one order of magnitude smaller than the
spin of the primary (table 2.1.2).

The spin isochronism (ch. 9) holds for bodies as different as small asteroids
(mass~10^{18} g) and the giant planets (mass~10^{30} g). The conclusion from
this is that the spin of most of the asteroids has not changed very much,
at least not in a systematic way, since their formation.

To what extent the spins of the terrestrial planets have been braked is
uncertain. The very slow rotations of Mercury and Venus may be due to
a braking produced by solar tides (in combination with resonance effects;
see ch. 13). The spin of Mars is unexpectedly slow. This cannot be due to
tidal effects from its satellites because they are too small to take up an
appreciable momentum. The large solar distance makes it unlikely that
solar tides could be very efficient, but perhaps such an effect cannot be
ruled out.

Pluto is reported to have a very slow rotation (6 days). We know too
little about this planet to speculate about the factors influencing its spin.

The spin of the planets is discussed further in ch. 13.

10.5 ON THE POSSIBILITY OF RECONSTRUCTING
THE HETEGONIC PROCESSES

We have reasons to believe that a series of dramatic events between 4 and
5 billion years ago produced the solar system. To reconstruct these events
it is necessary to determine how the system has changed since its origin.
Unless we are able to compensate for changes in the solar system after its
formation, we have little chance of understanding the primordial processes.
As we shall see later, there is a rapidly increasing body of chemical information relating to the formation of the solar system. But also from a dynamic
point of view there is, as discussed above, a surprisingly large amount of
data referring to the initial formation. With a few notable exceptions we
find that the large bodies of the solar system (planets and satellites) are, at
present, in a state that is not very different from that after they had just
formed.

In the literature there are numerous suggestions of changes in the structure of the solar system. In some instances dramatic changes in the orbits
of planets and satellites are proposed. Most of these suggestions would
never have been published if the authors had investigated the dynamic
implications.

Summing up, there is no indication of any major change in the planetary
orbits. Of the satellites, only the Moon and Triton have undergone large
orbital changes. Probably both were initially independent planets which

were later captured and brought to their present orbital position by tidal effects. There is no evidence that any of the normal (prograde) satellites have had their orbits appreciably changed.

Concerning the small bodies (asteroids, comets, meteoroids), the conclusion is different. As we have found, viscous effects including collisions are of importance in many cases, and this implies change in orbital elements. The retrograde satellites Jupiter 8, 9, 11, and 12 and the Saturnian satellite Phoebe belong to this category. Their capture into their present orbits may have taken place during the post-accretional phase, although it is perhaps more likely that it occurred late during accretion.

Suggestions have been made that the Martian satellites are recently captured asteroids. As they are the only bodies in the solar system that do not fit into the general matrix of ch. 23, it would certainly be agreeable from a theoretical standpoint to explain them in this way. This seems difficult, however. The presumably captured satellites mentioned above move in retrograde and highly eccentric orbits, drastically different from the low-eccentricity and low-inclination orbits of the Martian satellites.

PART B

The Accretion of Celestial Bodies

11

ACCRETIONAL PROCESSES

11.1 SURVEY OF PART B

In part A we have reviewed the observed features of the solar system and the general laws of physics that govern it. Relying upon these observations and laws, it was found possible to reconstruct with some confidence the state at the end of the hetegonic era.

In part B we shall try to determine what processes are responsible for producing the structure of the solar system that prevailed at that specific time. For reasons that have been outlined in chs. 1 and 7 and which will be discussed further in the following, the formation of the planets and satellites existing now and at the end of the hetegonic era must be due to accretion of smaller bodies, which in their turn ultimately must have accreted from single grains. This conclusion is in principle straightforward, mainly because the other types of processes proposed prove to be impossible. The concept of planetesimal accretion has been drawn upon as a qualitative basis many times in the past (Alfvén, 1942, 1943a, 1946; Schmidt, 1945; Safronov, 1954). However, to be thoroughly convincing it must also be supported by quantitative explanation of how orbiting grains with high relative velocities can interact to form larger bodies. We find that *jet streams* form an important intermediate stage in this evolution. The conditions for their development places important constraints on the conditions under which the original grains could have formed. The analysis of this earliest phase will consequently be treated (in parts D and C) only after the accretional evolution has been investigated in detail in the present part (B); this is in keeping with the actualistic principle (ch. 1) designed to keep us in as close contact with reality as possible.

This chapter contains a general analysis of accretion, which considers what lines of approach are of interest to follow up and which ones can be ruled out immediately. This analysis also defines the boundary conditions for the grain-producing plasma processes.

With the theory of jet streams (ch. 6) and of accretional processes studied in this chapter as starting points, a general theory of the accretion of planets and satellites is given in ch. 12. Some results of this theory can be checked by future space experiments that are within the present state of the art.

In ch. 13 the accretional theory of spins is presented and compared with the observed spin isochronism (sec. 9.7). This leads to an explanation of the spin periods of the different planets.

Chapter 14 treats the comet-meteoroid complex and considers how celestial bodies are accreted today. From this study of accretion we obtain important knowledge of accretional processes in general. The possibility of observing accretional processes that occur today in our neighborhood reduces the speculative element in our study of accretional processes in the hetegonic era.

Although part B concerns accretional problems in general, the formation of the Saturnian rings and the asteroids is not included. They represent a stage that has evolved very little from that established at the end of the preceding era of grain formation by condensation. Hence, they will conveniently be treated separately in part C (ch. 18).

11.2 GRAVITATIONAL COLLAPSE OF A GAS CLOUD

As we have seen in ch. 6, viscosity-perturbation of the Kepler motion produces an "apparent attraction" that may produce contractions in cosmic clouds. Before this was recognized, however, the only effect that could produce a contraction was believed to be the self-gravitation of the cloud. For this reason it is generally believed that stars are formed by gravitational contraction of vast interstellar clouds. The condition for contraction is given by the Virial Theorem, which requires that the potential energy of the cloud (assumed to be a uniform sphere of radius R) must exceed twice the thermal energy; i.e.:

$$\frac{3GM^2}{5R} > 2\left(\frac{3NkT}{2}\right) \qquad (11.2.1)$$

where M is the mass of the cloud; $N = M/m_a$ is the number of atoms with average mass m_a; k is Boltzmann's constant; and T is the temperature. If the average atomic weight is m_a/m_H we have

$$R \lesssim \chi \frac{m_a M}{m_H T} \qquad (11.2.2)$$

with $\chi = 2 \times 10^{-16}$ (cm K)/g.

As pointed out (e.g., by Spitzer (1968)), there are serious difficulties in understanding the formation of stars by this model. In particular, a large rotational momentum and magnetic flux oppose the contraction. It is far from certain that the model is appropriate.

However, we shall not discuss the problem of star formation here (it will be reserved for ch. 25), but rather the formation of planets and satellites. Laplace made the suggestion, admittedly qualitative and speculative, that these bodies were formed from gas clouds that contracted gravitationally. This idea has been adopted by a number of subsequent workers, without realization of its inherent inadequacy.

11.2.1 Objection to Gravitational Collapse As a Mechanism for the Formation of Planets and Satellites

11.2.1.1 Insufficient gravitation. If for an order of magnitude estimate we put $m_a/m_H = 10$ and $T = 100K$ for formation of planets and satellites, we find

$$R < KM \tag{11.2.3}$$

with $K = 10^{-17}$ cm/g. For the biggest planets with $M \approx 10^{30}$ g we find $R < 10^{13}$ cm, indicating, from these considerations alone, that Jupiter and Saturn may have been formed by this mechanism. But even in the mass range of Uranus and Neptune ($M \approx 10^{29}$ g) we run into difficulties because gravitational effects do not become important unless the clouds by some other means have been caused to contract to 10^{12} cm, which is less than 1 percent of the distance between the bodies. Going to the satellite systems or a hypothetical body consisting of all of the matter in the asteroid belt, we see immediately that gravitational contraction is out of the question. For a typical satellite mass (say, 10^{23} g), we find $R < 10^6$ cm (which means that the dimension of the gas cloud should be comparable to that of the present body). Hence, we conclude that the gravitational contraction of gas clouds is inadequate as a general model for the formation of the bodies in the solar system.

As another example that shows how negligible the gravitational attraction is in forming a satellite system, let us consider the inner part of the Saturnian satellite system. This system of secondary bodies is certainly one of the most regular with respect to systematic spacing of bodies and small inclinations and eccentricities of orbits. The masses of Mimas and Enceladus are of the order 10^{-7} of the mass of Saturn. At an orbital distance intermediate between Mimas and Enceladus, the gravitational attraction due to these bodies is less than 10^{-5} of the gravitational attraction of Saturn.

(Before the formation of the satellites the matter now forming them is likely to have been spread out over the whole orbit, which makes the ratios still smaller by one or more orders of magnitudes.)

A somewhat different way to express what is essentially the same objection is the following. The distance

$$r_L = r \left(\frac{M_{sc}}{3M_c} \right)^{1/3} \qquad (11.2.4)$$

to the interior and/or exterior Lagrangian points is a measure of the extension of the gravitational field of a secondary body with mass M in an orbit r around a central body of mass M_c. Only if the original extension of a gas cloud of mass M is smaller than r_L is a gravitational collapse possible. Table 11.2.1 gives the distance to Lagrangian points for the planets. Figure 11.2.1 shows the maximum possible extensions of gas clouds that could gravitationally collapse to form Mimas, Enceladus, and the terres-

TABLE 11.2.1

Distance to the Lagrangian Points of the Planets and Selected Satellites
Indicating Sphere of Gravitational Dominance

Planet	Orbital radius [a] 10^{12} cm	Mass [a] 10^{27} g	Distance to Lagrangian point [c] 10^{10} cm
Mercury	5.791	0.3299	2.206
Venus	10.821	4.870	10.11
Earth	14.960	5.967	14.96
Mars	22.794	0.6424	10.35
Jupiter	77.837	1899.	531.6
Saturn	142.70	568.	652.1
Uranus	286.96	87.2	700.2
Neptune	449.67	102.	1160.
Pluto	590	1.1	335.7
Satellite (planet)	10^{10} cm	10^{24} g	10^8 cm
Amalthea (Jupiter)	1.81	[b] 0.005	0.173
Io (Jupiter)	4.22	89.2	10.6
Mimas (Saturn)	1.86	0.04	0.532
Titan (Saturn)	12.2	137.	52.7
Iapetus (Saturn)	35.6	2.24	38.8

[a] Data taken from tables 2.1.1–2.1.2.
[b] Mass estimated using radius of 7×10^6 cm and density of 3.5 g/cm³.
[c] Calculated using eq. (11.2.4).

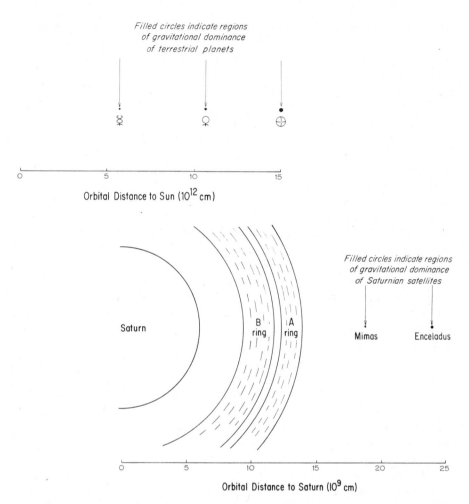

*Filled circles indicate regions
of gravitational dominance
of terrestrial planets*

☿   ♀   ⊕

Orbital Distance to Sun (10^{12} cm)

*Filled circles indicate regions
of gravitational dominance
of Saturnian satellites*

Saturn

B
ring

A
ring

Mimas   Enceladus

Orbital Distance to Saturn (10^9 cm)

FIGURE 11.2.1.—The inner region of the Saturnian satellite system (below). The small, filled circles (almost points) show the regions within which the gravitational fields of Mimas and Enceladus predominate. The regions of gravitational dominance of the terrestrial planets are shown above. The figure illustrates that gravitational collapse is not a reasonable mechanism for the formation of these bodies because of the minimal extension of their gravitational fields. The same conclusion holds for all satellites and planets, with the possible exception of Jupiter.

trial planets. It is obvious that the geometrical extensions of the gravitational fields of these bodies are much too small to make formation by collapse a viable suggestion.

Kumar (1972) also shows that, because of the limited extension of the Lagrangian points of Jupiter, the influence of solar tides would prevent any

175

gravitational collapse of the gas cloud from which Jupiter could be assumed to have formed. Since gravitational collapse can be excluded as a theory of Jovian origin, surely it must be excluded on similar grounds for all other secondary bodies in the solar system.

The Laplacian approach cannot be saved by assuming that the present satellites once were much larger ("protoplanets" and "protosatellites" as in Kuiper's theory (Kuiper, 1951)). As shown above, there are discrepancies of too many orders of magnitude to overcome in such a theory.

Hence we reach the *conclusion* that the self-gravitation of a cloud is, at least in many cases, much too small to produce a gravitational collapse. Much more important than the self-attraction is the *"apparent attraction"* which, according to sec. 6.4, is a result of a viscosity-perturbed Kepler motion and leads to a formation of jet streams as an intermediate stage in the accretion of celestial bodies.

11.2.1.2 Gravitational contraction and angular momentum. The formation of planets and satellites by gravitational contraction of a gas cloud also meets with the same angular momentum difficulty as does star formation. If a gas cloud with dimensions R is rotating with the period τ, its average angular momentum per unit mass is of the order of $2\pi R^2/\tau$. If it contracts, this quantity is conserved. If the present mass of, say, Jupiter once filled a volume with the linear dimensions β times Jupiter's present radius, its rotational period must have been of the order $\tau = \beta^2 \tau_{2\!\!\!\perp}$ where $\tau_{2\!\!\!\perp}$ is the present spin period of Jupiter. The maximum value of τ is defined by the orbital period, which for Jupiter is about 10^4 times the present spin period. Hence, we find $\beta < 100$, which means that the cloud which contracted to form Jupiter must be less than 10^{12} cm in radius. This is only 1 or 2 percent of half the distance between Jupiter and Saturn, which should be approximately the separation boundary between the gas forming Jupiter and the gas forming Saturn. (It is only 10 percent of the distance to the libration or Lagrangian point, which could also be of importance.) Hence, in order to account for the present spin period of Jupiter if formed by contraction of a gas cloud, one has to invent some braking mechanism. Such a mechanism, however, must have the property of producing the spin isochronism (sec. 9.7). No such mechanism is known.

11.3 PLANETESIMAL ACCRETION: ACCRETION BY CAPTURE OF GRAINS OR GAS

We have shown that the formation of planets and satellites by collapse of a gas cloud is unacceptable. This directs our attention to the alternative; namely, a gradual accretion of solid bodies (embryos or planetesimals) from dispersed matter (grains and gas). This process is often called planetesi-mal accretion and is a qualitative concept that can be traced back to the 18th century; for complete references see Herczeg (1968). Planets and satel-lites are assumed to have grown from such bodies as a rain of embryos and grains hit their surface, continuing until the bodies had reached their present size.

A number of direct observations support this concept. The saturation of the surfaces of the Moon, Mars, the Martian satellites, and Mercury with craters testifies to the importance of accretion by impact, at least in the terminal stages of growth of these bodies. Although now largely ob-literated by geological processes, impact craters may have also been a common feature of the Earth's primeval surface.

Second, the spin isochronism (sec. 9.7) can be understood at least qualita-tively as a result of embryonic accretion. The observed isochronism of spin periods requires that the same process act over the entire observed mass range of planets and asteroids, covering 12 orders of magnitude. Conse-quently, all seriously considered theories of planetary spin (Marcus, 1967; Giuli, 1968a and b) are based on the embryonic (planetesimal) growth con-cept.

Finally, the directly observable record in grain aggregates from space (now in meteorites) demonstrates that many of the grains, now preserved as parts of meteorites, condensed as isolated particles in space. After such initial existence as single particles, clusters of loosely (presumably electro-statically) bonded grains can be shown, by means of irradiation doses, to have existed over substantial time periods. These aggregates in their turn show evidence of alternating disruption and accretion before arriving at the most recent precursor states of meteorites; i.e., bodies several meters in size or possibly even larger.

This observational evidence, which is discussed in more detail in ch. 22, lends support to the concept that aggregation of freely orbiting grains into larger embryos constituted an important part of the hetegonic accretion process.

11.4 GRAVITATIONAL ACCRETION

As we have learned from sec. 7.3.1, the accretion process consists of two phases, nongravitational accretion and gravitational accretion.[1] We shall first discuss the latter phase.

When a particle hits the embryo, it causes secondary effects at its impact site. If the impacting particle is a solid body, it produces a number of ejecta,

---

[1] Gravitational accretion should not be confused with "gravitational collapse," which is a completely different process.

most of which are emitted with velocities predominantly smaller than the impact velocity. If the particle is large enough, it may split the embryo into two or more fragments. If the embryo is large enough, the escape velocity is almost the same as the impact velocity (see sec. 7.3.1) and we can be sure that only a small fraction of the ejecta can leave the embryo.

If the impacting particle is an ion, atom, or molecule it may be absorbed by the embryo, increasing its mass. However, it may also be reemitted either immediately or after some time delay with a velocity equal to its thermal velocity at the temperature of the embryo. As in typical situations in space, the temperature of a grain (or embryo) is much smaller than that of the surrounding plasma; the emission velocity is normally considerably smaller than the impacting velocity. Hence, gas will also be accreted when the escape velocity of the embryo is greater than the thermal velocity of the gas.

Gravitational accretion becomes increasingly rapid as the gravitational cross section of the embryo increases; eventually this leads to a runaway accretion. To distinguish this from the gravitational collapse with which it is totally unrelated, we shall call it "accretional catastrophe." A quantitative discussion of gravitational accretion, including the runaway process, is given in ch. 12.

11.5 NONGRAVITATIONAL ACCRETION

Gravitational accretion is rather straightforward, but nongravitational accretion is more difficult to understand. When an embryo is hit by a particle with a velocity much larger than the escape velocity, the ejecta at the collision may in principle have velocities in excess of the escape velocity and hence leave the embryo. At least at hypervelocity impacts the total mass of the ejecta may be much larger than the mass of the impinging particle. Hence, the impact may lead to a decrease in the mass of the embryo. Moreover, upon impact, the embryo may be fragmented.

For such reasons it is sometimes suggested that nongravitational accretion cannot take place. However, there seems to be no other process by which it is possible to generate bodies large enough to accrete further (by the help of gravitation). Hence, the existence of large (planet-sized) celestial bodies makes it necessary to postulate a nongravitational accretion.

To return to the example of the inner Saturnian satellites (fig. 11.2.1), the rings and the inner satellites must have been produced in closely related processes (see sec. 18.6). The ring has an outer limit because particles farther out have accreted to form the satellites instead of remaining in a dispersed state. Their incipient accretion must have been nongravitational. Also, as we shall see in sec. 18.8, conditions in the asteroid belt give further insight into the planetesimal accretion process.

The only small bodies we have been able to study more closely are Deimos and Phobos. They are completely saturated with craters that must have been produced by impacts which have not broken them up. As their escape velocities cannot have exceeded some 10 m/sec, they must have accreted essentially without the help of gravitation.

11.5.1 Objections to the Nongravitational Accretion Process

In the past, the major obstacle to understanding the incipient accretion process was the difficulty in visualizing how collisions could result in net accretion rather than in fragmentation. These difficulties have largely been eliminated by the first-hand data on collision processes in space obtained from studies of the lunar surface, the record in meteorites, and the grain velocity distribution in jet streams.

As pointed out by many authors (e.g., Whipple, 1968), the relative velocities between particles considered typical (for example, colliding asteroids) are of the order 5 km/sec, and, hence, collisions would be expected to result largely in fragmentation of the colliding bodies. At such velocities a small body colliding with a larger body will eject fragments with a total mass of several thousand times the mass of the small body. The probability of accretion would, under these circumstances, appear to be much smaller than the probability of fragmentation.

This is the apparent difficulty in all theories based on the embryonic accretion concept. Indeed, as will be shown in sec. 11.7.4, such accretion requires that the orbits of the grains have eccentricities of at least $e = 0.1$, and in some cases above $e = 0.3$. The relative velocity at collision between grains in such orbits is of the order

$$u \approx v_{orb} e \qquad\qquad (11.5.1)$$

where v_{orb} is the orbital velocity. Since v_{orb} is of the order 10 to 40 km/sec, u necessarily often exceeds 1 km/sec so that the collisions fall in the hypervelocity range.

11.5.2 Accretion in Jet Streams

The solution to this problem lies in the change of orbits that occurs as a result of repeated collisions between grains. This process has been analyzed in detail in ch. 6. The net result is a focusing in velocity space of the orbits and equipartition of energy between participating grains leading to relative velocities continuously approaching zero at the same time the particle population contracts into a jet stream. The process can be considered as a result of the "apparent attraction" caused by the viscosity-perturbation of Kepler motion.

An observational example of how such a reduction of relative velocities takes place in a jet stream has been given by Danielsson. In his study of the "profile" of some asteroidal jet streams (see fig. 4.3.6), he found that in certain focal points the relative velocities are as low as 0.2 to 1 km/sec. At such velocities collisions need not necessarily lead to mass loss, especially not if the surface layers of the bodies are fluffy. Furthermore, the velocities refer to visual asteroids, but, as the subvisual asteroids have a stronger mutual interaction, their relative velocities may be much smaller.

11.5.3 Electrostatically Polarized Grains

Charging and persistent internal electric polarization are found to be characteristic of lunar dust (Arrhenius et al., 1970; Arrhenius and Asunmaa, 1973). As a result, lunar grains adhere to each other with forces up to a few hundred dynes and form persistent clusters. This is probably a phenomenon common to all solids exposed to radiation in space. Hence, electrostatic forces were probably of similar importance during accretion. The nongravitational accretion in the hetegonic era may have been largely caused by electrostatic attraction (sec. 12.3).

11.5.4 Fluffy Aggregates

Meteorites provide evidence of the relative importance of various processes of disruption and accretion. The decisive importance of loosely coherent powder aggregates in absorbing impact energy is indicated by the high proportion of fine-grained material in chondrites, which form by far the largest group of meteorites. The low original packing density of this material is also suggested by evidence from meteors. Such fluffy aggregates probably represent the state of matter in jet streams at the stage when a substantial portion of the collision debris of the original grains has, through inelastic collisions, reached low relative velocities so that they can adhere electrostatically.

Hypervelocity impact of single grains on fluffy aggregates results in large excess mass loss (Vedder, 1972). In the subsonic range, however, it is possible and likely that an impinging particle will lose its energy gradually in penetrating the fluffy embryo so that few or no ejecta are thrown out. The impinging particle may partially evaporate in the interior of the embryo and hence preserve the fluffy structure.

The early stage of accretion can be considered to be at an end when an aggregate reaches a mass such that gravitational acceleration begins to control the terminal impact velocities. The catastrophic growth process that follows and leads to the accretion of planets and satellites has already been discussed in sec. 11.4 and will be discussed further in ch. 12.

11.6 ACCRETION OF RESONANCE-CAPTURED GRAINS

There are some regions in our solar system where planetesimal accretion may be in progress at the present time; namely, at some of the resonance points. We know three different regions in which several bodies are gravitationally captured in permanent resonances. These are

(1) and (2) The two libration or Lagrangian points ahead of and behind Jupiter where the Trojans are moving.

(3) The Hilda asteroids (20 asteroids), which are in 2/3 resonance with Jupiter.

In each of these three groups, the bodies are confined to movement in certain regions of space (secs. 8.5.3 through 8.5.4). Each of these groups probably includes a large number of smaller bodies. Some energy is pumped into these groups of bodies because the gravitational field is perturbed, in part due to the noncircular orbital motion of Jupiter and in part due to perturbations from other planets. Furthermore, other asteroids (and comets and meteoroids) pass the region and may collide with the members of the group, thereby feeding energy into it.

However, these sources of energy input are probably comparatively unimportant; consequently, we neglect them in the following idealized model. Hence, the only significant change in the energy of the group of bodies is due to mutual collisions, if such occur. If these collisions take place at hypervelocities, they lead to fragmentation. The number of bodies increases, but as the collisions are at least partially inelastic the total internal kinetic energy of the assembly decreases. According to our assumptions, there are no effects increasing the internal energy significantly, so the result will be that the relative velocities decrease until collisions occur only in the range in which accretion predominates. The result will be a net accretion. We would expect that all the matter in each of the groups would eventually accrete to form one body.

Therefore, if we treat the case where initially a large number of small grains (e.g., resulting from primordial condensation) were injected into the velocity space of one of our idealized groups, we could expect to follow in detail the accretional process from grains to planets. In the Hilda group, most of the mass is found in one object (Hilda herself). From this we may conclude that the accretional process is already far advanced.

There are a number of other resonances where only one small body is found to be trapped in resonance by a large body (ch. 8). Such cases are Thule (3/4 resonance with Jupiter), Pluto (3/2 resonance with Neptune), and Hyperion (4/3 resonance with Titan). These cases may represent a still more advanced state than that in the Trojan groups and the Hilda group with all of the observable mass gathered into one body. (There may, however, be small, still unknown companions.) We may also consider Mimas to be trapped by Dione, and Enceladus, trapped by Tethys, as similar cases.

It should be remembered that the libration amplitudes in some of the cases cited are small, in some cases less than 1°. As we have found in secs. 8.1 and 9.6, this is difficult to reconcile with the tidal theory of resonance capture because very efficient damping of the librations is needed. Our model of planetesimal accretion, on the other hand, provides a mechanism for energy loss through mutual collisions between the accreting bodies, which may result in a small libration. In fact, in the accretional state we have a number of bodies librating with different phase and amplitude. Their mutual collisions will decrease the libration of the finally accreted body.

A detailed analysis of the proposed model is desirable to demonstrate its applicability to real cases.

11.7 NECESSARY PROPERTIES OF AN ACCRETIONAL PROCESS

We shall now discuss the more general case of accretion. We start from the assumption that plasma containing a large number of grains is distributed in different regions around a central body. We require that the accretion of these grains shall finally lead to the formation of the celestial bodies we observe. From this requirement we can draw certain conclusions about the properties of the grains and about their dynamic state. We shall in this section confine ourselves to a discussion of the latter question.

We find that the celestial mechanical data that should be explained by a theory of accretion are as follows.

11.7.1 The Orbital Elements of the Bodies

The total angular momentum C_M of a celestial body should be the sum of the orbital momenta of all the grains that have contributed to the formation of the body. The eccentricity e and the inclination i of the orbits of the accreting grains change during the accretion because of collisions. The values of e and i of the resulting body depend upon the details of the mechanism of accretion, but are generally less than those of the grains.

11.7.2 The Spacing of the Bodies

The spacing ratio $q_n = (r_n+1)/r_n$ between two consecutive planetary or satellite orbits is given in tables 2.1.1 and 2.1.2. In the different groups it usually varies between about 1.18 (Mimas-Enceladus) and 2.01 (Saturn-Uranus). A theory of accretion should explain the values of q.

Of special interest is the fact that, with the exception of the group of the very small bodies, Jupiter 6, 10, and 7, there are no q values smaller than 1.15. It is important to clarify why the matter accumulated in, for example, the region of the Uranian satellites has accreted to form large bodies instead of, say, 100 satellites with spacings $q = 1.01$ or 1.02. If such a state were es-tablished, it would be just as stable as the present state with four bodies.

Hence, the gathering of primordial matter into a small number of bodies is an important fact for which the accretional model should account.

11.7.3. The Spin of the Bodies

The accretional mechanism should leave the bodies with the spins they had before tidal braking. Because all satellites and a few planets have been severely braked, the observational data we can use for checking a theory consist of the spin values of asteroids and the tidally unaffected planets. In particular, we have to explain the spin isochronism (sec. 9.7).

11.7.4 The Eccentricity of the Grain Orbits

From sec. 11.7.2 we can derive an interesting property of the orbits of the grains that form the raw material for the accretional process.

Suppose that the processes of grain capture and condensation have resulted in a large number of grains all moving around the central body in exactly circular orbits in the equatorial plane. Two spherical grains with radii R_1 and R_2 moving in orbits a_1 and a_2 can collide only if

$$\Delta a = a_2 - a_1 < R_1 + R_2 \qquad (11.7.1)$$

Since in the solar system R_1 and R_2 are usually very small compared with the spacing of the orbits, $R_1 + R_2 \ll \Delta a$, which means that we can have a large number of grains in consecutive circular orbits. At least in systems (e.g., the Uranian system) where the total mass of the satellites is very small compared to the mass of the central body, such a system would be perfectly stable from a celestial-mechanics point of view. Such a state would resemble the Saturnian rings and is conceivable even outside the Roche limit.

Hence, the fact that in each different group of bodies (see table 2.1.5) there are only a small number (3 to 6) of bodies shows that *the grains out of which the bodies were formed cannot have orbited originally in circles in the equatorial plane.*

Suppose next that we allow the original grains to orbit in circles with certain inclinations i. Then grains with the same angular momenta C but with different values of i will collide, but there will be no collisions between grains with different a values. In case the collisions are perfectly inelastic, they will result in grains with the C values unchanged but all with the same i values. Such a state is again dynamically stable but irreconcilable with the present state of the solar system.

Hence, we find that the *original grains must necessarily move in eccentric orbits.* (Originally circular orbits with different i values would result in eccentric orbits in the case where the collisions are not perfectly inelastic. This case is probably not important.)

An estimate of the minimum eccentricity is possible, but not without certain assumptions. Let us make the assumption (which later turns out to be unrealistic in certain respects) that a satellite or planet accretes by direct capture of grains.

If two adjacent embryos during the late stages of the accretional process move in circles with radii a_1 and a_2 and the spacing ratio is $q = a_2/a_1$, all grains must have orbits which intersect either a_1 or a_2. If not, there would be grains that are captured neither by a_1 nor by a_2, and these would finally accrete to a body between a_1 and a_2, contrary to our assumptions. As the ratio between the apocentric and pericentric distances is $(1+e)/(1-e)$ we find

$$\frac{1+e}{1-e} > q \qquad\qquad (11.7.2)$$

or

$$e > \frac{q-1}{q+1} \qquad\qquad (11.7.3)$$

Since in some cases (e.g., in the giant-planet group) $q = 2.0$, we find that at least for some groups $e \geq \frac{1}{3}$. For smaller q values such as $q = 1.2$ (in the inner Saturnian satellite group), we obtain $e > 0.09$. These results are not necessarily correct for a more complicated model of the accretion. However, as we shall find in ch. 12, it is essentially valid also for the two-step accretional process considered there.

11.8 THE PRESENT STATE OF ASTEROIDS, METEOROIDS AND COMETS, AND THE EXPLODED-PLANET HYPOTHESIS

We have found that the planetesimal approach requires a state characterized by a number of bodies moving in eccentric Kepler orbits. This state has a striking resemblance to the present state in the asteroidal belt. In fact, as shown in fig. 4.3.1, the eccentricities of the asteroid orbits vary up to about 0.30 or 0.35. There are very few asteroids with higher eccentricities. Thus, from this point of view it is tempting to identify the present state in the asteroidal region with the intermediate stage in a planetesimal accretion.

This is contrary to the common view that the asteroids are fragments of one or several planets, exploded by collisions. There are a number of other arguments against the explosion hypothesis:

(1) There is no doubt that collisions occur between asteroids. Arguments have been developed, particularly by Anders (1965), that the resulting fragmentation contributes to the observed size distribution of asteroids. However, Anders also points out that only the small-size part of the distribution is explained by fragmentation and that the large-size asteroids show another distribution which he attributes to "initial accretion" but which could equally well be explained as concurrent with the fragmentation.

(2) As discussed in sec. 11.5, it has been believed that collision of small objects could not lead to accretion; in this situation it appeared necessary first to postulate the formation of one or several large parent bodies by some undefined ad hoc process and then to decompose these to generate the wide size range of objects now observed. Obviously this approach does not solve the problem of accretion, which is only ignored or relegated to the realm of untenable hypotheses.

(3) It was long thought that meteorites could be produced from one or several parent "planets" of lunar size or larger that could have been located in the asteroid belt. The reasons for this assumption were mainly that several types of meteorites show evidence of heating of the accreted components. One way of interpreting this would be that they came from the interior of a planet, where heat would accumulate due to radioactive decay. The observed heating affects are, however, equally well, or better, explained by external sources (Wasson, 1972). The most obvious heating process is the dissipation of orbital energy by gas friction, as discussed in ch. 19. The monotonic decrease in power of the orbital thermal pulses would explain the diffusion profiles observed in the γ phase of nickel-iron meteorites (Wood 1964, 1967).

(4) The occurrence of microcrystalline diamond in meteorites, at one

time suggested to be due to high static pressure inside a planet, has been shown to be associated with and most likely caused by shock effects (Anders and Lipschutz, 1966); diamond can also grow metastably at low pressure from the gas phases (Angus et al., 1968).

(5) Finally, it was long thought that planetary-sized bodies with a fractionated atmosphere were needed to generate oxidized and hydrated minerals and some of the organic components observed in carbonaceous meteorites. It is now known, however, that extensive fractionation can occur in the pre-accretionary stages. This is illustrated by the variation in composition of comets, which have much higher oxygen/hydrogen ratios than, for example, the solar photosphere (sec. 21.6). Hydroxysilicates (such as chlorite) and ferriferrous iron oxide (magnetite) can form by direct condensation, and the classes of organic compounds observed in meteorites are readily synthesized in plasmas of the type observed in space and likely to have prevailed in the hetegonic era.

Hence, there appears to be nothing in the structure and composition of meteorites that indicates that their precursor bodies were ever larger than a few meters. (Further discussion of their possible maximum size is given in sec. 22.4).

In summary, there is no conceptual need for large bodies as predecessors of asteroids and meteorites. Furthermore, an assumption of such large bodies cannot be reconciled with the present dynamic state of the asteroids and with physically acceptable models for their formation. Most likely, the asteroids are generated by an ongoing planetesimal collision interaction process, where competing disruption and accretion result in net growth.

12

ON THE ACCRETION OF PLANETS
AND SATELLITES

12.1 PLANETESIMAL ACCRETION

According to the planetesimal (embryo) model of accretion, all planets and satellites have been formed by accretion of smaller bodies. The craters of the Moon, of Mercury, and of Mars and its satellites give clear evidence that an accretion of smaller bodies has been of major importance at least during the last phase of their formation. Theories of the spin of planets (see ch. 13) indicate that the planetesimal model is useful for the explanation of the rotation of planets. The isochronism of spin periods discussed in secs. 9.7 and 9.8 indicates that both planets and asteroids are likely to have been formed in this way.

The planetesimal accretion theory encounters some apparent difficulties. One of these is that, if planets are accreting by capturing grains moving in elliptic orbits in their neighborhood, one can calculate how long a time is needed before most of the grains are accreted to a planet or satellite. As shown by Safronov (1960), the time which Neptune and Pluto require to capture most of the grains in their environment is several times the age of the solar system. Safronov concludes from this that Neptune, for example, has only captured a small fraction of the matter accumulated in its neighborhood, and the rest is assumed to remain dispersed. This is not very likely. Although the matter in the asteroidal region has not accreted to a big planet, it is not dispersed. By analogy, if Neptune had not yet captured all the mass in its environment, one should expect the rest to be found as asteroid-like bodies. According to Safronov the "missing mass" must be some orders of magnitude larger than Neptune's mass. So much mass could not possibly be stored as asteroids because it should produce detectable perturbations of the orbits of the outer planets.

What appeared earlier to be a difficulty is that, according to practically all models of the embryonic state, it must have resembled the present state in the asteroidal region. In fact, if any embryo should be growing by accretion, it is necessary that a large number of asteroid-size bodies would be moving in Kepler orbits in its surrounding. But the relative velocities between visual asteroids can be as high as 5 km/sec. It is known that collisions at such hypervelocities usually lead to disruption or erosion so that larger bodies are fragmented into smaller bodies. Collisions are not likely to lead to an accretion of smaller bodies to larger bodies unless the relative velocity is below a certain limit v_{Lm} which is not very well known, but may be about 0.5 km/sec (see sec. 7.4 and also compare Gault et al., 1963).

As was shown in the preceding chapter, however, it is likely that in asteroidal jet streams the relative velocities go down to very low values. We conclude that for the subvisual bodies in the asteroidal region, low velocities may predominate leading to accretion.

12.2 A JET STREAM AS AN INTERMEDIATE STEP IN FORMATION OF PLANETS AND SATELLITES

The jet stream concept discussed in ch. 6 seems to resolve these difficulties. We shall devote this chapter to a study of this possibility.

There is strong indication (although perhaps not a rigorous proof) that a large number of grains in Kepler orbits constitute an unstable state (ch. 6). Even if the mutual gravitation between them is negligible (so that a gravitational collapse is excluded), mutual collisions tend to make the orbits of the colliding grains similar. Hence the "viscosity" of an assembly of grains in Kepler orbits introduces an "apparent attraction" that tends to focus the grains into a number of jet streams.

The general structure of the jet streams we are considering should resemble the jet streams found in the asteroidal region (ch. 4). There is also a similarity with meteor streams, although their eccentricities are usually very large. Although there is strong indication that the jet-stream mechanism (ch. 6) is producing asteroidal and meteor streams, this is not yet proven with such certainty that our discussion here should be dependent upon these phenomena. Hence, in this chapter, we shall treat the hetegonic jet streams independently of present-day observations of meteor and asteroidal streams; but later we will use such data to a certain extent.

According to the simplest model, a jet stream is a toroid with a large radius r_0 (equal to the orbital radius of a grain moving in a circular orbit around a central body) and a small radius $x = \beta r_0$. The stream consists of a large number of grains moving in Kepler orbits with semimajor axes close to r_0 and with eccentricities e and inclinations i of the order of β or less. If a particle moving in the circle r_0 has an orbital velocity v_0, for other particles in the jet stream this velocity is modulated by a randomly distributed velocity v ($|v| \ll |v_0|$). We will denote the average of $|v|$ by u and call it the *internal velocity* (approximately the average relative velocity) of the jet stream. This is the vector sum of differential velocities of the order $v_0 e$, $v_0 i$, and $(v_0 \Delta a)/2a$ produced by the eccentricities, inclinations, and differences in semimajor axes a of the individual orbits.

In our qualitative model we put

$$u = \beta v_0 \qquad \text{(12.2.1)}$$

and assume β to be constant. Hence

$$\frac{u}{v_0} = \frac{x}{r_0} \qquad \text{(12.2.2)}$$

The "characteristic volume" U of the jet stream is

$$U = 2\pi^2 r_0 x^2 = \tfrac{1}{2} G M_c T_K^2 \beta^2 = \tfrac{1}{2} r_0 T_K^2 u^2 \qquad \text{(12.2.3)}$$

or

$$U = \frac{2\pi^2 u^2 r_0^4}{G M_c} \qquad \text{(12.2.4)}$$

where

$$G M_c = \frac{4\pi^2 r_0^3}{T_K^2} = r_0 v_0^2 \qquad \text{(12.2.5)}$$

and $T_K = 2\pi r_0 / v_0$ is the Kepler orbital period.

   This structure of a stream should be compared with Danielsson's observed "profile" of an asteroidal jet stream (fig. 4.3.6). The cross section of our model, applied to a jet stream in the asteroid belt with $a = 2.2$, $u = 0.5$ km/sec, and $v = 20$ km/sec should, from eq. (12.2.2), have the radius $x = 0.055$ AU. As the figure shows, this is in fair agreement with observations.

12.3 ACCRETION OF AN EMBRYO

   According to our model, the accretion of large bodies takes place in two steps. The grains condensed in or were captured by a partially corotating plasma (chs. 16 and 17). The process results in grains in elliptic orbits. The precession of the ellipses will sooner or later bring them to collide with a jet stream in the region where they move. This will eventually lead to incorporation of the grains in the stream. Before incorporation has taken place, or in connection with this, an extraneous grain may make a hypervelocity collision with a grain in the jet stream and hence be vaporized, melted, or fragmented. Even if the grain is thus modified or loses its identity, the ultimate result is that its mass is added to the jet stream. The subsequent collisions will reduce the relative velocity of the grain, its fragments, or its recondensation products until they reach the internal velocity of the jet stream.

The result of a collision may either be fragmentation-erosion, leading to a decrease in the size of at least the largest of the colliding bodies, or accretion leading to larger bodies. These processes have not been studied very much in the laboratory, especially not for the type of bodies with which we are concerned. The processes depend very much upon impact velocity and the bodies' chemical composition, size, and physical properties (whether they are brittle or fluffy). We know from the studies of Gault and others that impact at supersonic velocities results in melting, vaporization, and fragmentation of a total mass of the order of 10^2–10^4 times that of the projectile. However, in the subsonic range these effects decrease rapidly with decreasing impact velocities.

At velocities exceeding the equivalent of the crushing energies of brittle solid bodies, collisions between such bodies still result in comminution of projectile and target. Below this range, of the order of 10–100 m/sec in the most common brittle solar-system materials, as many particles exist after the collision as existed before.

For accretion to take place, a force has to act between the particles which exceeds the rebound after collision. Such force can be supplied by electric and magnetic dipoles. The latter are restricted to ferromagnetic components; the effect of magnetic clustering can be seen in meteorites (fig. 22.7.1).

Adhesion and clustering due to electric polarization is probably the most important process for initial accretion in a jet stream; it also determines the persistent clustering and particle adhesion on the lunar surface (Arrhenius and Asunmaa, 1973, 1974; Asunmaa et al., 1970; Asunmaa and Arrhenius, 1974). The equivalent relative particle velocities below which accretion by this process can take place are estimated at 1–10 m/sec.

Once electret clusters, such as in the lunar dust, have formed in a jet stream, capture of subsonic particles in such clusters would probably become effective. Ballistic observations indicate that projectiles in the velocity range of a few hundred m/sec effectively dissipate their energy within fluffy targets. Hence we assume here that 0.5 km/sec is a reasonable value for the limiting velocity v_{Lm} below which particles can add mass to fluffy aggregates. It would be important to clarify such capture phenomena in a more quantitative fashion by appropriate experiments.

If $u<v_{Lm}$, grains inside the jet stream will accrete. Their size will be statistically distributed. In our model we choose the biggest embryo and study how it accretes by capturing smaller grains. We assume it to be spherical with radius R. This is a reasonable assumption for the later stages of accretion, but probably not very adequate for the earlier stages. However, no major error is likely to be introduced by this assumption.

In case such an embryo is immersed in a stream of infinitely small particles, which have the pre-accretional velocity u in relation to the embryo, the capture cross section is, according to sec. 7.3,

$$\sigma = \pi R^2 \left(1 + \frac{v_{es}^2}{u^2}\right) \tag{12.3.1}$$

where v_{es} is the escape velocity. From eq. (7.3.2) we find that the "time of escape"

$$t_{es} = \frac{R}{v_{es}} = \left(\frac{3}{8\pi G\Theta}\right)^{1/2} = \frac{1340}{\Theta^{1/2}} \text{ sec } (g/cm^3)^{1/2} \tag{12.3.2}$$

is independent of R. Hence for $v_{es} \gg v_{Lm}$ the capture cross section is proportional to R^4.

We cannot be sure that eq. (12.3.1) holds for the case where the embryo is moving in a Kepler orbit in a gravitational field. As shown by Giuli (1968a,b), an embryo moving in a circular orbit will accrete grains under certain conditions. His calculations are confined to the two-dimensional case when all grains move in the same orbital plane as the embryo. As shown by Dole (1962), if the grains also move in circles (far away from the embryo), there are 14 different "bands" of orbits which lead to capture. Of these only four are broad enough to be of importance. Hence eq. (12.3.1) can at best be approximately true. Unfortunately the three-dimensional case of Giuli's problem has not yet been solved; hence a qualitative comparison between eq. (12.3.1) and his exact calculations is not possible. A quantitative comparison seems to indicate that eq. (12.3.1) gives reasonable values for the capture cross section. We shall therefore use it until a more precise relationship has been developed.

We denote by ρ the space density of condensable substances. The jet stream may also contain volatile substances that are not condensing to grains, but according to sec. 11.4 these are also accreted by an embryo as soon as the escape velocity becomes much larger than the thermal velocity.

The plasma condensation of grains and the plasma capture (sec. 21.12) of preexisting grains takes place essentially outside the jet streams, and the orbiting grains resulting from this (sec. 17.5) are captured by the jet streams. Also, the noncondensable substances may partly be brought into the jet streams. It is not necessary to make any specific assumption here about the amount of volatile substances. (Indirectly they may contribute to the damping of the internal velocities and help to dissipate the kinetic energy.)

The growth of the embryo is, from eq. (7.3.5)

$$\frac{dR}{dt} = \frac{u\rho}{4\Theta}\left(1 + \frac{v_{es}^2}{u^2}\right) \tag{12.3.3}$$

When the embryo has grown large enough so that v_{es} equals u, gravitational accretion becomes important. The value of the radius of the embryo at this transition state between nongravitational and gravitational accretion is

$$R_G = t_{es}u \tag{12.3.4}$$

Substituting eqs. (12.3.2) and (12.3.4) into eq. (12.3.3) we have

$$\frac{dR}{R_G\left(1 + \frac{R^2}{R_G^2}\right)} = \frac{u\rho}{4\Theta R_G}\,dt = \frac{\rho}{4\Theta t_{es}}\,dt \tag{12.3.5}$$

Integration yields

$$\frac{R}{R_G} = \tan\left(\frac{\rho(t - t_0)}{4\Theta t_{es}}\right) \tag{12.3.6}$$

We now define a time t_a when accretion would produce an embryo of infinite radius if the supply of grains were continuous. Setting $R/R_G = \infty$ we have

$$\infty = \tan\left(\frac{t_a}{4\Theta t_{es}}\right) = \tan\frac{\pi}{2} \tag{12.3.7}$$

and

$$t_a = \frac{2\pi\Theta t_{es}}{\rho}$$ (12.3.8)

Setting $R = R_G$ in eq. (12.3.6) we obtain

$$t - t_0 = \frac{t_a}{2}$$ (12.3.9)

Hence, in a medium of constant density and constant u an embryo increases in diameter from zero to infinity in the finite time t_a. Half this time is needed for reaching R_G, the size at which the gravitation of the embryo becomes important. As $t - t_0$ approaches t_a, dR/dt approaches infinity, and the increase becomes catastrophic.

12.4 MASS BALANCE OF THE JET STREAM

Let us assume that in a certain region there is a constant infall and ionization of gas and solid particles during a time t_{inf} resulting in production of grains that are all captured in a jet stream. In the jet stream an embryo is accreting, so that finally all the emplaced mass is accumulated to one secondary body—a planet if the region we consider is interplanetary space or a satellite if it is space around a planet. The final mass of the accreted body is denoted by M_{sc} (mass of final secondary body). Hence the rate of mass injection into the jet stream is M_{sc}/t_{inf}. We assume that this mass is uniformly distributed over the volume U of the jet stream. The jet stream loses mass to the embryo which is accreting according to

$$\frac{dM_{em}}{dt} = 4\pi R^2 \Theta \frac{dR}{dt}$$ (12.4.1)

Hence we have

$$U\frac{d\rho}{dt} = \frac{M_{sc}}{t_{inf}} - \frac{dM_{em}}{dt} = \frac{M_{sc}}{t_{inf}} - 4\pi R^2 \Theta \frac{dR}{dt}$$ (12.4.2)

Incorporating eqs. (12.3.5) and (12.3.8), we find

$$U\frac{d\rho}{dR} = \frac{t_a 2 R_G M_{sc}}{t_{inf}\pi(R_G^2 + R^2)} - 4\pi\Theta R^2 \qquad (12.4.3)$$

12.5 ENERGY BALANCE IN A JET STREAM

The jet stream we consider is fed by an infall of condensed grains, each having a relative velocity v in relation to the jet stream. The rate of energy input to the jet stream is $M_{sc}v/2t_{inf}$. On the other hand, the jet stream loses energy through internal collisions. In our qualitative model we assume that the mass is distributed in N identical spherical grains, each with radius R_{gn}, a cross section $\sigma_{gn} = \pi R_{gn}^2$, and a mass $m_{gn} = \frac{4}{3}\pi\Theta_{gn}R_{gn}^3$. Their number density is

$$N_{gn} = \frac{N}{U} = \frac{2N}{r_0 T_K^2 u^2} \qquad (12.5.1)$$

They collide mutually with the frequency $\nu_{gn} = N_{gn}u\sigma_{gn}$, where u is the internal velocity of the jet stream. We assume that at each collision a fraction α of the kinetic energy $W_{gn} = \frac{1}{2}m_{gn}u^2$ is lost. Hence the energy loss rate per grain is

$$\frac{dW_{gn}}{dt} = -\alpha\nu_{gn}W_{gn} \qquad (12.5.2)$$

which gives

$$\frac{du}{dt} = -\frac{\alpha\nu_{gn}u}{2} = -\frac{\alpha\pi R_{gn}^2 N}{r_0 T_K^2} \qquad (12.5.3)$$

or

$$\frac{du}{dt} = -\frac{3\alpha M_j}{4\Theta_{gn}r_0 T_K^2 R_{gn}} \qquad (12.5.4)$$

where M_j is the total mass of the jet stream.

According to our assumption in sec. 12.3 there is a limiting velocity v_{Lm} such that, if $u > v_{Lm}$, collisions result in net fragmentation and thus a decrease in grain size R_{gn} accompanied by an increase in the loss of kinetic energy of the jet stream.

The conclusion is that within wide limits a jet stream will adjust itself in such a way that the losses due to collisions in the stream are balanced by the injected energy. The process will tend to make $u = v_{Lm}$. Hence the volume U of the jet stream is likely to remain constant, and the energy balance is produced by a change in the size of the grains in the stream.

When injection stops, there is no energy input to the jet stream. Collisions will decrease the internal velocity. As $u = \beta v_0 = 2\pi r_0 \beta / T_K$ we have

$$\frac{d\beta}{dt} = - \frac{3\alpha M_j}{8\pi\Theta_{gn}r_0^2 T_K R_{gn}} \tag{12.5.5}$$

Eventually all the mass in the jet stream is accreted to one spherical, homogeneous body, the radius of which is R_{sc}. Assuming the density of this body to be Θ_{gn}, we put

$$M_j = \frac{4\pi\Theta_{gn}R_{sc}^3}{3} \tag{12.5.6}$$

and we find

$$\frac{d\beta}{dt} = - \frac{\alpha R_{sc}^3}{2R_{gn}r_0^2 T_K} \tag{12.5.7}$$

If R_{gn} is constant, the thickness of the stream will decrease linearly and reach zero after a time

$$t_j = \frac{2 T_K r_0^2 R_{gn}}{\alpha R_{sc}^3} \tag{12.5.8}$$

12.6 ACCRETION WHEN THE INFALL INTO THE JET STREAM IS CONSTANT

We have found reasons for putting $u = $ constant, and hence $U = $ constant. If the injection starts at $t = 0$, and we neglect the mass accreted by the embryo, we have the average density of the jet stream

$$\rho = \frac{M_j t}{U t_{inf}} \tag{12.6.1}$$

Introducing this into eq. (12.3.5) we obtain

$$\frac{dR}{R_G \left(1 + \dfrac{R^2}{R_G{}^2}\right)} = \frac{M_j t \, dt}{4 \Theta U t_{es} t_{inf}} \tag{12.6.2}$$

or after integration

$$\tan^{-1}\left(\frac{R}{R_G}\right) = \frac{M_j t^2}{8 \Theta U t_{es} t_{inf}} \tag{12.6.3}$$

Equating ρ to M_j/U, eq. (12.3.8) becomes

$$t_a = \frac{2 \pi t_{es} \Theta U}{M_j} \tag{12.6.4}$$

Substituting eq. (12.6.4) into eq. (12.6.3) gives

$$\frac{R}{R_G} = \tan\left(\frac{\pi t^2}{4 t_{inf} t_a}\right) \tag{12.6.5}$$

These equations are valid only for $t \leq t_{inf}$. To obtain an approximate value for the time t_c after which there is a catastrophic increase of the embryo, we allow R/R_G to approach ∞ and substitute $t = t_c$, giving

$$t_c = (2 t_{inf} t_a)^{1/2} \qquad (12.6.6)$$

We have two typical cases, both of which are illustrated in fig. 12.6.1.

(1) $t_c \ll t_{inf}$. The density in the jet stream increases in the beginning linearly, and the radius of the embryo increases as t^2, its mass, as t^6. The linear increase in jet-stream density continues until the embryo rather suddenly consumes most of the mass in the stream. The catastrophic growth of the embryo stops even more rapidly than it has started, and for $t > t_c$ the embryo accretes mass at about the rate it is injected $(dM_{em}/dt) \approx (M_{sc}/t_{inf})$.

(2) $t_c \gg t_{inf}$. The injection stops before any appreciable accretion has taken place. The jet stream begins to contract because no more energy is fed into it to compensate the loss due to collisions. When it has contracted so much that its density is large enough, accretion sets in. This accretion is also catastrophic.

12.7 DISCUSSION

Our derivation of the accretion of celestial bodies in jet streams is based on a number of simplifying assumptions: There is not, as yet, any detailed general theory of jet streams; further, the relation between volatile and less volatile substances is far from clear. Such an approach is usually dangerous in astrophysics and it is likely that the present theory will have to be re-vised when sufficient observational facts become available. We may, how-ever, receive some observational support from a comparison with asteroidal jet streams (sec. 4.3.3), to some extent with meteor streams (secs. 14.2 through 14.4), and with the record in meteorites (sec. 22.6).

In Danielsson's profile of the asteroidal jet stream Flora A (fig. 4.3.6), the cross section of the stream is approximately $\sigma_j = 0.04$ AU². All orbits are confined within this surface, but most of them within about half of it $(\sigma_j = 0.02$ AU²). As $\sigma_j = \pi x^2 = \pi \beta^2 r_0^2$ (sec. 12.2) and the semimajor axis for the Flora A jet stream is 2.2 AU, setting $r_0 = 2.2$ AU we find for $\sigma_j = 0.04$ AU², $\beta = 0.052$, and for $\sigma_j = 0.02$ AU², $\beta = 0.036$. As the orbital velocity of the Flora A jet stream is 20 km/sec, the β value should be, from eq. (12.2.1), 0.025 assuming a u of 0.5 km/sec. This is in any case the right order of mag-nitude. With our present knowledge of the collisional properties of the grains (and with our qualitative treatment) we cannot expect a better agree-ment.

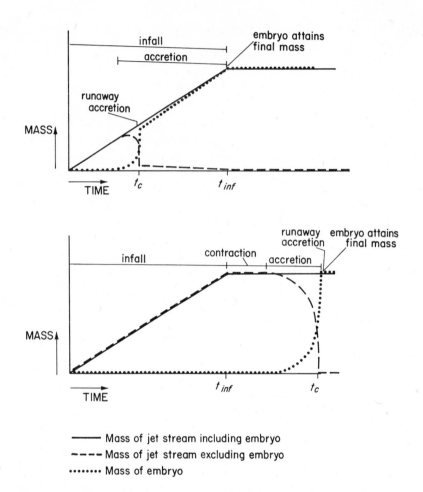

FIGURE 12.6.1.—Schematic representation of the accretion of an embryo from a jet stream. Plasma emplacement and infall of grains to the jet stream occurs during the time t_{inf}. The accreting embryo at first acquires mass slowly but then reaches catastrophic accretion at time t_c when all mass present in the jet stream is accreted by the embryo. For the case $t_{inf} > t_c$, a slow rate of accretion continues after the runaway accretion occurs. The slow accretion continues until plasma emplacement has ceased. For the case $t_{inf} < t_c$, as illustrated in the lower graph, after emplacement ceases and contraction of the jet-stream volume by negative diffusion increases the density in the jet stream, accretion commences and culminates in catastrophic accretion.

It should be observed that Danielsson also has found other jet streams with much larger spread. This does not necessarily contradict our conclusions because these could be interpreted as jet streams in formation from a number of bodies that initially had a larger spread. In order to check our conclusions a much more detailed study is obviously necessary.

12.8 NUMERICAL VALUES

Table 12.8.1 presents calculated values of t_a, t_c, and ρ for the planets. Equations (12.6.4) and (12.2.4) were used to obtain t_a:

$$t_a = \left(8.4 \times 10^3 \, \frac{\sec \text{g}^{1/2}}{\text{cm}^{3/2}} \, \frac{2\pi^2 u^2}{GM_c} \right) \frac{\Theta_{sc}^{1/2} r_0^4}{M_{sc}} \qquad (12.8.1)$$

The large radius of the jet stream r_0 is approximated by the present semimajor axis of each planet. To evaluate the constant term in eq. (12.8.1) we have used $u = 0.5$ km/sec and the solar mass as M_c. The values of t_c are calculated from eq. (12.6.6) assuming an infall time t_{inf} of 3×10^8 yr.

The table also contains information on the semimajor axis, mass, and density of each planet as well as the volume and density for each planetary jet stream. To facilitate intercomparison these values, excepting planetary

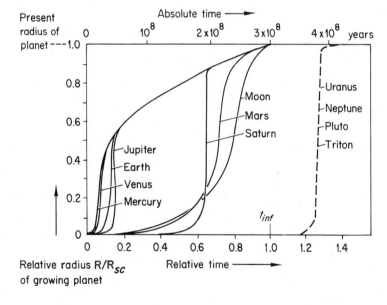

FIGURE 12.9.1.—The growth of planetary radii with respect to time. Runaway accretion occurs early for Mercury, Venus, Earth, and Jupiter. The time of runaway accretion approaches that of the duration of mass infall for Saturn, Mars, and the Moon. (From Ip, 1974c.) For Uranus, Neptune, Pluto, and Triton, runaway accretion occurs only after infall has ceased and the jet stream has contracted due to negative diffusion; this growth is schematically represented by the dashed curve.

TABLE 12.8.1

Values of t_a, t_c, and ρ and Related Parameters Characterizing the Accretion of the Planets[a]

	$\dfrac{r_{sc}}{r_\oplus}$	$\dfrac{U_{sc}}{U_\oplus}$	$\dfrac{M_{sc}}{M_\oplus}$	Θ_{sc} (g/cm³)	$\dfrac{\rho_{sc}}{\rho_\oplus}$	t_a (yr)	t_c (yr)
Mercury	0.386	0.0222	0.0568	5.46	2.54	0.78×10^6	22×10^6
Venus	0.720	0.269	0.826	5.23	3.03	0.63×10^6	20×10^6
Earth	1.00	1.00	1.00	5.52	1.00	2.0×10^6	34×10^6
Moon	1.00	1.00	1.0123	3.35	0.0123	130×10^6	270×10^6
Mars	1.52	5.34	0.108	3.92	0.0202	82×10^6	220×10^6
Jupiter	5.19	726	318	1.31	0.438	2.2×10^6	36×10^6
Saturn	9.53	8 250	95.1	0.7	0.0115	61×10^6	190×10^6
Uranus	19.1	133 000	14.6	1.30	1.09×10^{-4}	8.8×10^9	$>300 \times 10^6$
Neptune	30.0	810 000	17.1	1.66	2.12×10^{-5}	51×10^9	$>300 \times 10^6$

[a] Values for orbital radius, mass, and average density are taken from tables 2.1.1 and 2.1.3.

density, are given relative to Earth. As calculated from eq. (12.2.4), the jet stream volume for the Earth $U_\oplus$ is 1.9×10^{37} cm³.

12.9 CONCLUSIONS ABOUT THE DIFFERENT TYPES OF ACCRETION

Table 12.8.1 shows that the values of t_a fall into three groups (fig. 12.9.1). Mercury, Venus, Earth, and Jupiter all have values around 10^6 yr, which must be much shorter than t_{inf}. Uranus and Neptune have values that are larger than the age of the solar system; hence $t_a > t_{inf}$. There is an intermediate group, consisting of the Moon, Mars, and Saturn with $t_a \approx 10^8$ yr. This is probably of the same order of magnitude as t_{inf}. In any case we cannot be sure whether t_{inf} or t_a is the larger quantity.

Our conclusion is that there are three different pathways of accretion.

(1) *Early runaway accretion.* For Mercury, Venus, Earth, and Jupiter the catastrophic growth of the embryo took place early in the time period of infall of matter into the circumsolar region.

(2) *Late runaway accretion.* For the Moon, Mars, and Saturn the catastrophic growth took place near the end of the infall.

(3) *Delayed runaway accretion.* Uranus and Neptune cannot have accreted until, after the end of the infall, their jet streams eventually contracted so that β had decreased considerably from its original value.

12.10 EARLY TEMPERATURE PROFILE OF ACCRETED BODY

When a grain in the jet stream is brought to rest on the surface of a growing embryo, the impact velocity is

$$v_{imp} = (u^2 + v_{es}^2)^{1/2} \qquad (12.10.1)$$

Upon impact the kinetic energy of the grain is almost entirely converted into heat energy. In order to study the temperature of the accreting body we calculate the thermal power per unit surface area w_T delivered by impacting grains

$$4\pi R_{em}^2 w_T = \frac{v_{imp}^2}{2} \frac{dM_{em}}{dt} \qquad (12.10.2)$$

where the mass of the impacting grain is equated to dM_{em}. Defining u and v_{es} as in eqs. (12.3.4) and (12.3.2) we have

$$w_T = \frac{1 + \dfrac{R_G^2}{R^2}\, dM_{em}}{8\pi t_{es}^2\, dt} \tag{12.10.3}$$

or assuming the density of the embryo to remain constant we have, from eq. (12.3.5),

$$w_T = \frac{\rho(u^2 + v_{es}^2)^2}{8u} \tag{12.10.4}$$

which shows that for $R \gg R_G$ the heat *delivered per cm² sec* is proportional to the mass increase of the *whole* embryo. The function dM_{em}/dt is shown in fig. 12.6.1 and dR/dt in fig. 12.9.1. Hence w_T has a maximum at $t \approx t_c$. If w_T is balanced by radiation from the surface of the accreting body, its surface temperature should vary similarly to w_T. This means that the maximum temperature is reached when a fraction γ of the mass is accumulated:

$$\gamma = \frac{t_c}{t_{inf}} = \left(\frac{2t_a}{t_{inf}}\right)^{1/2} \quad \text{for } (t_a < t_{inf}) \tag{12.10.5}$$

Hence in an accreted body the region at a radial distance $R = \delta R_{sc}$ (where R_{sc} is the final radius) has received most heat:

$$\delta = \gamma^{1/3} = \left(\frac{2t_a}{t_{inf}}\right)^{1/6} \quad \text{for } (t_a < t_{inf}) \tag{12.10.6}$$

For the Earth $t_a = 2 \times 10^6$ yr. If as above we tentatively put $t_{inf} = 3 \times 10^8$ yr, we have

$$\delta = \left(\frac{4}{300}\right)^{1/6} = 0.5 \tag{12.10.7}$$

Hence the different layers were accreted with different temperatures: The innermost part was cold, the layers for which $\delta = 0.5$ were hot, and again the outer parts were cold. The value $\delta = 0.5$ depends on a guess for t_{inf}, but is rather insensitive to this value. If we choose for example $t_{inf} = 10^8$ or 10^9 yr, δ is changed to 0.58 or 0.40, respectively.

We know neither the chemical composition nor the heat conductivity of the Earth's interior very well (sec. 20.5.1). Also, the content of radio-active substances, which could contribute to the heating of the interior, is unknown. We are not in conflict with any facts or plausible conclusions if we assume that neither the radioactive heating nor the thermal conductivity has changed the temperature structure in a drastic way. Hence our results may give a simple explanation for the fact that only an intermediate part of the Earth is melted, whereas both the inner core and the mantle are solid. According to our result, the outer core was heated most intensely, whereas both the central region and the outer layers were formed cool.

As the heat per unit surface is proportional to dM_{em}/dt, the average formation temperature of a celestial body is proportional to M_{sc}/t_{inf}. If we assume t_{inf} to be similar for the different bodies, the formation tempera-ture (under the condition of similar accretion processes) is proportional to their present masses.

12.11 CONCLUSIONS ABOUT THE TEMPERATURE PROFILE OF PLANETS

The equations for w_T have been integrated numerically by Ip (1974c). His results for the different planets are shown in fig. 12.11.1. From this we can draw the following general conclusions about the internal temperatures of the planets.

(1) The giant planets were formed with a hot region in the interior. The heat structures of these planets differ in the respect that, while the heat maximum of Jupiter occurs at about half the radius, this maximum for Saturn occurs somewhat further out. In both cases there is a cold accre-tional phase later. For both Uranus and Neptune substantial heat was de-livered also to the outermost layers.

If the primeval heat profile of these planets is conserved at least to some extent, it may be an essential factor affecting their average density. To what extent such a conservation is possible depends on the thermal conductivity in the interior, which is unknown (sec. 20.2).

(2) Venus should have about the same heat structure as the Earth, but with the melted region closer to the center (see fig. 12.11.1). Mercury should have a temperature maximum still closer to its center, but due to its small-ness the temperature is much lower.

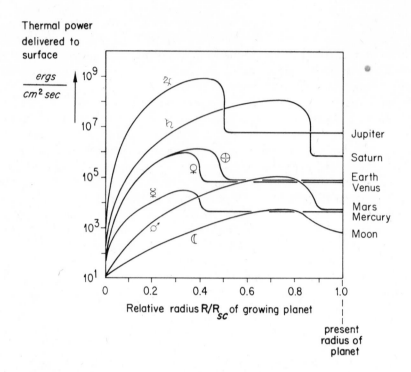

FIGURE 12.11.1.—Thermal profiles of the growing planets. (From Ip, 1974c.)

(3) The average heating power on Mars should have been one order of magnitude less than for the Earth. The temperature maximum should be rather close to the surface (perhaps at 0.9 of its radius), where, if at all, a liquid region may have existed. The Moon has a similar heat profile.

In all cases subsequent radioactive heating and thermal conduction may have modified the early heat profile, as is indeed indicated by the fact that the interior of the Moon now appears partially molten and that local volcanism has occurred on Mars.

12.12 THE ACCRETIONAL HOT-SPOT FRONT

Our conclusions about the low average formation temperature of some celestial bodies or specific zones in them should not be interpreted as meaning that their constituent matter has never been melted. On the contrary, for large celestial bodies every part, with the exception of the central cores, has been heated above the melting point repeatedly. One can attribute these processes to a front of "accretional hot spots" which sweeps through the body outwards.

Suppose that an energy W_m is needed to melt a mass M of a certain substance. We define a velocity v_m by the condition

$$W_m = \frac{Mv_m^2}{2} \tag{12.12.1}$$

As soon as a body of this substance has a velocity $v > v_m$ its kinetic energy suffices to melt it if converted into heat. For most substances v_m is of the order of 10^5 cm/sec.

If a body with mass M_1 and velocity v hits a target of the same composition its kinetic energy suffices to melt a mass

$$M_2 = \zeta M_1 \tag{12.12.2}$$

where

$$\zeta = \frac{v^2}{v_m^2} \tag{12.12.3}$$

A fraction of its energy will be used for the production of shock waves, the ejection of fragments from the place of collision, and the emission of radiation, but eq. (12.12.2) gives the correct order of magnitude.

We see that it is doubtful whether in a body as small as the Moon ζ has become much larger than unity. For planets like the Earth it may be 10 to 100 for the last phase of accretion.

When the matter melted by an impacting body has cooled down it may be remelted many times by the impact of other bodies in its close neighborhood. The impacting matter will, however, increase the radius of the embryo, and finally the volume we are considering, originally located at the surface, is buried so deeply that no new impact will be able to melt it. Before this is achieved *it is likely to be molten ζ times* (because all impacting matter melts ζ times its own mass).

In retrospect we can picture this as an accretional front of hot spots, discontinuous in time and space and moving outward with the surface layer of the growing protoplanet. All matter is heated ζ times before the front has passed. The factor ζ increases in proportion to R_{sc}^2 (R_{sc} is the radius of the growing protoplanet). The front is able to melt all material as soon as $\zeta \gg 1$, which probably occurs at about 10^8 cm from the center. As long as the impact frequency is low the impacts produce locally heated regions that radiate their heat differentially (sec. 12.13) and cool down again. The accretional heat front will leave a cool region behind it. This is what is likely to have been the case in the Earth's central core and in the mantle, and also in the entire Moon. If, on the other hand, the impact frequency is large, the heated regions have no time to cool. The accretional heat front will leave a hot region behind it. According to the interpretation in sec. 12.11 this is how the Earth's outer core became molten.

12.13 DIFFERENTIATION EFFECT OF THE ACCRETIONAL HEAT FRONT

In a volume of matter melted by impact of large embryos, a chemical separation would be expected to take place due to the heavy components' sinking and the light components' floating in the reservoir of liquid or liquids generated by melting. This phenomenon is common in the interior of the present crust of the Earth, where the heating, however, comes from sources other than impact. Gravitative differentiation in a planetary accretional heat front, as suggested here and by Alfvén and Arrhenius (1970b) has been observed on the Moon (see, for example, Urey et al., 1971).

Furthermore, in melt systems of this kind, ions with liquid-solid distribution coefficients favoring their concentration in the liquid will remain in the light residual melt and become removed to the top of the reservoir. Particularly, ions with large radii are included in this process; examples are potassium, barium, the rare-earth elements (particularly in divalent state), and the actinides, including the (next to potassium) most important radioactive heat sources, uranium, thorium, and plutonium.

By reiteration of differentiation every time a new impact occurs in the same region, the accretional hot-spot front will produce a differentiated crust on a global basis. In this way a limited amount of differentiated material may be brought the entire distance from the interior of the body to the surface. The lower limit at which this effect occurs is given by $\zeta \approx 1$.

The heavy components, such as dense magnesium silicates, transition metal oxides, sulfides, and metal, will sink down in the locally heated regions, but if the heat front leaves a solidified region below it the heavy component cannot sink more than the thickness of the heated region. This thickness will depend on the size of the impinging embryo and the impact rate. Typically it seldom exceeds a few kilometers.

Hence the accretional heat front may bring light components and associated heavy ions from the interior to the surface, but it will *not* bring dense components downward more than a very small distance. The change in the proportion of dense materials from that in the accreting planetesimals is thus mainly a secondary effect of the displacement of the light component.

The gravitative differentiation in the accretional hot-spot front explains why the outer layers of both the Earth and the Moon contain unusually large amounts of low-density components and radioactive elements. It is well known that the interior of the bodies must have a much lower content of such elements because, otherwise, the total heating of the bodies would be very large. Since in the Moon's core $\zeta < 1$, it should not be effectively depleted of radioactive elements. This may explain why the lunar interior is partially melted.

The constraints imposed by the accretional phenomena on the evolution of the Earth are discussed in more detail in ch. 26.

13

SPIN AND ACCRETION

13.1 GRAIN IMPACT AND SPIN

When an embryo grows by accreting grains, the spin of the embryo is determined by the angular momentum (in relation to the center of gravity of the embryo) which the grains transfer to the embryo. Suppose that a spherical embryo has a radius R_{em}, average density Θ_{em}, and moment of inertia Ξ_{em}, and that it is spinning with a period τ_{em} and angular velocity $\Omega_{em} = 2\pi/\tau_{em}$. Its spin angular momentum is

$$\mathbf{C}_\tau = \Xi_{em}\,\Omega_{\mathbf{em}} \tag{13.1.1}$$

We put

$$\Xi_{em} = M_{em}R_{\Xi}{}^2 = M_{em}R_{em}{}^2\alpha_{\Xi}{}^2 = \tfrac{4}{3}\pi\Theta_{em}\alpha_{\Xi}{}^2R_{em}{}^5 \tag{13.1.2}$$

where R_{Ξ} is the radius of gyration and α_{Ξ} the normalized radius of gyration. If the density of the spherical body is uniform, we have

$$\alpha_{\Xi}{}^2 = 0.4 \tag{13.1.3}$$

For celestial bodies with central mass concentration, $\alpha_{\Xi}{}^2$ is smaller (see table 2.1.1).

Suppose that a grain with mass m_{gn} impinges with the velocity v_{imp} on the embryo at an angle ψ with the vertical. At impact, the spin angular momentum of the embryo changes by the amount

$$\Delta\mathbf{C}_\tau = (\mathbf{R_{em}} \times \mathbf{v_{imp}})m_{gn} \tag{13.1.4}$$

where $\mathbf{R_{em}}$ is the vector from the center of the embryo to the impact point. The absolute value of $\mathbf{\Delta C_\tau}$ is

$$\Delta C_\tau = m_{gn} R_{em} v_{imp} \sin \psi \qquad (13.1.5)$$

Depending on the angle between $\mathbf{C_\tau}$ and $\mathbf{\Delta C_\tau}$, the impact may increase or decrease the spin of the embryo.

We shall discuss the two-dimensional case where impacting particles orbit in the same plane as the embryo, and $\mathbf{\Delta C_\tau}$ is perpendicular to this plane. In this case $\mathbf{\Delta C_\tau}$ is parallel to $\mathbf{C_\tau}$. We further assume $\Delta C_\tau \ll C_\tau$. Then we have from eq. (13.1.1)

$$\Delta C_\tau = \Xi_{em} \Delta \Omega_{em} + \Omega_{em} \Delta \Xi_{em} \qquad (13.1.6)$$

Assuming that after the impact the accreted mass m_{gn} will be uniformly distributed over the surface of the embryo (so that it keeps its spherical shape) we have

$$m_{gn} = 4\pi \Theta_{em} R_{em}{}^2 \Delta R_{em} = \frac{3M_{em}\Delta R_{em}}{R_{em}} \qquad (13.1.7)$$

and

$$\Delta \Xi_{em} = \tfrac{4}{3}\pi \Theta_{em} \alpha_{\overline{z}}{}^2 5 R_{em}{}^4 \Delta R_{em} = \frac{5\Xi_{em}\Delta R_{em}}{R_{em}} = \frac{5\Xi_{em}m_{gn}}{3M_{em}} \qquad (13.1.8)$$

From eqs. (13.1.2) and (13.1.5 through 13.1.7) we find

$$\Delta C_\tau = R_{em} v_{imp} \sin \psi 3 M_{em} \frac{\Delta R_{em}}{R_{em}}$$

$$= M_{em} R_{em}{}^2 \alpha_{\overline{z}}{}^2 \Delta \Omega_{em} + 5\Xi_{em} \frac{\Delta R_{em}}{R_{em}} \Omega_{em} \qquad (13.1.9)$$

or

$$\frac{\Delta\Omega_{em}}{\Delta R_{em}} = \frac{3v_{imp}\sin\psi}{\alpha_{\bar{z}}^2 R_{em}^2} - \frac{5\Omega_{em}}{R_{em}} \qquad (13.1.10)$$

13.2 ACCRETION FROM CIRCULAR ORBITS BY NONGRAVITATING EMBRYO

The general problem of finding the spin of an accreting body is a very complicated many-body problem that is far from solved. Important progress has been made in the treatment of the two-dimensional problem when all the accreting grains are confined to move in the embryo's orbital plane. There is no obvious reason why a three-dimensional treatment (where the accreting grains move in orbits out of the embryo orbital plane) should not give the same qualitative results as the two-dimensional treatment, but this has not yet been checked by calculation. The conclusions we draw in the following sections are made with this reservation.

We shall start by treating the simple but unrealistic case where an assembly of grains moves in circular Kepler orbits (in an exact inverse r^2 field or in the invariant plane of a perturbed field). We put the mass dm of the grains between the rings r and $r+dr$ equal to $dm = \rho dr$. A small embryo is orbiting in the circle r_0 with a velocity $v_0 = r_0\omega_0$. The radius of the embryo is R_{em}; its density is Θ_{em} (assumed to be uniform). We suppose that the accreted mass is immediately uniformly distributed over the surface of the embryo. (It should be observed that we assume the embryo to be a sphere but that the distribution of the grains is two-dimensional.)

As $\omega^2 r^3$ is constant, a grain at the distance $r_0 + \Delta r_{gn}$ will have the angular velocity $\omega_0 + \Delta\omega_{gn}$. If $\Delta r_{gn} \ll r_0$ we have

$$\Delta\omega_{gn} = -\frac{3\omega_0\Delta r_{gn}}{2r_0} \qquad (13.2.1)$$

It will hit the embryo at the distance Δr_{gn} from the spin axis with the relative velocity

$$u = r_0\Delta\omega_{gn} = -\tfrac{3}{2}\omega_0\Delta r_{gn} \qquad (13.2.2)$$

If the mass of the grain is m_{gn}, the angular momentum imparted to the embryo at impact is

$$\Delta C_{\tau} = m_{gn} u \Delta r_{gn} = -\tfrac{3}{2}\omega_0 \Delta r_{gn}^2 m_{gn} \qquad (13.2.3)$$

As $m_{gn} = \rho d(\Delta r_{gn})$ we find that, when all the matter in the ring $r_0 - R_{em}$ to $r_0 + R_{em}$ is accreted, the embryo has the angular momentum

$$C_{\tau} = -\frac{3\omega_0\rho}{2} \int_{-R_{em}}^{+R_{em}} \Delta r_{gn}^2 \, d(\Delta r_{gn}) = -\omega_0\rho R_{em}^3 \qquad (13.2.4)$$

and hence the spin velocity

$$\Omega_{em} = \frac{C_{\tau}}{\Xi_{em}} = -\frac{\omega_0\rho R_{em}^3}{MR_{em}^2\alpha_{\bar{z}}^2} \qquad (13.2.5)$$

As the accreted mass is $M = 2\rho R_{em}$

$$\Omega_{em} = -\frac{\omega_0}{2\alpha_{\bar{z}}^2} \qquad (13.2.6)$$

Hence the nongravitational accretion from circular grain orbits gives a *slow retrograde rotation*.

One would think that the case we have treated would be applicable at least to accretion by very small bodies. This is not the case for the following reason. It is possible to neglect the effect of gravitation on accretion only if

$$u_{\infty} \gg v_{es} \qquad (13.2.7)$$

where u_{∞} is the velocity of a grain at large distance and

$$v_{es} = \left(\frac{2GM_{em}}{R_{em}}\right)^{1/2} = \left(\frac{8\pi\Theta_{em}G}{3}\right)^{1/2} R_{em} \qquad (13.2.8)$$

Substituting eqs. (13.2.2) and (13.2.8) into eq. (13.2.7) we have

216

$$\frac{3\omega_0 \Delta r_{gn}}{2} \gg \left(\frac{8\pi\Theta_{em}G}{3}\right)^{1/2} \Delta r_{gn} \tag{13.2.9}$$

or

$$\omega_0 \gg \left(\frac{32\pi G\Theta}{27}\right)^{1/2} \tag{13.2.10}$$

Even if Θ is as small as 1 g/cm³, we have $\omega_0 \gg 0.5 \times 10^{-3}$ per sec, which is an unrealistic value.

13.3 GRAVITATIONAL ACCRETION

In the case of gravitational accretion[1] by the embryo (see chs. 7 and 12), the velocity v_{imp} of an impacting grain will equal or exceed the escape velocity v_{es} of the embryo. In case the internal velocity or relative velocity within the jet stream is negligible, we have

$$v_{imp} \approx v_{es} = \left(\frac{8\pi\Theta_{em}G}{3}\right)^{1/2} R_{em} \tag{13.3.1}$$

This is an important typical case which we shall discuss.

Equation (13.1.10) indicates how the spin of a spherical embryo ($\alpha_{\bar{z}}^2 = 0.4$) changes during accretion. If $\Delta\Omega = 0$ we have

$$\Omega_{em} = \frac{3v_{imp} \sin \psi}{2R_{em}} = \frac{\Omega_{es}3 \sin \psi}{2} \tag{13.3.2}$$

where we have introduced eq. (13.3.1) and put

$$\Omega_{es} = \left(\frac{8\pi G\Theta_{em}}{3}\right)^{1/2} = \frac{v_{es}}{R_{em}} \tag{13.3.3}$$

---

[1] The term gravitational accretion should not be confused with the gravitational instability of a gas cloud which, as shown in sec. 11.2, is not applicable to the formation of celestial bodies in the solar system, excepting the Sun.

Hence if the accretion occurs in such a way that sin ψ, or rather the weighted mean of it, remains constant, and if we put

$$Z = \tfrac{3}{2} \overline{\sin \psi} \tag{13.3.4}$$

where

$$\overline{\sin \psi} = \frac{\int dm_{gn} \sin \psi}{\int dm_{gn}} \tag{13.3.5}$$

then the spin will tend toward the value

$$\Omega_{em} = Z\Omega_{es} \tag{13.3.6}$$

This value is independent of R_{em}. If, however, after the accretion there is a density redistribution inside the body so that its relative radius of gyration changes from $(0.4)^{1/2}$ to a value α_Z, Ω_{em} will change to

$$\Omega_{em}' = \frac{0.4\Omega_{em}}{\alpha_Z^2} \tag{13.3.7}$$

Hence we see that this accretional model has a very important property: *The spin of a body produced by planetesimal accretion is independent of the size of the body* for a constant angle of incidence ψ. A model with this property explains at least in a qualitative way the *spin isochronism* (see sec. 9.7); i.e., the remarkable fact that the spin of bodies of mass ranging from 10^{18} to 10^{30} g does not show any systematic dependence on the size of the body.

Spin isochronism lends empirical support for the type of planetesimal accretion theory we are discussing. It is also a strong argument against the idea of protoplanets with properties very different from the present planets, and it is impossible to reconcile spin isochronism with the hypothesis of planet and satellite origin by gravitational collapse of a precursor cloud.

The planetesimal model used above is too simplified to be applicable. We shall therefore discuss two other more realistic models which also account for the similarity of spins among accreted bodies.

13.4 GIULI'S THEORY OF ACCRETION

In order to find the numerical value of Ω_{em} we must calculate Z. As stated above, we confine ourselves to a two-dimensional model. The problem is a many-body problem and can only be solved by using computers. This has been done by Giuli (1968a,b). He starts from the general planetesimal picture of accretion and assumes that the embryo of a planet (e.g., the Earth) orbits in a circle around the Sun. At the same time there is a uniform distribution of grains which when at large distance from the Earth

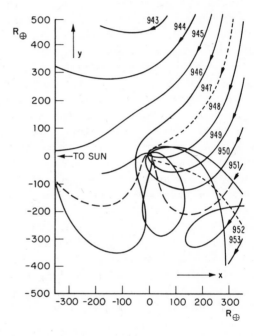

FIGURE 13.4.1—Planetesimal orbits in a rotating coordinate system x,y, in Earth radii, centered on the Earth (according to Dole). Small bodies (planetesimals) which originally move in circular orbits around the Sun with orbital radii greater than 1 AU will gradually be overtaken by the Earth. In a rotating coordinate system which fixes the Earth at the origin and the Sun on the abscissa to the left at a distance of 1 AU (thus assuming the Earth has a circular orbit), the particles will approach the Earth and will move in the complicated trajectories depicted in the figure. If their heliocentric orbital radii fall within seven ranges of values ("bands") all very close to the dashed line, they will hit the Earth. Otherwise, they will depart from the neighborhood of the Earth and return to heliocentric (but noncircular) orbits. Seven similar bands exist for particles with initial orbital radii less than 1 AU. (From Dole, 1962.)

move in Kepler orbits around the Sun. When a grain comes into the neighborhood of the embryo, it is attracted gravitationally. If it hits the embryo, it is assumed to stick. The mass of the embryo will increase, and at the same time the grain transfers angular momentum to the embryo. The ratio between angular momentum and mass determines the spin of the embryo.

Dole (1962) has demonstrated that in order to hit an embryo moving in a circular orbit around the Sun the grains must be moving within certain "bands," defined in terms of their orbital elements. He calculates these for the case of grains which, before approaching the Earth, move in circular orbits around the Sun (see fig. 13.4.1). Giuli has made similar calculations which also include grains moving in eccentric orbits. (Like Dole, he restricts his calculations to the case of particles moving in the orbital plane of the embryo.) Further, he has calculated the spin which a growing planet acquires when it accumulates mass in this way.

He finds that a planet capturing exclusively those grains moving in circular orbits will acquire a *retrograde* rotation. However, if accretion takes place also from eccentric orbits, the rotation will be *prograde* (assuming equal grain density in the different orbits). This result is essentially due to a kind of resonance effect that makes accretion from certain eccentric orbits very efficient. In the case of the accreting Earth, such orbits are ellipses with semimajor axes *a* greater than 1 AU which at perihelion graze the planet's orbit in such a way that the grain moves with almost the same velocity as the Earth. There is also a class of orbits with $a < 1$ AU, the aphelion of which gives a similar effect. In both cases a sort of focusing occurs in such a way that the embryo receives a pronounced prograde spin.

Consider a coordinate system *xy* which has its origin at the center of the Earth. The Sun is at a great distance on the $-x$ axis. The coordinate system rotates with the period of 1 yr. Using 1 AU as unit length and 1 yr$/\omega\pi$ as time unit, the equations of motion for particles moving in Kepler orbits close to the Earth can be written approximately:

$$\frac{d^2y}{dt^2} = -\frac{M_\oplus x}{M_\odot r^3} + X \tag{13.4.1}$$

$$\frac{d^2x}{dt_2} = -\frac{M_\oplus y}{M_\odot r} + Y \tag{13.4.2}$$

$$X = 2\frac{dy}{dt} + 3x \tag{13.4.3}$$

$$Y = -2\frac{dx}{dt} \tag{13.4.4}$$

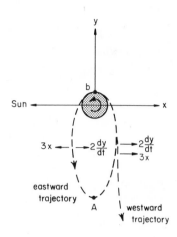

FIGURE 13.4.2.—Particles shot out tangentially to the east with approximately the escape velocity from the point b on the Earth's equator (at 0600 hrs local time) will move in an ellipse with apogee at A. The motion is disturbed only minimally by the Coriolis force ($2dy/dt$) and by the tidal effect from the Sun ($3x$) because these forces are anti-parallel. Particles shot out tangentially to the west under the same conditions experience parallel Coriolis and solar gravitational forces which deflect the trajectory from the elliptic orbit. (From Alfvén and Arrhenius, 1970b.)

The rotation of the coordinate system introduces the Coriolis force ($2dy/dt$), ($2dx/dt$) and the inhomogeneity of the solar gravitation, the force ($3x$, 0). These forces together disturb the ordinary Kepler motion around the planet. Capture is most efficient for particles moving through space with approximately the same speed as the Earth. These particles will hit the Earth at approximately the escape velocity v_{es}. We can discuss their orbits under the combined gravitation of the Earth and the Sun in the following qualitative way. (See fig. 13.4.2.)

Let us reverse time and shoot out particles from the Earth. In case a particle is shot out from the 6-hr point of the Earth ($x = 0$, $y = R_\oplus$) in the eastward direction with slightly less than the escape velocity, it will move in an ellipse out in the $-y$ direction toward its apogee A. The Coriolis force $2dy/dt$ and the solar gravitation gradient $3x$ will act in opposite directions so as to minimize the net disturbance. On the other hand, on a particle shot out in the westward direction from the 6-hr point the two forces will add in such a way as to deflect it from the ellipse far out from the Earth's gravitational field, where it will continue with a very low velocity.

Reversing the direction of motion we find that particles from outside can penetrate into the Earth's field in such a way that they hit the 6-hr point of the Earth's equator from the west but not from the east. Hence the particles form a sort of a jet which gives a prograde spin.

Similarly, particles moving inside the Earth's orbit can hit the 18-hr point only from the west, and they also give a prograde momentum.

Thus we have an efficient capture mechanism for two jets both giving prograde rotations (see fig. 13.4.3). They derive from particles moving in the solar field with about $a = 1.04$ AU and $a = 0.96$ AU and an eccentricity

FIGURE 13.4.3.—Planetesimals originally moving in slightly eccentric Kepler ellipses in
the solar field may hit the Earth in two jets,
both giving prograde rotation.

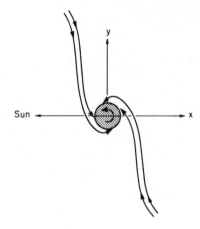

of 0.03. Most other particles hit in such a way that on the average they give a retrograde momentum.

Applied to the Earth, the net effect of the process is, according to Giuli, a prograde spin with a period of 15 hr, a value which is of the correct order of magnitude but larger by a factor of two or three than the Earth's spin period before the capture of the Moon (5 or 6 hr). Giuli finds that a body with the radius $0.1R_\oplus$ and the same density will acquire the same period. It is likely (although not proven mathematically) that the spin period is proportional to $\Theta^{-1/2}$ (Θ = density of the body, assumed to be homogeneous). The value of $\tau\Theta^{1/2}$ which is obtained in this way is

$$\tau\Theta^{1/2} = 35 \ \frac{\text{hr } g^{1/2}}{\text{cm}^{3/2}} \qquad (13.4.5)$$

This value is larger by a factor of about three than the average for all planets, including asteroids, which are not affected by tidal braking.

Giuli's calculations are based on the simplest possible planetesimal model, namely, that an embryo grows by accretion of those grains which hit it; collisions between the grains, for example, are not taken into account. It is highly satisfactory that this simple model gives the correct order of magnitude for the spin. It is reasonable to interpret this agreement as strong support for the theory of planetesimal accretion.

It should be mentioned that, if for some reason a planet accretes mainly from grains moving in orbits with small eccentricities, it should have a retrograde rotation. This means that if there is some reason to assume that Venus has accreted in this way, its retrograde rotation might be explained. We shall discuss this in sec. 13.6.3.

13.5 STATISTICAL THEORY OF ACCRETION

In Giuli's theory it is assumed

(1) That each planetesimal accreted by an embryo has a mass that is infinitely small compared to the mass of the embryo, and

(2) That planetesimals hit randomly.

There is no reason to doubt the second assumption, but whether the first one is correct depends on the type of accretion. As we have seen in ch. 12, there are three different cases: Runaway accretion may be early, late, or delayed. We shall discuss these three cases in sec. 13.6.1.

13.5.1 Accretion Prior to Runaway Accretion

When planetesimals are accreting prior to runaway accretion their size distribution will no doubt be a continuous function, probably of the kind we find among the asteroids. The body we call the "embryo" is not fundamentally different from the other grains: it is *primus inter pares*. Hence, the largest planetesimals it is accreting are, although by definition smaller, not necessarily very much smaller than the embryo. If a planetesimal with a mass $m = \gamma M_{em}$ hits the embryo, one single planetesimal with a reasonably large γ can change the state of rotation drastically. Take as an extreme case that the planetesimal hits the embryo tangentially with the escape velocity. In fact it will give the embryo an additional angular velocity

$$\Omega_{em} = Z'\Omega_{es}$$ (13.5.1)

where

$$Z' = \frac{m}{M_{em}\alpha_{\bar{z}}^2}$$ (13.5.2)

and $\alpha_{\bar{z}}^2$ typically equals 0.33 (see table 2.1.1). The Giuli process gives to an order of magnitude $Z = 0.1$. In order to make Z' comparable we need only have $\gamma = m/M_{em} = 3$ percent.

Hence, even one planetesimal with only a few percent of the mass of the embryo can under favorable conditions completely change the state of rotation of the embryo.

Levin and Safronov (1960), Safronov (1958 and 1960), and Safronov and Zvjagina (1969) on one hand, and Marcus (1967) on the other, have considered the question of the relative sizes of bodies that collide randomly. Their results are not in quantitative agreement with each other, but they all show that statistical accretion should give a spin that on the average is of the same absolute magnitude as in Giuli's case, but directed at random.

Whereas an accretion from small grains (such as Giuli's mechanism) gives spin axes perpendicular to the orbital plane, the random accretion of large planetesimals gives a random distribution of spin axes. It is possible that this mechanism of statistical accretion is applicable to the spin of asteroids. However, for the small asteroids the escape velocity is very small and our models may meet difficulties because the approach velocities must be correspondingly small. It is possible that such low impact velocities are reconcilable with jet-stream accretion, but the problem no doubt needs further clarification.

13.6 JET-STREAM ACCRETION AND PLANETARY SPINS

We have found (ch. 12) that after exhaustion of the parent jet stream by runaway accretion an embryo accretes planetesimals that are very small. This means that the premises of Giuli's theory are applicable. Before and during the runaway phase, however, the embryo accretes planetesimals, some of which are of a size comparable to that of the embryo. Hence, a random spin vector due to the statistical arrival of large planetesimals is superimposed upon the spin vector which in the Giuli case is perpendicular to the orbital plane. The absolute value of the random vector is probably on the average about the same as the regular spin vector (see fig. 13.6.1).

13.6.1 Early, Late, and Delayed Runaway Accretion; Spin Inclination

Combining the above conclusions with the results on accretion in jet streams from ch. 12, we first discuss the cases involving an early runaway phase (Jupiter, Earth, Venus, and Mercury). Random spin is received by the growing embryo only before and during runaway accretion while it adds the first small part, typically 10 percent of its mass and 3 percent of its spin. Hence during most of the accretion the condition of infinitely small grains is satisfied, which means that the inclination of the equatorial plane towards the orbital plane should be small. This is indeed what is found for the case of the spin axis of Jupiter, the inclination of which is only 3°. Venus has a retrograde spin, for reasons that will be discussed in sec. 13.6.3, but the inclination of the axis of spin is only $i_r = 1°$ ($= 180° - 179°$). In the case of the Earth, we should use the spin before the capture of the Moon.

We do not know this value with certainty, but different theories for the evolution of the Earth-Moon system give low inclination values. Gerstenkorn (1969), for example, sets $i_\tau = 3°$. The inclination of Mercury's spin may be influenced by its resonance capture.

The bodies which had a late runaway accretion (Saturn, Mars, and the Moon) have typically obtained 75 percent of their mass by accretion of a small number of bodies of relatively large size (statistical accretion). Only the last 25 percent of mass is accreted from small bodies (Giuli accretion). However, the Giuli accretion influences the spin more decisively because, due to the larger radius of the embryo, impacting planetesimals impart more spin angular momentum. Hence we would expect a superimposed random vector from statistical accretion of about one-half the regular vector from Giuli accretion. We find that both for Mars and for Saturn the spin axes inclinations are substantial (25° and 26°). We know nothing about the primeval spin of the Moon.

During a delayed accretion the entire process takes place by collision of large bodies (statistical accretion), so in this case we should have a large random spin vector. This applies to Uranus with $i_\tau = 98°$ and Neptune with $i_\tau = 29°$, which indeed have the largest spin inclinations among all planets, although the difference between Neptune and Saturn is not large (see fig. 13.6.1).

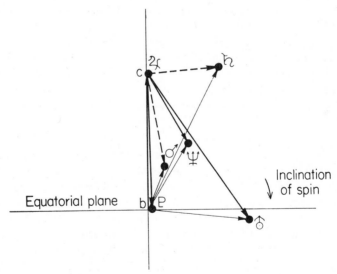

FIGURE 13.6.1.—*Spin vectors of the planets* are represented by the light lines (length $\alpha_{\bar{z}}^2 \Omega / \Theta^{1/2}$). The Giuli-type accretion gives a vector bc equal to Jupiter's spin. The statistical accretion should give the vectors from c to the dots representing the different planets. Dashed lines represent "late runaway accretion," the heavy lines, "delayed runaway accretion."

The number of planets we can apply our discussion to is only half a dozen. Our accretion mechanism involves a statistical element, but our sample is of course too small for any statistical analysis. However, we have found that the inclinations are smallest in cases where we should expect low values, and highest in the case of Uranus, where we should expect the random factor to dominate. This may be as far as it is possible to carry the analysis.

13.6.2 Spin Period

Concerning the absolute value of the spin vector the problem is less clear. In case embryos are accreting by the mechanism outlined in sec. 13.3, we should expect $\tau\Theta^{1/2}$ to be constant. The model implies that the accreted body is homogeneous. If a differentiation takes place *after* the accretion, τ should change as $\alpha_{\bar{z}}^2/0.4$, so that the relevant quantity becomes $\tau\Theta^{1/2}/\alpha_{\bar{z}}^2$. However, it is possible that the accreting embryo becomes inhomogeneous even at an early stage. Moreover the Giuli model is more complicated than the model of Sec. 13.3. Further, Giuli has only treated the two-dimensional case, and we have no theory for three-dimensional accretion. We should also observe that the conditions in a jet stream may be different from what has been assumed in the model of the theory of spin. This means that we must make much more sophisticated theoretical calculations before a quantitative comparison with observations can be made. We shall here confine ourselves to the following remarks:

(1) Assuming $\tau\Theta^{1/2}/\alpha_{\bar{z}}^2$ to have the same value for the primitive Earth as the present value for Jupiter, we find $\tau_{\oplus} = 6$ hr. This is higher than the Gerstenkorn value (sec. 13.6.1) but not in conflict with any observational data. It would speak in favor of a lunar capture in a polar or prograde orbit (see ch. 24).

(2) The period of Mars, which only by coincidence is similar to the period of the Earth today, is longer than expected by perhaps a factor of three. It may be futile to look for an explanation for this, other than the statistical character of the largest part of the Martian accretion history. In fact, accepting the Jovian accretion as normal for a nonrandom accretion, the vector from Jupiter to the other planets in fig. 13.6.1 should represent the random contribution. We see that the vector Jupiter-Mars is only about half the vector Jupiter-Uranus. In view of the fact that the entire Uranian accretion but only about half the Martian accretion is to be considered random, we have no reason to classify the slow Martian rotation as abnormal.

The same reasoning applies to the extremely slow rotation of Pluto ($\sim$6 days).

13.6.3 The Retrograde Rotation of Venus

As Giuli has shown, accretion exclusively from grains in circular orbits gives a retrograde spin, whereas, if grains in eccentric orbits are also accreted, the spin may become prograde. If we can show that the planetesimals from which Venus accreted moved in more circular orbits than the bodies from which the other planets accreted we may solve the problem of the anomalous rotation of Venus. A suggestion along these lines has recently been made by Ip (1974a).

14

RELATIONS BETWEEN COMETS
AND METEOROIDS

14.1 BASIC PROBLEMS

The properties of the comet-meteoroid population have been described in ch. 4. It was pointed out that the definite correlation between comets and meteor streams, as defined in sec. 4.6.2, showed that they must be genetically related. We have to consider, however, whether the meteoroids derive from comets, comets are accreted from meteor streams, or the processes are reciprocal. In fact, the basic questions to be answered are

(1) What is the physical nature of the cometary nucleus? (a) Does it invariably consist of one single monolith? Or (b) could it, in some instances, consist of a larger number of bodies and lack physical coherence?

(2) What is the genetic relationship between comets and the meteor streams with which they are associated? (a) Do the stream meteoroids invariably derive from the associated comets or (b) is the process the reverse one? Or (c) are both processes possible?

(3) Is there a net dispersion or accretion during the lifetime of a comet?

(4) What is the origin of short-period comets?

(5) What is the origin of long-period comets?

Several other questions with regard to the chemical composition of the nucleus, the mechanisms for the production of the observed radicals and ions, and the nature of the interaction between comets and solar wind are also of genetic importance.

14.2 POSITIVE AND NEGATIVE DIFFUSION; METEOR STREAMS AS JET STREAMS

The answers to all these questions are basically connected with the problem of how a swarm of particles in similar orbits will develop. There has long been a general belief that collisions (and other types of interaction) between such particles will result in dispersion. As we have seen in ch. 6, this is correct only under the assumption that the collisions are elastic (or have at least a minimum of elasticity). However, an assemblage of particles in periodic orbits whose collisions are sufficiently inelastic will behave in the contrary way; i.e., pass from a dispersed to a less dispersed state (sec. 6.6).

As we do not know the collisional properties of meteoroids in space, it is impossible to decide whether the diffusion in a stream of particles is positive or negative. This cannot be clarified by the study of the present collisional properties of meteorites that have fallen down on the Earth because any loose surface material, which may control the collisional behavior of meteorite parent bodies, has been lost during the passage of the meteorites through the atmosphere.

Study of the composition and texture of meteorites (ch. 22) demonstrates, however, that most groups consist of grains that were originally free from each other or loosely attached and that the material became compacted and indurated in the course of their evolution, so that durable pieces could survive travel to Earth.

Luminosity and deceleration studies of stream meteoroids in the Earth's atmosphere lead to the conclusion that the majority of these have mean bulk densities under 1.0 g/cm^3, independent of mass (Verniani, 1967, 1973). This suggests that they are fluffy and probably have low elasticities, as further discussed in Sec. 7.4.

The first alternative (positive diffusion) leads necessarily to the more generally accepted theory of the comet-meteor stream complex (Kresák, 1968) which supposes that stream meteoroids derive from a monolithic block of ice and dust (Whipple's "icy conglomerate") and must diffuse both along and normal to the stream to be ultimately dispersed into interplanetary space (sporadic meteors). Such a theory bypasses the question of identifying a physically acceptable mechanism by which the monolithic cometary nucleus would have formed initially.

According to the second alternative (negative diffusion), a meteor stream can be kept together or contract under the condition that the self-focusing effect exceeds the disruptive effects due to planetary perturbations and solar radiation (Poynting-Robertson effect, etc.). As shown by Mendis (1973) and by Ip and Mendis (1974), this seems likely to occur under very general conditions. Hence a meteor stream may behave as a typical jet stream discussed in ch. 6. Their analysis also shows that the strong focusing by inelastic collision may be preceded by a transient phase of expansion of the stream. Due to its very large accretion cross section, a meteor stream may also be able to collect a significant amount of interplanetary dust and gas (Mendis, 1973).

14.3 ACCRETIONAL MECHANISM IN METEOR STREAMS

As the density in present-day meteor streams is much smaller than that in the jet streams discussed in ch. 12, it is possible that the accretional mechanism is of a somewhat different type.

Trulsen (1971) has shown that planetary perturbations of meteor streams, rather than producing a general disruption, may cause density waves that build up slowly. If a number of such waves are forming, very large density increases can be caused statistically at some points, leading to the formation of a dense cloud of particles. These particles would ultimately agglomerate into a number of large aggregates which may accrete to form one body. This view then leads not to a model with a singular state of the cometary nucleus (as Whipple's "icy conglomerate" or Lyttleton's "sand bank"), but rather to a hierarchy of states ranging from a dispersed cloud of small particles to a single nucleus, with the latter the most likely final stable state.

Therefore, although many comets possibly do have a single central nucleus, perhaps of the Whipple type, it seems likely that there are comets with more than one nucleus or consisting of a more or less loose swarm of bodies of varying size. Indeed, the very dusty, gas-deficient comets may belong to the latter type. There are several instances of observation of comets with multiple nuclei (Richter, 1963, p. 152; Lyttleton, 1953; Mrkos, 1972). Whether these are the remnants of a single nucleus or merely the precursors of one is an open question. The latter alternative is consistent with accretion theory which explains how bodies such as monolithic cometary nuclei, asteroids, satellites, and planets can form in the first place.

14.4 OBSERVATIONS OF COMET FORMATION IN A METEOR STREAM

The formation of comets in meteor streams is supported by a number of observations. The comet P/Temple-Tuttle ($T \approx 33.2$ yr) was first recorded as a diffuse but bright object as recently as 1866 (Lovell, 1954), although the associated Leonid meteor stream was known for centuries earlier. Comet P/Swift-Tuttle ($T \approx 120$ yr) was bright enough on its first apparition to be easily seen with the naked eye, being a second-magnitude object at its brightest (Vsekhesviatsky, 1958). Although this spectacular short-period comet appeared as such for the first time only as late as 1862, its associated meteor stream, the Perseids, has been observed for over 12 centuries (Lovell, 1954). Under these circumstances it seemed reasonable to contemporary scientists to question the assumption that meteor streams always form from comets and to consider the possibility that these new comets were forming from the ancient meteor streams (Nordenskiöld, 1883, p. 155).

Several reputable observers in the past claimed to have actually witnessed the formation of cometary nuclei; see review in Lyttleton (1953). More recently, Mrkos (1972) reported that in the most recent apparition of P/Honda-Mrkos-Pajdusakova no nucleus was originally detectable although the comet came very close to Earth (<0.3 AU) and hence could be observed in detail. As the comet progressed in its orbit away from the Earth, not just one center of light but several appeared. Mrkos states that similar behavior also has been observed in earlier apparitions of this comet, which is probably also associated with a meteor stream (α Capricornids).

14.5 LONG- AND SHORT-PERIOD COMETS

The origin of long-period comets will later be discussed in the same general context as the formation of planets (ch. 19); the long-period comets are thus assumed to derive from assemblages of planetesimals in similar orbits.

As for the origin of short-period comets, the commonly accepted view has been that they derive from long-period comets that pass near one of the massive planets (especially Jupiter) and lose energy in the process. While a single close approach to Jupiter by the observed distribution of long-period comets cannot produce the observed distribution of short-period comets (Newton, 1891; Everhart, 1969), Everhart (1972) has recently shown that such a distribution could be the cumulative result of many hundreds of passages near Jupiter by near-parabolic comets having low inclinations and initial perihelia near Jupiter's orbit.

It is, however, doubtful if Everhart's calculations can resolve the crucial problem with regard to the origin of short-period comets; namely, the large observed number of these objects. Joss (1972) has shown, on the basis of Oort's comet cloud and the injection rate of new comets from this cloud into the inner solar system, that the above calculations fail by several orders of magnitude to explain the observed number of short-period comets. Delsemme (1973), however, has shown that if one also takes into account the intermediate period distribution and looks at the number of comets reaching perihelion per unit time, this difficulty is mitigated. However, due to the large number of assumptions inherent in Delsemme's calculation, it is not entirely convincing that the difficulty has been completely removed. One can also get around this difficulty, but only at the expense of introducing a new *ad hoc* hypothesis; namely, the existence of another population of long-period comets besides the observed one. This population would be distributed in a disc close to the ecliptic with dimension $\lesssim 10^4$ AU and containing over 10^9 objects (Whipple, 1964; Axford, 1973); further discussion of this type of assumption is given by Mendis (1973).

Comets, since they exist, must obviously have previously been forming by some accretional process despite competing disruptive processes. If we assume that the same processes are operating today, and hence that comets may accrete from dispersed particles in similar orbits (meteor streams), then the crucial difficulty with regard to the observed number of short-period comets is overcome as has been shown by Trulsen (1971) and Mendis

(1973). Meteor streams, according to this view, do not necessarily only represent a sink for short-period comets as has been generally believed, but they could also form a source. It is possible that a steady state may be maintained with the average rate of formational focusing of particles into short-period comets equaling the average rate of dispersion of cometary material into meteor streams (Mendis, 1973).

14.6 INFERENCES ON THE NATURE OF COMETS FROM EMISSION CHARACTERISTICS

The assumption of ices as important bonding materials in cometary nuclei rests in almost all cases on indirect evidence, specifically the observation of atomic hydrogen (Lyman α emission) and hydroxyl radical in a vast cloud surrounding the comet, in some cases accompanied by observation of H_2O^+ or neutral water molecules. In addition, CH_3CN, HCN, and corresponding radicals and ions are common constituents of the cometary gas envelope. These observations can be rationalized by assuming (Delsemme, 1972; Mendis, 1973) that the cometary nuclei consist of loose agglomerates containing, in addition to silicates (observed by infrared spectrometry (Maas et al., 1970)) and also water ice with inclusions of volatile carbon and nitrogen compounds.

It has been suggested by Lal (1972b) that the Lyman α emission could be caused by solar wind hydrogen, thermalized on the particles in the dust cloud surrounding the comet. Experiments by Arrhenius and Andersen (1973) irradiating calcium aluminosilicate (anorthite) surfaces with protons in the 10-keV range resulted in a substantial ($\sim$10 percent) yield of hydroxyl ion and also hydroxyl ion complexes such as CaOH.

Observations on the lunar surface (Hapke et al., 1970; Epstein and Taylor, 1970, 1972) also demonstrate that such proton-assisted abstraction of oxygen (preferentially O^{16}) from silicates is an active process in space, resulting in a flux of OH and related species. In cometary particle streams, new silicate surfaces would relatively frequently be exposed by fracture and fusion at grain collision. The production of hydroxyl radicals and ions would in this case not be rate-limited by surface saturation to the same extent as on the Moon (for lunar soil turnover rate, see Arrhenius et al. (1972)).

These observations, although not negating the possible occurrence of water ice in cometary nuclei, point also to refractory sources of the actually observed hydrogen and hydroxyl. Solar protons as well as the products of their reaction with silicate oxygen would interact with any solid carbon and nitrogen compounds characteristic of carbonaceous chondrites to yield volatile carbon and nitrogen radicals such as observed in comets. Phenomena such as "flares," "breakups," "high-velocity jets," and nongravitational acceleration are all phenomena that fit well into a theory ascribing them to the evaporation of frozen volatiles. However, with different semantic labels the underlying observations would also seem to be interpretable as manifestations of the focusing and dispersion processes in the cometary region of the meteor stream, accompanied by solar wind interaction.

14.7 ANALOGIES BETWEEN COMETARY AND ASTEROIDAL STREAMS

The main-belt asteroid population does not interact very much with the comet-meteoroid population but some analogous phenomena seem to occur there. The reason for this is that in both cases the interaction of a large number of small bodies produce similar results.

Among the main-belt asteroids there are a number of asteroidal *jet streams* (sec. 4.3.3). Each jet stream contains a number of visual asteroids which have almost the same values of semimajor axis *a*, inclination *i*, eccentricity *e*, and longitudes of the pericenter and node, ϕ_P and ϕ_Ω, and hence move in approximately similar orbits. Figure 4.3.6 is a profile of such a jet stream showing an example of dense distribution of orbits in space, which means that relative velocities between the bodies are small.

Each one of the large number of asteroidal *families* is characterized by their similarity in *a, e,* and *i*, but, in contrast to a jet stream, ϕ_Ω and ϕ_P differ. Hence the orbits of the bodies in a family do not keep together but are spread out in space. If the bodies in a jet stream move according to celestial mechanics, unperturbed by interaction between the bodies, the secular perturbations from the planets will cause the orbits to precess at a rate that is a function of the orbital parameters, but *a, i,* and *e* will vary only within narrow limits. The spread of the parameters in a jet stream will produce random orientation of their ϕ_Ω and ϕ_P after a time of the order 10^5–10^6 yr. In analogy with the asteroidal jet streams and families, many meteor streams are well focused also in ϕ_Ω and ϕ_P, even though they may lack an observable comet, while others (more rarely) have ϕ_Ω and ϕ_P widely scattered.

The traditional view is that an asteroidal family is the product of an "exploded" asteroid or consists of the debris of a collision between two asteroids. From this point of view one would be inclined to regard a jet stream as an intermediate stage in this development of a family. The debris will first keep together, with the orbital parameters being similar for all orbits, and later be spread out with random ϕ_Ω and ϕ_P.

From a qualitative point of view such a development is quite reasonable. It is more doubtful whether it is acceptable quantitatively. A detailed analysis will be necessary before this can be decided. The profiles of a number of jet streams must be analyzed and the number of jet streams must be reconciled with the length of time they can keep together.

For reasons we have discussed in sec. 7.3.3, accretion must be the dominant process in the asteroidal belt, and it seems reasonable to regard the asteroidal jet streams as products of the general jet-stream mechanism studied in ch. 6. This means that collisions between particles will perturb their motion in such a way that the orbits become more similar. However, this presumably cannot be done by interaction between the visual asteroids alone. There is obviously no reason to believe that the asteroids which have so far been observed are all that exist. To the contrary, the mass spectrum of asteroids is very likely to extend to subvisual asteroids, of which the majority will be very much smaller; how small is not known (see ch. 7). As, in practically all mass spectra of small bodies, the smallest bodies represent the largest cross section, the collisions between the subvisual asteroids will be much more frequent than those between the visual asteroids. Hence the subvisual members of a jet stream will be most important for the exchange of momentum between the bodies in the stream. In other words, it is the collisions between the subvisual asteroids which keep an asteroidal jet stream together.

Hence a reasonable sequence of evolutionary processes in the asteroidal belt would be the following.

A large number of small grains are focused together and form jet streams, which later accrete more grains. Within each stream, the relative velocities are gradually reduced so much by collisions that accretion of larger bodies begins, and, after some time, leads to formation of visual asteroids in the jet stream. As the process proceeds, the majority of the small grains are accreted by the largest bodies, so that eventually there is not enough collisional interaction to keep the jet stream focused. Planetary perturbation will then cause the members of the stream to precess with different velocities and a family with random ϕ_Ω and ϕ_P values is produced.

Throughout this development, there are high-velocity collisions between members of different jet streams and/or asteroids that are not members of jet streams. Such collisions will produce debris that sooner or later will be incorporated in existing streams or form new jet streams. The net result may be a progressive concentration of mass into a decreasing number of large bodies.

Evolution in the asteroidal belt is obviously a very complex process with various types of resonances complicating the situation still further, and what has been proposed here is only an attempt to present a reasonable sequence. Much theoretical work and much more observational data are needed before it is possible to decide to what extent these speculations are realistic.

14.8 COMPARISON WITH THE ACCRETION OF PLANETS AND SATELLITES

We have seen that, because of the low density in meteor streams, the mechanism of planetary and satellite accretion is not applicable. One may turn the question around and ask whether we need the accretional mechanism of ch. 12 at all. Perhaps the accretion of planets and satellites may also be due to density waves.

It seems likely that density waves may have been important, especially during the initial phase of accretion of planets and satellites. Thus it is possible that the application of the theory of cometary accretion will be a useful supplement to the theory for nongravitational accretion. It is less likely that the effects of density waves would have been significant in the runaway process and in the subsequent phase of accretion. Moreover, density waves are due to planetary perturbation and should be more easily produced in highly eccentric jet streams than in circular streams. On the other hand, the accretion of the outermost planets (delayed runaway accretion) implies jet streams of very low densities. It is possible that the cometary accretion mechanism may be more directly applicable in that case.

PART C

Plasma and Condensation

15

PLASMA PHYSICS AND HETEGONY

15.1 SUMMARY OF PARTS A AND B AND PLAN FOR PARTS C AND D

In the preceding two parts of this monograph we have treated the most recent phases in the formation of planets and satellites. In doing so, we have adopted the *actualistic principle*. Starting from the present properties of planets and satellites, we have traced their history back in time in an attempt to find how these bodies have accreted from smaller bodies. The formation of *jet streams* is an essential intermediate stage in this sequence of hetegonic events.

Our preceding treatment has shown that the essential features of the present structure of the solar system can be understood if an original population of grains with certain properties is postulated. In a general way we can say that

(1) The grains should have *dynamic* properties such that after accretion they form celestial bodies with the orbits and spins that we observe today (with the exception of instances where post-accretional events such as tidal interaction have played a part).

(2) The grains should have such *chemical* and *structural* properties as to explain the properties in the present small celestial bodies (comets, asteroids, meteoroids) as well as the composition of planets and satellites.

It is the purpose of this and the following chapters to investigate by what processes a population of grains with these required properties could have originated.

15.1.1 Applicability of Hydromagnetics and Plasma Physics

It is reasonable to assume that the formation of the solar system involved a gaseous nebula. The first question to answer is whether this medium could be analyzed without considering electromagnetic effects.

The criterion for justified neglect of electromagnetic effects in the treatment of a problem in gas dynamics is that the characteristic hydromagnetic parameter L is much less than unity.

$$L = \frac{Bl\sigma_E P_B^{1/2}}{c^2 \rho^{1/2}} \ll 1 \qquad (15.1.1)$$

where P_B, σ_E, and ρ are the magnetic permeability, the electrical conductivity, and the density of the medium, respectively; B is the magnetic field strength; l is the linear extent of the medium; and c is the velocity of light (Alfvén and Fälthammar, 1963, pp. 102–103). In cosmic problems involving interplanetary and interstellar phenomena L is usually of the order 10^{15}–10^{20} (table 15.1.1). In planetary ionospheres it reaches unity in the E layer. Planetary atmospheres and hydrospheres are the only domains in the universe where a nonhydromagnetic treatment of fluid dynamic problems is justified.

TABLE 15.1.1

Characteristic Quantities for Laboratory and Cosmic Plasmas

	Linear dimension l (cm)	Magnetic field strength B (G)	Density ρ (g/cm³)	Conductivity σ_E (esu)	Characteristic hydromagnetic parameter L
Laboratory experiments:					
Mercury	10	1×10^4	13.5	9.20×10^{15}	0.3
Sodium	10	1×10^4	0.93	9.37×10^{16}	10.8
Iodized gas (hydrogen)	10	1×10^3	1×10^{-10}	4.8×10^{14}	5.3×10^2
Cosmic plasmas:					
Earth's interior	2×10^8	10(?)	10	7×10^{15}	5×10^3
Sunspots	1×10^9	2×10^3	1×10^{-4}	4×10^{14}	9×10^7
Solar granulation	1×10^8	1×10^2	1×10^{-7}	7×10^{13}	2.5×10^6
Magnetic variable stars	1×10^{12}	1×10^4	1(?)	7×10^{15}	7.8×10^{10}
Interstellar space (more condensed regions)	1×10^{22}	1×10^{-5}(?)	1×10^{-24}(?)	7×10^{12}(?)	7.8×10^{20}
Interplanetary space	1×10^{13}	1×10^{-4}	1×10^{-23}	7×10^{14}(?)	2.5×10^{14}
Solar corona	1×10^{11}	1(?)	1×10^{-18}(?)	7×10^{15}(?)	7.8×10^{14}
Dark clouds	1×10^{13}	1×10^{-6}	1×10^{-20}	5×10^{12}	5.6×10^8

(From Alfvén and Fälthammar, 1963.)

In a circumstellar region such as that where our solar system was formed, partial ionization is necessarily impressed on any dilute gas not only by electromagnetic radiation from the star but also by electron collision caused by currents associated with the emplacement of matter and the transfer of angular momentum. In fact, any theory of the formation of a solar system must envisage that the formative processes necessarily released gravitational energy amounting to several thousand eV per atom. Such a large release of energy must lead to a considerable degree of ionization (unless highly improbable processes are postulated; see further ch. 23). As mentioned already in sec. 1.4.4 these theoretical arguments are supported by observations of strong magnetic fields and plasma chemistry effects in dark clouds. Hence a careful study of hydromagnetics and plasma physics is an absolute necessity for understanding the origin of the solar system.

When treating the medium out of which the solar system formed we choose to use the convenient term "plasma" instead of "partially ionized gas" also to semantically emphasize the necessity of taking magneto-hydrodynamic effects into account and to stress the generality of thermal disequilibrium between grains and gas. This term also points out the fact that much knowledge about the basic hetegonic processes can be obtained from laboratory plasma research and, for example, magnetospheric research; these important sources of validation have not been used in other studies of the evolution of the solar system.

The degree of ionization in hetegonic plasmas and in cosmic plasmas in general may vary over a wide range, depending on the specific process considered. It is of importance down to very low values; in a plasma of solar photospheric composition with a degree of ionization as low as 10^{-4}, for example, the major part of the condensable components is still largely ionized.

Thus the model we are trying to construct is essentially a model of a plasma that produces grains with the dynamic and chemical properties mentioned above. (The primeval plasma may have also contained preexisting grains (sec. 5.3).)

More specifically, in the present chapter we analyze the general requirements of a hetegonic model for the production of grains, whereas in chs. 16 and 17 we suggest a specific model derived essentially on the basis of the dynamics and properties of cosmic plasmas. This model is applied to interplanetary and transplanetary condensation in chs. 18 and 19.

In comparison to parts A and B, the treatment in this and following parts is necessarily more hypothetical and speculative. There are two reasons for this:

(1) We go further back in time.

(2) Plasma physics, which is essential to any realistic discussion of processes in space and hence also to the discussion of the formation of grains,

is a much more complicated and less well developed field than is celestial mechanics, which was the basis of parts A and B.

One of our problems then is how we should proceed in order to reduce the hypothetical character of our analysis as much as possible. This requires first a clarification of what is actually known in cosmic plasma physics and also where the major uncertainties lie (secs. 15.2 and 15.3).

15.2 RELATION BETWEEN EXPERIMENTAL AND THEORETICAL PLASMA PHYSICS

Because plasma physics is essential to the understanding of the early phase of evolution of the solar system, we give here a brief survey of its present state. Plasma physics started along two parallel lines, one mainly empirical and one mainly theoretical. The investigations in the field that was called "electrical discharges in gases," now more than a hundred years old, was to a high degree experimental and phenomenological. Only very slowly did it reach some degree of theoretical sophistication. Most theoretical physicists looked down on this complicated and awkward field in which plasma exhibited striations and double layers, the electron distribution was non-Maxwellian, and there were many kinds of oscillations and instabilities. In short, it was a field that was not at all suited for mathematically elegant theories.

On the other hand, it was thought that with a limited amount of work, the highly developed field of kinetic theory of ordinary gases could be extended to include ionized gases. The theories that thus emerged were mathematically elegant and claimed to derive all the properties of a plasma from first principles. The proponents of these theories had very little contact with experimental plasma physics, and all the poorly understood phenomena that had been observed in the study of discharges in gases were simply neglected.

In cosmic plasma physics, the modern experimental approach was initiated by Birkeland (1908), who was the first to try to bring together what is now known as laboratory plasma physics and cosmic plasma physics. Birkeland observed aurorae and magnetic storms in nature and tried to understand them through his famous terrella experiment. He found that when his terrella was immersed in a plasma, luminous rings were produced around the poles (under certain conditions). Birkeland identified these rings with the auroral zones. As we know today, this was essentially correct. Further, he constructed a model of the polar magnetic storms supposing that the auroral electrojet was closed through vertical currents (along the magnetic field lines). This idea also is essentially correct. Hence, although Birkeland could not know very much about the complicated structure of the magnetosphere, research today follows essentially Birkeland's lines, supplemented, of course, with space measurements; see Dessler (1968), Boström (1968; 1974), Cloutier (1971), and Fälthammar (1974).

Unfortunately, the progress along these lines did not proceed uninterrupted. Theories about plasmas, at that time called ionized gases, were developed without any contact with the laboratory plasma work. In spite of this, the belief in such theories was so strong that they were applied directly to space. One of the results was the Chapman-Ferraro theory, which soon became accepted to such an extent that Birkeland's approach was almost completely forgotten, and for 30 or 40 years it was seldom even mentioned in textbooks and surveys. All attempts to revive and develop it were neglected. Similarly, the Chapman-Vestine current system, according to which magnetic storms were produced by currents flowing exclusively in the ionosphere, took the place of Birkeland's three-dimensional system.

The dominance of this experimentally unsupported theoretical approach lasted as long as a confrontation with reality could be avoided. Such a confrontation was ultimately brought about by the conclusion from the theoretical approach that plasmas could easily be confined in magnetic fields and heated to such temperatures as to make thermonuclear release of energy possible. When attempts were made to construct thermonuclear reactors the result was catastrophic. Although the theories were generally accepted, the plasma itself refused to behave accordingly. Instead, it displayed a large number of important effects that were not included in the theory. It was slowly realized that new theories had to be constructed, but this time in close contact with experiments.

This "thermonuclear crisis" did not affect cosmic plasma physics very much. The development of theories could continue in this part of the field since they dealt largely with phenomena in regions of space where no real verification was possible. The fact that the basis of several of these theories had been proven to be false in the laboratory had little effect; this fact was either ignored or met with the arguments that failure in the laboratory would not necessarily imply failure in space.

The second confrontation came when space missions made the magnetosphere and interplanetary space accessible to physical instruments. The first results were interpreted in terms of the generally accepted theories or new theories were built up on the same basis. However, when the observational technique became more advanced it became obvious that these theories were not applicable. The plasma in space was just as complicated as laboratory plasmas. Today, in reality, very little is left of the Chapman-Ferraro theory and nothing of the Chapman-Vestine current system (although there are still many scientists who support them). Many theories that have been built on a similar basis are likely to share their fate.

15.3 THE FIRST AND SECOND APPROACH TO
COSMIC PLASMA PHYSICS

15.3.1 General Considerations

As a result of new factual knowledge, the "first approach" has been proven to describe only the properties of the "pseudo-plasma," a fictitious medium, which has rather little to do with real plasma. Hence we must now take a "second approach" (Alfvén, 1968). The characteristics of the two approaches are summarized in table 15.3.1.

15.3.2 Pseudo-Plasma Versus Real Plasma

The basic difference between the first and second approaches is to some extent illustrated by the terms *ionized gas* and *plasma* which, although

TABLE 15.3.1
Cosmic Electrodynamics

First approach (pseudo-plasma)	Second approach (real plasma)
Homogeneous models	Space plasmas often have a complicated inhomogeneous structure
Conductivity $\sigma_E = \infty$	σ_E depends on current and often suddenly vanishes
Electric field $E_{||}$ along magnetic field $= 0$	$E_{||}$ often $\neq 0$
Magnetic field lines are "frozen-in" and "move" with the plasma	Frozen-in picture is often completely misleading
Electrostatic double layers are neglected	Electrostatic double layers are of decisive importance in low-density plasma
Instabilities are neglected	Many plasma configurations are unrealistic because they are unstable
Electromagnetic conditions are illustrated by magnetic field line pictures	It is equally important to draw the current lines and discuss the electric circuit
Filamentary structures and current sheets are neglected or treated inadequately	Currents produce filaments or flow in thin sheets
Maxwellian velocity distribution	Non-Maxwellian effects are often decisive. Cosmic plasmas have a tendency to produce high-energy particles
Theories are mathematically elegant and very "well developed"	Theories are not very well developed and are partly phenomenological

(From Alfvén and Arrhenius, 1973.)

in reality synonymous, convey different general notions. The first term gives an impression of a medium that is basically similar to a gas, especially the atmospheric gas we are most familiar with. In contrast to this, a plasma, particularly a fully ionized magnetized plasma, is a medium with basically different properties: Typically it is strongly inhomogeneous and consists of a network of filaments produced by line currents and surfaces of discontinuity. These are sometimes due to current sheaths and, sometimes, to electrostatic double layers.

If we observe an aurora in the night sky we get a conspicuous and spectacular demonstration of the difference between *gas* and *plasma* behavior. Faint aurorae are often diffuse and spread over large areas. They fit reasonably well into the picture of an *ionized gas*. The degree of ionization is so low that the medium still has some of the physical properties of a gas that is homogeneous over large volumes. However, in certain other cases (e.g., when the auroral intensity increases), the aurora becomes highly inhomogeneous, consisting of a multitude of rays, thin arcs, and draperies a conspicuous illustration of the basic properties of most magnetized plasmas.

In the solar atmosphere the border between the photosphere and the chromosphere marks a transition similar to that between the two auroral states. The photosphere can be approximated as a homogeneous medium, at least to some extent, but in the chromosphere and upwards we have a typical plasma, a basic property of which is inhomogeneity manifest in filaments, streamers, and flares. To describe the chromosphere by means of homogeneous models and according to the pseudo-plasma theories is a fundamental mistake that has often led to conclusions and conjectures that are totally divorced from reality.

15.3.3 Some Laboratory Results Relevant to Cosmic Physics

Following Birkeland, the first laboratory experiments with reference to cosmic physics had the character of *scale-model experiments* (Malmfors, 1945; Block, 1955, 1956, 1967; Danielsson and Lindberg, 1964, 1965; Schindler, 1969; Podgorny and Sagdeev, 1970; Ohyabu and Kawashima, 1972; Fälthammar, 1974; and Boström, 1974). Such investigations demonstrated, however, that no real scaling of cosmic phenomena down to laboratory size is possible, partly because of the large number of parameters involved which obey different scaling laws. Hence, laboratory experiments should aim at clarifying a number of basic phenomena of importance in cosmic physics rather than trying to reproduce a scaled-down version of the cosmic example. There is now a trend to shift from *configuration simulation* to *process simulation*.

Laboratory experiments have already demonstrated the existence of a number of such basic phenomena which had been neglected earlier, particularly the following:

(1) Quite generally a magnetized plasma exhibits a large number of *instabilities*. Lehnert (1967a) lists 32 different types, but there seem to be quite a few more.

(2) A plasma has a tendency to produce *electrostatic double layers* in which there are strong localized electric fields. Such layers may be stable, but often they produce oscillations. The phenomenon is basically independent of magnetic fields. If a magnetic field is present, the double layer *cuts* the *frozen-in* field lines. A survey of the laboratory results and their application to cosmic phenomena (especially in the ionosphere) has been given by Block (1972) and by Fälthammar (1974).

(3) If a current flows through an electrostatic double layer (which is often produced by the current itself), *the layer may cut off the current.* This means that the voltage over the double layer may reach any value necessary to break the circuit (in the laboratory, say 10^5 or 10^6 V; in the magnetosphere, 10^4–10^5 V; in solar flares, even 10^{10} V). The plasma "explodes," and a high-vacuum region is produced (Carlqvist, 1969; Babic et al., 1971; Torvén, 1972; Boström, 1974) (see also fig. 15.3.1).

(4) Currents parallel to a magnetic field (or still more in absence of magnetic fields) have a tendency to *pinch*; i.e., to *concentrate into filaments* and not flow homogeneously (Alfvén and Fälthammar, 1963,

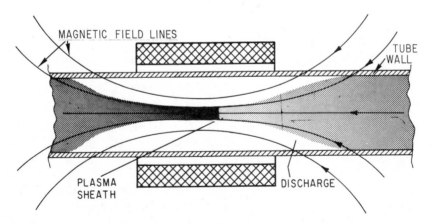

FIGURE 15.3.1.—Electrostatic double layers or sheaths are often produced in a plasma. The figure shows an electrostatic discontinuity produced spontaneously. The only function of the magnetic field is to keep the discharge away from the walls in order to ensure that the observed phenomena are not due to wall effects. Over the double layer a voltage drop is produced which sometimes suddenly becames large ($\sim 10^5$ V) and may disrupt the discharge.

FIGURE 15.3.2.—Simple model of a filamentary current structure in a low-density plasma. Currents flow parallel to the magnetic field. The lines in the figure represent both current paths and magnetic field lines. The magnetic field derives partly from an external axial field and partly from the toroidal field produced by the current itself (see Alfvén and Fälthammar, 1963). The current is strongest at the axis and becomes weaker further away from the axis as depicted by the decreasing thickness of the lines.

p. 193) (see also fig. 15.3.2). This is one of the reasons why cosmic plasmas so often exhibit filamentary structures. The beautiful space experiments by Lüst and his group (see Haerendel and Lüst, 1970) are illustrative in this connection (although not yet fully interpreted).

(5) The inevitable conclusion from phenomena (1) through (4) above is that *homogeneous models are often inapplicable*. Striation in the positive column of a glow discharge and filamentary structures (arc and discharge lightning at atmospheric pressure, auroral rays, coronal streamers, prominences, etc.) are typical examples of inhomogeneities. Nature does not always have a *horror vacui* but sometimes a *horror homogeneitatis* resulting in an *amor vacui*. For instance, a magnetized plasma has a tendency to separate into high-density regions such as prominences and coronal streamers and low-density "vacuum" regions; e.g., the surrounding corona.

(6) If the relative velocity between a magnetized plasma and a non-ionized gas surpasses a certain critical velocity, v_{crit}, obtained by equating the kinetic energy $\frac{1}{2}m_a v_{crit}^2$ to the ionization energy eV_{Ion} (V_{Ion}=ionization voltage, m_a=atomic mass), so that

$$v_{crit} = \left(\frac{2eV_{Ion}}{m_a}\right)^{1/2} \tag{15.3.1}$$

the interaction becomes very strong and leads to a rapid ionization of the neutral gas. The phenomenon is of importance in many thermonuclear experiments as well as in space, and we discuss it in detail in ch. 21.

(7) The *transition* between a fully ionized plasma and a partially ionized plasma, and vice versa, is often *discontinuous* (Lehnert, 1970b). When the input energy to the plasma increases gradually, the degree of ionization jumps suddenly from a fraction of 1 percent to full ionization. Under certain conditions, the border between a fully ionized and a weakly ionized plasma is very sharp.

(8) *Flux amplification:* If the toroidal magnetization in an experimentally produced plasma ring exceeds the poloidal magnetization, an instability is produced by which the poloidal magnetization increases at the expense of toroidal magnetization (Lindberg et al., 1960; Lindberg and Jacobsen, 1964). This phenomenon may be of basic importance for the understanding of how cosmic magnetic fields are produced (Alfvén, 1961; Alfvén and Lindberg, 1974) (see also fig. 15.3.3).

(9) When a plasma moving parallel to a magnetic field reaches a point

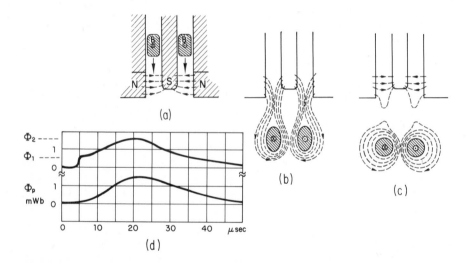

FIGURE 15.3.3.—Geometry of the Lindberg plasma ring experiment. (a) Before leaving the gun, the plasma has a toroidal magnetization *B*. It is shot through the radial field *N—S*. (b) On leaving the gun, the plasma ring pulls out the lines of force of the static magnetic field. (c) Plasma ring with captured poloidal field. If the toroidal magnetic energy is too large, a part of it is transferred to poloidal magnetic energy (through kink instability of the current). (d) The poloidal magnetic flux Φ_p during the above experiment. The upper curve shows how the ring, when shot out from the gun, first acquires a poloidal flux Φ_1. An instability of the ring later transforms toroidal energy into poloidal energy thus increasing the flux from Φ_1 to Φ_2. The upper and lower curves represent the flux measured by two loops at 15 and 30 cm distance from the gun, respectively.

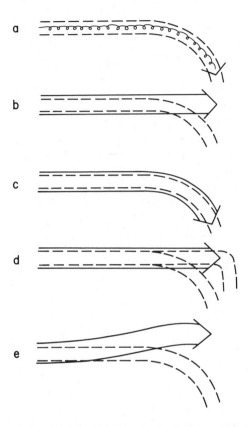

FIGURE 15.3.4.—(a) In a magnetic field which has a downward bend,
charged particles shot parallel to the field will follow the bend. If
instead a plasma beam is shot, one would expect either that it (b)
produces an electric polarization so that it can continue along a
straight line, (c) follows the bend as in (a), or (d) continues to move
straight forward bringing the "frozen-in" field lines with it. (e) In the
quoted experiment the plasma does not obey any of these theories;
instead, the plasma bends in the opposite direction to that of the
magnetic field. In hindsight, this is easily understood as being due to
an electric field transmitted backward by fast electrons (Lindberg and
Kristoferson, 1971.)

where the field lines bend, a laboratory plasma may *deviate in the opposite
direction* to the bend of the field lines (Lindberg and Kristoferson, 1971)
(see also fig. 15.3.4), contrary to what would be natural to assume in most
astrophysical theories.

(10) *Shock* and *turbulence* phenomena in low-pressure plasmas must
be studied in the laboratory before it will be possible to clarify the cosmic
phenomena (Podgorny and Sagdeev, 1970).

(11) Further physical experiments of importance include studies of *magnetic conditions at neutral points* (Bratenahl and Yeates, 1970).

Condensation of solid matter from plasma differs from condensation of a saturated or supersaturated gas at low temperature. This is partly because of the pronounced thermal disequilibrium that develops between radiation-cooled solid grains and a surrounding, optically thin, hot gas. Important effects may also arise because of the marked chemical differences between neutral and ionized components of mixed plasmas.

Cosmic plasmas contain at least 20 elements controlling the structural and major chemical properties of the solid materials that form from them. With this degree of complexity, condensation experiments in partially ionized media are a necessary complement to theoretical considerations if we wish to understand the chemical record in primordial solid materials. Such experiments are discussed by Arrhenius and Alfvén (1971) and by Meyer (1969, 1971).

Thus we find that laboratory investigations begin to demonstrate many basic plasma properties previously unknown or neglected. These properties differ drastically from those assumed in many astrophysical theories. The difference between the laboratory plasma and the plasma of these theories may in some cases be due to the dissimilarity between laboratory and space, but more often it reflects the difference between a hypothetical medium and one that has physical reality. The treatment of the former leads to speculative theories of little interest except as intellectual exercises. The latter medium is basic to the understanding of the world we live in.

The study of cosmic physics in intimate connection with laboratory physics is now well under way in the field of magnetospheric physics. A recent review of the results is given by Fälthammar (1974). Of special interest are the investigations by Boström (1974), which show that substantial voltage drops may occur along the geomagnetic field lines in the lower magnetosphere, so that the ionosphere is decoupled from the magnetosphere. These effects are relevant to understanding the concept of partial corotation, which is introduced in ch. 17.

15.4 STRATEGY OF ANALYSIS OF HETEGONIC PLASMAS

What has been said in the preceding section makes it evident that it is essential to work in close contact with laboratory plasma physics and chemistry. Furthermore, the study of present-day cosmic phenomena is essential. We cannot hope to construct a reasonable model of hetegonic plasma processes by abstract reasoning alone; but it is conceivable that we can extrapolate from present situations to hetegonic conditions. Hence our strategy should be the following:

(1) *Fundamental principle:* Premagnetohydrodynamic models (Laplace, von Weizsäcker, Kuiper, Berlage, Cameron, and others) and "first-approach" theories (Hoyle) are of limited interest. We should follow the "second approach" as defined above. This implies that we should rely to a large extent on laboratory and space experiments, especially those which are specifically aimed at the clarification of hetegonic problems.

(2) *Extrapolation from magnetospheric physics:* The transfer of angular momentum from a rotating magnetized central body to a surrounding plasma has some similarity to the present situation in the terrestrial magnetosphere. The hetegonic situation differs from this in two respects: (a) The plasma density must have been much higher. (b) The present solar wind effects (magnetic storms, etc.) may not necessarily be very important.

An extrapolation of our knowledge of the magnetosphere encounters difficulty because this field is not yet very advanced. Space research has certainly supplied us with a wealth of observations, but the theories are not yet well developed. Most theories are of the pseudo-plasma type and hence of limited interest. Systematic attempts to transfer laboratory plasma knowledge to the magnetosphere (according to the principle of the "second approach") have been made by Lindberg, Block, and Danielsson. The works of these authors have been referred to elsewhere in our discussion; a survey of recent results is given by Fälthammar (1974).

(3) *Extrapolation from solar physics:* In some respects the hetegonic phenomena can be extrapolated from the sunspot-prominence phenomena. As in the photosphere there are a magnetic field **B** and rotational motion **v**, there are generally fluctuating voltages. Between two points *a* and *b* there is a voltage difference

$$V = \int_a^b (\mathbf{v} \times \mathbf{B})\, \mathbf{dr} \qquad (15.4.1)$$

If *a* and *b* are connected by a magnetic field line, an electric discharge along this field line from *a* to the point *b* may take place (fig. 15.4.1; see also Stenflo, 1969). The current circuit is closed by currents in the photosphere.

The current along the magnetic field line is the basic phenomenon in prominences. A *filamentary current* of this type has the property of sucking ionized matter from the environment into itself. This phenomenon is somewhat similar to the pinch effect (Alfvén and Fälthammar, 1963). As a result, the density in the prominence is orders of magnitude larger than in the surrounding corona. At the same time, the temperature is orders of magnitude lower ($\sim 10^4$ K in the prominence compared to $\sim 10^6$ K in the corona).

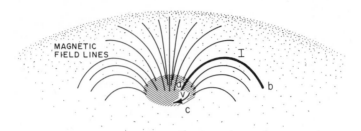

FIGURE 15.4.1.—The rotational motion *v* and the magnetic field in a sunspot may give
rise to a voltage between the points *a* in the sunspot and *b* outside the sunspot, causing
a discharge current *I* to flow along the magnetic field line from *a* to *b*. The circuit is
closed through currents below the photosphere from *b* to *c* (and back to *a*).

A typical value of the current in a prominence is 10^{11} amp (Carlqvist,
1969). As the currents in the magnetosphere are typically of the order
10^5–10^6 amp and the linear dimensions are not very different, in both cases
of the order of 10^{10} cm, the solar situation merely represents a high-current
and high-density version of the magnetospheric situation. As we shall see,
the hetegonic situation generally implies very high currents. Hence to some
extent the hetegonic magnetosphere is similar to the present-day solar
corona. In some hetegonic planetary magnetospheres, the linear dimensions
of the filamentary structures would be comparable to the present-day solar
prominences, whereas, in the hetegonic solar corona (the supercorona), the
dimensions should be three or four orders of magnitude larger.

Unfortunately, most of theoretical solar physics is still in the state of
the "first approach" and hence of limited use for our purpose. Still, the
analogy between the solar prominences and the hetegonic filamentary structures is important because it may reduce the hypothetical ingredients of
the model. Hence, a reasonable model is that of a rotating magnetized
central body surrounded by a network of prominence-like structures joining the surface of the central body with a surrounding plasma.

It is interesting to note that Chamberlin (1905) and Moulton (1905)
connected their "planetesimal" theories with solar prominences, although
in a different way.

(4) *Extrapolation from dark clouds and stellar envelopes:* During
the era of formation of planets and satellites, the amounts of gas falling into
the circumsolar region from surrounding regions of space probably gave
rise to coronal-type concentrations in a volume comparable to the size of
the solar system. The production or capture of solid particle condensates
in the filamentary structures extending through this medium must have
been high enough to produce at least the total mass of companion bodies
(10^{30} g) in a time period of the order of 10^8 yr. In the dark clouds, observable

today, gas and dust densities occur which are sufficient to permit gravitational accretion of the necessary mass in 10^7–10^8 yr.

Other objects which conceivably have a bearing on solar system formation are stars with optically thin envelopes of silicate dust. The relatively common occurrence of these attests to the substantial duration of the phenomenon. The fact that the central stars in such systems are of widely varying types ranging from early to late types of stars (Neugebauer et al., 1971; Stein, 1972) suggests that, in general, the circumstellar matter is gathered by the star from outside rather than being ejected from the star itself.

At the present time it is uncertain how close the parallelism may be between dark clouds, circumstellar envelopes and our solar system in its formative state. The continued, refined investigation of these objects is of great interest from a hetegonic point of view. Particularly important is the information which is being gathered about plasma phenomena such as magnetic fields and the ion-molecule reactions in optically opaque dark clouds.

Figure 15.4.2 is an attempt to illustrate the general scheme along which astrophysical theories should be developed in order to be realistic and consistent with observations.

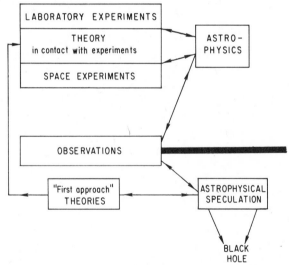

FIGURE 15.4.2.—An illustration of the present strategic situation in astrophysics. Before we are allowed to combine them with observations, the "first-approcah" theories must be processed through the laboratory where many of their ingredients will no doubt be filtered away. This is the only way of building up astrophysics with a minimum of speculation. We have to learn again that science without contact with experiments is an enterprise which is likely to go completely astray into imaginary conjectures.

15.5 REQUIRED PROPERTIES OF A MODEL

In part B we studied the accretion of grains to asteroids, planets, and satellites. In sec. 11.7 we derived some properties the grains must have had. We shall try here to find a model of the process that provides a suitable original population of grains for the accretional process. As we have found, the requirements for such a model are essentially as follows.

(1) In the environment of a central body, a large number of grains should be produced which move in Kepler orbits in the same sense as the spin of the central body. This implies a transfer of angular momentum from the central body to the medium surrounding it (see chs. 16 and 17).

(2) The orbits of the grains are bound initially to be ellipses with considerable eccentricites. In sec. 11.7.4 values of $e > 0.1$ or $e > 0.3$ have been suggested.

(3) The structure and chemical composition of these grains should be consistent with those components of meteorites which appear to be primordial condensates; furthermore, the composition should also be consistent with that of the bodies later formed from them by accretion (i.e., those we observe today) (chs. 20–22).

(4) The space density of matter should vary in the way indicated by figs. 2.5.1 through 2.5.4. This means that we cannot accept a state where the density distribution has any resemblance to a uniform Laplacian disc. To the contrary, both around the planets and around the Sun there should be certain regions with high density surrounded by (or interspaced with) regions with much lower density.

(5) As the transfer of angular momentum is necessarily a slow process, the medium to be accelerated must be supported against the gravitation of the central body until the centrifugal force is large enough to balance the gravitational force (sec. 16.4).

(6) The orbital axis of each system is close to the spin axis of its central body. Thus, regardless of the fact that the spin axis of Uranus is tilted 97°, all its satellites lie in the equatorial plane of the planet, not in the ecliptic plane.

The requirements (1), (5), and (6) specifically suggest that the model we are looking for must employ hydromagnetic effects. Indeed, there are well-known hydromagnetic processes that are able to transfer angular momentum from a magnetized rotating central body to a surrounding plasma (Alfvén, 1943b; Alfvén and Fälthammar, 1963, p. 109). Furthermore, the magnetic fields may support a plasma against gravitation (Alfvén and Fälthammar, 1963, p. 111), at least for a certain length of time (until instabilities develop). However, the mass that can be suspended with reasonable values of the magnetic field is orders of magnitude smaller than the total distributed solar-system mass, as will be shown in ch. 16. This implies that the mass density existing in the cloud at any particular time during the hetegonic age must be orders of magnitude lower than the total distributed mass density. This is possible if *plasma is continually added to the nebula from outside and is concurrently removed from the cloud by condensation and accretion*. This state will be discussed in sec. 16.5.

In the following chapters we shall show that the angular momentum transfer, support of the cloud, and capture or condensation of grains with the specific properties observed in meteoric material can all be attributed to some rather simple hydromagnetic processes.

15.6 SOME EXISTING THEORIES

As was stated at the outset, we are abstaining in this work from consideration of theories that do not offer an explanation of the basic structural similarities within the four well-developed hetegonic systems within our solar system. At this point it seems worthwhile, however, to mention briefly some of the existing theories on the origin of the planetary system alone that have received attention in the literature over the past three decades. A somewhat arbitrarily chosen list includes the work of von Weizsäcker (1944), Berlage (1930–1948), Kuiper (1951), Cameron (1962, 1963, 1973), Hoyle (1960, 1963), Hoyle and Wickramasinghe (1968), McCrea (1960), Schmidt (1944–1956), and ter Haar (1948). Detailed reviews of the work of some of these authors may be found in ter Haar (1967).

Most of these theories start by postulating properties of the primeval Sun for which there is little observational evidence. Hence the basic assumptions of these theories are highly speculative. Furthermore, hydromagnetics and plasma effects are usually neglected making these theories (see sec. 15.1) primarily interesting only from a historical point of view.

However, the importance of electromagnetic processes in the primordial solar cloud is recognized by ter Haar (1949), Hoyle (1960, 1963) and Hoyle and Wickramasinghe (1968), although Hoyle introduces these processes in a highly implausible way. His theory of hydromagnetic angular momentum transfer from the Sun is based on the concept of "frozen-in" field lines, a concept that is applicable in space only under exceptional circumstances. In this theory, a highly spiralized magnetic field is essential, implying that a large magnetic energy is stored in a toroidal magnetic field (fig. 15.6.1). Such a configuration is, however, unstable, as shown by Lundquist (1951). Consequently, it is not surprising that this phenomenon has never been observed in space or in the laboratory. The process that precludes it has been demonstrated experimentally by Lindberg et al. (1960) and Lindberg and Jacobsen (1964) (for details see sec. 15.3.3 and fig. 15.3.3), who showed that,

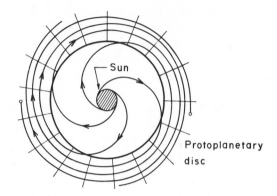

FIGURE 15.6.1.—Schematic representation of Hoyle's theory. According to Hoyle (1960), the rotation of the primeval Sun would have produced highly spiralized magnetic field lines both in the Sun and in its surroundings. The figure shows only five turns but Hoyle's theory requires 100 000 turns storing an energy of 5×10^{45} ergs. Hoyle claims that this magnetic energy caused the protoplanetary disc to expand and form the planetary system. If Hoyle's mechanism were physically reasonable, it would have had important technological applications. But as shown both theoretically (Lundquist, 1951) and experimentally (Lindberg et al., 1960; see also fig. 15.3.3), such a configuration is unstable and can never be achieved.

if the toroidal component of a magnetic field becomes too large compared to the poloidal component, an instability occurs which transfers energy from the toroidal to the poloidal field. (In the solar wind the toroidal field is likely to be larger than the poloidal field at large solar distances, but this does not necessarily produce a similar instability because the magnetic energy is much smaller than the kinetic energy.)

If we forget for a moment the question of hydromagnetic processes, a theory that has some elements of special interest is that of Schmidt (1944 to 1959). This is essentially a planetesimal accretion theory and treats what, in some respects, has been covered in part B along similar lines. The theory assumes that the Sun captured swarms of small particles and bodies from interstellar clouds. Schmidt's theory, further developed by B. J. Levin, E. Ruskol, and V. Safronov, has attracted considerable interest as a theory for the formation of satellites and particularly for the formation of the Moon.

In ch. 24 it is shown that the Moon is not relevant in discussing the formation of satellites around the planets. But it is not immediately obvious that Schmidt's theory cannot be applied to the regular satellite systems. According to this theory, the matter now forming the satellites was injected into the neighborhood of the central body in parabolic or hyperbolic orbits which, through viscous effects (mutual collisions), were transformed into the present nearly circular orbits. Hence the picture is similar to the conditions we have discussed (Alfvén, 1942, 1943a, 1946) prior to formation of jet streams. However, a main difference is that the grains we have treated acquire their angular momenta from the plasma from which they are condensing or in which they are captured electromagnetically. In Schmidt's theory, the angular momentum is due to an asymmetric injection of dust grains from "outside."

A number of objections can be raised against this process.

(1) The asymmetric injection is an ad hoc assumption. It has not been shown that any reasonable dynamic distribution of grains in space can lead to such an asymmetry.

(2) The grains collected by a system should give the central body a certain angular momentum per unit mass and, at the same time, give the satellites angular momenta per unit mass which are two or three orders of magnitude larger (see figs. 2.3.1–2.3.4). It is difficult to see how this could be achieved by the mechanism invoked.

(3) The spin axis of Uranus is tilted by 98°. (In secs. 13.5–13.6 we ascribe this to the statistical accretion which gives the planets their spins.) The Uranian satellite system is perhaps the most regular and undisturbed of all systems, with the remarkable property that the satellites move *in the equatorial plane of Uranus* with circular orbits of negligible eccentricity and inclination. The angular momentum transferred by the Schmidt mechanism should produce satellites moving in the orbital plane of the planet.

(4) The cloud of dust which captures the injected dust must extend far beyond the present orbits of the satellites. Suppose that a cloud with radius R captures grains from "infinity." We know from sec. 13.5 that the value of Z in eqs. (13.3.4–13.3.6) is not likely to be more than about 10 percent. This means that the momentum which the cloud gains does not suffice to support the final orbits at a distance larger than $r = Z^2 R = R/100$. For the outermost Saturnian satellite Iapetus, $r_{Iapetus} = 3.56 \times 10^{11}$ cm. This means that the cloud must extend a distance of 3.56×10^{13} cm. This is far outside the libration or Lagrangian point which can be taken as the outer limit of the gravitational control of Saturn.

It seems unlikely that these objections to Schmidt's theory of satellite formation can be resolved without introducing too many ad hoc assumptions. On the other hand, the jet streams in which the satellites are formed must, according to our model, necessarily capture some of the grains of the planetary jet stream in which the central body is accreting. Hence Schmidt's mechanism deserves further attention. For example, a satellite may accrete a considerable number of grains that would have impacted on the planet if they had not been captured by the satellite.

16

MODEL OF THE HETEGONIC

PLASMA

16.1 MAGNETIZED CENTRAL BODY

The simplest assumption we could make about the nature of the magnetic field in the hetegonic nebula is that the field derives from a magnetized central body. This implies that the formation of satellites around a planet and the formation of planets around a star cannot take place unless the central body is magnetized. We know that the Sun and Jupiter are magnetized. Mars is not magnetized now. The magnetic states of Saturn and Uranus, which are also surrounded by secondary bodies, are not known. However, for our study, it is not essential that the central bodies be magnetized at present but only that they possessed sufficiently strong magnetic fields in the hetegonic era (see sec. 16.3 and table 16.3.1). This must necessarily be introduced as an ad hoc assumption. This assumption can in some cases be checked experimentally by analysis of remanent magnetization in preserved primordial ferromagnetic crystals in the way it has been done for crystals that now are gathered in meteorites (Brecher, 1971, 1972c; Brecher and Arrhenius, 1975).

A considerable amount of work has been done on theories of the magnetization of celestial bodies, but none of the theories is in such a state that it is possible to calculate the strength of the magnetic field. However, the theories give qualitative support to our assumption that the central bodies were magnetized during hetegonic times. It should also be noted that certain stars are known to possess magnetic fields of the order of several thousand G, and one (HD215441) even as high as 35 000 G (Gollnow, 1962).

To make a model of the state of the plasma surrounding such a body, we assume that the central body is uniformly magnetized parallel or antiparallel to the axis of rotation. In case there are no external currents, this is equivalent to assuming that *the magnetic field outside the body is a dipole field with the dipole located at the center of the body and directed parallel or antiparallel to the spin axis.*

As we shall find later, neither the strength nor the sign of the dipole appears explicitly in our treatment. The only requirement is that the strength of the magnetic field be sufficient to control the dynamics of the plasma.

We shall also see later that only moderate field strengths of the planets are required to produce the necessary effect. The dipole moment of the Sun must have been much larger than it is now (table 16.3.1), but this does not necessarily mean that the surface field was correspondingly large, since the latter would depend on the solar radius and we know very little about the actual size of the Sun in the hetegonic era (ch. 25).

16.2 ANGULAR MOMENTUM

For understanding the evolutionary history of the solar system, it is important to examine the distribution of angular momentum in the system. Figures 2.3.1–2.3.4 show that the specific angular momenta of the respective secondary bodies exceed that of the spinning central body by one to three orders of magnitude.

This fact constitutes one of the main difficulties of all Laplacian-type theories; these theories claim that the secondary bodies as well as the central body derive from an initial massive nebula which, during its contraction, has left behind a series of rings that later form the secondary bodies. Each of these rings must have had essentially the same angular momentum as the orbital momentum of the secondary body formed from it, whereas the central body should have a specific angular momentum which is much less. No reasonable mechanism has been found by which such a distribution of angular momentum can be achieved during contraction. The only possibility one could think of is that the central body lost most of its angular momentum after it had separated from the rings.

In the case of the Sun, such a loss could perhaps be produced by the solar wind. Using the present conditions in the solar wind, an e-folding time for solar rotational braking has been claimed to be in the range $3–6 \times 10^9$ yr (Brandt, 1970). The currently accepted age of the Sun is about 5×10^9 yr. Thus, allowing for error in the estimate, it is not unlikely that solar wind emission may have been an efficient process for the loss of solar angular momentum. However, the above value is very uncertain since there is, as yet, no way of deciding whether the solar wind had its present properties at all times in the past. Emission of the solar wind depends on some hydromagnetic processes that are not very well understood.

It is possible that one or more links in this complicated causality chain has varied in such a way as to change the order of magnitude of the rate of loss of angular momentum. Hence, on the basis of the solar wind braking hypothesis, it is possible that the newborn Sun had about the same angular momentum as it has now, but it may have been larger by an order of magnitude or more.

There are speculations about an early period of intense "solar gale." These speculations are mainly based on an analogy with T-Tauri stars but aside from the uncertainties in interpreting the T-Tauri observations the relation between such stars and the formation of planets is questionable. Furthermore, the record of irradiation of primordial grains gives no evidence of the steepness changes in the corpuscular energy spectrum, which ought to accompany a strong enhancement of solar wind emission (see also sec. 5.5).

These uncertainties point out how difficult it is to draw any conclusions about the hetegonic process from the study of the formation of planets around the Sun. It is much safer to base our discussion on the formation of satellites around the planets.

In all the satellite systems we find that the specific angular momentum of the orbital motion of satellites is orders of magnitude higher than that of the spinning central planet. A braking of this spin by the same hypothetical process as suggested for the Sun is out of the question since this would require a mechanism that would give almost the same spin period to Jupiter, Saturn, and Uranus, in spite of the fact that these planets have very different satellite systems. From the spin isochronism discussed in secs. 9.7–9.8 we have concluded instead that the planets could not have lost very much angular momentum. We have also found that Giuli's theory of planetary spins (ch. 13) strongly supports the theory of planetesimal accretion which is fundamentally different from the picture of a contracting Laplacian nebula.

16.3 THE TRANSFER OF ANGULAR MOMENTUM

The transfer of angular momentum from a rotating central body is a problem that has attracted much interest over the years. It has been concluded that an astrophysically efficient transfer can only be produced by hydromagnetic effects. Hydromagnetic transfer was studied by Ferraro and led to his law of isorotation. Lüst and Schlüter (1955) demonstrated that a hydromagnetic braking of stellar rotation could be achieved.

The Ferraro isorotation law assumes that not only the central body but also the surrounding medium has infinite electrical conductivity, which means that the magnetic field lines are frozen in. However, recent studies of the conditions in the terrestrial magnetosphere indicate the presence of components of electric field parallel to the magnetic field ($E_{||}$) over large distances in a few cases (Mozer and Fahleson, 1970; Kelley et al., 1971). Such electric fields may occur essentially in two different ways. As shown by Persson (1963, 1966), anisotropies in the velocity distribution of charged particles in the magnetosphere in combination with the magnetic field gradient will result in parallel electric fields under very general conditions. However, $E_{||}$ may also be associated with Birkeland currents in the magnetosphere, which are observed to have densities of the order of 10^{-6}–10^{-4} amp/m^2 (Zmuda et al., 1967; Cloutier et al., 1970). Such currents have a tendency to produce electrostatic double layers. A review by Block (1972) gives both theoretical and observational evidence for the existence of such layers, preferentially in the upper ionosphere and the lower magnetosphere.

The existence of an electric field parallel to the magnetic field violates the conditions for frozen-in field lines (see Alfvén and Fälthammar, 1963, p. 191). It results in a decoupling of the plasma from the magnetic field lines. Hence the state of Ferraro isorotation is not necessarily established, and the outer regions of the medium surrounding the central body may rotate with a smaller angular velocity than does the central body itself.

16.3.1 A Simplified Model

We shall study an idealized, and in certain respects (see sec. 16.3.2) unrealistic, model of the hydromagnetic transfer of angular momentum from a central body with radius R_c, magnetic dipole moment μ, and spin angular velocity Ω (fig. 16.3.1).

Seen from a coordinate system fixed in space, the voltage difference between two points b_1 and b_2 at latitude λ_1 and λ_2 of a central body has a value

$$V_b = \int_{b_1}^{b_2} [(\Omega \times R_c) \times B] \, ds$$

$$= \frac{\mu\Omega}{R_c} (\cos^2 \lambda_2 - \cos^2 \lambda_1) \qquad (16.3.1)$$

Similarly, if there is a conducting plasma element between the points c_1 and c_2 situated on the lines of force through b_1 and b_2, but rotating around the axis with the angular velocity ω, there will be a voltage difference induced between c_1 and c_2 given by

$$V_c = \int_{c_1}^{c_2} [(\omega \times r) \times B] \, dr$$

$$= \frac{\mu\omega}{R_c} (\cos^2 \lambda_2 - \cos^2 \lambda_1) \qquad (16.3.2)$$

If we have Ferraro isorotation (i.e., if the magnetic field lines are frozen into the medium), ω will be equal to Ω, and hence $V_c = V_b$. If, however, there

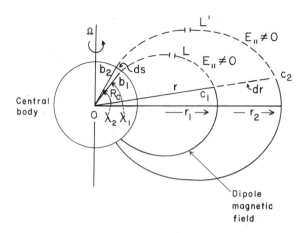

Dipole
magnetic
field

FIGURE 16.3.1.—In the absence of Ferraro isorotation, the angular velocity ω in the outer
regions of the magnetosphere is different from the angular velocity Ω of the central body.
This results in a current flow in the loop $b_1b_2c_2c_1b_1$ (shown by broken lines) which may
result in the electrostatic double layers L and L'. Along part of the paths b_1c_1 and b_2c_2,
the electric field has nonzero parallel components resulting in a decoupling of the plasma
from the magnetic field lines.

is no isorotation, $\omega \neq \Omega$ and hence $V_c - V_b$ will be nonzero, resulting in a
current flow in the circuit $b_1c_1c_2b_2b_1$. In the sectors c_1c_2 and b_1b_2 this current
together with the magnetic field gives rise to a force $\mathbf{I} \times \mathbf{B}$ which tends to
accelerate ω and retard Ω (in the case $\omega < \Omega$), thus transferring angular momentum and tending to establish isorotation. The current $\mathbf{I}$ flows outward
from the central body along the magnetic field line b_1c_1 and back again along
the field line b_2c_2. In a time dt the current between c_1 and c_2 transfers the
angular momentum

$$C = dt \int_{c_1}^{c_2} [\mathbf{r} \times (\mathbf{I} \times \mathbf{B})] dr = I \ dt \int_{c_1}^{c_2} Br \ dr = \frac{Q\Phi}{2\pi} \qquad (16.3.3)$$

where $Q = I \ dt$ is the charge passing through the circuit $b_1c_1c_2b_2b_1$ in time
dt and Φ is the magnetic flux enclosed between the latitude circles at λ_1
and λ_2.

Suppose that the plasma is situated in the equatorial plane of a central
body between r_1 and r_2 and condenses and forms a secondary body with
mass M_{sc} moving in a circular orbit of radius r and Kepler period T_K. Its
orbital momentum C_{sc} is

$$C_{sc} = M_{sc}rv = \frac{2\pi M_{sc}r^2}{T_K} = \frac{GM_cM_{sc}T_K}{2\pi r} \tag{16.3.4}$$

where $GM_c = 4\pi^2r^3/T_K^2$ and G and M_c represent the gravitational constant and the mass of the central body, respectively.

In an axisymmetric model with a constant current I flowing during a time t_I we have

$$Q = It_I \tag{16.3.5}$$

and

$$\Phi = 2\pi\mu \left(\frac{1}{r_1} - \frac{1}{r_2}\right) \tag{16.3.6}$$

The current I produces a tangential magnetic field B_ϕ which at r $(r_1 < r < r_2)$ is $B_\phi = 2I/r$. This cannot become too large in comparison to B. One of the reasons for this is that if the magnetic energy of B_ϕ exceeds that of B by an order of magnitude, instabilities will develop (see sec. 15.3, especially the reference to Lindberg's experiment). For an order of magnitude estimate we may put

$$I = \alpha Br \tag{16.3.7}$$

which together with eqs. (16.3.3) and (16.3.5–16.3.6) gives

$$C = \alpha \frac{\mu^2}{r^2} t_I \left(\frac{1}{r_1} - \frac{1}{r_2}\right) = \beta \frac{\mu^2}{r^3} t_I \tag{16.3.8}$$

where r is a distance intermediate between r_1 and r_2 and α and β constants of the order unity (which we put equal to unity in the following).

Putting $C = C_{sc}$ we obtain from eqs. (16.3.4) and (16.3.8) a lower limit μ_{Lm} for μ:

TABLE 16.3.1

Minimum Values of Magnetic Fields and Currents for Transfer of Angular Momentum

Central body	Secondary body	Mass of secondary body M_{sc} (g)	Orbital radius of secondary body r (cm)	Orbital period of secondary body T_K (sec)	$\dfrac{M_{sc}r^5}{T_K}$	Dipole moment μ_{Lm} (G cm³)	Equatorial surface field B (G)	Current I (amp)
Sun	Jupiter	1.9×10^{30}	0.778×10^{14}	3.74×10^{8}	0.15×10^{92}	0.97×10^{38}	(see table 16.3.2)	1.6×10^{11}
Sun	Neptune	1.03×10^{29}	0.45×10^{15}	5.2×10^{9}	3.6×10^{92}	4.8×10^{35}		0.23×10^{11}
Jupiter	Callisto	0.95×10^{26}	1.88×10^{11}	1.44×10^{6}	1.5×10^{76}	3.1×10^{30}	9	9×10^{8}
Saturn	Titan	1.37×10^{26}	1.22×10^{11}	1.38×10^{6}	0.27×10^{76}	1.3×10^{30}	6	9×10^{8}
Uranus	Oberon	2.6×10^{24}	0.586×10^{11}	1.16×10^{6}	1.54×10^{72}	3.1×10^{28}	2	0.9×10^{6}

μ_{Lm} = minimum dipole moment of central body calculated from eq. (16.3.9).

B = minimum equatorial surface field.

I = current which transfers the momentum.

Note: If the angular momentum is transferred by filamentary currents (produced by pinch effect), the values of B and I become smaller, possibly by orders of magnitude.

$$\mu_{Lm}^2 = \frac{GM_cM_{sc}r^2\gamma}{2\pi} = \frac{2\pi M_{sc}r^5}{t_I T_K} \tag{16.3.9}$$

with

$$\gamma = \frac{T_K}{t_I} \tag{16.3.10}$$

To estimate the necessary magnetic field we assume that t_I is the same as the infall time t_{inf} and introduce $t_I = 10^{16}$ sec $(3 \times 10^8$ yr), a value we have used earlier (ch. 12), and obtain table 16.3.1.

From the study of spin isochronism (sec. 9.7) and planetesimal accretion we know that the size of the planets cannot have changed very much since their formation. As it is likely that the satellites were formed during a late phase of planet formation, it is legitimate to use the present value of the planetary radii in calculating the minimum surface magnetic field. From table 16.3.1 we find that surface fields of less than 10 G are required. There is no way to check these values until the remanent magnetism of small satellites can be measured, but with our present knowledge they seem to be acceptable. The value Jupiter must have had when it produced its satellites is of the same order of magnitude as its present field.

As we know next to nothing about the state of the Sun when the planets were formed, we cannot make a similar calculation for the solar surface field. We can be rather confident that the solar radius was not smaller than the present one, and the formation of Mercury at a distance of 5.8×10^{12} cm places an upper limit on the solar radius. A dipole moment of 5×10^{38} G cm³ implies the values of the surface field shown in table 16.3.2.

In the absence of magnetic measurements from unmetamorphosed bodies in low-eccentricity orbits (such as asteroids), it is impossible to verify any of these values. If carbonaceous chondrites are assumed to be such samples, field strengths of the order of 0.1 to 1 G would be typical at a solar distance

TABLE 16.3.2
Minimum Solar Equatorial Field
for Different Radii of the Primeval Sun

$R=$	10^{11}	3×10^{11}	10^{12}	3×10^{12} cm
$B=$	5×10^5	18 000	500	18 G

of 2–4 AU (Brecher, 1972a, c; Brecher and Arrhenius, 1974, 1975). If this field derived directly from the solar dipole, its value should be 10^{40}–10^{41} G cm^3; i.e., more than two orders of magnitude higher than the value in table 16.3.1. However, the field causing the magnetization of grains now in meteorites may also have been strengthened locally by currents as shown by De (1973) and Alfvén and Mendis (1973) and discussed further in ch. 17. As stars are known to possess surface fields as high as 35 000 G, at least the values in table 16.3.2 corresponding to $R > 3 \times 10^{11}$ cm do not seem unreasonable.

Table 16.3.1 also gives the value of the current I which transfers the angular momentum. It is calculated from

$$I = \frac{\mu_{Lm}}{r^2} \qquad (16.3.11)$$

which is obtained from eq. (16.3.7) by putting $\alpha = 1$ and $B = \mu_{Lm}/r^3$. For the planets, I is only one or two orders of magnitude larger than the electric currents known to flow in the magnetosphere. For the Sun, it is of the order of the current in one single prominence. Hence the required currents are within our experience of actual cosmic plasmas.

16.3.2 Discussion of the Model

The model we have treated is a steady-state, homogeneous model and subject to the objections of secs. 15.2 and 15.3. It is likely that we can have a more efficient momentum transfer; e.g., through hydromagnetic waves or filamentary currents. This means that the magnetic dipole moments need not necessarily be as large as found here. It seems unlikely that we can decrease these values by more than one or two orders of magnitude but that can be decided only by further investigations. On the other hand, we have assumed that all the plasma condenses to grains and thus leaves the region of acceleration. This is not correct in the case where most ingredients in the plasma are noncondensable. If, for example, the plasma has a composition similar to the solar photosphere, only about 1 percent of its mass can form grains. As the behavior of volatile substances is not yet taken into account, some modification of our model may be necessary. We may guess that if the mass of volatile substances is 1000 times the mass of condensable substances, the magnetic fields and currents may have to be increased by a factor $\sqrt{1000} \approx 33$. Hence a detailed theory may change the figures of table 16.3.1 either downward or upward by one or two orders of magnitude.

16.4 SUPPORT OF THE PRIMORDIAL CLOUD

Closely connected with the problem of transfer of angular momentum is another basic difficulty in the Laplacian approach, namely, support of the cloud against the gravitation of the central body. As soon as the cloud has been brought into rotation with Kepler velocity, it is supported by the centrifugal force. In fact, this is what defines the Kepler motion. But the acceleration to Kepler velocity must necessarily take a considerable amount of time, during which the cloud must be supported in some other way.

Attempts have been made to avoid this difficulty by assuming that the Laplacian nebula had an initial rotation so that the Kepler velocities were established automatically. This results in an extremely high spin of the Sun, which then is supposed to be carried away by a "solar gale." This view could be theoretically possible when applied to the planetary system but lacks support in the observational record of early irradiation of grains (see secs. 5.5 and 16.2). When applied to the satellite systems the proposed mechanism fails also in principle. One of the reasons is that it is irreconcilable with the isochronism of spins.

A plasma may be supported by a magnetic field against gravitation if a toroidal current I_ϕ is flowing in the plasma so that the force $|\ I_\phi \times \mathbf{B}\ |$ balances the gravitational force $(GM_cM_B)/r^2$, where M_B is the total mass of plasma magnetically suspended at any particular time. Let us assume for the sake of simplicity that the plasma to be supported is distributed over a toroidal volume with large radius r and small radius $r/2$. If N and m are the number density and the mean mass of a plasma particle in this volume, the condition for balance is expressed by

$$2\pi r I_\phi B = \frac{2\pi r G M_c m N}{r^2}\frac{\pi r^2}{4} \qquad (16.4.1)$$

or

$$I_\phi = \frac{\pi G M_c m N}{4B} \qquad (16.4.2)$$

The magnetic field produced by this current is approximately homogeneous within the toroidal volume and has a value

$$B_\phi \approx \frac{I_\phi}{r} = \frac{\pi G M_c m N}{4Br} \qquad (16.4.3)$$

Once again we note that, if this field B_ϕ becomes too large compared to B, the dipole field will be seriously disturbed and instabilities will develop. For stability, B_ϕ must be of the same order of, or less than, B. Let us put $B_\phi = \delta B$, with $\delta \leq 1$. If for B we use its equatorial value at a distance r (i.e., $B = \mu/r^3$), we obtain from eq. (16.4.3)

$$\mu^2 = \frac{GM_c M_B r^2}{2\pi\delta} \tag{16.4.4}$$

which gives the value of the dipole moment μ necessary for the support of the plasma. If $\delta = 1$, we get a lower limit μ_{lm} to μ. Comparing μ_{lm} with μ_{Lm} as given by eq. (16.3.9) we find that M_{sc} and M_B in these two equations are equal if μ_{lm} is larger than μ_{Lm} by a factor $\gamma^{-1/2}$. In the case of Sun-Jupiter, this is $(3\times10^8/10^{16})^{-1/2}\approx5500$; for the satellite systems this factor is of the order of 10^5. Hence the magnetic fields required to suspend the entire distributed mass of the planetary and satellite systems together with a complement of hydrogen and helium during transfer of angular momentum are unreasonably large. (This conclusion is not affected by the uncertainty discussed at the end of sec. 16.3 which is applicable here.) Consequently there is no way to suspend the total mass of the plasma until it is accelerated to Kepler velocity.

16.5 THE PLASMA AS A TRANSIENT STATE

We have found that only a small fraction M_B of the final mass M_{sc} of a planet or satellite can be supported by the magnetic field at any particular time. This means that the plasma density ρ at any time can only be a small fraction γ_B of the distributed density ρ_{dst} (mass of the final secondary body divided by the space volume from which it derives; see sec. 2.4)

$$\gamma_B = \frac{\rho}{\rho_{dst}} = \frac{M_B}{M_{sc}} \tag{16.5.1}$$

This can be explained if matter is falling in during a long time t_{inf} but resides in the plasma state only during a time $t_{res} \ll t_{inf}$. This is possible if t_{res} is the time needed for the plasma to condense to grains. Since during each time interval t_{res} an amount of matter M_B condenses to grains, we have

$$M_{sc} \frac{t_{inf}}{t_{res}} = M_B \tag{16.5.2}$$

so that

$$\gamma_B = \frac{M_B}{M_{sc}} = \frac{t_{res}}{t_{inf}} \tag{16.5.3}$$

It is reasonable that the characteristic time for the production of grains in Kepler orbit is the Kepler period T_K. Hence we put $t_{res} = T_K$ which together with eqs. (16.3.10) and (16.5.3) gives

$$\gamma_B = \gamma \tag{16.5.4}$$

This means that the instantaneous densities are less than the distributed densities by 10^{-7} for the giant planets to 10^{-11} for the satellite systems. Hence from figs. 2.4.1–2.4.4 we find that the *plasma densities we should consider (compare sec. 2.4) are of the same order of magnitude as the present number densities in the solar corona* (10^2–10^8 cm^{-3}).

It should be observed that these values refer to the *average* densities. Since the plasma is necessarily strongly inhomogeneous, the *local* densities at some places are likely to be several orders of magnitude higher. Indeed the differences between the local and average densities should be of the same order as (or even larger than) the density differences between solar prominences and the solar corona in which they are embedded.

This is important because both the time of condensation of a grain and its chemical and structural properties depend upon local conditions. Assuming that the primordial components of meteorites were formed in the hetegonic nebula, one can place some limits on the properties of the medium from which they formed. The densities suggested in this way, mainly from the vapor pressures of the grain components (Arrhenius, 1972; De, 1973), are much higher than ρ but still lower than ρ_{dst}.

16.6 CONCLUSIONS ABOUT THE MODEL

We can now restate the requirements of our model in the following way:
(1) Gas should be falling into the environment of the central body in

such a way as to account for the density distribution in the solar system. This is satisfied by the infall mechanism we are going to study in ch. 21. In short, this implies that neutral gas falling under gravitation toward the central body becomes ionized when it has reached the critical velocity for ionization. The ionization prevents a closer approach to the central body and the plasma is suspended in the magnetic field.

(2) Angular momentum is transferred from the central body to this plasma. A state of *partial corotation* is produced. This will be studied in ch. 17.

(3) The condensation of the nonvolatile substances of the plasma produces grains with chemical and structural properties exemplified by primordial components in meteorites. This condensation should take place in an environment permeated by a magnetic field of the order of 0.1–1 G in the case of the planetary system (Brecher, 1972a,c; Brecher and Arrhenius, 1974, 1975). It is, however, also possible that a major portion of the primordial grains are of interstellar origin and became electromagnetically trapped in the circumsolar plasma.

(4) The grains should acquire such a dynamic state that they move in eccentric Kepler orbits thus satisfying the prerequisites for planetesimal accretion. Many-particle systems in this state are termed jet streams; the characteristic energy and mass balance in such systems are described in chs. 6 and 12.

The plasma state necessarily coexists with the jet streams. In fact, the grains and the plasma out of which they condense will interact mutually. As a population of orbiting grains has a "negative diffusion coefficient" (Baxter and Thompson, 1971, 1973), the grains originally distributed through a given volume will tend to form a number of separate jet streams. Once a jet stream is formed it will collect new grains as they condense in its environment. Inside the jet streams, the grains accrete to larger bodies and eventually to planets and satellites. A perspective of the various processes is represented by fig. 16.6.1. There are a number of jet streams in the equatorial plane, and these are joined with the central body by plasma regions somewhat similar to the present-day solar prominences but having much greater dimensions if the central body is the Sun. We shall refer to these regions as *superprominences*.

16.7 THE HETEGONIC NEBULAE

In Laplacian-type theories, the medium surrounding the primordial Sun is called the "solar nebula" or "circumsolar nebula" and forms the precursor for the planets. In contrast to Laplacian theories, we are not developing a theory of the formation of planets alone, but a general hetegonic

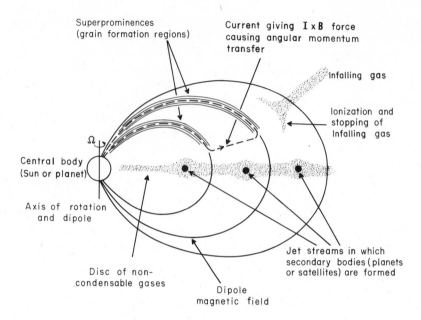

FIGURE 16.6.1.—A sketch of the series of hetegonic processes leading to formation of
secondary bodies around a spinning magnetized central body (not drawn to scale).
The dipole magnet is located at the center of the central body and is aligned with the spin
axis. The gas falling from "infinity" into the environment of the central body becomes
ionized by collision with the magnetized plasma when its free-fall velocity exceeds the
critical velocity for ionization, and the ionized gas then remains suspended in the magnetic field. The rotation and magnetic field together with the conducting plasma surrounding the central body give rise to a homopolar emf which causes a current flow
in the plasma. This current I together with the magnetic field B give rise to a force
$I \times B$ which transfers angular motion from the central body to the surrounding plasma.
The current also produces prominence-like regions of gas (by pinch effect) which are
denser and cooler than the surrounding regions, and in these regions the condensation
of grains takes place. Through viscous effects, the population of grains evolves into a
number of jet streams while the noncondensable gases form a thin disc in the equatorial
plane.

theory applicable both to the formation of planets around the Sun and the
formation of satellites around planets. Since the term "solar nebula" only
refers to one of these systems, "hetegonic nebulae" is a preferable term
where reference is made to the entire system.

In retaining the term "nebula" it is important to definitely disassociate
it from the 19th-century concept; i.e., a homogeneous disc of nonionized
gas with uniform chemical composition described by prehydromagnetic
dynamics. For a number of reasons that we have discussed earlier this concept is obsolete. In terms of modern theory and observation we need instead

to consider the central bodies to be surrounded by a structured medium of plasma and grains throughout the period of formation of the secondary bodies. The results of the preceding analysis combined with some of the results discussed in subsequent chapters lead to a rather complex pattern which we shall now describe.

The space around the central body may be called a supercorona, characterized by a medium that is similar to the present solar corona but much larger in extent due to the flux of gas from outside into the system during the formative era. It is magnetized, primarily by the magnetic field of the central body. Its average density, to show the proper behavior, would be of the same order as that of the solar corona (10^2–10^8 cm^{-3}). This supercorona consists of four regions of widely differing properties (fig. 16.6.1). Note that the central body may be *either the Sun or a planet*.

(1) *Jet streams:* The theory of these is given in ch. 6. They fill up a very small part of this space. The small diameter of the toroid is only a few percent of the large diameter and hence they occupy 10^{-3}–10^{-4} of the volume. They are fed by injection of grains condensed in large regions around them. The accretion of satellites or planets takes place in the jet streams (see chs. 11–12).

(2) *Low-density plasma regions:* Most of the space outside the jet streams is filled with a low-density plasma. This region with a density perhaps in the range 10–10^5 cm^{-3} occupies most of the volume of the supercorona. The supercorona is fed by infall of matter from a source at large distance ("infinity"). The transfer of angular momentum from the central body is achieved through processes in this plasma; there is a system of strong electric currents flowing in the plasma which results in filamentary structures (superprominences).

(3) *Filamentary structures or superprominences:* The plasma structurally resembles the solar corona with embedded prominences produced by strong currents. These stretch from the surface of the central body out to the most distant regions to which angular momentum is transferred by the currents. As in the solar corona, the filaments have a density that is orders of magnitude larger and a temperature that is much lower than those of the surrounding medium. As high plasma density favors condensation, most of the condensation takes place in the filaments. When condensed grains leave the filaments, they possess a tangential velocity which determines their Kepler orbits; their interaction leads to the formation of jet streams. At the same time, plasma from the low-density regions is drawn into the filaments by the pinch effect.

(4) *Noncondensable gas clouds:* As the injected matter contains a large fraction of noncondensable gases—presumably they form the main constituent—there is an increasing supply of such gases in the filaments and in the interfilamentary plasma. When partial corotation is established,

this gas is accumulated close to the equatorial plane. Part of the gas is retained in the jet streams where the apparent attraction accumulates it (ch. 6). Hence accretion in the jet streams may take place in a cloud of noncondensable gases. When an embryo has become so large that its gravitation becomes appreciable, it may capture an atmosphere from the gas supply of the jet stream.

It is likely that the jet streams cannot keep all the gas. Some of it may diffuse away, possibly forming a thin disc of gas that may leak into the central body or transfer gas from one jet stream to another. In fig. 16.6.1 the gas is assumed to form toruses around the jet streams which flatten out to discs. It is doubtful whether any appreciable quantity of gas can leak out to infinity because of momentum considerations.

The behavior of the noncondensable gases is necessarily the most hypothetical element in the model because we have very little, essentially indirect, information about it.

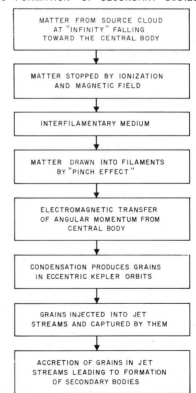

SEQUENCE OF PROCESSES LEADING
TO FORMATION OF SECONDARY BODIES

MATTER FROM SOURCE CLOUD
AT "INFINITY" FALLING
TOWARD THE CENTRAL BODY

MATTER STOPPED BY IONIZATION
AND MAGNETIC FIELD

INTERFILAMENTARY MEDIUM

MATTER DRAWN INTO FILAMENTS
BY "PINCH EFFECT"

ELECTROMAGNETIC TRANSFER
OF ANGULAR MOMENTUM FROM
CENTRAL BODY

CONDENSATION PRODUCES GRAINS
IN ECCENTRIC KEPLER ORBITS

GRAINS INJECTED INTO JET
STREAMS AND CAPTURED BY THEM

ACCRETION OF GRAINS IN JET
STREAMS LEADING TO FORMATION
OF SECONDARY BODIES

FIGURE 16.7.1.—Sequence of processes leading to the formation of secondary bodies around a central body.

The diagram in fig. 16.7.1 outlines the sequence of processes leading to the formation of secondary bodies around a central body. These processes will be discussed in detail in the following chapters.

16.8 IRRADIATION EFFECTS

Analyses of particle tracks and surface-related gases in meteorites demonstrate that individual crystals and rock fragments become individually irradiated with accelerated particles (ch. 22). This irradiation evidently took place before material was permanently locked into the parent bodies of the meteorites of which they are now a part. Considerable fluxes of corpuscular radiation with approximately solar photospheric composition must have existed during that period of formation of meteorite parent bodies when individual crystals and rock fragments were free to move relative to each other; that is, during the time of embryonic accretion. This process may still be going on as, for example, in the asteroidal and cometary jet streams.

With present information it is not possible to fix the point in time when this irradiation began or to decide whether it was present during or soon after the era of gas infall and condensation of primordial matter. Hence the specific irradiation phenomena are not a critical part of our treatment of these early phases. On the other hand, the properties of our model are such that particle acceleration into the keV ("solar wind") and MeV or GeV ("solar flare") ranges in general is expected.

In sec. 15.4 our model is characterized as a synthesis of phenomena now observed in the Earth's magnetosphere and in the solar corona. This implies that we should expect the model to exhibit to a certain extent other related properties of these regions. It is well known that in the magnetosphere there are processes by which particles are accelerated to keV energies (as shown by the aurora and by direct space measurements). In the van Allen belts there are also particles accelerated by magnetospheric processes to MeV energies. Furthermore, it is well known that solar activity, especially in connection with flares, produces MeV-GeV particles ("solar cosmic rays").

Our superprominences should produce similar effects in the whole region where transfer of angular momentum takes place and grains are condensing. Hence in our model grains necessarily are irradiated in various ways. Even nuclear reactions may be produced. All these effects will occur independently of whether the Sun was hot or cool or had an activity of the present type. In fact, the only required properties of the central body, be it the Sun or a planet, are gravitating mass, spin, and magnetization.

A detailed theory of irradiation effects is difficult and cannot be worked out until the theory of both the magnetosphere and solar activity is much more advanced than today. When this stage is reached the irradiation effects will probably allow specific conclusions. Already, present studies of the irradiation record in the constituent grains of meteorites make it possible to place limits on total dosage and energy spectra of the primordial grain irradiation (see, e.g., Macdougall et al., 1974).

16.9 THE MODEL AND THE HETEGONIC PRINCIPLE

In ch. 1 it was pointed out that, because the general structure of the satellite systems is so similar to that of the planetary system, one should aim at a general hetegonic theory of formation of secondary bodies around a central body. This is a principle that has been pronounced repeatedly over the centuries and no one seems to have denied it explicitly. It is an extremely powerful principle because of the severe constraints it puts on every model. In spite of this it has usually been neglected in the formulation of solar-system theories.

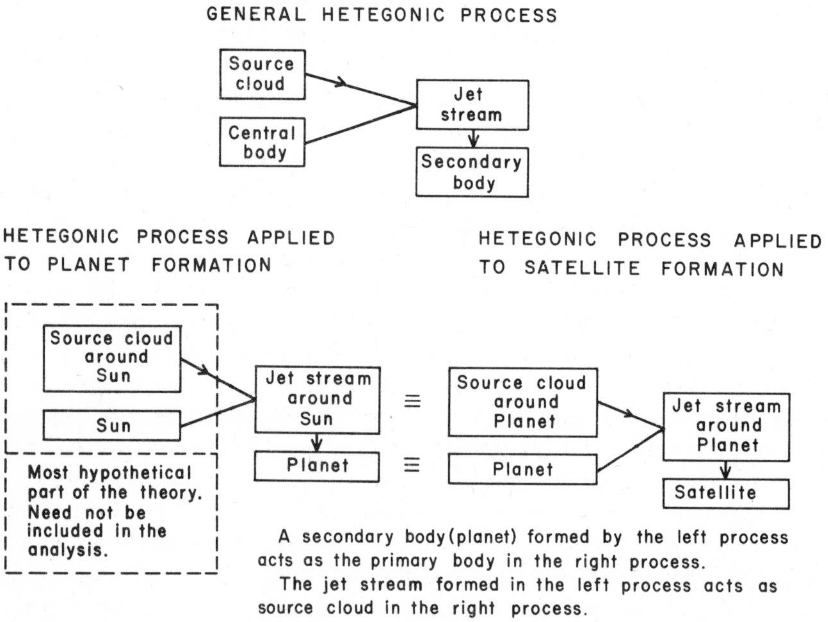

GENERAL HETEGONIC PROCESS

HETEGONIC PROCESS APPLIED TO PLANET FORMATION

HETEGONIC PROCESS APPLIED TO SATELLITE FORMATION

A secondary body (planet) formed by the left process acts as the primary body in the right process.
The jet stream formed in the left process acts as source cloud in the right process.

FIGURE 16.9.1.—Diagram showing how the speculative character of a theory is reduced by the hetegonic principle which implies that all theories should be applicable to both planetary and satellite systems. This eliminates the need to rely on hypotheses about the early Sun and ties the theory closer to observations.

Earlier we used the hetegonic principle for a choice between alternative explanations of the resonances in the satellite systems (sec. 9.6). The diagram in fig. 16.9.1 shows how the principle is applied to the two similar series of processes leading to the formation of secondary bodies from a primeval dispersed medium. The chain of processes leading to the formation of planets around the Sun is repeated in the case of formation of satellites around the planets, but in the latter case a small part (close to the planet) of the planetary jet stream provides the primeval cloud out of which the satellites form. Hence there is only one basic chain of processes, as summed up in fig. 16.7.1, which applies to the formation of both planets and satellites. This means that a complete theory of jet streams (including not only grains but also the gas component) must give the initial conditions for satellite formation.

Hence we can *explore the hetegonic process without making detailed assumptions* about the properties of the early Sun. This is advantageous because these properties are poorly understood. Indeed, the current theories of stellar formation are speculative and possibly unrelated to reality. For example, the Sun may have been formed by a "stellesimal" accretion process analogous to the planetesimal process. The planetesimal process works over a mass range from 10^{18} g (or less) up to 10^{30} g (see secs. 9.7–9.8). One may ask whether to these 12 orders of magnitude one could not add 3 more so as to reach stellar masses (10^{33} g). Observations give no real support to any of the conventional theories of stellar formation and may agree just as well with a stellesimal accretion. As was pointed out in sec. 15.3, it is now obvious that many homogeneous models are misleading and have to be replaced by inhomogeneous models. The introduction of stellesimal accretion would be in conformity with the latter approach.

From fig. 16.9.1 and the discussion above, we conclude that we need not concern ourselves with the hypothetical question of whether the Sun has passed through a high-luminosity Hayashi phase or whether the solar wind at some early time was stronger than it is now. Neither of these phenomena could have influenced the formation of satellites (e.g., around Uranus) very much. The similarity between the planetary system and satellite systems shows that such phenomena have not played a major dynamic role.

Instead of basing our theory on some hypothesis about the properties of the early Sun, we can draw conclusions about solar evolution from the results of our theory based on observation of the four well-developed systems of orbiting bodies (the planetary system and the satellite systems of Jupiter, Saturn, and Uranus). This will be done in ch. 25.

What has been said so far stresses the importance of studying jet streams (see ch. 6). The theoretical analysis should be expanded to include the gas (or plasma) which is trapped by the apparent attraction. One should also investigate to what extent meteor streams and asteroidal jet streams are similar to those jet streams in which planets and satellites were formed. The formation of short-period comets is one of the crucial problems (see ch. 14).

As a final remark: Although the hetegonic principle is important and useful it should not be interpreted too rigidly. There are obviously certain differences between the planetary system and the satellite systems. The most conspicuous one is that the planets have transferred only a small fraction of their spin to satellite orbital momenta, whereas the Sun appears to have transferred most of its spin to planetary orbital momenta. The principle should preferably be used in such a way that the theory of formation of secondary bodies is developed with the primary aim of explaining the properties of the satellite systems. We then investigate the extent to which this theory is applicable to the formation of planets. If there are reasons to introduce new effects to explain the formation of planets, we should not hesitate to do this. As we shall see, there seems to be no compelling reason to assume that the general structure is different but there are local effects which may be produced by solar radiation.

TRANSFER OF
ANGULAR MOMENTUM
AND CONDENSATION OF GRAINS

17.1 FERRARO ISOROTATION AND PARTIAL COROTATION

We have shown in sec. 16.3 that a difference in angular velocity between a magnetized central body and the surrounding plasma may lead to a transfer of angular momentum.

From a purely hydromagnetic point of view the final state would be a Ferraro isorotation with $\omega = \Omega$. However, a transfer of angular momentum means an increase in rotational velocity of the plasma, with the result that it is centrifuged outwards. This will produce a region with low density between the central body and the plasma, and the density may decrease so much that anomalous resistance or the production of electrostatic double layers (see sec. 15.3.3) impedes a further transfer of angular momentum. In this way a state is established such that the rotational motion of an element of plasma is essentially given by the condition that the gravitational and the centrifugal forces balance each other. This state is called "partial corotation."

Partial corotation can be thought of as a transient state in the process of angular momentum transfer from the central body. This state is important if the time of transfer of angular momentum from the central body to a cloud of plasma is long compared to the time it takes for the cloud of plasma to find its equilibrium position on the magnetic field line; if the duration of transfer is much greater than the time needed to reach equilibrium, we can treat the partial corotation as a steady state.

We are especially interested in studying the state of motion of grains that are delivered from the plasma and put into a Kepler motion which is essentially independent of the plasma. Thus we should treat the transition through the size limit m_{Lm} of the grains which, according to sec. 5.4, controls whether the motion is essentially governed by electromagnetic forces (from the magnetized plasma) or by gravitation. The plasma is here (as in most regions in space) a "dusty plasma." A grain can pass the limit in three different ways. Its mass can increase due to condensation of refractory substances in the plasma or accretion of other grains. There can also be a change in the electrostatic potential of the grain. As we have seen in ch. 5 such changes are known from space research to occur in an erratic way, sometimes resulting in a jump of two or three orders of magnitude (between a few volts and 1000 volts). It is quite likely that such changes would also occur under hetegonic conditions.

In the following we shall treat the simple case for which the transition from plasma motion to a collisionally perturbed Kepler motion takes place in a time which is short compared to one Kepler period.

If gas is falling in and becoming ionized at a constant rate, and the condensation products are also removed at a constant rate, a state of time-independent partial corotation may be established. The condition for this is that the rate of transfer of angular momentum equals the angular momentum required to put the infalling gas into rotation. The transfer of angular momentum may be regulated by the density of the plasma in the depleted region between the central body and the plasma element to be accelerated. This density determines the maximum current which transfers the momentum.

In the next section we discuss the state of equilibrium motion of an element of plasma situated in a magnetic flux tube which we have earlier referred to as superprominence (see fig. 16.6.1).

17.2 PARTIAL COROTATION OF A PLASMA IN MAGNETIC AND GRAVITATIONAL FIELDS

We have found that it is important to study the fundamental behavior of a corotating plasma in the environment of a central body with mass M_c and a magnetic dipole moment μ, coaxial with the rotational axis (of the central body and of the plasma).

Consider a volume of plasma located at (r, λ) and in the state of partial corotation with angular velocity ω. We assume that the plasma temperature is so low that pressure effects and diamagnetic effects are negligible. The plasma is subject to three forces:

Gravitational force $\qquad \mathbf{f_G} = \dfrac{GM_c}{r^3}(-\mathbf{r})$ $\qquad\qquad\qquad$ (17.2.1)

Centrifugal force $\qquad \mathbf{f_c} = (\omega^2 r \cos \lambda)\mathbf{x}$ $\qquad\qquad\qquad$ (17.2.2)

Electromagnetic force $\qquad \mathbf{f_B} = \mathbf{I} \times \mathbf{B}$ $\qquad\qquad\qquad$ (17.2.3)

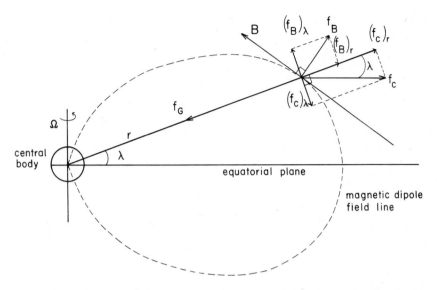

FIGURE 17.2.1.—Partial corotation. Equilibrium between gravitational force f_G, centrifugal force f_c, and electromagnetic force f_B implies that $f_G + f_c + f_B = 0$. Because $(f_c)_\lambda + (f_B)_\lambda = 0$, the geometry of the magnetic dipole field requires that $(f_c)_r = 2(f_B)_r = 2/3(-f_G)$. (From Alfvén et al., 1974.)

where **x** is a unit vector perpendicular to the axis of rotation, **B** the magnetic field, and **I** the current in the plasma (fig. 17.2.1).

The condition for equilibrium is

$$F = f_G + f_c + f_B = 0 \qquad (17.2.4)$$

The components of **B** along the r and λ axes are

$$B_r = \frac{2\mu}{r^3} \sin \lambda \qquad (17.2.5)$$

and

$$B_\lambda = \frac{\mu}{r^3} \cos \lambda \qquad (17.2.6)$$

289

As the ϕ components of F, f_c and f_G are zero we obtain:

$$\frac{I_\lambda}{I_r} = \frac{B_\lambda}{B_r} \tag{17.2.7}$$

showing that currents along the magnetic field lines are possible (under the condition that they do not perturb the dipole field too much). Further, $F_\lambda = 0$ gives:

$$f_c \sin \lambda = (f_B)_\lambda = I_\phi \frac{2\mu}{r^3} \sin \lambda \tag{17.2.8}$$

or (if $\lambda \neq 0$)

$$f_c = \frac{2\mu I_\phi}{r^3} \tag{17.2.9}$$

Finally $F_r = 0$, and consequently

$$f_G = f_c \cos \lambda + I_\phi \frac{\mu}{r^3} \cos \lambda \tag{17.2.10}$$

From eq. (17.2.9) follows:

$$f_c \cos \lambda = 2 I_\phi \frac{\mu}{r^3} \cos \lambda \tag{17.2.11}$$

Substituting eq. (17.2.11) into eq. (17.2.10) we see that the r component of the centrifugal force is twice the r component of the electromagnetic force and hence $2/3$ of the gravitational force. From eqs. (17.2.10) and (17.2.11) follows a theorem for the partial corotation of a plasma: *The gravitational force is balanced, 2/3 by the centrifugal force and 1/3 by the electromagnetic force.*

This law does not hold in the plane $\lambda=0$ where eq. (17.2.8) allows any rotational velocity.

We now find the tangential velocity $v_\phi=r\omega\cos\lambda$ characteristic of the state of partial corotation. From eqs. (17.2.1–17.2.2) and (17.2.10–17.2.11) follows

$$\frac{2}{3}\frac{GM_c}{r}=r^2\omega^2\cos^2\lambda=v_\phi^2 \qquad (17.2.12)$$

The state of rotation described in eq. (17.2.12) will be referred to as *partial corotation*.

17.2.1 Relation Between Ferraro Isorotation and Partial Corotation

If the conductivity of the central body and of the plasma is infinite, all parts of the plasma must rotate with the same angular velocity Ω as the central body. Under these conditions eq. (17.2.4) is satisfied only at the surface given by eq. (17.2.12), where

$$r_s=\left(\frac{2GM_c}{3\Omega^2\cos^2\lambda}\right)^{1/3} \qquad (17.2.13)$$

and at the surface

$$\lambda=0 \qquad (17.2.14)$$

If $r<r_s$, gravitation dominates and the plasma will fall down on the central body.

If $r>r_s$, centrifugal force dominates and the plasma will "fall down" to the equatorial plane.

Applying our model to cases of cosmic interest we will find under both conditions that the main opposing force is the pressure gradient which we have neglected. The result is that the plasma separates at $r=r_s$, the inner part becoming an ionosphere around the central body and the outer part forming a ring in the equatorial plane.

17.3 A PLASMA IN PARTIAL COROTATION

Comparing (17.2.12) with a circular Kepler motion with radius r characterized by

$$v_K{}^2 = \frac{GM_c}{r} \qquad (17.3.1)$$

we can state as a general theorem: *If in the magnetic dipole field of a rotating central body a plasma element is in a state of partial corotation, its kinetic energy is two-thirds the kinetic energy of a circular Kepler motion at the same radial distance.*

This factor 2/3 derives from the geometry of a dipole field and enters because the centrifugal force makes a smaller angle with a magnetic field line than does the gravitational force. The plasma element is supported against gravitation in part by the centrifugal force and in part by the current I_ϕ which interacts with the magnetic field to give a force. The above treatment, strictly speaking, applies only to plasma situated at nonzero latitudes. The equatorial plane represents a singularity. However, as this plane will be occupied by a disc of grains and gas with a thickness of a few degrees, the mathematical singularity is physically uninteresting.

Table 17.3.1 compares the energy and angular momentum of a circular Kepler motion and a circular motion of a magnetized plasma.

TABLE 17.3.1

Comparison Between Kepler Motion and Partial Corotation

	Circular Kepler motion	Partial corotation of magnetized plasma
Gravitational energy	$-\dfrac{GM_c}{r}$	$-\dfrac{GM_c}{r}$
Kinetic energy	$\dfrac{1}{2}\dfrac{GM_c}{r}$	$\dfrac{1}{3}\dfrac{GM_c}{r}$
Total energy	$-\dfrac{1}{2}\dfrac{GM_c}{r}$	$-\dfrac{2}{3}\dfrac{GM_c}{r}$
Orbital angular momentum	$(GM_cr)^{1/2}$	$(\tfrac{2}{3}GM_cr)^{1/2}$

If the plasma has considerable thermal energy, diamagnetic repulsion from the dipole gives an outward force having a component which adds to the centrifugal force. This makes the factor in eq. (17.2.12) smaller than two-thirds. It can be shown that this effect is of importance if the thermal energy $W_T = \delta k(T_e + T_i)$ (where δ is the degree of ionization, k is Boltzmann's constant, and T_e and T_i are the electron and ion temperatures) is comparable to the kinetic energy of a plasma particle $W = \frac{1}{2} m v_\phi^2$. Choosing arbitrarily the environment close to Saturn to give an example of the effect, we put $m = 10 m_H = 1.7 \times 10^{-23}$ g, $v_\phi = 2 \times 10^6$ cm/sec ($=$ orbital velocity of Mimas) and $\delta = 10$ percent. We find that $W_T/W = 1$ percent, if $T_e = T_i = 15\ 000$K. This indicates that the temperature correction is probably not very important in the case we have considered.

17.4 DISCUSSION

It is a well-known observational fact that in solar prominences matter flows down along the magnetic flux tube to the surface of the Sun, presumably under the action of gravitation. The plasma cannot move perpendicular to the flux tube because of electromagnetic forces. The solar prominences are, however, confined to regions close to the Sun and this state of motion is such that the centrifugal force is unimportant. In contrast our super-prominences would extend to regions very far away from the central body (see fig. 16.6.1), roughly to the regions where the resulting secondary bodies would be located. In these superprominences the components of the centrifugal force and the gravitational attraction parallel to the flux tube may balance each other, keeping the plasma in a state of dynamic equilibrium; i.e., the state of partial corotation. This state is analyzed in some further detail by De (1973).

17.5 CONDENSATION OF THE PLASMA:
THE TWO-THIRDS LAW

If a grain in the plasma is transferred through the limit m_{Lm} (sec. 5.4) its motion changes from the type we have investigated, and under certain conditions its trajectory will be a Kepler ellipse. We shall confine the discussion to the simple case of the grains which have grown large enough, or have had their electric charge reduced, so that they are influenced neither by electromagnetic forces nor by viscosity due to the plasma. Furthermore, this transition is assumed to be instantaneous so that the initial velocity of a grain equals the velocity of the plasma element from which it derives.

As the initial velocity of the grain is $(2/3)^{1/2}$ of the circular Kepler velocity at its position, a grain at the initial position (r_0, λ_0, ϕ_0) will move in an ellipse with the eccentricity $e = 1/3$ (see fig. 17.5.1). Its apocenter A is situated at (r_0, λ_0, ϕ_0) and its pericenter P at (r_P, λ_P, ϕ_P).

$$r_P = \frac{r_0}{2} \qquad\qquad (17.5.1)$$

$$\lambda_P = -\lambda_0 \qquad\qquad (17.5.2)$$

$$\phi_P = \phi_0 + \pi \qquad\qquad (17.5.3)$$

The ellipse intersects the equatorial plane $\lambda = 0$ at the nodal points $(r_\Omega, 0, \phi_0 + \pi/2)$ and $(r_\Omega, 0, \phi_0 - \pi/2)$ with

$$r_\Omega = \frac{2r_0}{3} \qquad\qquad (17.5.4)$$

When the grain reaches r_Ω its angular velocity equals the angular velocity of a body moving in a Kepler circle with radius r_Ω in the orbital plane of the grain.

If we assume that grains are released only from a ring element (r_0, λ_0) of plasma, all of them will then cross the equatorial plane at the circle $r_\Omega = 2r_0/3$. Suppose that there is a small body (*embryo*) moving in a circular Kepler orbit in the equatorial plane with orbital radius r_Ω. It will be hit by grains, and we assume for now that all grains hitting the embryo are retained by it. Each grain has the same angular momentum per unit mass as the embryo. However, the angular momentum vector of the embryo is parallel to the rotation axis, whereas the angular momentum vector of the grain makes an angle λ_0 with the axis. In case λ_0 is so small that we can put $\cos \lambda_0 = 1$, the embryo will grow in size but not change its orbit. (If $\cos \lambda_0 < 1$, the embryo will slowly spiral inward while growing.)

Seen from the coordinate system of the embryo, the grains will arrive with their velocity vectors in the meridional plane of the embryo. These velocities have a component parallel to the rotation axis of the central body, equal to $(2GM_c/3r_0)^{1/2} \sin \lambda_0$, and a component in the equatorial plane of, and directed toward, the central body, equal to $(GM_c/12r_0)^{1/2}$.

The existence of an embryo in the above discussion is assumed merely to illustrate the importance of the circular orbit with radius $2r_0/3$ in the equatorial plane. All the grains which are released at a distance r_0 from the center will cross the equatorial plane at the circumference of this circle, irre-

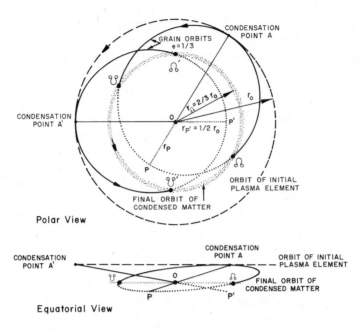

Polar View

Equatorial View

FIGURE 17.5.1.—The condensation process. The outer dashed line represents the circular orbit of a plasma element in the partially corotating plasma. Condensation produces small solid grains which move in Kepler ellipses with eccentricity $e = 1/3$. Two such grain orbits are shown, one originating from condensation at A and the other, at A'. The condensation point A, which hence is the apocenter of the former orbit, has the spherical coordinates (r_0, λ_0, ϕ_0). The pericenter P is at $r_P = r_0/2$, $\lambda_P = -\lambda_0$, $\phi_P = \phi_0 + \pi$, and the nodal points are at $r_{\Omega} = 2r_0/3$, $\lambda_{\Omega} = 0$, and $\phi_{\Omega} = \phi_0 \pm \pi/2$. Collisions between a large number of such grains result in the final (circular) orbit of solid particles in the equatorial plane. The eccentricity $1/3$ of the initial grain orbit and the radius $2r_0/3$ of the final orbit of condensed matter are direct consequences of the plasma being in the state of partial corotation (see secs. 17.3–17.5).

spective of the value of λ_0 (under the condition that we can put cos $\lambda_0 = 1$). These grains will collide with each other and coalesce to form increasingly larger embryos until these are large enough to accrete smaller grains. The large bodies thus produced will move in a circular orbit in the equatorial plane with radius $2r_0/3$.

17.5.1 Conclusions

Summarizing our results, we have found that a plasma cloud in the dipole field of a rotating central body need not necessarily attain the same angular velocity as the central body. If in the region between the plasma cloud and the central body the density is so low that the parallel electric field may differ from zero, a steady state characterized by a partial corotation described in table 17.3.1 is possible. If at a central distance r_0 grains condense out of such a plasma, they will move in ellipses with a semimajor axis $3r_0/4$ and an eccentricity $e = 1/3$. Mutual collisions between a population of such grains will finally make the condensed matter move in a circle in the equatorial plane with the radius $2r_0/3$ (see fig. 17.5.1).

In the more general case, when condensation takes place over a wider range of latitudes and central distances in an extended region, one would expect that each condensate grain will ultimately be moving in a circle at a distance of $2/3$ times the distance where the condensation has taken place. This may occur under certain conditions, but is not generally true because collisions between the grains are no longer restricted to the equatorial plane. There will be competitive processes through which grains accrete to become larger embryos moving in eccentric orbits. However, the semimajor axes of these orbits are $2/3$ the weighted mean of the radius vector to the points of condensation (see ch. 18).

17.6 ENERGY RELEASE DURING ANGULAR MOMENTUM TRANSFER

The transfer of angular momentum from the central body to the surrounding plasma is accompanied by a conversion of kinetic energy into heat. Suppose that a central body with a moment of inertia Ξ is decelerated from the spin angular velocity Ω to $\Omega - \Delta\Omega$ by accelerating a mass m, at orbital distance r, from rest to an angular velocity ω. Then we have

$$\Xi \Delta\Omega = mr^2\omega \qquad (17.6.1)$$

The energy released by this process is

$$W = \frac{\Xi}{2}(\Omega^2 - [\Omega - \Delta\Omega]^2) - \frac{mr^2\omega^2}{2} \qquad (17.6.2)$$

Assuming $\Delta\Omega \ll \Omega$ we have

$$W = \Xi\Omega\Delta\Omega - \frac{mr^2\omega^2}{2} \qquad (17.6.3)$$

and with eq. (17.6.1) we find

$$W = mr^2\omega^2 \left(\frac{\Omega}{\omega} - \frac{1}{2}\right) \tag{17.6.4}$$

As has been studied previously in detail (Alfvén, 1954), the ionized gas will fall toward the central body along the magnetic lines of force, but at the same time its ω value is increased because of the transfer of momentum from the central body. When the velocity ωr has reached approximately the Kepler velocity, the gas will move out again. The bodies that are formed out of such a nebula move in Kepler orbits. Hence, the final result is that ωr equals the Kepler velocity, so that

$$mr^2\omega^2 = \frac{GM_cm}{r} \tag{17.6.5}$$

This gives

$$W = \frac{GM_cm}{r}\left(\frac{\Omega}{\omega} - \frac{1}{2}\right) \tag{17.6.6}$$

If to this we add the kinetic energy of the falling gas, GM_cm/r, we obtain the total available energy,

$$W' = \frac{GM_cm}{r}\left(\frac{\Omega}{\omega} + \frac{1}{2}\right) \tag{17.6.7}$$

This energy is dissipated in the plasma in the form of heat. In fact, this may have been the main source of heating and ionizing of the circumsolar and circumplanetary nebulae during the hetegonic era.

Equation (17.6.7) gives the energy release which necessarily accompanies any process by which a mass m initially at rest is put into orbit by transfer of spin angular momentum from a central body. If the transfer is effected by electromagnetic forces, the energy is normally released by electric currents which ionize and heat the plasma. As typically W is much larger than the sum of ionization energies for all the atoms in m, often several hundred times (see ch. 23), the energy released in the process of putting a mass into orbit is amply sufficient for producing a high degree of ionization. This emphasizes the conclusion in sec. 15.6 that hydromagnetic processes necessarily must control the formative processes in the solar system.

18

ACCRETION OF THE CONDENSATION PRODUCTS

18.1 SURVEY

The accretion of grains to larger bodies is one of the main problems in the theory of formation of planets and satellites. In parts A and B we have found that this process takes place in two steps, the first one leading to the formation of jet streams and the second one, studied in chs. 6 and 12, leading to the formation of large bodies inside the jet streams.

The first three chapters (15–17) of part C represent an attempt to trace the plasma processes that have led to the formation of grains. In ch. 17 we found that under certain conditions a state called partial corotation may be established, which places grains in Kepler orbits with eccentricity of 1/3. Whether the conditions for partial corotation were really satisfied during hetegonic times can be ascertained only by looking for evidence in the solar system today that may have derived from such a state.

This chapter shall be devoted to such evidence. More specifically, we shall study the intermediate process (namely, the accretion of grains and the formation of jet streams) and compare the products of these processes with observations.

The study is facilitated by the fact that in certain parts of the solar system we find intermediate products of these processes. In the asteroidal region as well as in the Saturnian ring system accretion has not led to the formation of large bodies, a process which necessarily obliterates much of the stored information. In the asteroidal region the reason for this seems to be the extremely low space density of the condensed matter (see sec. 4.3.4), whereas in the Saturnian ring system the formation of large bodies has been prevented because the region is situated inside the Roche limit.

Hence we shall in this chapter treat the development of a population of orbiting grains with the aim of developing three theories:

(1) A theory of the formation of the Saturnian rings.

(2) A theory of the formation of the asteroid belt.

(3) A theory of the formation of jet streams as an intermediate stage in the formation of satellites and planets.

We have tried to develop the first of the above theories in secs. 18.5–18.6, the second in secs. 18.7–18.8, and the third in sec. 18.10.

18.2 EVOLUTION OF ORBITS DUE TO COLLISIONS

The accretion of grains to larger bodies has been treated in part B where observations were predominately analyzed with the aid of celestial mechanics. Here we shall treat the same problem, but as a starting point we choose the state of partial corotation and the motion of grains resulting from it. As we shall discover, it is possible to unify the two pictures.

In a partially corotating plasma, grains are placed in Kepler ellipses with $e = 1/3$ (fig. 17.5.1). The major axis of such an ellipse passes through the point of condensation (the apocenter) and the central body (focus), and the minor axis is located in the equatorial plane. The pericentric distance is $1/2$, and the distance of the nodes is $2/3$ of the apocentric distance.

We shall study the development of an assembly of such grains under the action of gravitational forces alone. Pursuing the ideas of ch. 5, we assume that the interaction of the grains with the plasma is negligible, and that electromagnetic forces do not influence their motion. The meaning of these assumptions has already been analyzed quantitatively in ch. 5.

Under the idealized assumptions of a spherical homogeneous central body with a single grain orbiting around it, the orbit of this grain will remain unchanged with time. If the central body assumes an ellipsoidal shape due to rotation, this will result in a secular change (precession) in the orientation of the orbit of the grain (see ch. 3). In a realistic case, one must also consider the gravitational perturbations from other neighboring celestial bodies, whether full grown or embryonic. Such perturbations also produce precession. (At the same time they produce long period changes in the eccentricity and inclination of the orbit, but these are of small amplitude and not very important in this connection.) If other grains are present in the same region of space, the gravitation from their dispersed mass also produces secular disturbances of the same type.

However, the most important systematic change in the orbits of an assembly of grains is due to their mutual collisions, which are inelastic, or at least partially so. At such a collision, kinetic energy is converted into heat but the sum of the orbital angular momenta of the two colliding grains does not change. Collisions may also result in fragmentation or in accretion.

The general result of inelastic collisions within a population of grains with intersecting orbits is that the eccentricities of the orbits decrease with time, and so do the inclinations in relation to the invariant plane of the population (fig. 18.2.1). In our model of condensation of grains, the angular momentum of the population of grains ultimately derives from the rotation of the central body. Assuming the process of condensation to be symmetrical with respect to the equatorial plane, the invariant plane of the population will be coincident with the equatorial plane.

If gas is present in the region, the effect of viscosity on the motion of the

eccentricity

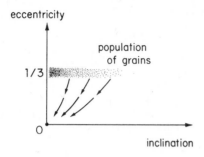

population
of grains

1/3

0

inclination

FIGURE 18.2.1.—Development of a population of grains originally orbiting in ellipses with eccentricity $e = 1/3$ and varying inclinations i. The final state with $e = 0$ and $i = 0$ is either a thin disc of grains or a group of planets (or satellites), in circular orbits in an equatorial plane.

grains may be important, particularly in the case of small grains. If we consider the gas molecules as extremely small "grains," the presence of gas essentially means an enrichment of population in the low end of the mass spectrum of the grains. However, we must observe that collisions between molecules may be perfectly elastic, whereas collisions involving grains and aggregates are always more or less inelastic.

Using the terminology of secs. 3.2–3.4, we can state that collisions and viscosity make both the axial oscillations and the epicycle motion decrease, eventually leaving the grains in unperturbed circular orbits.

One example of this state is the Saturnian ring system, where a large number of small bodies form an extremely thin disc (thickness ∼2 km or less), each body moving in a circle with an angular velocity that decreases outward according to Kepler's laws. A general survey of the state of the Saturnian rings may be found in Cook et al. (1973). Other examples of relatively unperturbed circular motion are the different groups of planets or satellites (see sec. 18.10). Each one of the bodies in a group is likely to have formed from a single population of grains that evolved through mutual collisions. Most of the planets and satellites move in almost circular orbits with small inclinations.

The asteroids represent an intermediate stage in this evolution. The present eccentricities are on the average about one-half of the original value 0.33, and the present inclinations probably represent a similar decrease in relation to the unknown primeval distribution.

18.3 THE ROCHE LIMIT

Suppose that a small solid sphere of radius R and density Θ moves in a circular orbit of radius r around a spherical central body of radius R_c and density Θ_c, the mass of the latter body being much larger than that of the former. Consider an infinitely small test particle of mass m on the surface of the sphere closest to the central body. The particle is acted upon by the gravitation f_G of the sphere

$$f_G = \frac{4\pi G\Theta R}{3} \tag{18.3.1}$$

and by the tidal force f_t from the central body

$$f_t = \frac{4\pi}{3} G\Theta_c R_c^3 \left[\frac{1}{(r-R)^2} - \frac{1}{r^2} \right] \approx \frac{4\pi}{3} G\Theta_c \left(\frac{R_c}{r} \right)^3 2R \tag{18.3.2}$$

The tidal force exceeds the gravitation if

$$\frac{r}{R_c} < \chi \left(\frac{\Theta_c}{\Theta} \right)^{1/3} \tag{18.3.3}$$

with

$$\chi = 2^{1/3} \approx 1.26 \tag{18.3.4}$$

When, instead of the small solid sphere, there is a self-gravitating body consisting of a perfect fluid, the tidal force will deform it from a sphere and, if it is orbiting at a large distance, it will become an ellipsoid. If the orbital radius is decreased the body will become increasingly deformed with the long axis pointing toward the central body and, at a sufficiently small distance, it will become unstable because the tidal force exceeds the self-gravitation of the body. This distance r_R is the well-known Roche limit defined by

$$\frac{r_R}{R_c} = \Lambda \left(\frac{\Theta_c}{\Theta} \right)^{1/3} \tag{18.3.5}$$

with

$$\Lambda = 2.44$$

The outer border of the Saturnian ring system is located at $r = 1.37 \times 10^8$ cm which gives $r/R_b = 2.28$. As Saturn's average density is $\Theta_b = 0.70$ g/cm³, the outer border could be identified with the Roche limit under the following conditions:

(1) The density of the grains is $\Theta = 0.70(2.44/2.88)^3 = 0.75$ g/cm³.

(2) The grains behave like drops of a perfect fluid.

(3) The gravitational field of all adjacent grains can be neglected.

We have no independent way of determining the density of the grains, so (1) may or may not be true.

According to some authors, the material in the rings is likely to occur as loosely bound particles in the form of spindle-shaped aggregates with their long axes tangent to their orbits; that is, at right angles to what is supposed in the Roche theory. Other authors have proposed similar elongated aggregates but with their long axes perpendicular to the equatorial plane. So (2) is probably not satisfied.

The mass of the ring is so small that it does not perturb the Saturnian gravitational field very much. The tidal effect, however, is produced by the field gradient, and adjacent grains may very well produce local perturbations. Hence it is doubtful whether (3) is satisfied.

The conclusion is that the identification of the outer border of the ring with the Roche limit is not very convincing from a theoretical point of view.

However, from an observational point of view there is no doubt that the outer limit of the ring marks the border between one region where matter does not accrete to larger bodies and another region where it does accrete to satellites. We shall call this limit the "modified Roche limit" (r_{MR}). It is reasonable that this limit is determined by the tidal disruption, but the theory for this is much more complicated and possibly rather different from the classical Roche theory.

Inside r_{MR} matter will be much more dispersed than outside so that the mean free path between collisions will be much smaller in this region than outside of r_{MR}.

18.4 MODEL OF ORBIT DEVELOPMENT

Consider a state when the condensation or plasma capture of grains has proceeded for some time and a large number of grains has been produced. Inside r_{MR} collisions between the grains have damped their radial and axial oscillations so that they move in circular orbits and form a thin disc in the equatorial plane. Newly condensed grains moving in orbits with nonzero inclination will pass this plane twice in every orbital revolution. Sooner or later such a new grain will collide with a disc grain knocking the latter out of the disc. The two grains will continue to oscillate about the plane of the disc, but will collide again with other disc grains. After some time the oscillations are damped out and all grains will be incorporated in the disc.

In the model we are going to develop we assume that inside r_{MR} disturbances caused by the arrival of a newly formed grain are so small and so rapidly damped out that every new grain essentially interacts with a thin disc of grains that condensed earlier.

Outside r_{MR} the collisions between the grains lead to accretion, first to larger aggregates or embryos and eventually to satellites. If this process is rapid enough, the mean free path between collisions may continue to be so long that the grains do not settle into the equatorial plane before new grains arrive. Hence collisions may also take place outside the equatorial plane. This may lead to a formation of jet streams. Although the theory of formation of jet streams is not yet worked out well enough to specify in detail the conditions for this, the general discussion in ch. 6 indicates that when condensation takes place outside the limit r_{MR} a series of jet streams will probably form.

At the same time collisions will often result in production of extremely small grains by fragmentation or recondensation of vapor. As these small grains mutually collide they may form a thin disc (possibly with a small total mass) even outside the r_{MR} limit, and coexisting with the jet streams.

Hence our model of orbit development should deal with two regions: one for $r < r_{MR}$, in which the accretion leads to the formation of a thin disc, and the other for $r > r_{MR}$, where it leads to the formation of jet streams.

18.5 ACCRETION INSIDE r_{MR}

As found in sec. 17.5, a grain generated at (r_0, λ_0, ϕ_0) in a coordinate system with the equatorial plane as the reference plane and the origin at the center of the central body will intersect the equatorial disc at $(2r_0/3, 0, \phi_0 + \pi/2)$. We center our attention on a condensation so close to the equatorial plane that we can put $\cos \lambda_0 \approx 1$ (but we exclude a very thin region close to the plane because of the singularity for $\lambda = 0$ (see sec. 17.2). In this case the angular momentum of a new grain with reference to the axis of the coordinate system is the same as that of the disc grains at $r = 2r_0/3$. Hence the tangential component of its velocity at collision with a disc grain equals the tangential velocity of the disc grain so that, seen from the disc grain, the velocity of the new grain lies in the meridional plane. Its component parallel to the axis is $(2GM_c/3r_0)^{1/2} \sin \lambda_0$ and the component in the equatorial plane is $(GM_c/12r_0)^{1/2}$.

Let us first discuss the case in which the collision between the new grain and the disc grain is almost perfectly inelastic, by which we mean that the relative velocity between two grains after collision is small but not zero.

Such a collision does not change the angular momentum of either grain, but only their velocity components in the meridional plane. After the collision, the grains will return to the equatorial plane at the point $(2r_0/3, 0, \phi_0 + 3\pi/2)$, where they may collide again with other disc grains. In this way new disc grains will be set in motion, but they will all reach the equatorial plane again at $(2r_0/3, 0, \phi_0 + \pi/2)$. A repetition of this process will result in more and more disc grains being set in motion with decreasing amplitude, so that the perturbation caused by the new grain is damped out and the grain is incorporated into the disc.

It is important to observe that this whole process *affects only the disc grains at* $r = 2r_0/3$. The rest of the disc remains entirely unaffected (see fig. 17.5.1). This means that the *disc can be regarded as a kinematic image of the condensing plasma* diminished in the proportion 2/3.

We shall now discuss the limitations of our idealized model.

(1) If the collision between the grains is only partially inelastic, part of the momentum contained in velocity components in the meridional plane may cause a change in the angular momentum. This will also cause a "diffusion" of the perturbation to grains closer or more distant than $2r_0/3$. In a realistic case this diffusion may not be very important.

(2) If $\cos \lambda_0 < 1$, disc grains at $2r_0/3$ will be hit by new grains with smaller angular momenta. This will cause the grains to slowly spiral inward as they orbit around the central body. However, if the grains reach a region where they are not hit by new grains, the inward motion stops.

(3) The idealized case is applicable if the disc is opaque so that the new grain collides with a disc grain at its first passage. If the disc is not opaque, so that the grain is not likely to collide until after many transits, we must introduce the restriction that the collision should take place before a considerable change in the orbit of the new grain has taken place. Such a change may be due to precession, but it may also be produced by collisions outside the equatorial plane.

(4) The collision may also result in accretion or in fragmentation. In the latter case, all the fragments will move in orbits which bring them back at the point of fragmentation where they may collide again. Thus the fragments will in course of time be incorporated in the disc by the mechanism discussed above. The same is true of accretion. The entire process may be visualized as damping of oscillations around a circular orbit at $r = 2r_0/3$ (sec. 3.3).

18.6 STRUCTURE OF THE SATURNIAN RINGS

We shall apply our models of condensation and orbit evolution to the Saturnian ring system. This consists of three rings: The outermost is called

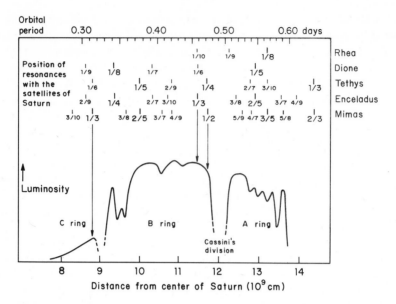

FIGURE 18.6.1.—Photometric curve of the Saturnian rings (according to Dollfus, 1961). The abscissa gives the distance from the center of Saturn in cm. The top scale gives the orbital period of the particles. The periods, which are integral fractions of the periods of the inner Saturnian satellites, are marked in the upper part of the diagram. According to the resonance theory, the density minima in the ring system should be produced by resonance with these satellites. The lack of correlation between low-integer resonances and structural features shows that this is not the case.

the A ring and is separated by a dark region called *Cassini's division* from the B ring which is the brightest of the rings. Inside the B ring is the very faint C ring, also known as the crape ring on account of its darkness.

The photometric curve given by Dollfus (fig. 18.6.1) shows that near the outer edge of the A ring there is a series of light maxima and minima. A double minimum exists near the inner edge of the B ring. In the middle of the B ring two minima are visible. The rings lie in the equatorial plane of the planet and consist of numerous small particles that orbit around the planet with the orbital period increasing outward in accordance with Kepler's law. The thickness of the rings is about 2 km (Cook et al., 1973).

18.6.1 The Resonance Theory of the Ring Structure

The suggestion has been made in the past that the structure of the ring system is produced by resonance effects with the inner satellites. Different investigators have claimed that Cassini's division is due to a resonance with Mimas resulting in removal of particles from the dark region; the particles are removed because their period is exactly $1/2$ of the period of Mimas. The resonance corresponding to $1/3$ of the period of Enceladus also falls close to Cassini's division. In a similar way the sharp change in intensity between the B ring and the C ring should be connected with the $1/3$ resonance with the period of Mimas. A list of claimed resonances has been given by Alexander (1953, 1962).

Figure 18.6.1 shows a plot of all resonances with denominators ≤ 10. The resonances with denominators ≤ 5 are marked with heavy lines. A number of resonance points of Mimas and Tethys are similar because the period of Mimas is half the period of Tethys. The same is the case for the pair Enceladus-Dione. It should be remembered that the periods of Mimas, Enceladus, Tethys, and Dione are approximately proportional to $2/3/4/6$; see table 8.5.1.

As was pointed out in sec. 8.7, a comparison between the calculated resonance points and the observed pattern of the ring system does not show any obvious connection. The $1/2$ resonance of Mimas definitely falls inside Cassini's division. Half the period of Mimas differs by 1.2 percent from the period of the outermost particles of the B ring and by 4 percent from that of the innermost particles of the A ring. The difference between the $1/3$ resonance with Enceladus and Cassini's division is still larger. Nor is there any obvious connection between other markings, bright or dark, and the resonance points.

In this respect the Saturnian rings are strikingly different from the asteroid belt, where there are very pronounced gaps corresponding to integral fractions of Jupiter's period (the Kirkwood gaps). For example, near the resonances $1/3$ and $2/5$ of Jupiter's period there is a complete absence of observed asteroids (see figs. 4.3.3 and 18.6.2). As Cassini's division has been attributed to resonances that are displaced by a few percent, it is of interest to see whether a similar asymmetry exists for the asteroids. We see from figs. 4.3.3 and 18.6.2, with reference to the resonance points the asymmetry of the gaps, if any, is only a fraction of 1 percent. The half-width is about 1.5 percent. Hence with the same relative breadth any resonance gaps corresponding to $1/2$ Mimas' and $1/3$ Enceladus' periods would be altogether within the B ring and outside Cassini's division. Further, there is not the slightest trace of a resonance gap in the B ring corresponding to either $2/5$ of Mimas' period or $1/3$ of Enceladus' period.

Therefore, from an observational point of view there is no real similarity between the asteroid gaps on one side and the low-density regions of the Saturnian rings on the other. In fact, fig. 18.6.1 indicates that if anything is characteristic for Cassini's division it is that not a single resonance point falls in that region.

The reason why the low-density regions of the Saturnian rings show no similarity to the Kirkwood gaps is likely to be the much smaller magnitude

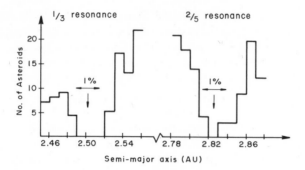

FIGURE 18.6.2.—The number of asteroids as a function of the semimajor axis showing gaps in the asteroid belt. The vertical arrows mark the orbital distances where the period of an asteroid is 1/3 or 2/5 of the period of Jupiter. The horizontal arrows extend 1 percent of the orbital distance for each resonance indicating the close correspondence of resonance points to these Kirkwood gaps. The reason why there are resonance gaps in the asteroid belt but not in the Saturnian rings is that the mass ratio Jupiter/Sun is 10 000 times larger than the mass ratio Mimas/Saturn.

of the perturbing force. The masses of Mimas and Enceladus are of the order of 10^{-7} of the Saturnian mass, whereas the mass of Jupiter is about 10^{-3} of the solar mass. As by definition the ratio of the relative distances from the perturbed bodies to the central body and to the perturbing body is the same in the two cases, the relative magnitude of the perturbing force is about 10^{-4} times less in the Saturnian rings than in the asteroidal belt.

Hence it seems legitimate to doubt whether Mimas and Enceladus are large enough to produce any phenomenon similar to the asteroid gaps. In fact the sharpness of a resonance effect is generally inversely proportional to the perturbing force. Hence we should expect the relative breadth of a Kirkwood gap in the Saturnian rings to be 10^{-4} of the breadth in the asteroid population. As the latter is of the order of 1 percent, the dark marking in the Saturnian rings should have a relative breadth of 10^{-4} percent, which is well below the limit of observability. These objections to the resonance theory also apply to its recent development by Franklin and Colombo (1970).

Further, it should be noted that the resonance theories have so far not been able to give an acceptable explanation of why the B ring is brighter than the A ring.

Concerning the sharp limit between the B ring and the C ring it has been claimed that the 1/3 resonance of Mimas should be responsible for the very large positive derivative of the light curve. However, the 1/3 resonance of Enceladus is situated somewhat inside Cassini's division in a region where the derivative of the light curve is slightly negative. There is no obvious reason why the same type of resonance with different satellites should produce such different results. Furthermore, in the asteroid belt the 1/3 resonance with Jupiter produces a sharp gap, but the mass densities on both sides of the gap are about equal (fig. 4.3.4).

18.6.2 Can the Structure of the Saturnian Rings Be of Hetegonic Origin?

Our conclusion is that the resonance theory has not succeeded in explaining the main characteristics of the Saturnian rings. Furthermore, it is difficult to imagine that any other force acting at the present time could produce the observed structure. We therefore ask ourselves whether the structure of the rings could have been produced when the rings were formed and preserved for 4 or 5 billion years to the present time.

Such a view implies, however, that at least some parts of the solar system have an enormous degree of dynamic stability. Many scientists may object to this idea. Nevertheless, we have already found that except in the cases when tidal braking has been important (Earth, Neptune, and perhaps Mercury) planetary spins have probably not changed very much since hetegonic times (see secs. 9.7 and 9.8). Furthermore, as found in sec. 8.1, the orbit-orbit resonances must also have been produced at the time the bodies were formed. The general conclusions in ch. 10 indicate that with a few exceptions there has been very little dynamic change in the solar system since its formation. Hence there should be no a priori objections to the view that the present structure of the Saturnian rings was produced when the rings were formed and that even the fine structure may have originated during formation.

18.6.3 Hetegonic Theory of the Saturnian Rings

Several independent arguments, experimental as well as theoretical, suggest that the hetegonic era of the solar system must have extended over a time period of the order 3×10^8 yr (see secs. 12.8–12.9). In the Saturnian region, the matter which at present constitutes the satellites and the rings would consequently have been introduced around the planet during an extended period of time. This emplacement can be envisaged as a continuous infall of gas, or an injection of a series of gas jets, during a period perhaps as long as 3×10^8 yr. The gas became ionized upon reaching critical velocity (ch. 21), was brought into a state of partial corotation (ch. 17), and the condensable components of the resulting plasma condensed to grains. It is also possible that a significant fraction of the condensable material consisted of transplanetary dust, which at infall became electromagnetically trapped by the plasma emplaced around the planet. However, these processes are relatively very rapid; at any given moment only a very small fraction of the total mass now forming the secondary bodies in the solar system could have been present as plasma or neutral gas. Hence the process was producing grains more or less continuously during a very long time.

In sec. 18.5 we discussed some basic processes in the formation of the rings under the assumption that they formed from a partially corotating plasma. The result was that the grains which at present are orbiting at a central distance r originally condensed out of a plasma at a distance $3r/2$. The disc forms a "kinematic image" of the plasma diminished by a factor of $2/3$. Therefore, if we want to find the place of origin of present grains, we should enlarge the present orbits by a factor $3/2$. The result is shown in fig. 18.6.3. We find that Cassini's division is projected into the region where Mimas moves, and the border between the B ring and the C ring coincides with the outer edge of the A ring. Remembering that the grains, condensed at a certain distance, interact only with disc grains at $2/3$ of this distance, we may interpret the figure in the following way.

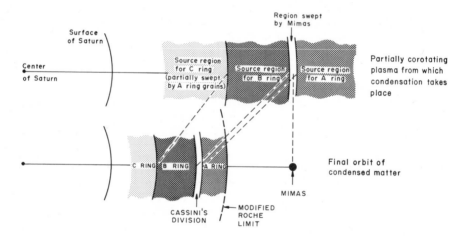

FIGURE 18.6.3.—Condensation of grains from a partially corotating plasma in the environment of Saturn. The condensation is assumed to take place essentially from the neighborhood of the equatorial plane (but only a negligible part in the plane itself). The figure refers to a state in which part of the plasma has already condensed so that Mimas (or its parent jet stream) and the rings already exist, although with only a small part of their present masses. The upper part of the figure refers to the plasma which has not yet condensed. The plasma near the orbit of Mimas condenses on this satellite (or on the jet stream in which it accretes), leaving the "region swept by Mimas" void of plasma. Similarly, the plasma in the region of the extant A ring (and B ring) condenses directly on the grains of the ring. When the grains produced by condensation fall down to $\frac{2}{3}$ of their original central distances, the state depicted in the lower part of the figure is produced. Cassini's division is derived from the region swept by Mimas. The C ring has a reduced intensity because part of the plasma has condensed on the already existing grains of the A ring.

18.6.4 Theory of Cassini's Division

In the region where Mimas moves, a large part of the revolving plasma will condense on Mimas (or perhaps rather on the component grains of the jet stream within which Mimas is forming). Hence in this region there will be little plasma left to form the grains which later would be found at 2/3 of the central distance to Mimas. In other words, we may interpret Cassini's division as what we may call the *hetegonic shadow* of Mimas.

The plasma outside the orbit of Mimas condenses to grains which, having fallen to 2/3 of their initial distance, form the present A ring. However, before they reach this position they have to pass through Mimas' jet stream and part of them will be captured by it. The grains condensing from plasma inside Mimas' orbit fall down to 2/3 of their initial position without passing through Mimas' orbit and form the B ring. This may explain why the B ring is brighter than the A ring.

18.6.5 Theory of the Limit Between the B and C Rings

If the radial distance of the limit between the B and C rings is magnified by a factor 2/3, it coincides with the radial distance of the outer edge of the A ring. The reason for this is that plasma falling into the region inside r_{MR} will rapidly be gathered by the grains already existing there as the growing A ring, thus depleting the plasma which gives rise to C ring grains. In the same way as Mimas produces Cassini's division as its hetegonic shadow at 2/3 of its central distance, the outer edge of the A ring is imaged at 2/3 of its distance.

The qualitative picture in fig. 18.6.3 can be refined and compared directly with observation: See fig. 18.6.4. In the upper left corner the ordinate of the light curve has been reversed and the abscissa reduced by a factor of 2/3. The depletion of plasma causing the hetegonic shadow should depend on the total surface area of the matter, which is proportional to the luminosity. The figure shows that the drop in intensity from the B ring to the C ring occurs almost exactly where we expect the hetegonic shadow to appear. In fact Dollfus' value for the outer limit of the A ring is 13.74×10^9 cm and for the border between the B ring and C ring 9.16×10^9 cm. The ratio between these values happens to be exactly $1.50 = 3/2$.

18.6.6 Discussion

Considering Cassini's division as the hetegonic shadow of Mimas, we find that the fall-down ratio must be slightly higher than 1.5; namely, about 1.55 ($= 1/0.65$). It is doubtful whether we should attribute very much significance to such a slight deviation. If we look for a refinement of the theory, the

313

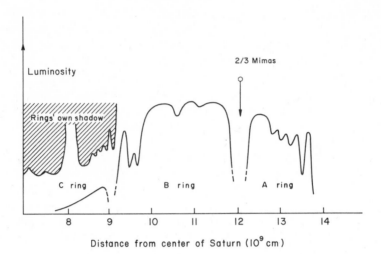

FIGURE 18.6.4.—Hetegonic effects in the Saturnian ring system. Dollfus' photometric profile compared with Mimas' orbital distance reduced by a factor 2/3 (or 0.65). Cassini's divison may be the "hetegonic shadow" of Mimas. In the left corner, the photometric profile is turned upside down and reduced by the factor 2/3 ("ring's own shadow"). The rapid drop in intensity between the B ring and C ring coincides with the beginning of this shadow.

deviation from the value 3/2 of the simple theory can be explained in two ways. It may be an indirect effect of the production of a shadow (Alfvén, 1954) or it may be due to condensation at such a large distance from the equatorial plane that $\cos \lambda_0 < 1$. In contrast, in the resonance theory of Cassini's division it is difficult to see why there should be any deviation from the theoretical resonance, which, as mentioned, is clearly outside Cassini's division.

18.7 ACCRETION OUTSIDE r_{MR}

A model of accretion outside the modified Roche limit must necessarily include a number of hypotheses because we do not know under what conditions a collision results in fragmentation or in accretion, or to what degree it is inelastic. Also, the theory of jet streams is not very well developed, and, in fact, cannot be, until the collision response is quantitatively clarified.

These uncertainties were not very serious for a theory of accretion inside r_{MR}, mainly because the condensed grains almost immediately reached their final location. It is more serious outside r_{MR} because the eventual formation of planets and satellites involves a long chain of processes. Our approach must necessarily be partly phenomenological and essentially provisional.

According to the model in sec. 18.4, outside r_{MR} most of the condensed grains will be captured into jet streams. This does not exclude the existence of a thin disc in the equatorial plane consisting of very small grains resulting from fragmentation and impact vapor condensation; such a disc would not substantially affect the formation of jet streams.

Important aspects of the formation of planets and satellites may be clarified by studying the present state of the asteroidal belt. As has been pointed out in sec. 11.8, this state may be considered as an intermediate "planetesimal" state in planet formation, or in any case as being related to this state. The reason why matter has not gathered into one single body in this region is likely to be the extremely low distributed density of matter condensed there. Indeed, the distributed density is about 10^{-5} of the density in the regions of the giant planets and the terrestrial planets (sec. 2.5). This may mean that accretion takes 10^5 times longer for completion in the asteroidal belt. Hence, even if the time for complete accretion of the terrestrial planets were as short as 10^7 yr, planet formation in the asteroidal belt would require a time longer than the present age of the solar system. There is also the possibility that, due to the low density, accretion never will proceed to the single planet state in the asteroid belt.

Hence the study of the asteroidal region is very important because it will clarify essential features of planetesimal evolution. However, we need not necessarily assume that it is in all details an analog of an early state in, for example, the terrestrial region before the formation of the Earth. Not only the space density but also the structure and composition of the grains and the progression of the collisional processes may be different.

18.8 FORMATION OF THE ASTEROID BELT

In this section we shall study whether the essential features of the asteroid belt can be interpreted as a result of condensation from a partially corotating plasma.

There are certain similarities between the asteroidal belt and the Saturnian rings, but the structure differs in the following respects:

(1) The asteroidal belt is very far outside r_{MR}. No tidal disruption prevents the buildup of larger bodies.

(2) The space density is very low so that collisions are rare. The time scale for development is very large.

(3) Whereas the reason why the grains forming the Saturnian rings have not accreted to larger bodies is that they are moving inside the Roche limit, in the asteroid belt, the bodies have not yet accreted to planets because the density is very low.

(4) Jupiter produces a large number of resonance gaps (Kirkwood gaps)

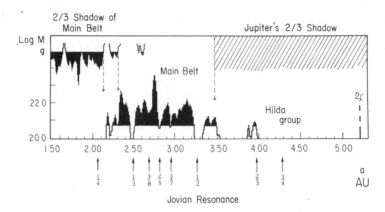

FIGURE 18.8.1.—The smoothed (*M*, *a*) diagram of fig. 4.3.4. Mass distribution in units of grams per radial distance interval of $\Delta a = 0.01$ AU. To emphasize the significance of the log scale, high-density regions are darkened. In analogy with fig. 18.6.4, the diagram, diminished by a factor 2/3 and turned upside down, is shown in the upper part of the diagram demonstrating the "hetegonic shadow" effect which produces the inner cutoff of the asteroidal belt. Similarly Jupiter's shadow, which generates the outer cutoff, is shown, as well as the position of Jupiter. Kirkwood gaps from Jovian resonances are also marked. (From Alfvén et al., 1974.)

of which there are no analogs in the Saturnian rings for reasons discussed in sec. 18.6.1.

The outer border of the main groups of asteroids is situated at a solar distance of 2/3 the distance of Jupiter (figs. 4.3.3 and 18.8.1). On condensing, the grains move in ellipses with $e = 1/3$; hence those grains which form outside the orbit of Jupiter repeatedly cross Jupiter's orbit and there is a high probability that either they are captured by Jupiter (or the jet stream in which Jupiter is forming) or their orbits are perturbed so that they will not ultimately be found at 2/3 of their place of origin. For this reason there are very few asteroids outside 2/3 of Jupiter's orbit. This means that there is no real correspondence to the A ring of the Saturnian system. Mimas, with a mass of only 10^{-7} of the Saturnian mass, has reduced the intensity of the A ring (compared to the B ring), but only to a limited extent.

The inner limit to the asteroid belt is given by its "own hetegonic shadow," just as is the inner limit of the *B* ring around Saturn. The very few asteroids below $a = 2.1$ AU should be an analog to the very faint *C* ring.

18.8.1 Detailed Comparison With (*M*, *a*) Diagram

In ch. 4 both the (*N*, *a*) and the (*M*, *a*) diagrams of the asteroids (figs. 4.3.3–4.3.4) are shown. As the theory in the present chapter refers to the mass distribution, it is preferable in connection with the present discussion to use the (M, a) diagram. This also has the advantage that, in contrast to the (N, a) diagram, this diagram is practically definitive; the discovery of new asteroids may change the (N, a) diagram, but, as the new asteroids necessarily are very small, the (M, a) diagram cannot be changed appreciably.

Here we subject the (M, a) diagram to the same analysis as the Saturnian rings diagram (fig. 18.6.4) by turning it upside down and diminishing and translating it by a factor 2/3. Also Jupiter's shadow (translated to 2/3 of Jupiter's orbital distance) is plotted.

We see that the (M, a) diagram gives a clear definition of the asteroid belt, giving very sharp inner and outer limits. Except the Hilda group which is due to a Jupiter resonance, there are no asteroids inside 2.1 AU or outside 3.50 AU in the diagram because their mass is very small. Looking at fig. 18.8.1, we see that the outer limit of the belt agrees within 1 percent with 2/3 of Jupiter's orbital distance. At almost exactly 2/3 of the outer limit there is a sharp drop in intensity (at 2.32 AU). The inner limit of the belt (at 2.16 AU) agrees just as satisfactorily with 2/3 of the limit (at 3.22 AU) where the density begins to be large (at the lower edge of the 1/2 resonance). It is more doubtful whether the Hildas show a shadow effect.

18.9 CONCLUSIONS ABOUT PARTIAL COROTATION

We have found in sec. 17.5 that condensation from a partially corotating plasma should produce bodies at a final distance of 2/3 of the point of condensation. We have looked for observational confirmation of a fall-down ratio of 2/3 and have found several examples. In the Saturnian ring system the ratio 2/3 is found at two different places, and in the asteroidal belt in three places. We can regard this as a confirmation that partial corotation plays a decisive role in the condensation process.

18.9.1 Remarks on the Deformation of the Magnetic Field Produced by the Plasma

The theory of partial corotation implies a fall-down by a factor 2/3 only under the condition that the shape of the dipole field is not disturbed too much by currents in the plasma when it is being supported by the magnetic field and brought into corotation.

In the case of the Saturnian magnetic field, we know that it must have been strong enough to support the plasma condensing to form Titan and Iapetus very far out. Because a dipole field decreases as r^{-3} we can be confident that in the region very close to Saturn where the ring was formed it was strong enough to control the motion of the relatively thin plasma with-out being modified appreciably.

Similar arguments hold for the asteroidal belt. As the average distributed density in the asteroidal belt is 10^{-5} of the density in the Jovian region, a solar magnetic field strong enough to support the plasma forming Jupiter is unlikely to be appreciably different from a dipole field in the asteroidal region.

Hence in both cases where we have found evidence for a 2/3 fall-down ratio, we have good reasons to believe that the dipole field was unperturbed.

18.10 SATELLITE AND PLANET FORMATION

Evolution of an asteroid-like assembly of bodies will lead to a general de-crease in inclinations and eccentricities and eventually to an accretion of larger bodies. Since the space density in the present asteroidal region is very small, the time scale of development in this region is very long. In regions where the accumulation of primeval condensing plasma was much larger than in the asteroidal region, a more rapid development took place, leading to the formation of groups of densely populated jet streams of grains inside which satellites or planets formed.

18.10.1 The Groups of Secondary Bodies

In ch. 2 we found that the regular bodies in the solar system form several groups consisting of a number of similar bodies with regular orbital spacing (tables 2.1.1–2.1.2 and 2.5.1). Examples of such clearly distinguishable groups are

(1) The four Galilean satellites of Jupiter.

(2) The five Uranian satellites.

(3) The giant planets.

The identification of other groups is less clearcut:

(4) In the Saturnian satellite system, all the inner satellites out to Rhea have orbits with spacings roughly proportional to their distances from the planet, and their sizes increase in a fairly regular way with the distance. These satellites form an unbroken sequence of secondary bodies from the outer edge of the ring system out to Rhea. This sequence may be considered as a group.

(5) The distance between Rhea and the next outer satellite Titan is very large, and the disparity of masses between these two satellites is great. It is thus possible that Titan forms an outer group with the two other outer satellites Hyperion and Iapetus, but this group is not at all as regular as the inner group.

(6) Another irregular group consists of the Jovian satellites 6, 7 and 10.

There are still a few more prograde satellites: One is the fifth satellite of Jupiter, Amalthea. Both its large distance to the Galilean satellites and its much smaller mass makes it impossible to count this as a member of the Galilean group. If we want to classify all the satellites, Amalthea must be considered as the only known member of a separate group. Further, the highly eccentric Neptunian satellite Nereid may be a remnant of an early group of regular satellites destroyed by the capture of Triton (McCord, 1966; Alfvén and Arrhenius, 1972a). Finally, the very small Martian satellites may be counted as a group of regular satellites.

As grains initially move in orbits with $e = 1/3$ after condensation, the ratio between their apocentric and pericentric distances is 2. Hence as long as the relative spacings between bodies are smaller than 2, we can be sure that the grains will be captured, sooner or later, by one of the bodies. Inside a group the relative spacings normally do not exceed 2 (for Uranus/Saturn, it is 2.01). This means that we may have had a production of grains in the entire region of space covered by the present groups of bodies, and all this mass should now be found in those bodies.

However, the spacings *between* the groups, as we have defined them, is always greater than a factor 2. For Jupiter/Mars the ratio between their orbital radii is 3.42; for Titan/Rhea it is 2.32; for Io/Amalthea, 2.33; and for Jupiter 6/Callisto, 6.09. This means that there are regions in the gaps between groups where grains, if formed, cannot be captured by any body. From this we conclude that *there must have been regions between the groups where no appreciable condensation took place*. In other words, *the different plasma clouds from which the groups have been formed were distinctly separated by regions where the density was very low*.

One such region is found between Jupiter and Mars. From the study of the asteroids we know that the density in this region was several orders of magnitude lower than the density within the regions of the giant planets and the terrestrial planets. Similar intermediate regions where the plasma must have had an extremely low density are found between Titan and Rhea, Io and Amalthea, and Jupiter 6 and Callisto. It is possible that in these regions a number of very small bodies, similar to the asteroids, may be found. The same is possible in the region between the group of Uranian satellites and the planet itself, and also outside the orbit of Oberon.

In theories of the Laplacian type it is postulated that the secondary bodies around a central body derive from a homogeneous disc. We have found that the distribution of mass in both the planetary system and the satellite systems is very far from such uniformity. Mass is accumulated at certain distances where groups of bodies are formed, but between the groups there are spacings which are practically devoid of matter. The formation of groups of bodies is shown schematically in fig. 18.10.1.

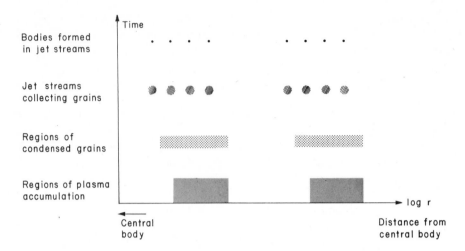

FIGURE 18.10.1.—Diagram of the formation of a group of bodies. Infalling gas is stopped and ionized at different distances from the central body. The two regions in the figure may receive plasma simultaneously or during different epochs. Condensation of the plasma is rapid during the total infall period. Condensed grains are collected in jet streams which increase their mass during the whole infall period. Grains are stored in the jet streams as single particles and embryos (often for a long period of time) until they are finally accreted by the largest embryo. In each region of plasma infall, 3–5 bodies are formed.

According to Laplacian theories the explanation of the low-density region between Mars and Jupiter is that, because of the large mass of Jupiter, the condensation would have been disturbed inside its orbit. This is very unlikely. The solar distance of the asteroids ($a = 2.1$–3.5 AU) is about half the distance to Jupiter ($a = 5.2$ AU). As Jupiter's mass is 10^{-3} of the Sun's mass, the Jovian gravitation cannot be more than 0.1 percent of the solar gravitation in the asteroidal region. Certainly, as this is a perturbation of the Newtonian field, it produces a precession of the perihelion and the nodes of bodies orbiting in this region. Hence it may contribute to the disruption of the jet streams. However, the disruptive effect of Jupiter on jet streams active during the formation of Saturn would have been about equally large, and the same effect produced by Saturn during the accretion of Jupiter would also have been of the same order of magnitude. Hence a theory that attributes the absence of large bodies in the asteroidal region to the large size of Jupiter will run the risk of explaining away either Saturn or Jupiter.

18.11 ACCRETION OF VOLATILE SUBSTANCES

The mechanism of accretion we have considered is based on the behavior of solid grains. In the first place it is a theory of those celestial bodies which consist mainly of nonvolatile elements. Such bodies are the terrestrial planets, including the Moon, and the asteroids. We know very little about the chemical composition of the satellites except that it is highly variable; existing data will be discussed in ch. 20. At least the smallest of them consists entirely of materials condensable at their solar distances since their masses are not large enough to keep an atmosphere. Some of the better known satellites of Jupiter have a mean density indicating that rocky material forms a substantial fraction of their mass; others must consist largely of icy or liquid components (Lewis, 1971b). The Saturnian satellite Titan, with a size almost twice that of our Moon, is capable of retaining a thin atmosphere.

In the case of the giant planets, which perhaps mainly consist of volatile substances, the planetesimal accretion mechanism needs supplementation. This is a general complication with all planetesimal theories, and has attracted much attention already. Öpik (1962) has tried to solve the problem through the assumption that the accretion of Jupiter (and the other giants) took place at such an extremely low temperature as to make even hydrogen solid. This means that Jupiter should have accreted from hydrogen snowflakes. The temperature which according to Öpik is necessary for this process is about 4K, which seems to be unreasonably low. In our mechanism, in which gas density is lower than that assumed by Öpik, the required temperature would be even lower. Hence it is necessary to envisage direct accretion of gas from an interplanetary medium.

To keep an atmosphere a body must possess a certain minimum mass. As Mars has an atmosphere but the Moon has none, we can conclude that under the conditions prevailing in the region of the inner planets the critical size should be of the order 10^{26} g. When through the accretion of solid grains an embryo has reached this mass, it is able to attract gas efficiently from the interplanetary medium and to retain it as an atmosphere, which eventually may contain more mass than the solid core. The giant planets may have accreted from a large number of planetesimals which were big enough to have an atmosphere.

As none of the asteroids has reached the critical size, we have no hope of studying this process by observations in the asteroidal region. Hence the accretion of gas by a growing embryo is necessarily a more hypothetical process than those for which we can find analogies in present-day phenomena. The present very low density of gas in interplanetary space together with the action of the solar wind practically prevents planets from gravitationally accreting gas today.

This process should be considered in relation to the jet-stream model discussed in chs. 6 and 12. The accretion of gas from an interplanetary medium may also occur in two steps. A jet stream could also have the property of drawing in gas from its environment so that it has an "atmosphere." This means that the gas density inside a jet stream may be much larger than in the interstream medium. When an embryo inside a jet stream has reached the critical state (see sec. 11.4), it would then be accreting gas from a region with relatively high gas pressure.

The presence of gas as a dissipative medium in some jet streams is suggested by the state of preservation of particles in carbonaceous chondrites. In these meteorites the characteristic products of collision melting and vaporization (chondrules) are a minor component or are entirely absent. Crystals magnetized before accretion have escaped collisional heating above the Curie temperature (Brecher, 1972a,b,c). The highly embrittled skin of isotropically irradiated crystals in gas-rich meteorites has been protected against destruction in the process of accretion of the parent body embryos (Wilkening et al., 1971). Hence it is necessary to assume that the lowering of relative velocities, required for accretion, was substantially aided by viscous energy losses other than inelastic collisions.

It is believed that at least Jupiter consists mainly of hydrogen and helium which necessarily must have been acquired by direct accretion of gas from space or from the atmosphere of a jet stream. This means that the orbital characteristics should be determined by a gas accretion process and not by a solid grain accretion. The accretion mechanism that we have discussed would, accordingly, have to be substantially modified in the case of the giant planets, or at least for Jupiter. A detailed analysis of this problem is very important but must be left to future investigations. (In case it turns out that the hydrogen-helium model of Jupiter is not correct, such an investigation loses much of its motivation.)

19

TRANSPLANETARY
CONDENSATION

19.1 INTERPLANETARY AND TRANSPLANETARY CONDENSATION

In the preceding chapters we have studied planetary formation as the end product of two processes active in interplanetary space:

(1) Transfer of angular momentum from the Sun to a surrounding plasma.

(2) Condensation of the plasma.

There is necessarily a spatial limit to the first process because of the limitation of the distance to which the Sun can transfer angular momentum. There may also be an outer limit to the region in which condensation takes place, but it is unlikely that this coincides with the limit of momentum transfer. As we shall find, it is likely that condensation also took place far outside the transfer limit, giving a condensate with small angular momentum.

In this chapter we shall study this process, which we shall call *transplanetary condensation* since (by definition) it took place outside the region of the planets. The processes we discuss are basically the same as those we have studied earlier. Hence *no new assumptions* are necessary. The transplanetary condensation is essentially *a corollary to our theory of planet formation*.

As we shall find, the transplanetary condensation gives two important results:

(1) The formation of the comet-meteoroid population.

(2) The enrichment of condensable elements in the A, B, and C clouds (ch. 21). This process may have been essential in determining the chemical composition of the planets (and satellites).

19.2 LIMIT BETWEEN INTERPLANETARY AND TRANSPLANETARY SPACE

The planets acquired their prograde orbital motion from hydromagnetic transfer of solar angular momentum (chs. 16–17). There must be an outer limit to this transfer because the solar magnetic field can dominate only out to a point where it becomes equal to magnetic fields of other origin. Usually the field outside the solar system is referred to as the "galactic magnetic field." This is a misleading term because the galaxy has the linear dimension 10^{23} cm and we are concerned with a region that is 10^{-8} to 10^{-6} less than this. The conditions in this close neighborhood of our solar system are unlikely to be representative of the galaxy as a whole. We will call this region the *transplanetary region*. The field outside the region where the solar field dominates will be called the *transplanetary field*.

If the solar magnetic dipole moment is $\mu_\odot$, the field at a distance r_{Lm} is $B_\odot = \mu_\odot / r_{Lm}^3$. Denoting the transplanetary field by B_{Tp} we find

$$r_{Lm} = \left(\frac{\mu_\odot}{B_{Tp}} \right)^{1/3} \tag{19.2.1}$$

As $\mu_\odot$ and B_{Tp} are likely to vary with time, r_{Lm} will change. The maximum value r_{Tp} which r_{Lm} reaches during a period of plasma emplacement defines the outermost region to which the Sun has ever been able to transfer angular momentum. We define this as the limit between *interplanetary space* and *transplanetary space*. Assuming that Pluto is the outermost member of the solar system, this limit should, according to ch. 17, be related to the orbital distance r_p of Pluto by

$$r_{Tp} = \frac{3r_p}{2} \approx 10^{15} \text{ cm} \tag{19.2.2}$$

19.3 CONDENSATION OF BODIES IN ALMOST-PARABOLIC ORBITS

As we have found, bodies with prograde orbits are formed in interplanetary space but a similar condensation in transplanetary space, and also anywhere outside r_{Lm}, gives rise to a population with small and randomly distributed angular momenta. Introducing this difference in angular momentum we can apply the interplanetary processes that we have analyzed in chs. 16–17 to transplanetary space:

(1) Grains condense from the plasma, especially in dense regions. (Moreover, this medium may have already contained appreciable amounts of interstellar dust at an early stage.) The condensates in this region can be identified with *sporadic meteors* in long-period orbits.

(2) The grains are focused into jet streams (ch. 6). Some of these may

be identified with the observed *long-period meteor streams,* but most of them are difficult to observe.

(3) In these jet streams an accretion of larger bodies takes place (chs. 11 and 14). We identify these accreted bodies with *long-period comets.*

The concept of transplanetary condensation has been criticized on the premise that the plasma density far from the Sun is likely to have been very small and hence the time of condensation of a small grain would have been extremely large. This objection was based on the concept of a homogeneous model and was invalidated when it became apparent that space plasmas usually are inhomogeneous. In fact, even if there might be objections to a high *average* density, the density is likely to have been orders of magnitude larger *locally.* (See ch. 15.) Condensation of grains can take place in such high-density regions. Further, the grains may be focused into jet streams by the mechanisms discussed in ch. 6.

Hence, although we are far from a detailed theory of transplanetary condensation there is no obvious objection to such an approach and, as we shall see, quite a few observed phenomena are indicating that such a condensation must have taken place.

However, even if these processes have the same general character for transplanetary condensation as for interplanetary condensation, they do differ in certain aspects. We can understand fairly well that grains which condensed from a partially corotating plasma in interplanetary space are focused into jet streams. It is not so obvious that in transplanetary space grains in randomly distributed orbits will evolve into randomly distributed jet streams. This mechanism has to be investigated carefully. Further, formation of comets in a meteor stream does not necessarily proceed by the same mechanism as the formation of planets and satellites. The Trulsen (1972a) mechanism, involving a number of superimposed density waves, is probably more important.

19.4 BODIES WITH LONG-PERIOD ORBITS

As we have seen in ch. 4, the comet-meteoroid complex consists of two populations: the short-period population and the long-period population. Of the latter we know only those bodies which have their perihelia close to the Sun (less than 1 AU for meteoroids, less than a few AU for comets). These move in almost parabolic orbits with aphelia far out from the Sun. Typical orbits are given in table 19.4.1.

A body with aphelion at 20 000 AU spends about 1 million yr very far from the Sun in what Oort (1963) has called the cometary reservoir. It then makes a quick visit to the solar environment, spending about 80 yr inside the orbit of Pluto and about 4 yr inside the orbit of Jupiter. After

TABLE 19.4.1
Long-Period Orbits

Aphelion	Semimajor axis	Period
200 AU $=3\times10^{15}$ cm	100 AU	1000 yr
20 000 AU $=3\times10^{17}$ cm	10 000 AU	1 000 000 yr

this rapid excursion, it returns to a million-year rest in the reservoir. For a body with aphelion at 200 AU the period of time in interplanetary space is essentially the same. If a slight correction is made for selection effects, the orbits of the long-period bodies are found to be completely random (Porter, 1963), from which one concludes that the cometary reservoir is at rest in relation to the Sun. It is not completely clarified whether this conclusion is based on a selection effect, due to the fact that only those bodies which have their perihelia close to the Sun can be observed.

Oort (1963) has suggested that the long-period comets were produced in the inner regions of the planetary system and ejected by Jupiter. Detailed orbital evolution calculations (Everhart, 1974) show that this mechanism is impossible. This result is also fatal to Whipple's theory (1972) of an origin in the Uranus-Neptune region. One is forced to conclude that the comets were formed by some process in the transplanetary region.

19.5 DIFFUSION OF ALMOST-PARABOLIC ORBITS: ENCOUNTERS WITH PLANETS

A body in an almost-parabolic orbit with perihelion inside Jupiter's orbit and aphelion far outside the orbit of Jupiter has a chance of 3×10^{-8} of colliding with Jupiter for every turn into the central region of the solar system. The chance for an approach close enough to cause a noticeable change in orbit (diffusion of aphelion) is given by Öpik as 0.5×10^{-3} (Öpik, 1963).

Consider a body with an orbital period T_K yr, which was generated in the hetegonic era. If $T_K > 2\times10^6$ yr it will have made less than 2×10^3 visits to the central parts of the solar system, and it is not very likely to have been seriously perturbed by Jupiter. Hence, most of the very long-period population will still be in approximately the primeval state. This is consistent with the randomly distributed orbits of long-period meteoroids and comets. However, stellar perturbations of the cometary reservoir may invalidate this conclusion.

With decreasing T_K there is an increase in the chance that a close approach to Jupiter (or some other planet) has taken place during the lifetime of the body. This leads to a diffusion which becomes more rapid the smaller the orbital period. For an order-of-magnitude approximation we can put the diffusion time equal to $2 \times 10^3 T_K$ (see above). Hence the aphelia of orbits inside 10^{16} cm, corresponding to Kepler periods of some hundred years, will diffuse with a time scale of the order of less than a million years.

For bodies with perihelia outside the region of the terrestrial planets, the main risk of destruction is collision with Jupiter. For orbits with perihelia closer to the Sun, Venus and Earth provide another main collision risk with probability for a hit of the order of 3×10^{-8} per turn. As bodies in near-parabolic orbits with apherlia in interplanetary space have periods less than 100 yr, this means that most bodies which condensed in interplanetary space (but outside the temporary position of r_{Lm}) in the hetegonic era have been destroyed, unless they have diffused into orbits of longer periods.

19.6 GENETIC RELATIONS OF THE COMET-METEOROID COMPLEX

What we have found suggests a family history of comets and meteoroids as shown in fig. 19.8.2. The primeval transplanetary condensation produced the long-period meteoroids, of which many have been focused into jet streams (long-period meteor streams). Accretion inside these, probably due to density waves, produces the long-period comets. All these bodies move in almost-parabolic orbits with random distribution.

Planetary encounters of long-period meteoroids perturb their orbits into short-period, predominantly prograde orbits with lower eccentricities. These meteoroids are focused into short-period meteor streams, and short-period comets then accrete within these streams. The ultimate fate of the largest of these comets may be Apollo-Amor-type bodies ("burned-out comets"), which eventually collide with a planet.

In principle short-period comets could also derive from long-period comets which are "captured" by Jupiter. This is the same process that has produced short-period meteoroids from long-period meteoroids. However, the probability of this process is too small by several orders of magnitude to be of any importance.

In fact, the transition probability between almost-parabolic and captured orbits is of the order 10^{-6}. (This should not be confused with the probability for a diffusion of the aphelion of a long-period orbit due to scattering by Jupiter.) As the period of Jupiter-crossing captured bodies is 10–100 yr, this means that a diffusion between different orbits takes place in 10^7–10^8 yr. This is lower than the mean life of a body like a meteoroid in interplanetary space, which is of the order of 10^8 yr, with the result that the population of the different orbits will be roughly equal.

In striking contrast to the long lifetime of short-period meteoroids is the short lifetime of short-period comets, which according to observations is only 100–10 000 yr. This means that a diffusional equilibrium between long-period and short-period comets cannot be established. In other words, Jupiter is inefficient as a scatterer of long-period comets into short-period orbits. If the short-period comets were exclusively due to capture of long-period comets their number would be three or four orders of magnitude less than observed.

This constitutes a serious inadequacy in the capture theory for short-period comets (Mendis, 1973). This difficulty can be circumvented by the ad hoc assumption of a special cometary reservoir close outside Jupiter, but there is no independent evidence for this. Further, an intrinsic difficulty of this theory is that it takes for granted the existence of long-period comets. Its only ambition is to refer the origin of short-period comets one step backward.

Within the approach used here, the short-period comets are considered to accrete from short-period meteor streams by the same process that produces the long-period comets as accretions in the long-period meteor streams. In this approach both types of objects follow a pattern of evolution which basically is the same as that of planets and satellites.

19.7 CONCLUSIONS ABOUT THE METEOROID POPULATIONS

In view of the fact that the time constant for collision of short-period bodies with planets is short compared to the age of the solar system, most of these bodies in interplanetary space must either have condensed there long after the formation of the solar system or diffused into this region at a later time. The first alternative is not attractive, because no independent argument seems to exist for such a late condensation. The second alternative is quite acceptable because the time for orbit diffusion is rather short, as found in sec. 19.5. In fact, as the time constant for orbit diffusion is much shorter than the time constant for collisional destruction, we may expect the meteoroid orbits to be in diffusional equilibrium, a result which may be checked observationally.

This means that the short-period meteoroids may very well originate from long-period meteoroids, perturbed ("captured") by Jupiter. As we have seen, the capture theory of short-period comets is *not* acceptable because quantitatively it is in error by a factor of 10^4. However, the same theory can be directly applied to meteoroids, where it probably works very well.

Hence the theory of Jupiter capture of long-period bodies into short-period orbits is applicable to meteoroids, but *not* to comets. The reason for this is that the lifetime of meteoroids in interplanetary space is of the order of millions of years (i.e., long compared to the diffusion time), whereas the lifetime of short-period comets is known to be short, in the range 100 to 10 000 yr, which is short compared to the diffusion time constant for transition between long-period and short-period orbits.

What we have found suggests a genealogy of meteoroids and comets as outlined in sec. 19.8.2 and fig. 19.8.2.

19.8 GENEALOGY OF THE BODIES IN THE SOLAR SYSTEM

19.8.1 Traditional Approach

Figure 19.8.1 shows the traditional view of the genetic relationships between the bodies in the solar system. The asteroids are assumed to be debris of one or more exploded planets, which, like other planets, derive from a Laplacian solar nebula.

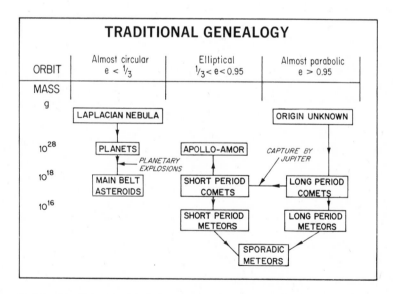

FIGURE 19.8.1.—Traditional view of genetic relationships between different types of bodies in the solar system.

The elliptic population, consisting of short-period comets and meteoroids, is supposed to derive from Jovian capture and deflection of long-period comets into short-period orbits. These comets disintegrate, giving rise to part of the short-period meteoroid population and, after scattering, a portion of sporadic meteoroids.

Long-period comets produce long-period meteoroids and sporadic meteoroids by a similar process. The origin of the long-period comets is accepted as unknown or is accounted for by hypotheses which are not integrated in a general hetegonic framework (see, e.g., Oort, 1963; Whipple, 1972; Cameron, 1973).

19.8.2 Present Analysis

Figure 19.8.2 and table 19.8.1 present the genealogy which results from the present analysis. The primeval condensation providing the source material for all the bodies takes place in both interplanetary and transplanetary space. (Some of the transplanetary material may derive from condensation at large distances in space and time.)

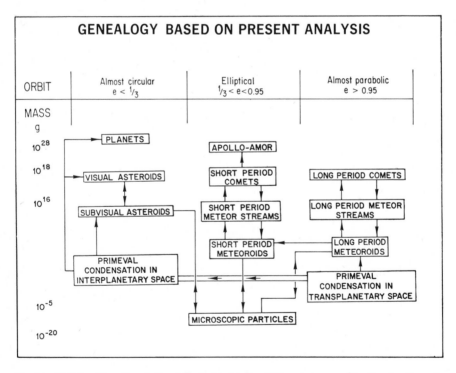

FIGURE 19.8.2.—Genetic relationships between the different types of bodies in the solar system. This genealogy is based on the present analysis.

TABLE 19.8.1
Orbital Populations in the Solar System

ALMOST CIRCULAR $e < 1/3$	ELLIPTIC $1/3 < e < 0.95$	ALMOST PARABOLIC $e > 0.95$
Summary	*Summary*	*Summary*
Originate from primeval interplanetary condensates augmented from the transplanetary reservoir. The angular momentum transfer process and viscous dissipation ultimately result in almost circular orbits of planets, asteroids, and satellites.	Because of collision with planets the lifetime is short and no primeval condensate remains today. The origin of elliptic orbits is diffusion by planetary perturbation of long-period meteoroids into short-period orbits.	Originate from primeval condensation in transplanetary space, beyond the influence of the solar magnetic field. Angular momentum is small.
Planets and satellites	*Short-period meteoroids*	*Long-period meteoroids*
Infinite lifetime and no orbital evolution	Arise mainly from scattered long-period meteoroids; asteroid debris can, in principle, contribute, but the transition probability is small.	Formed by accretion of condensates in the transplanetary reservoir. If the period is >5000 yr, planets do not perturb the orbit; if <5000 yr, meteoroids may be scattered into increasingly prograde short-period orbits.
Visual Asteroids		
Slow evolution, on a time scale of 10^{11} yr, possibly toward formation of several planets.	*Short-period meteor streams*	*Long-period meteor streams*
	Formed from short-period meteoroids.	Formed from long-period meteoroids.
Subvisual asteroids	*Short-period comets*	*Long-period comets*
Predominantly produced by accretion from small particles, but also from asteroid collisions. They interact mutually with other populations.	Accreted in short-period meteor streams. Long-period comets can, in principle, be captured by Jupiter into short-period orbits, but transition probability is very small.	Accreting in long-period meteor streams.
		Microscopic particles
Microscopic particles	*Apollo-Amor asteroids*	Originate from asteroid and meteoroid collisions and cometary debris. Interact with all the populations.
Originate from asteroid and meteoroid collisions and cometary debris. Interact with all the populations.	Residue of short-period comets.	
	Microscopic particles	
	Originate from asteroid and meteoroid collisions and cometary debris. Interact with all the populations.	

The interplanetary condensation produces grains accreting to embryos (planetesimals) which, in turn, accrete to planets in the dense regions. In less dense regions the material is still in an embryonic stage of accretion, in the form of asteroids, visual and subvisual.

The transplanetary condensation primarily produces meteoroids in almost-parabolic orbits. Some of these meteoroids will interact with the interplanetary condensates, contributing condensable components to this region. Long-period meteoroids can diffuse (by "Jupiter capture") into short-period orbits. Short-period meteoroids constitute the major component of the elliptic population. Both long-period and short-period meteoroids undergo the same evolution, forming meteor streams and eventually comets.

The micrometeoroids may have genetic relations with all the populations.

PART D

Physical and Chemical Structure of the Solar System

20

CHEMICAL STRUCTURE OF
THE SOLAR SYSTEM

20.1 SURVEY

In the theories derived from the Laplacian concept of planet formation it is usually postulated that both the Sun and the planets—satellites are often not even mentioned—derive from a solar nebula with a chemical composition assumed to be uniform and characterized by "cosmic abundances" of elements. The Sun and the giant planets are supposed to have condensed directly from the solar nebula and are thought to have the same composition as this nebula. The solar photosphere has been proposed as the closest available approximation to this composition (Suess and Urey, 1956). The terrestrial planets should consist of the refractory ingredients of the nebula condensing in the inner regions of the solar system.

We have summarized earlier a number of objections to Laplacian-type theories, including the difficulty that not even bodies as large as Jupiter can condense directly from a nebula (sec. 11.2). The only reasonable alternative was found to be the planetesimal approach. To the objections discussed earlier we should add that the composition of the solar system appears far from uniform. It is well known that densities derived from mass and size indicate substantial differences in chemical composition among the different outer planets, among the terrestrial planets, and among the small bodies in the solar system. The notable variability in surface composition of asteroids supports this conclusion.

The marked differences in composition among the various groups of meteorites and comets also point at fractionation processes operating on matter in the solar system, before or during the formative stage. The observational evidence for the chemically fractionated state of the solar system will be discussed in this and the next chapter.

20.2 SOURCES OF INFORMATION ABOUT CHEMICAL COMPOSITION

The empirical knowledge we have about the chemical composition of the solar system may be categorized with regard to level of certainty:

(1) *Surface layers and atmospheres*. The surface layers of the Earth
and Moon have been analyzed under well-defined conditions. The data
refer to less than 10^{-3} of the total mass of these bodies. Fragmentary information from landed instruments has been obtained from Venus.

The surface layers of the Sun have been analyzed by remote spectroscopy; however, the error limits are generally large in comparison to elemental fractionation factors characteristic of planetary processes (Aller, 1967;
Urey, 1972; Worrall and Wilson, 1972). Independent indications derive
from analysis of corpuscular radiation from the Sun (Price, 1973), but they
clearly represent material fractionated at the source. The composition of
solar wind is found to vary up to a factor of 3 (S) to 10 (He) from assumed
solar abundances.

Emission, absorption, and polarization of electromagnetic radiation by
planets, satellites, and asteroids give some qualitative information about
the structure and chemical composition of their surface layers (of the order
of a fraction of a millimeter up to a few centimeters in depth) and of their
atmospheres (Dollfus, 1971b; Gehrels, 1972a; Chapman, 1972a; Newburn
and Gulkis, 1973).

(2) *Bulk composition*. Our knowledge of the bulk composition of the
planets and satellites is extremely uncertain. Parameters that yield information on this question are

(a) Mass and radius, from which average density can be calculated.

(b) Moment of inertia, which allows conclusions about the density
distribution.

(c) Seismic wave propagation, electric conductivity, heat flow, magnetic properties, and free oscillations, which have been studied in the case of
Earth and Moon. The resulting data can be inverted to model internal
structure and, indirectly, composition, but generally with a wide latitude
of uncertainty.

In the case of Jupiter, the observation of a net energy flux from the
interior also places a limit on the internal state.

Extrapolation of bulk composition from chemical surface properties of
Earth, Moon, and Sun has been attempted but is necessarily uncertain.

Several hundred meteorites have been analyzed. These are of particularly great interest since they are likely to approximate the bulk composition of both the bodies from which they came and the parent streams of
particles from which these bodies accumulated. A major limitation of this
material as a record of the formative processes in the solar system comes
from the fact that the regions of origin and the genetic interrelation of
different types of meteorites are uncertain (chs. 22 and 19).

20.3 CHEMICAL DIFFERENTIATION BEFORE AND AFTER THE ACCRETION OF BODIES IN THE SOLAR SYSTEM

The solar system is generally considered to have formed by emplacement of gas and possibly solid dust in some specific configuration in space and time. Regardless of the details assumed with regard to this configuration and the state of its component matter, it appears highly unlikely that such an emplacement, which by definition involves the release of an enormous amount of energy, would proceed without accompanying chemical separation effects (see secs. 21.11 and 21.12). It is also improbable that the subsequent thermal evolution of each emplaced portion of matter would take place without some degree of chemical separation of the components. Hence the solid condensates, forming in the solar system in different regions and at different times as precursor material of the subsequently accreting bodies, were probably chemically different from each other.

If we could precisely determine the chemical differences among bodies from known and widely separated regions in the solar system, planets, satellites, comets, and the Sun, it should be possible to study in detail the effects of fractionation processes active in the hetegonic era. However, direct chemical measurements of the bulk composition of large celestial bodies do not exist; in the course of accretion and subsequent thermal evolution all such bodies must have become stratified, and we are unable to obtain samples deeper than a thin outer layer. We know with certainty that even a body as small as the Moon has thoroughly altered the primordial material from which it accreted. Consideration of accretional heating as a function of terminal velocity of the source particles at impact suggests that the effect of the accretional hot-spot front would be considerable for bodies larger than a few hundred kilometers (sec. 12.12). Hence even the surfaces of the largest asteroids would not be representative of the bulk composition of these bodies. For this same reason we have no certain knowledge of the deep interior chemical composition of any planet, not even our own (secs. 20.4(1) and 20.5.1).

On the other hand, bodies with sizes of tens of kilometers and smaller are likely not to have been subject to accretional and post-accretional differentiation of this kind, and it should be possible to determine their bulk composition from samples of surface material. The small asteroids and comets and the matter trapped in the Lagrangian points of the larger planets (such as the Trojan asteroids of Jupiter) are possible sources for such samples. The meteorites (ch. 22) in all likelihood constitute samples of such small bodies.

20.4 UNKNOWN STATES OF MATTER

As stated in sec. 20.2, in most cases the measurement of the average density is our main source of information about the bulk chemical composition of a body. However, interpretation of the mean density in terms of chemical composition is often difficult because we know so little about the state of matter at high pressure. Nor do we have satisfactory information about the properties of solid bodies aggregated in low gravitational fields.

(1) *Matter at high pressure.* Static pressure experiments with satisfactory calibration extend into the range of a few hundred kilobars (Drickamer, 1965), corresponding to pressures in the upper mantle of the Earth. In transient pressure experiments using shock waves, pressures in the megabar range can be reached (see, e.g., McQueen and Marsh, 1960). Although such experiments are useful in studying elastic compression effects, their general applicability is more questionable in studies of materials undergoing high-pressure phase transformations. The reason is that the material in the shock front is strongly heated, and the relaxation time for phase transformations may be long compared to the duration of the pressure pulse.

Under these circumstances it is difficult to predict with certainty the structure and composition of matter in the deep interior of the planets. The interpretation of the nature of the cores of the Earth and Venus, for example, has important consequences with regard to the inferred chemical composition of these planets. Lodochnikov (1939) and Ramsey (1948, 1949) proposed that the high density of the core of the Earth and the high bulk density of Venus could be due to pressure-induced transformation of magnesium-iron silicate into a high-density phase. If this were the case, the Earth's core and mantle could have the same chemical composition. Although the formation of an unknown high-density phase may possibly have escaped detection in transient compression experiments, it has been considered unlikely (see, e.g., Samara, 1967) that such a density change could assume the magnitude required, about 70 percent, at the core-mantle boundary. Recent experiments (Simakov et al., 1973) suggest, however, that minerals which already possess close-packed structures before the shock experiment undergo phase transitions of this kind at shock pressures in the megabar range.

The alternative explanation is that the Earth's core consists of material with higher mean atomic mass than that of the mantle; for example, nickel-iron with some lighter elements such as silicon or sulfur (Birch, 1964; Ringwood, 1966; Murthy and Hall, 1970; Lewis, 1971a). Much of the uncertainty concerning the properties of materials in the pressure range typical of the terrestrial planets could probably be clarified in the near future due to progress in high-pressure experimental studies. This would, however, not solve the problems of the state of matter in the giant planets.

(2) *Grain aggregates.* According to ch. 11, planets and satellites must have formed from smaller bodies (planetesimals) and ultimately from small condensed particles. Such particles can accumulate to form larger bodies only if they are held together by an attractive force. Since gravity is negligible in the incipient growth stages, the main initial cohesive effect is likely to have been provided by electric charge and vapor deposition, as exemplified by the lunar soil. The nature of such aggregates and the dynamic conditions of their formation are discussed in secs. 7.4 and 22.6–22.7. High porosity and hence low bulk density may thus have been common in the initial stages of planetesimal accretion and still occur today in bodies that have remained at a small size. A major portion of the solid matter inter-

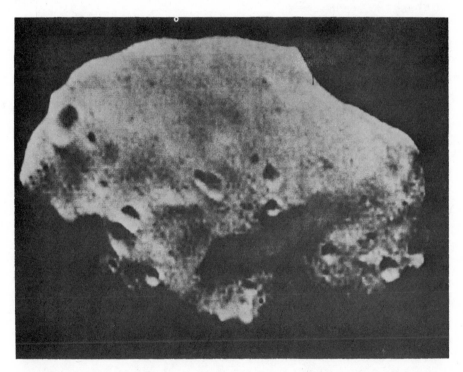

FIGURE 20.4.1.—Impact cratering of the Martian satellite Phobos. In suitable illumination craters such as *A* above can be seen to have rims of substantial height above the surrounding terrain. Since ejecta with velocities exceeding a few meters per second will leave the satellite, the crater cones cannot be generated by fallout from the impact as is the case on Earth, Mars, and the Moon. The dimensions of the cones also appear larger than the elevation of crater rims observed on the Earth as a result of shock rebound. A possible explanation of this phenomenon is that Phobos, or at least its outer regions, consists of aggregate material with low bulk density, and that impacting projectiles dissipate their energy largely below the target surface. (NASA Photograph 71–H–1832.)

cepted by Earth appears to have fluffy texture with mean bulk densities below 1.0 g/cm^3. Such materials are destroyed during passage through the atmosphere (Verniani, 1969, 1973; McCrosky, 1970).

Although gravitational compaction would be practically absent in bodies of small size, shock compaction of the original texture would be expected as a result of collisions leading to repeated breakup and reaccumulation during the evolution of jet-stream assemblages of such bodies. Evidence of a wide variety of such effects is given by textures in meteorites ranging from complete melting (achondrite parent rocks formed from melts; e.g., Duke and Silver, 1967) and shock-induced reactions and phase changes (Neuvonen et al., 1972) to less dense packing (10–20 percent porosity) without fusion bonding between the particles, such as in carbonaceous meteorites (see fig. 7.1.1) and some chondrites.

The largely unexplored fluffy state in some small bodies in the solar system could have important consequences for their response to collision and hence for the processes of disruption, accretion, and chemical fractionation (secs. 7.4 and 22.6).

The Martian satellites are the first small objects in space studied with sufficient resolution to record discrete surface features. The two satellites are saturated with impact craters and these have characteristics that suggest the possibility of porous target material (fig. 20.4.1).

20.5 THE COMPOSITION OF PLANETS AND SATELLITES

Physical data available for the planets and satellites are listed in table 20.5.1, together with estimated uncertainties.

In many respects the information from the Earth is most reliable. For this reason we shall begin with the data and theories relating to the composition of our own planet.

20.5.1 Earth

In the Earth and Moon, the only sampled terrestrial planets, the surface composition implies that oxygen is the most abundant element to considerable depth. At a depth of a few hundred kilometers in the Earth, the density is likely to be controlled essentially by close-packed oxygen ions.

The steep increase in density indicated at the core-mantle boundary has been interpreted in different ways:

(1) One suggestion is that the boundary represents a pressure-induced phase transformation associated with a substantial decrease in specific volume and with band gap closure resulting in metallic conductivity. The

general background of this proposition has been discussed in sec. 20.4(1). Objections against it are partly based on the results of model experiments which have failed to produce the high-density silicate phase. These results are, however, not entirely conclusive since the experiments employ transient shock rather than static pressure; hence, transformation with relaxation times longer than the shock duration would not necessarily be reproduced.

(2) To avoid the assumption of a hypothetical high-density silicate phase, the other current interpretation assumes that the core differs distinctly from the mantle in chemical composition and consists mostly of nickel-iron alloyed with 10–20 percent of light elements such as silicon or sulfur. This hypothesis requires a mechanism to explain the heterogeneous structure of the Earth. It also implies a high concentration of iron in the source material from which the Earth was formed.

Four types of mechanisms have been suggested to account for the proposed separation of an oxygen-free metal core from a mantle consisting mainly of silicates:

(1) *A metallic core developed as a result of accretional heating.* The progression of the accretional hot-spot front has been discussed in secs. 12.11–12.12; this analysis shows that (a) the Earth's inner core should have accreted at low temperature; (b) runaway exhaustion of the source material in the terrestrial region of space would have coincided roughly with the formation of the outer core; and (c) the mantle accreted at a low mean temperature but with local heating at each impact causing light melts to migrate outward with the surface of the growing planetary embryo. Hence heavy differentiates including metal would not be able to sink further than to the bottom of locally melted pools. Large-scale simultaneous melting and sinking of metal over large radial distances would be limited to the still-liquid outer core, entirely melted in the runaway phase of accretion.

Complete melting of the entire planet at catastrophic accretion has been proposed by Hanks and Anderson (1969) as a means for gravitational separation of a metallic core. This approach, however, does not take into account a distribution of matter preceding accretion, which satisfies the boundary conditions for obtaining the present structure of the planet and satellite systems. Furthermore, it meets with the same objection as any scheme involving complete melting of the Earth, further discussed in (2) below.

(2) *The Earth' core developed during or after the accretion of the planet.* This type of theory has been developed in detail by Elsasser (1963) and Birch (1965). Elsasser suggested that the Earth accreted as a homogeneous body consisting of a mixture of metal, silicates, and sulfides, similar to meteorite material. The interior of the planet heated up gradually due to radioactivity decay, reaching the melting point of iron (or the eutectic point in the iron-sulfide system at about 44 atomic percent S (Murthy and Hall, 1970; Lewis 1971a)) at a depth below the surface determined by the pressure

TABLE 20.5.1

Physical Data for the Planets, Former Planets (Moon and Triton), and Asteroids

	Mean orbital radius r_{orb} from Sun (10^{12} cm)	Radius (10^8 cm)	Mass (10^{27} g)	Average density (g/cm³) Best estimate	Upper limit	Lower limit
Mercury	[a] 5.791	[b] 2.434 ±0.002	[b] 0.3299 ±0.0029	[b] 5.46	[h] 5.53	[h] 5.40
Venus	[a] 10.821	[b] 6.050 ±0.005	[b,f] 4.870	[b] 5.23		
Earth	[a] 14.960	[a] 6.378	[a] 5.976	[b] 5.52		
Moon	[j] ~14–20	[a] 1.738	[b] 0.0735	[b] 3.35		
Mars	[a] 22.794	[b] 3.400	[b] 0.6424	[b] 3.92		
Vesta	[i] 35.331	[d] 0.285 ±0.015	[e] 0.00024 ±0.00003	[h] 2.5	[h] 3.3	[h] 1.9
Ceres	[i] 41.402	[d] 0.567 ±0.042	[e] 0.00119 ±0.00014	[h] 1.6	[h] 2.2	[h] 1.1
Jupiter	[c] 77.837	[c] 71.60	[c] 1899.	[c] 1.31		
Saturn	[c] 142.70	[c] 60.00	[c] 568.	[c] 0.70		
Uranus	[c] 286.96	[c] 25.40	[c] 87.2	[c] ~1.3		
Neptune	[c] 449.67	[c] 24.75 ±0.06	[c] 102.	[c] 1.66		
Triton	[j] ~450	[c] 1.88 ±0.65	[c] 0.135 ±0.024	[c] ~4.8	[h] 20.1	[h] 1.6
Pluto	[c] 590.00	[c,g] 3.20 ±0.20	[k] 0.66 ±.018	[c] 4.9	[h] 7.4	[h] 2.9

[a] Allen, 1963.   [b] Lyttleton, 1969.   [c] Newburn and Gulkis, 1973.
[d] Morrison, 1973.   [e] Schubart, 1971.   [f] Howard et al., 1974.
[g] Upper limit of radius obtained from near occultation.
[h] Average density is calculated from the mean values of mass and radius given in the table. The upper density limit is calculated by combining the lower estimated error limit for the radius and the upper estimated error limit for the mass, and vice versa for the lower density limit. Spherical shape is assumed for all calculations.
[i] *Ephemerides of Minor Planets* for 1969.
[j] The distances of interest in the present discussion are those at the time of formation. Since Moon and Triton are considered to be captured planets, their original orbital radius can only be approximated.
[k] Seidelmann et al., 1971; these authors suggest a mass error of 16–17 percent. We have here arbitrarily used a higher value (±25 percent) in order to, if anything, exaggerate the uncertainty margin of the density estimate.

TABLE 20.5.1 (Continued)

Physical Data for the Regular Satellites With Radii $>10^8$ cm

	Mean orbital radius r_{orb} (10^{10} cm)	Radius (10^8 cm)	Mass (10^{24} g)	Average density (g/cm³)		
				Best estimate	Upper limit	Lower limit
Jovian						
Io	[c] 4.22	[d] 1.83 ±0.01	[d] 89.2 ±1.1	[d] 3.5		
Europa	[c] 6.71	[d] 1.50 ±0.05	[d] 48.7 ±1.1	[d] 3.45	[d] 3.75	[d] 3.1
Ganymede	[c] 10.71	[d] 2.64 +0.01 −0.10	[d] 149. ±1.5	[d] 1.9	[d] 2.2	[d] 1.9
Callisto	[c] 18.84	[d] 2.50 ±0.08	[d] 106. ±3.2	[d] 1.6	[d] 1.75	[d] 1.5
Saturnian						
Enceladus	[c] 2.38	[c] 0.27 ±0.15	[c] 0.085 ±0.028	[c] ~1.0	[b] 16.	[b] 0.2
Tethys	[c] 2.94	[c] 0.60 ±0.10	[c] 0.648 ±0.017	[c] 0.7	[b] 1.3	[b] 0.4
Dione	[c] 3.77	[a] 0.58 ±0.10	[c] 1.05 ±0.03	[a] 1.4	[a] 2.0	[a] 0.8
Rhea	[c] 5.27	[a] 0.80 ±0.13	[e] 1.8 ±2.2	[a] 0.9	[b] 3.2	[b] 0.0
Titan	[c] 12.22	[c] 2.42 ±0.15	[c] 137. ±1.	[c] 2.3	[b] 2.8	[b] 1.9
Iapetus	[c] 35.62	[c] 0.85 ±0.10	[c] 2.24 ±0.74	[b] 0.9	[b] 1.7	[b] 0.4

[a] Morrison, 1974.
[b] Average density is calculated from the mean values of mass and radius given in the table. The upper density limit is calculated by combining the lower estimated error limit for the radius and the upper estimated error limit for the mass, and vice versa for the lower density limit. Spherical shape is assumed for all calculations.
[c] Newburn and Gulkis, 1973.
[d] Anderson et al., 1974.
[e] Murphy et al., 1972.

effect on melting. At further heating the point would be reached where the strength of the supporting silicate material became insufficient to sustain the gravitational instability due to the higher density of the iron (or iron-sulfide) liquid. At this point the liquid would drain toward the center of the Earth, releasing potential energy. The energy release would be sufficient to completely melt the entire planet.

This scheme encounters difficulties from the time constraints in the Earth's thermal evolution. On one hand the core formation process is not allowed to begin until radioactive heating has raised the initiating material to the melting-point range and the supporting silicate material to its yield temperature. On the other hand, preserved segments of the crust are found which are as old as 3.6 Gyr. It is questionable if these limitations would allow complete melting of the planet to occur at any time in its early history, even as early as the time of accretion (Majeva, 1971; Levin, 1972). Such an event would also generate a heavy atmosphere containing the major fraction of the planet's accreted volatiles (ch. 26). This would be likely to prevent cooling to such a temperature that an ocean could form even today; nonetheless evidence for condensed water and development of life are found in the earliest preserved sediments, exceeding 3 Gyr in age (see ch. 26).

Another observation of importance in connection with the question of core formation is the consistently high content ($\sim$0.2 percent) of Ni^{+2} in the magnesium silicates from the upper mantle. If the metallic iron, now assumed to form the core, at one time was homogeneously distributed as small particles throughout the protoplanet, such as in stone meteorites, the melting, migrating droplets of iron would be expected to reduce nickel ion in the silicate phase and to remove the resulting metallic nickel into solution in the melt (Ringwood, 1966); hence, a metallic core is generally thought of as consisting mainly of nickel-iron (see, e.g., Birch, 1964). Accretional melting indeed leads to such extraction of nickel, as demonstrated by the conditions in the lunar surface rocks. These are low in metallic nickel iron, and have an order of magnitude less nickel ion in the magnesium silicates than do terrestrial mantle rocks. Generation of core metal by accretional or post-accretional reduction of iron silicates with carbon (Ringwood, 1959) would doubtless be a still more efficient way to remove nickel from the silicate phases. Hence the presence of substantial concentrations of oxidized nickel in the Earth's mantle also speaks against melt extraction of a metallic core from an originally homogeneous planet.

(3) *The differentiation, ultimately leading to the formation of an iron core, is due to a solid grain interaction process in the Earth's jet stream.* It has been suggested that condensed nickel-iron metal particles would aggregate together at higher relative velocities, and hence at an earlier

time in the evolution of the jet stream than silicate grains. This would be due to the plastic properties of the metal (Orowan, 1969) or to a high accretion cross section caused by magnetization of the grains (Harris and Tozer, 1967). Such a selective accretion of metal grains, if possible at all, could only occur when relative velocities had been brought down to the subsonic range since hypervelocity impact invariably leads to breakup and vaporization in the metal grains (Gault et al., 1968; Neukum et al., 1970).

Observations in meteorites do not provide support for this type of mechanism as far as preferential accretion of metal by collisional or magnetic processes is concerned. Studies of the state of metal grains in chondrites such as those by Urey and Mayeda (1959) do not indicate collision-induced welding. Nor do any observations appear to exist of clustering of metal grains, characteristic of magnetic accretion. In contrast, such clustering is indeed observed for ferromagnetic iron-oxide crystals (magnetite) accreted in space and subsequently aggregated into carbonaceous chondrites (fig. 22.7.1; Jedwab, 1967; Kerridge, 1970; Brecher, 1972a). Arguments have been given by Banerjee (1967) against magnetostatic accretion of multidomain grains of nickel-iron. Finally, runaway accretion in the Earth's jet stream would take place at about $1/10$ of the present mass of the planet, corresponding to the mass of the core. Even if it had been possible to selectively accrete metal and leave silicate material behind in the jet stream during the formation of the inner core, all the material orbiting in the source region of the Earth, regardless of composition, would be swept up during the runaway accretion coinciding with the formation of the outer core (sec. 12.6).

(4) *The differentiation took place in conjunction with the gas emplacement and condensation processes.* A suggestion of this kind, now mainly of historical interest, was made by Eucken (1944a). It has recently been revived in modified form by Turekian and Clark (1969) but without application of the physical constraints of condensation (Arrhenius and De, 1973) or accretion dynamics (secs. 12.1–12.7). This type of hypothesis could in principle be made physically and chemically consistent if it is assumed ad hoc that the composition of condensable impurities in the region of the inner terrestrial planets changed with time, having higher iron content during the first $\sim 3 \times 10^7$ yr of infall (the order of magnitude of time required for accretion of the Earth's core; see secs. 12.8–12.9).

If it were conclusively demonstrated that the high densities of the Earth and Venus are due to a high content of iron, this fact would lend observational support to an assumption of a change with time of the composition of the source materials of these planets. At the present time such an assumption, although speculative, receives some support from the relationships discussed in sec. 21.12.2.

20.5.2 Mercury

Mercury with a radius of 0.38 $R_\oplus$ has a pressure at the center which is as low as that in the Earth's upper mantle (Lyttleton, 1969). In spite of this Mercury has a density as high as 5.46 g/cm³. This can be understood in terms of the general mechanism for fractionation in the inner solar system discussed in sec. 20.5.1.

20.5.3 Venus

The discussion of the composition of the Earth in sec. 20.5.1 applies also to Venus, which has 85.5 percent of the volume and 81.6 percent of the mass of the Earth. Its density, estimated at 5.25 g/cm³, is only 5 percent less than that of the Earth. With the assumption of a core of densified silicate, Venus could have the same composition as the Earth, the Moon, and Mars. If, on the other hand, as is likely, excess iron is needed to account for the high bulk density in both Earth and Venus, these two planets, together with Mercury, would be distinctly different from the Mars-Moon group (fig. 20.7.1a).

20.5.4 Moon and Mars

Since there are strong indications that the Moon is a captured planet (Alfvén, 1942, 1943a, 1946, 1954; Urey, 1952; Gerstenkorn, 1969; Alfvén and Arrhenius, 1972), it is here included in the discussion of planetary compositions.

The observed chemical composition of the lunar surface cannot be characteristic of the interior. If the high thorium and uranium contents of the surface rocks persisted at depth, the lunar interior would be extensively melted, but seismic observations indicate possible partial melting only in the central region below 10³ km (Toksöz et al., 1972).

Furthermore, rocks of the observed surface composition of the Moon would, in the interior and in a limited zone in the lower crust, seem to transform to high-density assemblages (seismic data may indeed indicate such a transformation in the lower crust (Toksöz et al., 1972)). If these high-density phases prevailed throughout the interior of the Moon its average density would be considerably higher than the observed value, 3.35 g/cm³ (Wetherill, 1968). Therefore, the higher content of radioactive elements in the outer crust as well as its basaltic-anorthositic composition suggests either that the Moon accreted sequentially from materials of different chemical compositions (Arrhenius, 1969; Arrhenius et al., 1970; Gast, 1971) or that a differentiation process selectively removed the critical components from the interior to the surface.

The latter explanation would appear possible since it is difficult to escape the conclusion that an accretional front of hot spots has swept through the mantles of the terrestrial planets including that of the Moon (secs. 12.9–12.12). Such a progressive zone melting would be likely to cause removal to the planetary surface region of components with low melting temperature range, low density, or large ionic radius (Vinogradov, 1962; Vinogradov et al., 1971). The crusts of the Earth and the Moon consist of such materials except that much of the volatile components appear to have escaped thermally in the low gravitational field of the Moon (see ch. 26).

The former suggestion, namely that the source material for the lunar interior differed in composition from the material that formed the outer layer of the Moon, may seem more ad hoc. However, support for such an assumption can be drawn from the closeness and possible overlap of the A and B regions where the source materials of the terrestrial planets condensed. These relationships are discussed in sec. 21.12.2.

Regardless of the cause of the lunar differentiation, the low mean density of the Moon (table 20.5.1) makes it clear that it differs chemically from Mercury, most likely by having a lower iron content. It is also possible that the Moon differs substantially from the Earth and Venus in bulk chemical composition. This possibility becomes certainty if it can be verified that the latter two planets owe their high densities to a high content of iron (see sec. 20.5.1).

The bulk density of Mars, 3.92 g/cm^3, suggests that the bulk proportion of heavy to light elements is similar to that of the Moon, and hence lower than those of Venus and the Earth (see fig. 20.7.1a).

20.5.5 Asteroids

These bodies are of sufficiently small size that pressure-induced phase changes can be neglected. On the other hand, asteroids of a size larger than about 100 km have gravitation that is probably large enough to effectively compact fluffy material. Hence some of the uncertainties in data interpretation discussed in sec. 20.4 do not apply to such large asteroids. Their densities, in the few cases where they are known at all, furnish suggestive information on gross chemical composition.

Mass determinations from gravitational perturbation of the orbits of other asteroids exist only for Vesta and Ceres (Schubart, 1971). These values, combined with the most accurate measurements of radii (Morrison, 1973) give a density of 1.6±0.5 g/cm^3 for Ceres and 2.5±0.7 g/cm^3 for Vesta. In bodies like these, several hundred kilometers in size, porosity can probably only be maintained in a small surficial region. The low densities, if correct, therefore suggest the presence of hydrous minerals or ice in the interior or (less likely) rocks virtually free of iron. Optical measurements by Chapman et al. (1971) indicate that the surface layer of Vesta consists of material with absorption properties closely similar to the meteorites known as calcium-rich eucrites (density 3.4–3.7 g/cm³) which are also similar to some common lunar rocks. Ceres, in contrast, has a lower albedo and more bluish color than Vesta and lacks diagnostic absorption bands; it does not bear close resemblance to any known type of meteorite (Chapman, 1972a).

The optical properties of the dusty surface material of the near-Earth object 1685 Toro (Gehrels, 1972b) are similar to those of the most common type of chondritic meteorite (Chapman, 1972b). In general, however, the asteroids show widely differing optical surface properties (Chapman et al., 1971). We do not yet know to what extent, if any, there is a corresponding variation in their bulk composition.

20.5.6 Jupiter and Saturn

These planets are so massive that our lack of knowledge of matter at high pressures precludes any detailed speculation about their chemical composition. Not even a meaningful comparison between Jupiter and Saturn can be carried out in view of the large difference in size between them.

Attempts have been made to construct models for the different giant planets (DeMarcus, 1958: DeMarcus and Reynolds, 1963; Reynolds and Summers, 1965), but the assumptions used are necessarily highly uncertain. Existing calculations are generally based on the arbitrary assumption that the composition of the source material of all planets and satellites is the same and, specifically, is that of the solar photosphere. Such assumptions are in conflict with the wide variation in bulk densities observed among small bodies in the solar system.

Furthermore, in order to draw conclusions about the chemical composition from the average density of a body it is necessary to know the internal temperature distribution. However, attempts to estimate interior temperatures are highly sensitive to the assumed composition and to the unknown properties of the elements in question at high pressure. If the interior of Jupiter is assumed to be at relatively low temperature and to consist of solid metallic hydrogen and helium, accretional heat could then effectively be removed by conduction. The discovery of excess energy emission from Jupiter (Hubbard, 1969; Bishop and DeMarcus, 1970) has, however, shown that this commonly accepted picture is unrealistic, and leaves us with a wide range of uncertainty regarding interior temperature and chemical composition. It should be noted that during planetesimal accretion the primordial heat distribution probably differed substantially for the individual planets (sec. 12.11; fig. 12.11.1). This distribution is likely to have affected the present-day internal temperature profile.

Finally, a strong magnetic field, as existing in Jupiter and possibly also in the other giant planets, could profoundly affect the heat transfer in a liquid or gaseous interior by inhibiting convection. Hence, the interior temperature of the giant planets may well be much higher than existing models have indicated, and the average atomic mass could also be correspondingly higher.

Although space missions to the giant planets will certainly provide additional information with direct or indirect bearing on the problem of the interior state, this problem is likely to remain in a speculative state for a long time. Suggestive information on the completely unknown composition of the nonvolatile material in the giant planets could perhaps be obtained from residues of the source material in their regions of formation. Small bodies in the Lagrangian points L_4 and L_5 (Trojan asteroids in the case of Jupiter) may consist of such material.

20.5.7 Uranus and Neptune

The uncertainties in chemical composition, further complicated by the unknown internal thermal states of Jupiter and Saturn, apply also to Uranus and Neptune. However, because of the close similarity in size (Neptune possibly being slightly smaller but definitely more massive than Uranus; see table 20.5.1), comparison of physical properties of this pair is, to some extent, meaningful. It is interesting to note that the density of Neptune (1.66 g/cm³) at a solar distance of 30 AU is larger than that of Uranus (1.3 g/cm³) at 19 AU, and both are much denser than Saturn at 9 AU (see fig. 20.7.1a).

20.5.8 Triton

The retrograde orbit of this body, now a satellite of Neptune, indicates that it was captured from a planetary orbit (McCord, 1966) and underwent an evolution partially similar to that suggested for the Moon (Gerstenkorn, 1969; Alfvén and Arrhenius, 1972). Mass and radius for Triton have been measured with estimated errors of ±18 percent and ±30 percent, respectively. A combination of the extremes would give a lower density limit of 1.6 g/cm³ and an upper exceeding 8 g/cm³; the "best" value is around 5 g/cm³.

20.5.9 Pluto

Considering even the largest estimated "possible" errors in the values for the mass and diameter of Pluto, it is difficult to escape the conclusion that its density considerably exceeds 2 g/cm³. A density of 4.8 g/cm³ (calculated assuming a radius of 3200 km, a value close to the definitive upper limit of 3400 km set by occultation measurements) is regarded as the best estimate

(Newburn and Gulkis, 1973, p. 253; and Seidelmann et al., 1971). Combining the occultation volume limit with a negative mass error of 25 percent of the best estimate gives a "minimum" density of 2.9 g/cm³. To bring the mass estimate into lower values it would be necessary to assume much larger errors in the mass estimates for Neptune and Saturn (Halliday, 1969) than are presently believed to be feasible (Newburn and Gulkis, 1973). The lower limit for the radius is less precisely defined than the upper limit, but it cannot be much different from the estimated best value since lowering of the radius rapidly results in unreasonably high densities (table 20.5.1).

Pluto, like Triton, is sufficiently small to rule out the possibility of unknown high-density phases in its interior. The relatively large bulk density of Pluto consequently indicates a substantial fraction of rocky material, and, if the best present estimate is close to reality, also a significant proportion of iron.

20.5.10 Bulk Density in Relation to Planetary Mass

The densities of the terrestrial planets, discussed above and summarized in table 20.5.1, have been plotted against planetary mass in fig. 20.5.1. A regular increase in density with increasing mass is found in the series Moon-

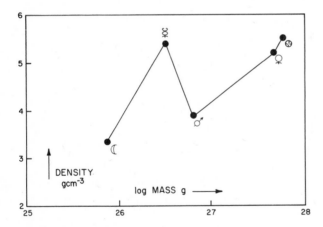

FIGURE 20.5.1.—Density of the terrestrial planets as a function of their mass. A smooth curve could be drawn through Moon-Mars-Venus-Earth indicating that all may have a similar composition. This would require the assumption that Moon-Mars-like material can be compressed to the high core densities indicated (~15–17 g/cm³) at the core pressures of Venus and the Earth (~1.5 Mb). But it is also possible that Moon and Mars have a heavy element content entirely different from that of Earth-Venus. The composition of Mercury must in any case be different from all the other bodies.

Mars-Venus-Earth. This density increase could possibly be due to compression including pressure-induced phase transformations; if this were the case, the chemical composition of all these bodies might be the same.

On the other hand, arguments can be made for a higher content of heavy elements in Venus and Earth than in the Moon and Mars (secs. 20.4(1) and 20.5.1). However, for Mercury it is in any case necessary to assume a difference in chemical composition, presumably a higher iron content.

The densities of the outer planets have been plotted as a function of their masses in fig. 20.5.2. Also in this group it is obvious that factors other than the mass determine the densities of the planets.

20.5.11 Compositions of Satellites

Except for the Moon, which is here considered as a planet, satellite mass and radius values are most reliable for the Galilean satellites of Jupiter. The reported values of their densities display marked differences, the two smaller inner satellites (Io and Europa) consisting of more dense material (3.1–3.75 g/cm³) than the outer ones (Ganymede and Callisto) (1.5–2.2 g/cm³) (table 20.5.1). This density variance probably indicates differences in the proportion of light elements in icy or liquid compounds to the heavier elements as

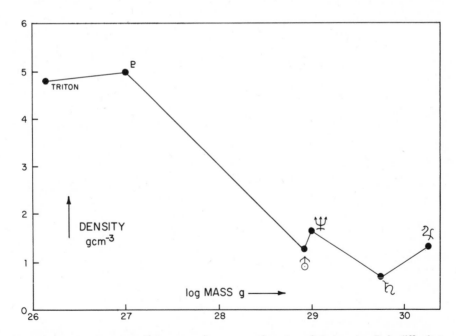

FIGURE 20.5.2.—Density of the outer planets as a function of their mass. It is difficult to believe that the density variation can be due to only the difference in mass.

found in earthy components (Lewis, 1971b), and demonstrates again the nonuniformity in composition of the source materials and bodies in the solar system.

The densities of the Saturnian satellites are poorly known except perhaps for Titan with a reported density of 2.3 g/cm³. The estimated densities for the other satellites (table 20.5.1), to the extent they can be relied upon, would suggest variations by a factor of four.

The densities of the Uranian satellites are completely unknown.

20.6 COMPOSITION OF THE SUN
20.6.1 Spectrometric Analysis

In principle, the composition of the solar photosphere, the chromosphere (including prominences), and the corona can be found by spectrometric analysis. This involves two steps; namely, measurement of line intensity profile, etc., which can be made with a high degree of accuracy, and, secondly, calculations of abundances from the spectrometric data based on models of the solar atmosphere. The models are usually homogeneous in the sense that they assume that light received by the spectrograph emanates from a region with density and temperature which are functions of only the height in the atmosphere.

As pointed out in sec. 15.3, homogeneous models are often misleading in astrophysics. In the case of the Sun, a homogeneous model is unrealistic, since we know that the solar atmosphere has a fine structure with elements of a size down to the limits of resolution and presumably still smaller. The differences in temperature and density between such elements are so large that the averaging introduced by the homogeneous model may cause gross errors. It is well known that solar magnetograph measurements are seriously in error, and in many cases it is even doubtful whether solar magnetograms can be interpreted at all. This is suggested by the fact that the "magnetic field" derived from solar magnetograms does not obey Maxwell's equations (Wilcox, 1972). It is possible that the major uncertainties in chemical analysis by means of spectral analysis (Worrall and Wilson, 1972) are due to the same inhomogeneity effects. This must be clarified before we can rely on spectrometric results for abundance estimates for more than an order-of-magnitude accuracy.

20.6.2 Analysis of Corpuscular Radiation From the Sun

Space measurements of solar wind composition and of solar cosmic rays have provided quantitative information on the chemical composition of the material emitted from the upper corona and of the flare regions (Price,

FIGURE 20.6.1—Coronal streamers, visible at solar eclipse. The photograph illustrates
the inhomogeneous nature of emission of solar material. Homogeneous models of the Sun
are often completely misleading.

1973). The abundances obtained from these measurements have no simple
relationship to the chemical composition of the regions from which they
derive because of selective processes during emission (see fig. 20.6.1). We
know very little about the fractionation processes themselves; however,
fluctuations in them are manifest by variations of two orders of magnitude
in the helium content of the solar wind (Hirschberg, 1973), and also by
variations in the heavier elements (Price, 1973; Price et al., 1973).

Long-term integration of the corpuscular flux may eliminate the effects
of short-term fluctuations in selective emission processes and give clues to
their nature. However, they leave unknown any permanent differences
between the composition of the Sun and the material that leaves it.

20.6.3 Significance of Solar Photospheric Abundance Data

For the reasons outlined above, elemental abundances in the accessible
layers of the Sun are known with much less accuracy than in samples of
the Earth, Moon, and meteorites analyzed under controlled conditions,
and it is difficult to assign a probable error to any individual elemental
abundance determinations (Urey, 1972).

It is often assumed that the bulk composition of the Sun is identical to some undifferentiated matter that was conjectured to be the source of other bodies in the solar system. This assumption derives from the Laplacian concept that all the matter of the solar system taken together once formed a dense solar nebula. It was further assumed that throughout the presumed process of contraction and dynamic differentiation of such a nebula, the chemical composition somehow remained uniform.

As has been discussed in detail in other sections of this work, theories of this type are unrealistic since they ignore many of the important facts concerning the observed present state of the solar system and do not incorporate modern knowledge of the behavior of particles and fields in space. Hence there is no reason to believe a priori that the Sun has a composition which accurately corresponds to that of the bulk of any satellite, planet, or group of meteorites. Indeed, this is demonstrated already by the observed variability in composition of rocky components among various bodies in the solar system (secs. 20.5 and 20.7). Furthermore, we do not know whether the surface composition of the Sun is representative of its bulk composition. Theories of the solar interior are not very useful since they seem to be seriously out of line with observation (Fowler, 1972).

The range of actual variation in chemical composition is hard to specify because we have sampled only a few of the relevant bodies, and most of these are strongly differentiated. An indication of the variations in composition is given by the range of densities of the small bodies in the solar system (sec. 20.5.11) and, on a smaller scale, by the differences in composition between unmodified primordial condensate components in meteorites from different parent jet streams.

In order to place limits on the differences between accurately measurable materials such as meteorites and approximately measurable materials such as solar photosphere, comparisons such as those in fig. 20.6.2a are useful. Carbonaceous chondrites of Type I (Wiik, 1956) have been chosen for the comparison since there is general agreement that they consist of primary condensate material (one of the necessarily many different types) which does not seem to have been significantly modified with regard to elemental composition after condensation.

Elemental abundance data on this type of meteorite were obtained from a methodologically critical review compiled from work by a number of analytical experts (Mason, ed., 1971). To avoid bias in selection of analyses, all reported measurements accepted in that review have been included without preferential selection. The solar abundances are taken from the evaluations by Müller (1968) and Grevesse et al. (1968). In the case of the solar abundances a potential bias may be caused by the presumption that the solar and meteoritic abundances ought to converge on a value, referred to as the "cosmic abundance." The literature indicates that marked deviations from such agreement become subject to more extensive scrutiny, revision, rejection, and exclusion than do the abundance ratio estimates which fall close to 1.0. The distribution shown in fig. 20.6.2a therefore probably represents a minimum dispersion.

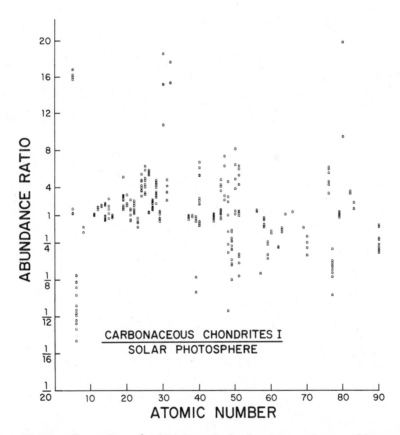

FIGURE 20.6.2a.—Comparison of solar photospheric abundance estimates with measurements on carbonaceous meteorites of Type I. Each analytical chondrite value, normalized to silicon, has been divided by each of the several current photospheric values. Four of the ratio values for mercury ($Z=80$) exceed 20 and are not shown in the diagram. Data compiled by L. Shaw. It has commonly been assumed that these two materials can be regarded as splits from a chemically homogeneous body "the solar nebula" having "cosmic abundances" of elements. Except for components with high vapor pressures or nuclear instabilities the compositions of these meteorites and of the solar photosphere then ought to approach identity, and the elemental abundance ratios should be close to 1. The strong scatter of data in the figure shows, however, that they do not provide a basis for the assumption of a close agreement between the solar photosphere and this group of meteorites (see also fig. 20.6.2b).

As shown by fig. 20.6.2b, for about 50 percent of all abundance pairs determined, the solar and meteoritic values are within a factor five of each other. About 10 percent of all elements deviate by more than a factor of 60. The most extreme cases are the relative concentrations of the noble gases (measured only in meteorites and not included in fig. 20.6.2b), mercury, thorium, uranium, and the rare earth elements. Particularly in the latter three cases it is difficult to tell what fraction of these deviations reflect real differences; the oscillator strengths are very poorly known and the solar data for these elements may have large experimental errors. The noble gas anomalies, on the other hand, are based on implanted vs. occluded components in meteorites and implanted solar emissions in lunar materials. These anomalies would consequently seem to reflect real fractionation of the kind expected in the emplacement and condensation process of solids (Signer and Suess, 1963; Jokipii, 1964; Arrhenius and Alfvén, 1971; Arrhenius, 1972).

It is clear from the comparison that observational uncertainties leave room for considerable differences in composition between the solar photosphere on one hand and various condensates such as the one represented

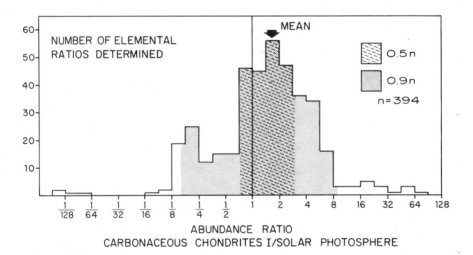

ABUNDANCE RATIO
CARBONACEOUS CHONDRITES I/SOLAR PHOTOSPHERE

FIGURE 20.6.2b.—Frequency distribution of abundance ratios from fig. 20.6.2a. The diagram shows that on the average there is about 50 percent probability for solar photospheric observations to agree within a factor of five with their meteorite counterparts, and a 90 percent probability for agreement within a factor of 60. Ratios for elements with atomic number ≤ 10 are not included in this diagram since they are affected by preferential nuclear instabilities or are highly volatile. Neither are the noble gases included because their abundances in solids are strongly permuted due to volatility and other factors; furthermore their photospheric abundances are not known. Two abundance ratios exceed 128 and are not shown in the graph. Data compiled by L. Shaw.

by carbonaceous meteorites, Type I, on the other. As indicated above there is no particular a priori reason why there should be any close agreement in composition between these materials. The differences in bulk densities among the individual planets and satellites discussed in sec. 20.5 are related to differences in abundances of the elements of which the bodies consist. Abundance differences of a factor of about four in the major condensable elements appear sufficient to explain the density differences among the small bodies in the solar system.

20.7 REGULARITY OF BULK DENSITIES IN THE SOLAR SYSTEM

Our analysis of the solar system is based on the "hetegonic principle" implying that we should investigate to what extent the same relationships hold for all bodies formed in orbit around a primary body. From this point of view it is important to compare the chemical composition of the satellite systems and the planetary system. This is admittedly difficult because we know little about the chemical compositions of the planets and still less about those of the satellites. The only comparison we can make is between their densities.

20.7.1 Density As a Function of Potential Energy

As we shall see in ch. 21, there are reasons to believe that the emplacement of plasma in different regions around a central body is regulated by the critical velocity for ionization of the neutral gas falling toward the body. This implies that we should expect the abundances of elements in a system to vary with the gravitational potential energy. For this reason, it is useful to plot densities of the celestial bodies as a function of this gravitational potential energy (the ratio of the mass M_c of the central body to the orbital radius r_{orb} of the body in question). In this way planets and satellites can be compared. Figure 20.7.1a shows gravitational potential energy as a function of density for the planets (including asteroids, Moon, and Triton), fig. 20.7.1b shows the satellite systems of Jupiter and Saturn, and fig. 20.7.1c shows a composite of planets and satellites. The parameter M_c/r_{orb} allows a direct comparison of the planetary system and the different satellite systems.

Looking at figs. 20.7.1a, b, and c, we can conclude that the bulk densities decrease from the high value for Mercury, Venus, and Earth (at $M_c/r_{orb} = 3 \times 10^{20}$ g/cm) to a minimum at a gravitational potential energy of about 10^{19} g/cm (the region of Saturn in the planetary system) and then rise again to higher values with decreasing gravitational potential energy.

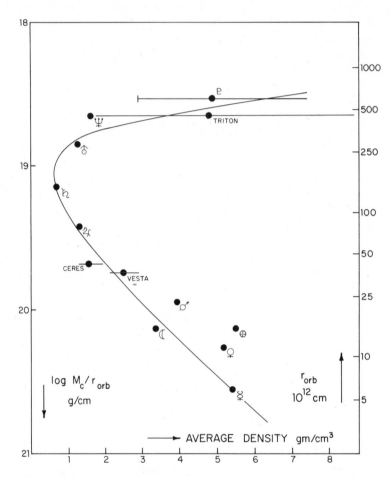

FIGURE 20.7.1a.—Average density of planets and former planets as a function of orbital distance r_{orb} from the Sun. The guideline through the population of density points is intended for intercomparison of this figure with figs. 20.7.1b and c. The ordinate is also given in terms of gravitational potential energy (mass, M_c, divided by orbital radius, r_{orb}); this makes it possible to directly compare the distribution of satellites with that of the planets. The gravitational potential energy is also a parameter which enters in an important manner in the discussion of the critical velocity phenomenon (see chs. 21 and 23). Since the Moon and Triton are captured planets, the Sun is regarded as their central body. Hence the Moon and Triton have the approximate gravitational potential energy of the Earth and Neptune, respectively. The horizontal lines through the points for Ceres, Vesta, Triton, and Pluto indicate the estimated range of uncertainty, with the vertical bar designating the lower limit for the density of Pluto as discussed in the text. Data from table 20.5.1.

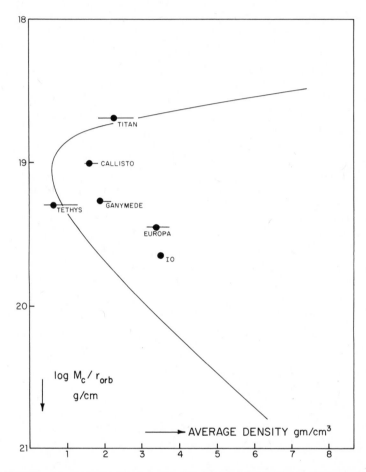

FIGURE 20.7.1b.—Average density as a function of gravitational potential energy, M_c/r_{orb}, for the regular satellite system of Jupiter and the two best known Saturnian satellites, Titan and Tethys. Solid circles denote density values based on the best estimates of radius and mass; horizontal lines indicate the estimated range of uncertainty. Data from table 20.5.1.

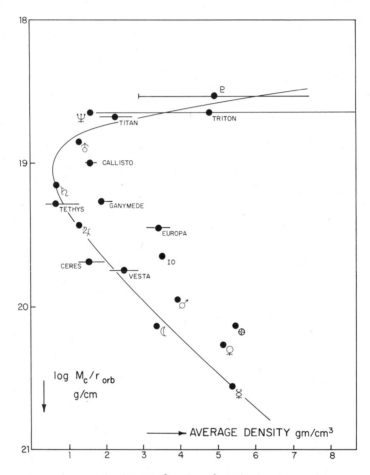

FIGURE 20.7.1c.—Average density as a function of gravitational potential energy, M_c/r_{orb}, for the planets and better known satellites. The distribution indicates that heavy substances accumulated both in the inner and outermost regions of the systems, whereas light substances dominate in the intermediate region. Symbols are those used in figs. 20.7.1a and b. Data from table 20.5.1.

20.7.2 Chemical Meaning of Bulk Densities

The chemical meaning of the bulk densities of the large planets is rather uncertain. Because of the insignificance of pressure effects, the values for Mercury, Mars, Moon, Triton, Pluto, the asteroids, and the satellites are in principle more reliable, although possible measurement error is high in several cases.

The interpretation of the densities of Uranus and Neptune also suffers from the uncertainties related to compression and temperature in the large planets but they can be better intercompared because of the closely similar size of these two planets.

In the case of the least dense objects, namely Ganymede, Callisto, Tethys, and the giant planets, it is likely that substantial amounts of volatile light elements in unknown proportions contribute significantly to the low density. This indicates that *heavy substances were accumulated both in the inner and the outermost regions of the systems, whereas light substances dominate in the intermediate region.*

20.7.3 Density as Influenced by Solar Radiation

There is a common notion that the density of a body in the solar system is an inverse function of solar distance; this decrease in density is thought to be due to the decrease in radiation temperature at greater solar distances, which enhances capability for retaining lower density volatile elements and compounds. The fact that Neptune's density is higher than that of Uranus (which, in turn, is higher than that of Saturn) proves that this view is not correct. Together with the suggestive densities of Triton and Pluto this indicates that the chemical composition changes such as to give increasing density with increasing solar distance in this part of the solar system.

20.7.4 Theoretical Implications of Bulk Densities in the Solar System

We have seen above that bulk densities vary among the bodies of the solar system. This variation substantiates that the solar system did not form from a homogeneous medium. Hence it does not make sense to refer to any specific body in the solar system as representative of an average "cosmic" composition of the source materials, and the Sun is no exception. Furthermore, we know very little about the bulk composition of the Sun (see sec. 20.6).

Other conclusions to be drawn from our survey of the bulk densities in the solar system are that the density of a given body is not a function of mass (see sec. 20.5.10) nor is it a monotonic function of the distance from the central body (see secs. 20.7.1 and 20.7.3).

Consequently, an explanation is needed for these variations in density, and presumably composition, in regions of different gravitational potential. A theory making detailed predictions of composition, however, cannot be verified because such detailed data are not yet available. An explanation of the variation of densities and compositions throughout the solar system, however, follows from consideration of plausible courses of the primordial emplacement of matter around the central bodies, such as discussed in ch. 21 and 23.

MASS DISTRIBUTION AND THE CRITICAL VELOCITY

21.1 MASS DISTRIBUTION IN THE SOLAR SYSTEM

21.1.1 Inadequacy of the Homogeneous Disc Theory

In theories of the Laplacian type it is assumed that the matter that formed the planets originally was distributed as a more or less uniform disc. The inadequacies of this type of approach have been discussed in secs. 2.4 and 11.2. For completeness a Laplacian-type theory applicable to the planetary system must also prove applicable to the satellite systems. Hence let us turn our attention to the empirical aspects of Laplacian theories as applied to the satellite systems.

As has been discussed in sec. 18.10, the distributed density (see secs. 2.4–2.5) for the group of inner Saturnian satellites (fig. 2.5.3) is reasonably uniform from the ring system out to Rhea, and within this group a uniform disc theory might be acceptable. But outside Rhea there is a wide region devoid of matter, followed by the giant satellite Titan, the very small Hyperion, and the medium-sized Iapetus. An even greater discrepancy between the homogeneous disc picture and the observed mass distribution is found in the Jovian satellite system (fig. 2.5.2). Although the Galilean satellite region is of reasonably uniform density there are void regions both inside and outside it. This same general density pattern also holds for the Uranian satellite system (fig. 2.5.4).

Thus the distributed densities of the satellite systems of Jupiter, Saturn, and Uranus do not substantiate the homogeneous disc theory. Obviously the planetary system does not show a uniform distribution of density. In fact the distributed density varies by a factor 10^7 (fig. 2.5.1).

In spite of this there are many astrophysicists who believe in a homogeneous disc as the precursor medium for the planetary system. The low density in the asteroid region is then thought of as a "secondary" effect, presumably arising from some kind of "instability" caused by Jupiter. However, under present conditions several big planets (e.g., of 10 to 100 times the mass of Mars) moving between Mars and Jupiter would be just as perfectly stable in all respects as are the orbits of the present asteroids. And no credible mechanism has been proposed explaining how Jupiter could have prevented the formation of planets in this region.

In addition to these obvious discrepancies between the implied uniform and the actually observed distributions of mass in the solar system, the whole disc idea is tied to the theoretical concept of a contracting mass of gas which could collapse to form both the central body and the surrounding secondaries via the intermediate formation of the disc. As has been pointed out in sec. 11.2, small bodies cannot be formed in this way and it is questionable whether even Jupiter is large enough to have been formed by such a collapse process. Another compelling argument against a gravitational collapse of a gas cloud is found in the isochronism of spins (secs. 9.7–9.8 and ch. 13). We have also found in ch. 20 that the chemical composition of the celestial bodies speaks against a Laplacian homogeneous disc. Other arguments against it are found in the detailed structure of the Saturnian rings and the asteroidal belt (see secs. 18.6 and 18.8). It is very unlikely that these features can be explained by a Laplacian model or by gravitational collapse.

21.1.2 Origin and Emplacement of Mass: Ejection of Mass

Since the concept of the homogeneous disc consequently is unrealistic when applied to any of the actual systems of central bodies with orbiting secondaries, we must look for other explanations of how the mass which now forms the planets and satellites could have been emplaced in the environment of the central bodies.

In principle, the mass which now constitutes the planets and satellites could either have been ejected from the central body or could have fallen in toward the central body from outside the region of formation. It is difficult to see how a satellite could have been ejected from its planet and placed in its present orbit. Such processes have been suggested many times, but have always encountered devastating objections. Most recently it has been proposed as an explanation of the origin of the Moon, but has been shown to be unacceptable (see Kaula, 1971; and ch. 24).

This process would be still less attractive as an explanation of, e.g., the origin of the Uranian satellites. In fact, to place the Uranian satellites in their present (almost coplanar circular) orbits would require all the trajectory control sophistication of modern space technology. It is unlikely that any natural phenomenon, involving bodies emitted from Uranus, could have achieved this result.

An ejection of a dispersed medium which is subsequently brought into partial corotation is somewhat less unnatural, but it also requires a very powerful source of energy, which is hardly available on Uranus, to use the same example. Moreover, even in this case, the launch must be cleverly adjusted so that the matter is not ejected to infinity but is placed in orbit at the required distances. Seen with the Uranian surface as launch pad, the outermost satellites have gravitational energies which are more than 99 percent of the energy required for escape to infinity.

21.1.3 Origin and Emplacement of Mass: Infall of Matter

Hence it is more attractive to turn to the alternative that the secondary bodies derive from matter falling in from "infinity" (a distance large compared to the satellite orbit). This matter (after being stopped and given sufficient angular momentum) accumulates at specific distances from the central body. Such a process may take place when atoms or molecules in free fall reach a kinetic energy equal to their ionization energy. At this stage, the gas can become ionized by the process discussed in sec. 21.4; the ionized gas can then be stopped by the magnetic field of the central body and receive angular momentum by transfer from the central body as described in sec. 16.3.

21.2 THE BANDS OF SECONDARY BODIES AS A FUNCTION OF GRAVITATIONAL POTENTIAL ENERGY

If the hypothesis assuming infall of matter is correct, then the matter that has fallen into the solar system would have accumulated at predictable distances from the central body. This distance is a function of the kinetic energy acquired by the matter during free fall under the gravitational attraction of the central body. Let us consider the positions of a group of secondary bodies as a function of their specific gravitational potential, $G\Gamma$, where

$$\Gamma = \frac{M_c}{r_{orb}} \tag{21.2.1}$$

and G is the gravitational constant, M_c is the mass of a central body, and r_{orb} is the orbital radius of a secondary body. The gravitational potential Γ determines the velocity of free fall and thus the kinetic energy of infalling matter at a distance r_{orb} from the central body. In fig. 21.2.1, we have plotted this energy as a function of M_c for the Sun-planet system as well as for all the planet-satellite systems.

We see from fig. 21.2.1 that:

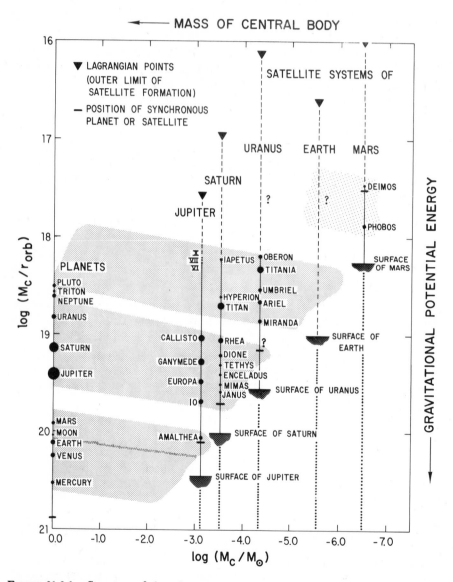

FIGURE 21.2.1.—Structure of the solar system in terms of the mass of the central bodies and the gravitational potential energy of the bodies orbiting around them. For a detailed analysis refer to secs. 21.2, 21.3, and 23.9.2. (From Alfvén and Arrhenius, 1972.)

(1) *The secondary bodies of the solar system fall into three main bands.*

(2) *Whenever a band is located far enough above the surface of a central body there is a formation of secondary bodies in the region.* These two important observational facts will be discussed in this and the following chapter.

Although there are some apparent exceptions to the general validity of these conclusions, cogent explanations can be offered for each discrepancy. Venus has no satellites, probably because of its extremely slow rotation and lack of a magnetic field. Both these properties, rotation and magnetic field of the central body, are the prerequisites for formation of secondary bodies, as was discussed in sec. 16.1. Further, we find no satellite systems of the normal type around Neptune and the Earth. The reason for this seems to be straightforward; both these bodies might very well have once produced normal satellite systems, but they have been destroyed by the capture of Triton (McCord, 1966) and of the Moon (ch. 24). Mercury has a very slow rotation and a weak magnetic field and is perhaps not massive enough for satellite formation. Whether Pluto has any satellites is not known.

We have not yet discussed the Martian satellites which fall far outside the three bands. From a formal point of view they may be thought to indicate a fourth band. However, the Martian satellite system is rudimentary compared to the well-developed satellite systems of Jupiter, Saturn, and Uranus, and the Martian satellites are the smallest satellites we know. In view of the rudimentary character of the Martian satellite system, we do not include this in our discussion of systems of secondary bodies. This question is further discussed by Alfvén and Arrhenius (1972) and in ch. 24.

In fig. 21.2.1 the satellite systems are arranged along the horizontal axis according to the mass of the central body. Groups of secondary bodies belonging to a particular band are generally located somewhat lower if the central body is less massive, thus giving the bands a slight downward slope. As a first approximation, however, we can consider the bands to be horizontal. (The reason for the slope is discussed in sec. 23.9.2).

We conclude from the gravitational energy diagram that *groups of bodies are formed in regions where the specific gravitational energy has values in certain discrete ranges.*

In fig. 21.2.1 we have also plotted the positions of synchronous secondary orbits as well as those of the Lagrangian points for the satellite systems. The position of a synchronous secondary orbit around a primary body is a *natural inner limit* to a system of secondary bodies, since any secondary body located inside this position would have to orbit faster than the central body spins. (As discussed in sec. 23.9.1, bodies may, under special conditions, orbit inside the limit.) Of all the secondary bodies in the solar system only Phobos orbits within the synchronous limit.

A natural outer limit for a satellite system is the Lagrangian point situated at a distance r_L from the planet, given by

$$r_L = r_{sc} \left(\frac{M_{sc}}{3M_\odot} \right)^{1/3} \tag{21.2.2}$$

where r_{sc} is the planetary distance from the Sun, M_{sc} is the planetary mass, and $M_\odot$ is the solar mass. Table 11.2.1 gives the distances to the Lagrangian points. Outside r_L, the gravitational attraction on a satellite due to the Sun exceeds that due to the planet. Hence a satellite must orbit at a distance much smaller than r_L in order not to be seriously perturbed by solar gravitation.

21.3 COMPARATIVE STUDY OF THE GROUPS OF SECONDARY BODIES

We have found in table 2.5.1 and sec. 18.10.1 that the regular bodies in the solar system belong to certain groups. Accepting the conclusions of sec. 21.2 we shall now attempt a more detailed study of these groups. Physical data for both the planetary and satellite systems are given in tables 2.1.1–2.1.3. Our general method is to compare each group of secondary bodies with its neighbors to the left and right within the same band of the gravitational potential energy diagram (fig. 21.2.1).

We start with the Jovian system which should be compared with the planetary system and the Saturnian system. The giant planets, the Galilean satellites of Jupiter, and the inner satellites of Saturn (Janus through Rhea) fall in the same energy interval (allowing for the general slope discussed earlier). There is a conspicuous similarity between the group of the four big bodies in the planetary and in the Jovian systems, the four giant planets corresponding to the four Galilean satellites. However, there is also a difference; whereas in the planetary system the innermost body in this group, Jupiter, is by far the largest one, the mass of the bodies in the Galilean satellite group slightly increases outward. In this respect the Jovian system is intermediate between the group of giant planets and the inner Saturnian satellites, where the mass of the bodies rapidly increases outward. The latter group consists of six satellites and the rings. (The difference in mass distribution among the inner Saturnian satellites, the Galilean group, and the giant planets is discussed in secs. 23.6–23.8).

The fifth Jovian satellite, Amalthea, orbits far inside the Galilean satellites. It falls in the same energy band as the group of terrestrial planets. We may regard it as an analog to Mars while the other terrestrial planets have no correspondents probably because of the closeness to the surface of Jupiter. The mass of Amalthea is unknown. Its diameter is estimated to be about 160 km. As the diameter of Io is about 3730 km its volume is about 10^4 times that of Amalthea. The mass ratio of these two satellites is unknown. The volume ratio of Io to Amalthea is of the same order as the volume of Jupiter to Mars, which is 9000, but the close agreement is likely to be accidental.

The outermost group of Jovian satellites, Jupiter 6, 7, and 10, is rudimentary. One may attribute the rudimentary character of this group to its closeness to the outer stability limit r_L for satellite formation, which is closer to this group than to any other group in the diagram. Although this group of Jovian satellites falls within the band including the outer Saturnian satellites and the Uranian satellites, it has no other similarity with these two groups.

In the planetary system the same band may have given rise to Pluto and Triton (the latter being later captured by Neptune in a similar way as the Moon was captured by the Earth).

The Uranian satellites form the most regular of all the groups of secondary bodies in the sense that all orbital inclinations and eccentricities are almost zero, and the spacings between the bodies are almost proportional to their orbital radii ($q = r_{n+1}/r_n \approx$ constant). The group is situated far outside the synchronous orbit and far inside the Lagrangian point. It should be noted that this is also the case for the Galilean satellites which also form a very regular group. In fact, these two groups should be studied as typical examples of satellite formation in the absence of disturbing factors.

Titan, Hyperion, and Iapetus are considered as a separate group which we refer to as the "outer Saturnian satellites." The assignment of these three bodies to one group is not altogether convincing and the group is the most irregular of all with regard to the sequence of satellite orbital radii and masses. However, it occupies a range of Γ values which closely coincides with that of the Uranian satellites. Furthermore, if we compare the group with both its horizontal neighbors, we find that the irregular group in the Saturnian system constitutes a transition between the rudimentary group in the Jovian system and the regular group in the Uranian system. In this respect there is an analogy with the Galilean group in which the almost equal size of the bodies is an intermediate case between the rapid decrease in size away from the central body in the giant planets and the rapid increase in size away from the central body in the inner Saturnian system. The probable reason for these systematic trends is discussed in secs. 23.6–23.8.

21.4 THEORETICAL BACKGROUND FOR THE BAND FORMATION

Attempts to clarify the mechanism which produces the gravitational energy bands (sec. 21.2) should start with an analysis of the infall of the gas cloud toward a central body. To avoid the difficulties inherent in all theories about the primitive Sun, we should, as stated in ch. 1 and sec. 16.9, base our discussion primarily on the formation of satellites around a planet.

The gas cloud we envisage in the process of satellite formation is a local cloud at a large distance from a magnetized, gravitating central body. This cloud, called the source cloud (see sec. 21.11.1) is located within the jet stream in which the central body has formed or is forming and is thus part of the gas content of the jet stream itself (see fig. 21.4.1). This cloud also contains grains from which the central body is accreting. For the sake of simplicity let us assume that initially the cloud is at rest at such a low tem-

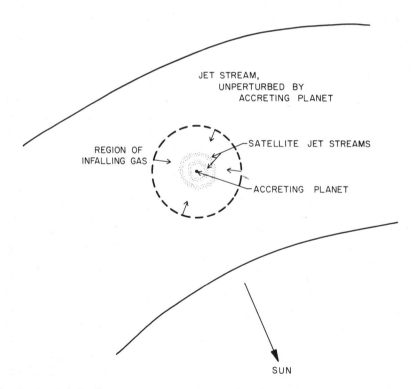

FIGURE 21.4.1.—Qualitative picture of the infall of gas from a jet stream toward a planet. The gas becomes ionized, is brought into partial corotation, and eventually forms satellite jet streams.

perature that the thermal velocity of the particles can be neglected compared to their free-fall velocity. Then every atom of the cloud will fall radially toward the center of the gravitating body. If the gas cloud is partially ionized, the ions and electrons, which necessarily have a Larmor radius which is small compared to the distance to the central body, will be affected by the magnetic field even at great distances from the central body, with the general result that their free fall will be prevented. Hence in our idealized case only the neutral component, the grains and gas, will fall in. The infall of grains is the basic process for the formation and growth of the central body (which acquires spin as a result of the asymmetry of this infall; for a detailed discussion see ch. 13).

Let us now consider the infall of gas in an idealized case in which the gas is not disturbed by the infall of grains. Probably such a situation occurs when the accretion of the central body is near completion. Hence we assume that for a certain period of time there is a constant infall of gas toward the central body which is assumed to be in approximately its present state.

Suppose that at some distance r from the central body there is a very thin cloud of plasma which also has negligible thermal velocity and which, due to the action of the magnetic field, is at rest. (The effect of rotation of the body is neglected here; it will be introduced in sec. 21.13.) The plasma density is assumed to be so low that the mean free path of the atoms exceeds the dimensions of the cloud. (For densities $\lesssim 10^3–10^4$, the mean free path is larger than the dimension of the satellite formation regions; i.e., $\leq$ planet-outermost satellite distance. However, the dimension of the cloud in question may be an order of magnitude or so smaller, allowing somewhat higher densities, but the mean free path would still be much greater than the dimension of the cloud.)

When the infalling atoms reach the plasma cloud, some will pass through it without colliding and some will make nonionizing collisions and be deflected, but neither of these processes will affect the conditions in the plasma cloud very much.

However, under the condition that the atoms arrive at the cloud with a sufficiently high velocity, atoms may become ionized at some of the collisions. Due to the magnetic field, the ions and electrons thus produced will rapidly be stopped and become incorporated in the plasma cloud. Hence the density of the plasma cloud will grow, with the result that it will capture infalling atoms at an increased rate. In an extreme case the density may become so high that the mean free path of atoms is smaller than the size of the cloud, resulting in a complete stopping of the infalling gas. (We assume that the magnetic field is strong enough to support the resulting dense plasma cloud; see secs. 16.3–16.5.)

Basic theoretical analysis of electric breakdown in a gas treats the conditions under which the electric field will give sufficient energy to an electron to produce new electrons so that an avalanche may start. The "original" existence of free electrons can be taken for granted. Our case is essentially similar. The existence of thin plasma clouds anywhere in space can be taken for granted. The question we should ask ourselves is this: What are the conditions under which the infalling atoms get ionized so frequently that the density of the original plasma cloud will grow like an avalanche? It is likely that the infall velocity is the crucial parameter. In our simple model the infalling gas cloud will be stopped at the distance r_{ion} where its velocity of fall reaches the value v_{ion}, such that

$$\frac{GM_cm_a}{r_{ion}} = \frac{m_av_{ion}^2}{2} \tag{21.4.1}$$

where m_a is the mass of an atom. At this distance the specific gravitational potential energy $G\Gamma$ will have the value $G\Gamma_{ion}$ with

$$\Gamma_{ion} = \frac{M_c}{r_{ion}} = \frac{v_{ion}^2}{2G} \tag{21.4.2}$$

Hence Γ_{ion} is a function only of v_{ion}. Because v_{ion} is the parameter which sets the lower limit for ionization of the infalling gas, v_{ion} may be considered as an analog to the breakdown electric field in the theory of electrical discharges.

The analogy between the stopping of an infalling cloud and the electric breakdown is in reality still closer. In fact, seen from the coordinate system of the infalling cloud, there is an electric field

$$\mathbf{E} = -\mathbf{v} \times \mathbf{B} \tag{21.4.3}$$

which increases during the fall because both the velocity of fall $\mathbf{v}$ and the dipole magnetic field $\mathbf{B}$ increase. If the electric field exceeds a certain critical value E_{ion}, a discharge will start via some (yet unspecified) mechanism for energy transfer to the electrons. This will lead to at least partial ionization of the falling gas cloud. In situations where the collision rate for the electrons is low the mechanism for transfer of energy from the electric field (i.e., from the falling gas) to the electrons is very complicated and not yet quite clarified (the electric field $-\mathbf{v} \times \mathbf{B}$ in the coordinate system of the gas cloud cannot directly accelerate the electrons; in a magnetic field the electron cannot gain more than the potential difference over a Larmor radius for every collision and this is very small). Nonetheless this mechanism has empirically been demonstrated and proven to be highly efficient in a variety of plasma experiments (see sec. 21.8 and references). Under certain (rather general) conditions, this will lead to a braking of the velocity of the cloud and possibly to stopping it. The discharge will occur when v exceeds the value v_{ion} which is connected with E_{ion} by

$$\mathbf{E_{ion}} = -\mathbf{v_{ion}} \times \mathbf{B} \tag{21.4.4}$$

Hence the ionization of the infalling cloud may also be due to the electric field's exceeding E_{ion}.

21.5 ATTEMPTS TO INTERPRET THE BAND STRUCTURE

If we equate the ionization energy eV_{ion} of an atom of mass m_a to its gravitational energy in the presence of a central body of mass M_c, we have

$$eV_{ion} = \frac{GM_c m_a}{r_{orb}} \tag{21.5.1}$$

or

$$\Gamma = \frac{M_c}{r_{orb}} = \frac{eV_{ion}}{Gm_a} \tag{21.5.2}$$

As we will see later there is a mechanism which converts the kinetic energy of an atom falling toward a central body to ionization energy. Hence, eq. (21.5.2) allows one to determine for an atom of known mass and ionization potential the orbital radius from the central body at which ionization can take place.

In table 21.5.1 we list a number of elements of cosmochemical importance along with their estimated relative abundance, average atomic mass, ionization potential, eV_{ion}, gravitational energy as given by eq. (21.5.2), and critical velocity which will be discussed in a later section. Just as the Γ values for the bodies in the solar system, as given by eq. (21.2.1), were plotted in fig. 21.2.1, so the Γ values for the elements as given by eq. 21.5.2 are plotted in fig. 21.5.1. Looking at this plot of gravitational potential

TABLE 21.5.1

Parameters Determining the Gravitational Energy Band Structure

Element [a]	Ionization potential V_{ion} (V)	Average atomic mass (amu)	Log gravitational potential energy log Γ (g/cm)	Atomic abundance [b] relative to Si $=10^6$	Critical velocity [c] V_{crit} (10^5 cm/sec)	Band
H	13.5	1.0	20.29	2×10^{10}	50.9	I
He	24.5	4.0	19.94	2×10^9	34.3	I
Ne	21.5	20.2	19.18	2×10^6	14.3	II
N	14.5	14.0	19.18	2×10^6	14.1	II
C	11.2	12.0	19.11	1×10^7	13.4	II
O	13.5	16.0	19.08	2×10^7	12.7	II
(F)	17.42	19.0	19.11	4×10^3	13.3	II
(B)	8.3	10.8	19.08	1×10^2	12.1	II
[Be]	9.32	9.0	19.18	8×10^{-1}	14.1	II
[Li]	5.39	6.9	19.04	5×10^1	12.2	II
Ar	15.8	40.0	18.78	1×10^5	8.7	III
P	10.5	31.0	18.70	1×10^4	8.1	III
S	10.3	32.1	18.70	5×10^5	7.8	III
Mg	7.6	24.3	18.60	1×10^6	7.7	III
Si	8.1	28.1	18.60	1×10^6	7.4	III
Na	5.12	23.0	18.30	6×10^4	6.5	III
Al	5.97	27.0	18.48	8×10^4	6.5	III
Ca	6.09	40.1	18.30	7×10^4	5.4	III
Fe	7.8	55.8	18.30	9×10^5	5.2	III
Mn	7.4	54.9	18.30	1×10^4	5.1	III
Cr	6.8	52.1	18.30	1×10^4	5.0	III
Ni	7.6	58.7	18.30	5×10^4	5.0	III
(Cl)	13.0	35.5	18.70	2×10^3	8.4	III
(K)	4.3	39.1	18.30	2×10^3	4.6	III

[a] Minor elements (abundance 10^2–10^4) are indicated by parentheses; trace elements (abundance $<10^2$) are indicated by brackets.

[b] The very fact that separation processes are active in interstellar and circumstellar space makes it difficult to specify relative abundances of elements except by order of magnitude and for specific environments (such as the solar photosphere, the solar wind at a given point in time, the lunar crust). This is further discussed in ch. 20. The abundances are the averages estimated by Urey (1972). Most values are based on carbonaceous chondrites of Type II which form a particularly well analyzed set, apparently unaffected by the type of differentiation which is characteristic of planetary interiors. Supplementary data for volatile elements are based on estimates for the solar photosphere and trapped solar wind. All data are normalized to silicon, arbitrarily set at 10^6.

[c] All values are calculated from eq. (21.6.1) using the data presented in this table.

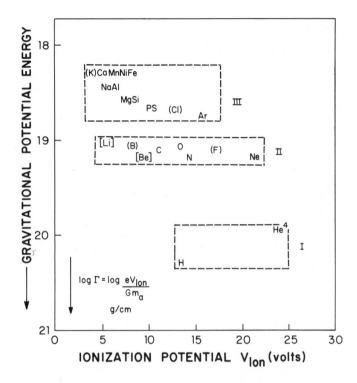

FIGURE 21.5.1.—The gravitational energy Γ and ionization potential of the most abundant elements. Roman numerals refer to row in the periodic table, with "III" including the fourth row. All elements in a band have approximately the same gravitational energy and v_{ion}, as discussed in secs. 21.4 and 21.5. Minor and trace elements are indicated, respectively, by parentheses and brackets.

energy versus ionization potential we find that *all the elements fall in one of three bands*. Hydrogen and helium give a value for Γ which falls in the region of the lowest band (which will be referred to as Band I, since this is comprised of elements of the first row of the periodic table). All the elements in the second row of the periodic table (Li-F), including C, N, and O, have values around $\Gamma \approx 10^{19}$ falling in the intermediate band (Band II), whereas all the common heavier elements found in the third and fourth row of the periodic table fall in the upper band (Band III). This means that if a gas dominated by any one of the most abundant elements falls in toward the central body, its kinetic energy will just suffice to ionize it when its gravitational potential energy reaches the values indicated by its appropriate band. For our discussion it is decisive that the value of the cosmically most abundant elements fall in a number of discrete bands rather than forming a random distribution.

This ionization is a collective phenomenon dependent upon the gas mixture in the source cloud. The gas as a whole will tend to be stopped in one band. In the light of the above discussion, we note that because of the discrete regions where the Γ values of the most abundant elements fall, the discrete bands of gravitational energy discussed in sec. 21.2 may be explained by *the hypothesis that they are related to these Γ values*. This relationship is discussed in detail in secs. 21.7–21.13.

21.6 THREE OBJECTIONS

When the preceding analysis was first made (Alfvén, 1942, 1943a, 1946) there were three objections to the ensuing hypothesis:

(1) There was no obvious mechanism for the transfer of the kinetic energy into ionization. The requirement that Γ_{ion} of eq. (21.4.2) and Γ of eq. (21.5.2) should be equal; i.e.,

$$v_{ion} = \left(\frac{2eV_{ion}}{m_a}\right)^{1/2} \tag{21.6.1}$$

was crucial to the hypothesis, but no reason was known for this equality to be true.

(2) There was no empirical support for the hypothesis that masses of gas falling in toward central bodies would have different chemical compositions.

(3) The chemical compositions of the bodies found in each gravitational potential energy band are not characterized by the elements giving rise to those bands. For example, the terrestrial planets fall in a band which corresponds to the Γ value for hydrogen and helium, but they contain very little of these elements. The band of the giant planets corresponds to C, N, and O, but these planets were believed to consist mainly of hydrogen and helium.

However, the above situation has changed drastically over three decades of theoretical studies and empirical findings. Although we are still far from a final theory, it is fair to state that objection (1) has been eliminated by the discovery of the critical velocity phenomenon as discussed in sec. 21.7–21.10. With reference to (2), we now know that separation of elements by plasma processes is a common phenomenon in space. We shall discuss such separation and variation of chemical compositions in sec. 21.11. In sec. 21.12 we shall consider objection (3) in light of the dependence of chemical composition on gravitational potential.

In the meantime, no alternative theory has been proposed which in terms

of known physical processes explains the positions of the groups of bodies
and which at the same time is consistent with the total body of facts describing the present state of the solar system.

21.7 SEARCH FOR A "CRITICAL VELOCITY"

Early attempts to theoretically analyze the stopping of an infalling cloud
were not very encouraging. Equating the gravitational and ionization
energies has no meaning unless there is a process by which the gravitational
energy can be transferred into ionization. Further, in an electric discharge
the energy needed to actually ionize an atom is often more than one order
of magnitude greater than the ionization energy of that atom, because in
a discharge most of the energy is radiated and often less than 10 percent is
used for ionization.

In view of the fact that, as stated in ch. 15, all theoretical treatments of
plasma processes are very precarious unless supported by experiments, it
was realized that further advance depended on studying the process experimentally. As soon as the advance of thermonuclear technology made it possible, experiments were designed to investigate the interaction between a
magnetized plasma and a nonionized gas in relative motion. Experimental
investigations have now proceeded for more than a decade. Surveys have
been made by Danielsson (1973) and Lehnert (1971).

21.8 EXPERIMENTS ON THE CRITICAL VELOCITY

Many experimental measurements of the burning voltage in magnetic
fields were made independently. They demonstrated the existence of a
limiting voltage V_{Lm} which if introduced into eq. (21.4.4) with $E_{ion} = V_{Lm}/d$
(d being the electrode distance) gives almost the same values of v_{ion} as are
calculated from eq. (21.6.1). This upper limit of the burning voltage is
directly proportional to the magnetic field strength but independent of gas
pressures and current in very broad regions. The presence of neutral gas,
however, is a necessity for this effect to occur; once a state of complete ionization is achieved these limiting phenomena no longer appear.

Of the first observations most were accidental. Indeed the effect sometimes appeared as an unwanted limitation on the energy storage in various
plasma devices, such as thermonuclear machines like the Ixion, the early
homopolars, and the F-machines (Lehnert, 1966).

21.8.1 Homopolar Experiments

One of the earliest experiments which was especially designed to clarify the phenomena occurring when a neutral gas moves in relation to an ionized gas was performed by Angerth, Block, Fahleson, and Soop (1962). The experimental apparatus, a homopolar device, is shown in fig. 21.8.1. In a vessel containing a gas at a pressure of the order of 5×10^{-3}–0.2 torr, or 10^{14}–10^{16} atoms/cm³, a radial electric field is established by connecting a capacitor bank between two concentric cylindrical electrodes. There is an almost homogeneous magnetic field of up to 10 000 G perpendicular to the plane of the lower figure. To have any reference to our problem, the gas density in the experiment should be scaled down in the same relation as the linear dimension is scaled up. As the densities during the formation of the planetary system should have been of the order of 10^{1}–10^{5} atoms/cm³, and the scaling factor is 10^{10}–10^{13}, the experiment is relevant to the astrophysical problem. The temperatures are determined by the plasma process both in the experiment and in the astrophysical problem and should therefore be equal.

A portion of the gas is ionized by an electric discharge. This ionized component is acted upon by a tangential force, resulting from the magnetic field and the radial electric field, and begins to rotate about the central

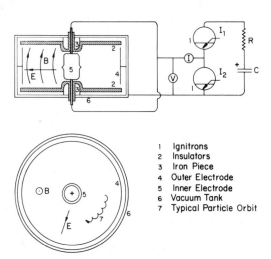

1	Ignitrons
2	Insulators
3	Iron Piece
4	Outer Electrode
5	Inner Electrode
6	Vacuum Tank
7	Typical Particle Orbit

FIGURE 21.8.1.—Homopolar apparatus. A voltage V is applied across an inner electrode (5) and an outer electrode (4) to give a radial electric field E. The electric field, in the presence of an axial magnetic field B, acts on the ionized portion of the gas to set it into rotation (7). The interaction between the rotating magnetized plasma and the nonionized, nonrotating gas (in contact with the wall) produces a voltage limitation indicating that the relative velocity of the two components attains a critical velocity v_{crit}. (From Angerth et al., 1962.)

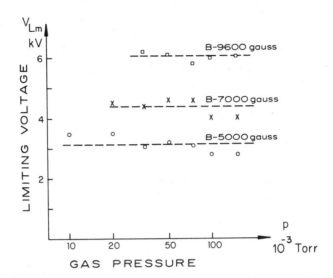

FIGURE 21.8.2.—The limiting value V_{Lm} of the burning voltage as a function of gas pressure for hydrogen in the homopolar experiment. V_{Lm} is independent of pressure, but proportional to the magnetic field B. (From Angerth et al., 1962.)

axis. The nonionized component remains essentially at rest because of the friction with the walls. Hence there is a relative motion between the ionized part of the gas and the nonionized gas. If the relative motion is regarded from a frame moving with the plasma, there is a magnetized ionized gas at rest which is hit by nonionized gas. We can expect phenomena of the same general kind as when a nonionized gas falls toward a central body through a magnetized ionized gas (a plasma).

The experiment shows that the ionized component is easily accelerated until a certain velocity, the "critical" velocity v_{crit}, is attained. This critical velocity cannot be surpassed as long as there is still nonionized gas. Any attempt to increase the burning voltage V_b above the limiting value V_{Lm} in order to accelerate the plasma results in an increased rate of ionization of the gas, but not in an increase in the relative velocity between the ionized and nonionized components. From a theoretical point of view the phenomenon is rather complicated. The essential mechanism seems to be that kinetic energy is transferred to electrons in the plasma and these electrons produce the ionization (see sec. 21.9).

The limiting value of the burning voltage was found to be independent of the gas pressure in the whole range measured (fig. 21.8.2) but dependent on the magnetic field (fig. 21.8.3), as one would infer from eq. (21.4.4). Further, the burning voltage was independent of the applied current; i.e.,

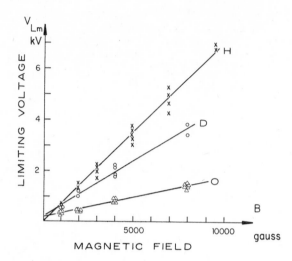

FIGURE 21.8.3.—Limiting voltage V_{Lm} versus the magnetic field B in the homopolar experiment. V_{Lm} is proportional to B and depends also on the chemical composition (O, D, H) of the gas being studied. (From Angerth et al., 1962.)

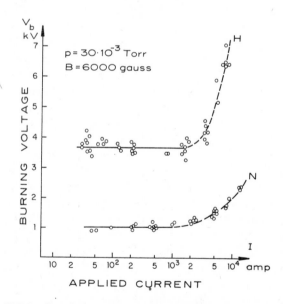

FIGURE 21.8.4.—Burning voltage V_b versus applied current I, for hydrogen and nitrogen in the homopolar experiment. V_b is independent of current (degree of ionization) up to a maximum value related to the complete ionization. The plateau defines the limiting voltage V_{Lm} related to the critical velocity. (From Angerth et al., 1962.)

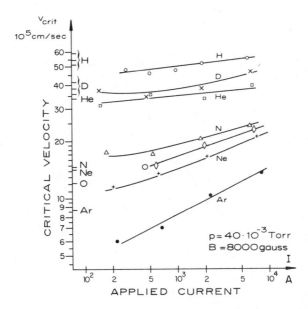

FIGURE 21.8.5.—Critical velocity v_{crit} versus applied current for seven gases studied in the homopolar experiment. (The slope of the Ar curve is related to the magnetic field's being too weak to make the ion gyro-radii small enough). The theoretical v_{crit} for each gas, as calculated from eq. (21.6.1), is indicated on the ordinate. (From Angerth et al., 1962.)

was equal to V_{Lm} until this exceeded a certain value (which is related to the degree of ionization; see fig. 21.8.4). Given the relationship of the burning voltage to the radial electric field and the value of the axial magnetic field, one can, from eq. 21.4.4, determine the critical velocity from the measured value of the limiting voltage V_{Lm}. The dependence of the critical velocity on the chemical composition of the gas was also investigated and found to agree with eq. 21.6.1. Within the accuracy of the experiment, this equation has been checked experimentally for H, D, He, O, and Ne (and also for Ar, but with less accuracy). The experimental results are shown in fig. 21.8.5, where one can observe that the plasma velocity remains rather constant while the applied current (and thus the energy input and degree of ionization) is changed over almost two orders of magnitude.

21.8.2 Plasma Beam Hitting Neutral Gas Cloud

The experiment most directly related to the cosmic situation was carried out by Danielsson (1970) and Danielsson and Brenning (1975). The experimental arrangement is shown in fig. 21.8.6. The hydrogen plasma is

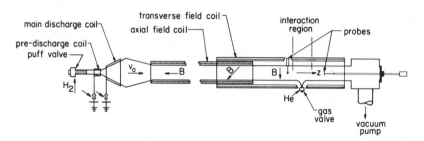

FIGURE 21.8.6.—Experimental arrangement for critical velocity measurement used by Danielsson. The left part is a plasma gun, emitting a magnetized plasma with a velocity v_0. In a long drift tube, the longitudinal magnetization is changed to transverse magnetization. A thin cloud of gas is injected through the gas valve. If v_0 is below the critical velocity, the plasma beam passes through the gas cloud with very little interaction because the mean free path is long. If v_0 is above the critical velocity, there is a strong interaction, bringing the velocity to near the critical value. At the same time, the gas cloud becomes partially ionized. (From Danielsson, 1969b.)

generated and accelerated in an electrodeless plasma gun (a conical theta pinch) and flows into a drift tube along a magnetic field. The direction of the magnetic field changes gradually from axial to transverse along the path of the plasma. As the plasma flows along the drift tube much of it is lost by recombination at the walls. A polarization electric field is developed and a plasma with a density of about 10^{11}–10^{12} cm^{-3} proceeds drifting across the magnetic field with a velocity up to 5×10^7 cm/sec. In the region of the transverse magnetic field the plasma penetrates into a small cloud of gas, released from an electromagnetic valve. This gas cloud has an axial depth of 5 cm and a density of 10^{14} cm^{-3} at the time of the arrival of the plasma. The remainder of the system is under high vacuum. Under these conditions the mean free path for direct, binary collisions is much longer than 5 cm so that the interaction according to common terminology is collisionless.

In the experiment it was observed that the velocity of the plasma was substantially reduced over a typical distance of only 1 cm in the gas cloud (see fig. 21.8.7). It was also found that this reduction in plasma velocity depends on the impinging velocity as shown in fig. 21.8.8. If the neutral gas was helium there was no change in velocity for the smallest impinging velocities (below $\sim 4 \times 10^6$ cm/sec) as the plasma penetrated the gas. For higher impinging velocities there was a relatively increasing deceleration of the plasma.

By investigation of radiation emission from the plasma and neutral gas it was found that the electron energy distribution changed drastically at the penetration of the plasma into the gas and that the ionization of the

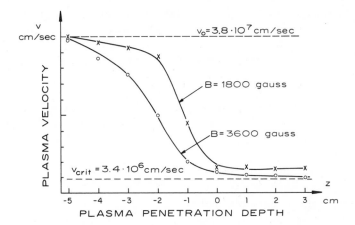

FIGURE 21.8.7.—Velocity retardation to near the critical value in the Danielsson experiment. Plasma deceleration with depth of penetration z in a neutral gas cloud of helium is shown. The front of the cloud is located at $z=-5$ cm, and the center, at $z=0$ cm. The plasma undergoes deceleration from the impinging velocity v_0 to near the critical velocity v_{crit} of helium. Data for two values of the magnetic field B are shown. (From Danielsson, 1969b.)

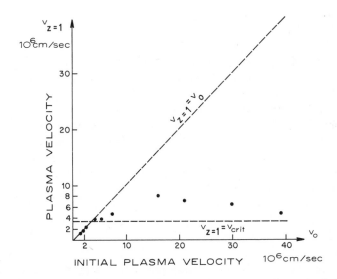

FIGURE 21.8.8.—Plasma deceleration as a function of impinging velocity in the Danielsson experiment. Plasma velocity $v_{z=1}$ in the neutral gas cloud of helium, 1 cm beyond the cloud center, as a function of the initial plasma vacuum velocity v_0 is shown. The critical velocity v_{crit} for helium is indicated. For v_0 less than v_{crit} there was no change in velocity; $v_{z=1}=v_0$. For v_0 greater than v_{crit} deceleration was marked; $v_{z=1}$ remained close to v_{crit}. (From Danielsson, 1969b.)

gas atoms was two orders of magnitude faster than anticipated from the parameters of the free plasma stream. The characteristic electron energy was found to jump from about 5 eV to about 100 eV at least locally in the gas cloud. This was inferred to be the cause of the ionization and deceleration of the plasma.

So far Danielsson's experiment has demonstrated that even in a situation where the primary collisions are negligibly few there may be a very strong interaction between a moving plasma and a stationary gas. In helium this interaction is active above an impinging velocity of 3.5×10^6 cm/sec and it leads to:

(1) Local heating of the electrons.
(2) Ionization of the neutral gas.
(3) Deceleration of the plasma stream.

21.8.3 Other Experiments

Analysis of a number of other experiments confirms these conclusions. In some of the experiments the critical velocity is much more sharply defined and hence better suited for a detailed study of the phenomenon. The experiment described above has the pedagogic advantage of referring most directly to the cosmic situation.

21.8.4 Conclusions

Experiments investigating the critical velocity or voltage limitation phenomenon have been conducted under a wide variety of experimental conditions (see Danielsson, 1973). These experiments have demonstrated that as the relative velocity increases a *critical velocity* v_{crit} is reached. When $v < v_{crit}$ there is a small and often negligible interaction between gas and plasma. With $v > v_{crit}$ very strong interaction sets in, leading to ionization of the gas. The onset of ionization is abrupt and discontinuous. The value of v_{crit} for a number of gases has been measured. Although under certain conditions there are deviations up to perhaps 50 percent, the general result is that v_{crit} is the same as v_{ion}, as given by eq. (21.6.1).

21.8.5 Possible Space Experiments

Experiments on the critical velocity phenomenon carried out in space are of particular interest since they give more certain scaling to large dimensions. The upper atmosphere provides a region where plasma-gas interaction of this kind could suitably be studied in the Earth's magnetosphere. The first observation of the critical velocity effect under cosmic conditions was reported by Manka et al. (1972) from the Moon. When an abandoned lunar excursion module was made to impact on the dark side of the Moon not very far from the terminator, a gas cloud was produced which when it had expanded so that it was hit by the solar wind gave rise to superthermal electrons.

21.9 THEORY OF THE CRITICAL VELOCITY

A considerable number of experiments representing a wide variety of experimental conditions have each demonstrated an enhanced interaction between a plasma and a neutral gas in a magnetic field. However, the theoretical understanding of the process is not yet complete although much progress has been made; a review is given by Sherman (1973). An initial theoretical consideration might reasonably suggest that an ionizing interaction between a gas and a plasma should become appreciable when the relative velocity reaches a value of $(2eV_{ion}/m_a)^{1/2}$ (as noted in sec. 21.6, eq. (21.6.1)) because the colliding particles then have enough energy for ionization. However, two serious difficulties soon become apparent: (1) The kinetic energy of an electron with the above velocity in the plasma is only $(m_e/m_a)eV_{Ion}$ (where m_e is the electron mass), or just a few millivolts, and (2) ionizing collisions between the ions and the neutrals will not occur unless the ion kinetic energy in the frame of reference of the neutral gas exceeds $2eV_{Ion}$. This second difficulty follows from the fact that, assuming equal ion and neutral masses and negligible random motion of the neutrals, the maximum inelastic energy transfer equals the kinetic energy in the center-of-mass system of the colliding particles. It is then evident that any theoretical justification of the critical-velocity hypothesis must explain how the ion and/or electron random velocities are increased.

Different theories have been suggested by Sockol (1968), Petschek (1960), Hassan (1966), Lin (1961), Drobyshevskii (1964), Lehnert (1966, 1967), and Sherman (1969, 1972). They all refer to different mechanisms of transfer of energy from the atoms/ions to the electrons. We shall not discuss these theories here, but only cite the rather remarkable conclusion which Sherman (1973) draws from his review. He states that for the most part the theories discussed are internally self-consistent. The different theories give a good description of those situations which satisfy the assumptions on which the theories are based. It is remarkable that several widely different theoretical models should all predict the values of E/B near to $(2eV_{ion}/m_a)^{1/2}$. Correspondingly, the experiments show that values of E/B near the critical value are observed over a wide range of experiments. The critical velocity hypothesis is then an experimentally confirmed relationship which is valid over a wide range of conditions, but it seems likely that more than one theoretical model is necessary to explain it.

If the atomic mass in eq. (21.6.1) is replaced by the electron mass m_e, we have a result which is a formal analog to the well-known law discovered by Franck and Hertz: $\frac{1}{2}m_e v_{ion}^2 = eV_{ion}$. The experimental and theoretical investigations demonstrate that a number of mechanisms exist which make the results of the Franck and Hertz experiment for pure electron interaction valid also for a plasma. The only difference is that here one additional step in the interaction is needed which transfers the energy from the atoms (or the ions, depending on the choice of coordinate system) to the electrons (Danielsson and Brenning, 1975).

Hence the critical velocity experiment may be considered as the "plasma version" of the classical Franck-Hertz experiment.

21.10 CONCLUSIONS ABOUT THE CRITICAL VELOCITY

We conclude from the survey of relevant experimental and theoretical investigations that the critical velocity v_{crit} at which a neutral gas interacts strongly with a magnetized plasma is

$$v_{crit} = v_{ion} = \left(\frac{2eV_{Ion}}{m_a}\right)^{1/2} \tag{21.10.1}$$

Hence if a gas of a certain chemical composition is falling toward a magnetized central body from a cloud at rest at infinity, it will become ionized when Γ has reached the value

$$\Gamma_{ion} = \frac{M_c}{r_{ion}} = \frac{v_{crit}^2}{2G} = \frac{eV_{Ion}}{Gm_a} \tag{21.10.2}$$

Consequently objection (1) of sec. 21.6 does not apply and eq. (21.6.1) is validated.

21.11 CHEMICAL COMPOSITION OF INFALLING GAS

Objection (2) of sec. 21.6 states that there is no empirical support for the hypothesis that masses of gas falling toward a central body would have different chemical compositions. In this section we shall discuss the theoretical conditions under which such chemical differentiation and fractionation could occur.

21.11.1 The Basic Model

Let us return to the simple model of sec. 21.4 which refers to a jet stream, partially ionized either by radiation or, more importantly, by hydromagnetic effects. We assume that the source cloud which contains all elements (e.g., in an abundance relationship more similar to some average "galactic" composition than now found in the satellites and planets) is partially ionized to such an extent that all elements with ionization potential higher than a certain value $V_{Ion}(t)$ are neutral, but all with an ionization potential lower than $V_{Ion}(t)$ are ionized. The Larmor radii of electrons and ions are all assumed to be negligible, but all mean free paths are assumed to be larger than the source-cloud dimension. The region which we call "source cloud" may be so defined. All neutral atoms will begin to fall toward the central body.

Let $V_{Ion}(t)$ decrease slowly with time (for example, through a general cooling of the plasma by radiation or a change in current such as that discussed by De (1973) in the case of solar prominences). When it has fallen below the ionization potential of helium, helium ions will begin to recombine to form a neutral gas which falls in toward the gravitating central body. Helium reaches its critical velocity of 34.4×10^5 cm/sec at a Γ_{ion} value (which we now realize, recalling eq. 21.10.2, to be equivalent to the Γ value) of 0.9×10^{20} g/cm (the upper region of Band I of fig. 21.11.1). The gas will at this point become ionized, forming a plasma cloud which will be referred to as the *A cloud*.

When $V_{ion}(t)$ decreases further, and has passed the ionization potential of hydrogen (which is nearly equal to the ionization potentials of oxygen and nitrogen), hydrogen, oxygen, and nitrogen will start falling out from the source cloud. Because hydrogen is by far the most abundant element, we can expect the infalling gas to behave as hydrogen and to be stopped at $\Gamma = 1.9 \times 10^{20}$ g/cm (the lower region of Band I) forming what we shall call the *B cloud*. In a gas consisting mainly of H, the elements O and N will not be stopped at their critical velocities because of the quenching effect of the hydrogen on the acceleration of electrons that would lead to ionization in pure oxygen or nitrogen gas.

Next will follow an infall dominated by carbon, which is stopped at a v_{crit} of 13.5×10^5 cm/sec and a Γ value of 0.1×10^{19} g/cm (Band II), forming the *C cloud*; and finally the heavier elements, mainly silicon, magnesium, and iron, will fall in to $\Gamma = 0.3 \times 10^{18}$ g/cm (Band III), producing the *D cloud* with a weighted mean critical velocity of 6.5×10^5 cm/sec.

21.11.2 The A, B, C, and D Clouds in the Solar System

From the above discussion one can consider the solar system as forming from four plasma clouds. The planets would form by accretion of planetesi-

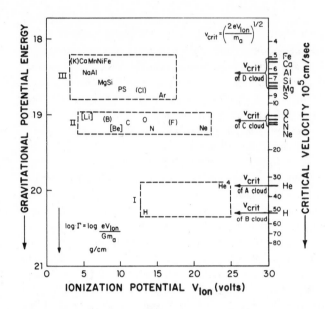

FIGURE 21.11.1.—Critical velocity and ionization potential of the most
abundant elements. The left-hand ordinate showing gravitational
potential energy Γ and the right-hand ordinate showing the critical
velocities of the controlling elements of the A, B, C, and D clouds
allow a comparison of Γ values and v_{crit} values.

mals and grains, the matter condensing from the plasma cloud in the specific
region of gravitational potential of each planet. The location of each plasma
cloud is determined by the critical velocity of its controlling elements as
depicted in fig. 21.11.1. Hence each plasma cloud can be characterized by
a dominant critical velocity. Figure 21.11.2 shows the gravitational potential energy bands labeled as plasma clouds A, B, C, and D with their respective critical velocities indicated.

We see from fig. 21.11.2 and the discussion in the previous section that
Mercury, Venus, and Earth formed from the B cloud, while Moon and Mars
accreted within the A cloud. As indicated in fig. 21.11.2, there was probably
an overlap and possibly an interchange of matter between the A and B
clouds in the region of the Earth and the Moon. The giant planets formed
within the C cloud, while Pluto and perhaps Triton accreted within the D
cloud. Referring to fig. 20.7.1a, we can see that, although there is a wide
range of densities in the solar system, the bodies which formed in the same
cloud have similar densities. This pattern can be understood on the basis
of relatively constant composition within each cloud, but variance of composition among the A, B, C, and D clouds.

Returning to fig. 21.11.2 we see that there were plasma clouds formed around each of the planets shown. Our hetegonic principle stresses that the same processes which formed the planetary system should also prove capable of forming the satellite systems. As depicted in fig. 21.4.1, the jet stream formed within a plasma cloud will provide material for a planet and will function as the source cloud for a series of plasma clouds that will form around that planet by the processes discussed in sec. 21.11.1. Thus, each planet with sufficient magnetization and spin will act as the central body around which A, B, C, and D clouds will form.

Formation of the plasma clouds depends upon attainment of critical velocity by the element determining the orbital distance of the cloud to the

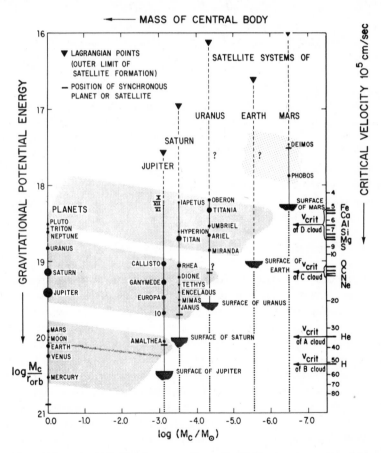

FIGURE 21.11.2.—Gravitational potential energy Γ as a function of the mass of the central body for the planetary and satellite systems. The right-hand ordinate showing critical velocity affords comparison of Γ values for the planets and satellites with v_{crit} values for abundant elements and the A, B, C, and D clouds.

central body. For planets of less mass, the inner clouds cannot form due to inadequate acceleration of the infalling gas from the source clouds. We see in fig. 21.11.2 that Jupiter is massive enough for an A cloud to form, but not for a B cloud to form. The Galilean satellites of Jupiter formed in the Jovian C cloud. The Saturnian inner satellites formed in the Saturnian C cloud, while the outer satellites formed in the D cloud around Saturn. The satellites of Uranus accreted in the Uranian D cloud.

Therefore all discussion of band formation, gravitational potential energy bands, and the plasma clouds A, B, C, and D refer to both planetary and satellite systems.

21.11.3 Refinement of the Basic Model

This is the simplest model that can produce chemically differentiated mass accumulation in the observed gravitational potential energy bands. Of course it is much too simple to be realistic. When discussing and developing it we have to take into account the following facts:

(1) There are a number of plasma processes which could produce chemical separation in a cosmic cloud (see Arrhenius and Alfvén, 1971).

(2) The critical velocity of a gas mixture has not yet been thoroughly studied. We expect that the value v_{crit} is determined by the most abundant constituent in the cloud.

(3) Other charged species besides single atomic ions have been neglected. The more complete picture including the expected distribution of molecular compounds is discussed below.

21.11.4 Effect of Interstellar Molecules

The elementary treatment given above suggests only the gross features of the emplacement band structure. This is modified to some extent by the fact that the elements in the source regions are likely to prevail not only as monatomic species but also, at least to some extent, as molecules and molecular ions. The experiments carried out with diatomic molecular gases (sec. 21.8) indicate that ionization at the critical velocity limit is preceded by dissociation and therefore that the limit is determined by the atomic mass and ionization potential. Only homonuclear molecules (H_2, D_2, N_2) have so far been investigated, but it is reasonable to assume that, in the case of heteronuclear molecules such as CH, CH_4, OH, and the multitude of other polynuclear molecules observed in dark clouds in space, the element with the lower ionization potential will determine the critical limit. The main effect expected from the presence of molecular precursors would therefore be transport and emplacement of stoichiometric amounts of hydrogen, accompanying carbon, oxygen, and nitrogen into the C cloud.

In the case of the commonly observed simple hydrides (CH, NH, OH, OH_2, CH_2, NH_2, NH_3), the ligated hydrogen contributes relatively little to the mass of the molecule. Furthermore, the molecular ionization potential is similar to or slightly lower than that of the core atom. Hence, even if there is an, as yet, undetermined effect of the molecular state, we would expect the critical velocity to remain close to that of the core atom.

In the case of molecules containing elements from rows 2 and 3 (SiO, AlO, MgO), the ionization potential of the molecule is substantially increased over that of the metal atom. Critical velocities (which are entirely hypothetical) calculated from mass and ionization potential of such molecules place them in the same band as the metals (the increased ionization potential is balanced by the mass increase). The effect, if any, would consequently be to contribute oxygen to the D cloud.

It is important to notice that in no case does molecular formation from abundant species of atoms lead to such an increase in ionization potential that penetration inside the C cloud is possible by this mechanism. Deposition in the A and B clouds therefore would depend entirely on transport of impurities, together with major amounts of helium and hydrogen, and on evaporation of solid grains falling toward the Sun, as discussed in sec. 21.12.

One can conclude from the above discussion that, although direct empirical evidence of source cloud composition during the formative era of the solar system is indeed lacking, there are many cogent theoretical possibilities to account for differing composition of the gravitational potential energy bands resulting from infall into the circumsolar region. Therefore objection (2) of sec. 21.6 is relevant only in its emphasis on the need for continued observation and experimentation.

21.12 THE CHEMICAL COMPOSITION OF THE SOLAR SYSTEM AND INHOMOGENEOUS PLASMA EMPLACEMENT

Objection (3) of sec. 21.6 states that the chemical compositions of the bodies found in each gravitational potential energy band are not characterized by those elements which theoretically give rise to each specific band. In this section we shall consider a more detailed theoretical model of band formation.

21.12.1 A Model of Band Formation

We are certainly far from a consistent model of the infall of plasma. The discussion here will therefore be confined to some basic principles.

As stated in chs. 15 and 16, homogeneous models are of little value in astrophysics. Hence if we assume that the source cloud is a homogeneous shell from which there is a symmetric and time-constant infall of gas (the simple model of the previous section), we may go completely astray. In-homogeneous models are necessarily rather arbitrary, and the final choice between possible models can be made only after extensive experiments in the laboratory and in space.

In almost any type of inhomogeneous model one should envisage a number

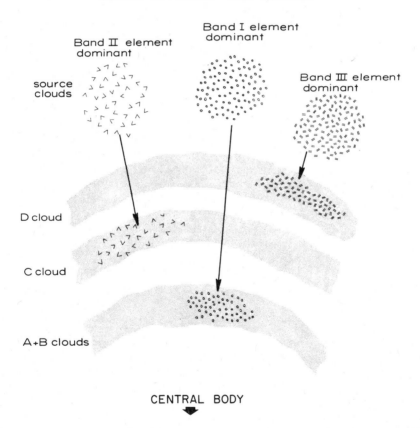

FIGURE 21.12.1.—Infall pattern for source clouds active during different time periods. The infalling gas from one source cloud will be dominated by one element. The mass of infalling gas will be stopped when the dominant element is ionized; i.e., in the cloud corresponding to the critical velocity value of that element's band. For example, a Band II element reaches its critical velocity at a value r_{ion} which falls within the C cloud.

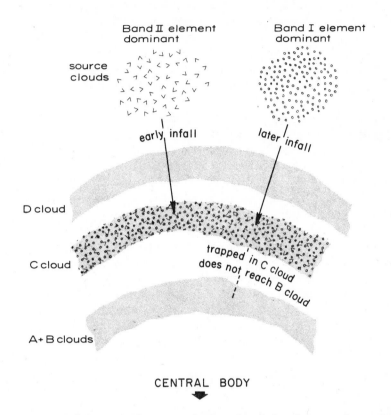

INFALL PATTERN FOR SOURCE CLOUDS
ACTIVE DURING THE SAME TIME PERIOD

Band II element
dominant

Band I element
dominant

source
clouds

early infall

later infall

D cloud

C cloud

trapped in C cloud
does not reach B cloud

A+ B clouds

CENTRAL BODY

FIGURE 21.12.2.—Infall pattern for source clouds active during the same time period. A
gas infall from a Band II element-dominated source cloud will be ionized and stopped
in the C cloud. If this plasma has not had time to condense, it will interact with any
infall from a Band I element-dominated source cloud. The Band I gas infall will be trapped
in the C cloud by the plasma there and not reach its own r_{ion} in the B cloud.

of source clouds from which a gas is falling down during finite periods (see
fig. 21.12.1). At a certain instant one or several clouds may be active. The
chemical composition of the gas falling in from a certain source cloud may
vary. For our model the most important question to ask is which element
dominates in such a way that it determines the value of the critical velocity
v_{crit} and hence the arresting value of the gravitational potential energy Γ_{ion}.

Suppose that, after there has been no infall for a long time, gas with a
certain value of Γ_{ion} begins to fall in from one source cloud. This gas will
then accumulate in the band characterized by Γ_{ion}. If another cloud with

a different characteristic Γ_{ion} begins to yield gas, this will accumulate in the correspondingly different region, under the condition that when the infall of the second cloud starts the first infall has already ceased, and there has been enough time for the accumulated plasma to condense. However, if this condition is not satisfied, the plasma from the first infall may interfere with the second infall.

Suppose, for example, that the first infall produced a plasma cloud in the C-cloud band, and that the second gas infall has a Γ value of the B band. Then it can reach the B region only if there is no plasma in the C region, because, if there is, the infalling gas, normally penetrating to the B region, will interact with the plasma in the C region (if it is dense enough; mean free path shorter than C-cloud thickness) and become ionized and hence stopped prematurely. Under certain conditions most of the new cloud will be trapped in the C region. See fig. 21.12.2.

Hence we see that an infall of hydrogen-rich material may be trapped in any of the bands. It arrives at the B cloud only if it is not hindered by plasma in any of the upper bands, but if a recent infall of gas into, e.g., the C cloud, has taken place, most of the gas that subsequently falls in may be trapped there. Then under certain conditions there may be, for example, more B-cloud gas trapped in the C region than there is C-cloud gas.

From this we can draw the important conclusion that although the stopping of infalling gas in a certain band depends on the v_{crit} value of a controlling element, an inhomogeneous model need not necessarily predict that this element should dominate the ultimate chemical composition of the cloud. Although the trigger element would be enriched to some extent, the ultimate chemical composition of the band need not necessarily deviate drastically from that of the source clouds.

21.12.2 Effects of Transplanetary Condensation on the Composition of Planets and Satellites

We have seen (ch. 19) that most of the condensates forming in the transplanetary region must have assumed highly eccentric orbits around the Sun. When penetrating through the regions where plasma is accumulated, these solids may partially evaporate and inject part of their mass into the plasma cloud. This ablation effect would become important when the infalling grains have been accelerated to high velocities relative to the plasma clouds and in regions where the plasma density is comparatively high. Hence one would expect contamination by grain ablation to be most pronounced in the A (helium) and B (hydrogen) regions, and a major fraction of the condensable ions gathered there may be such ablation products.

Furthermore, transplanetary dust accelerated through the B region would interact chemically with the hydrogen characteristic of that region. The physical ablation process would thus be accompanied by selective vaporiza-tion of species of SiO, MgO, OH, and SH, leaving the infalling solid grains with an increasing concentration of metallic iron, vaporizing toward the end of the trail, near the central body. Comparable chemical effects are ob-served in the interaction of the Moon (and possibly of comets) with the solar wind and in laboratory experiments exposing silicates and oxides to proton beams (sec. 14.6), atomic hydrogen, or molecular hydrogen in the temperature range above $\sim$1200K.

This ablation process is physically analogous to the observed ablation of meteors in the Earth's upper atmosphere—the velocity and composition of the particles being the same, the density of the medium being lower (iono-spheric), its extension much larger, and its chemical effect reducing rather than oxidizing.

Transplanetary material must also have collided with the grains and embryos in the jet streams, adding material to these.

The total effect of the interaction of transplanetary bodies with inter-planetary material (fig. 21.12.3) would thus include complete vaporization of some of the grains, capture and transfer of angular momentum to small dust particles in the plasma clouds, and, furthermore, collision, vaporiza-tion, fragmentation and ultimately accretion of some transplanetary ma-terial in the planetary jet streams. Larger meteoroid aggregates may have been heated and slowed down by friction in each perihelion passage in inter-planetary space with gradually decreasing peak temperature in each Kepler period because of the deceleration. Ultimately such objects would be cap-tured by a jet stream.

Chemical fractionation at ablation of transplanetary dust in the inner solar and planetary nebulae (A–B clouds) may be the explanation for the increasing density of secondary bodies toward the central bodies in the Jovian and planetary systems (sec. 20.7).

21.12.3 Fractionation Associated With or Following Condensation

All the fractionation processes so far discussed precede condensation of the solids from which the bodies in the solar system subsequently accumu-lated. In addition, it is likely that fractionation processes associated with the condensation and later evolution have influenced the chemical com-position of the present bodies. We do not know much about the state of the early Sun, for example, if it had a radiation field as intense as today (sec. 25.5). If this were so, volatile compounds such as water ice may have been prevented from condensing and accumulating in the inner part of the planetary system, as pointed out, for example, by von Weizsäcker (1944), Berlage (1948), and Urey (1952). In close proximity to the Sun, a high

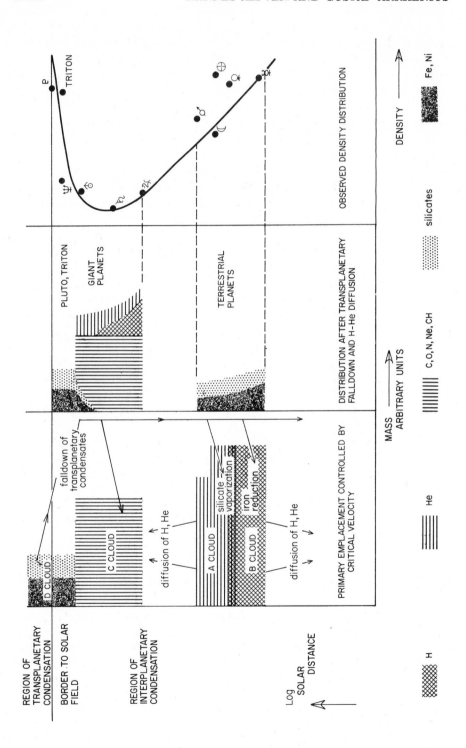

FIGURE 21.12.3.—Simplified diagram of the effect of transplanetary condensation on the chemical composition of the planets. The primary emplacement of plasma controlled by the critical velocity produced the A, B, C, and D clouds. The A and B clouds were enriched in He and H. The C cloud composition was enriched in C, O, N, and Ne, while the D cloud contained an excess of heavy elements. Part of the D cloud condensation took place outside the solar magnetic field and resulted in particles and embryos in almost parabolic orbits, passing through the interplanetary clouds. Due to ablation of these bodies in the massive A and B clouds, and chemical interaction with the hydrogen in the latter, substantial amounts of transplanetary D-type material were deposited in the inner part of the solar system (and in the corresponding regions of the satellite systems). The distribution after transplanetary falldown and H–He diffusion indicates the possible redistribution of heavy elements into the A- and B-cloud regions and the diffusion of H and He to the C region, where light gases could be partially accreted by giant planetary embryos. The observed density distribution among the planets (see fig. 20.7.1a) reflects the compositions of the respective clouds. The terrestrial planets, forming in the A and B clouds, have higher densities than the giant planets which formed in the C cloud. Pluto and Triton have higher densities indicative of the composition of the D cloud in which they accreted.

temperature of the radiation field could perhaps decrease the condensation rate of oxygen compounds with silicon and magnesium, which have high vapor pressures relative to iron. However, it is also possible that the solar radiation was negligible, and we must look for another explanation of some of the quoted facts. This is suggested by the similar trends of the density distribution (sec. 20.7) in the inner part of the solar system and in the Jovian satellite system, where effects of the radiation field can hardly be held responsible.

Another late fractionation effect is the gravitational retention of increasingly light gases by planets and satellites of increasing size. The embryos accreting to form the giant planets may, after having reached a few Earth masses, have been able to collect and retain substantial amounts of hydrogen and helium.

21.12.4 Conclusions About the Chemical Composition of Celestial Bodies

We are necessarily dealing with highly hypothetical phenomena which do not allow us to draw very specific conclusions. However, we here summarize the processes most likely to influence the bulk composition of the accreted bodies:

(1) The critical velocities of the element groups corresponding to clouds A, B, C, and D; this effect would also be responsible for the spacing of the groups of secondary bodies around their primaries.

(2) The vapor pressure of the solids that can form from the gases controlling the cloud formation; since hydrogen and helium are not condensable, the bodies formed in the A and B clouds consist largely of "impurities".

(3) The fractional vaporization of infalling transplanetary material in the dense A and B clouds, preferentially depositing refractory elements such as iron in the central reactive hydrogen cloud (B cloud).

(4) Trapping of infalling gases with high critical velocities in already established clouds.

(5) Fractionation at condensation, due to the gradient in the solar radiation field.

(6) Gravitational accumulation of hydrogen and helium by the giant planets.

It will require much work before we can decide between models giving similar composition to all the bands and models in which there are appreciable chemical differences among the regions. Such work should include interaction and fractionation experiments in hydrogen and in mixed plasmas as well as the sampling and analysis of comets and asteroids which possibly consist of materials representative of the primordial states.

What has been said in ch. 20 and sec. 21.12 shows the complexity of the problems relating to chemical composition of the celestial bodies. Although objection (3) (sec. 21.6) is no longer valid, we are still far from a detailed theory of chemical composition.

21.13 MODIFICATION OF CRITICAL VELOCITY IONIZATION DISTANCE DUE TO INTERACTION WITH A PARTIALLY COROTATING PLASMA

The simple model of sec. 21.4 could be developed in different directions. The falling gas need not necessarily interact with a plasma at rest. If, for example, the plasma is in the state of partial corotation (see ch. 17), its tangential velocity is (from table 17.3.1)

$$v_\phi = \left(\frac{2GM_c}{3r}\right)^{1/2} \tag{21.13.1}$$

Adding this vectorially to the velocity of fall

$$v = \left(\frac{2GM_c}{r}\right)^{1/2} \tag{21.13.2}$$

we get a resulting relative velocity v_{rel}

$$v_{rel} = \left(\frac{8GM_c}{3r_{rel}}\right)^{1/2} \tag{21.13.3}$$

When v_{rel} reaches the critical velocity v_{crit} the infalling gas can become ionized. Let us determine the orbital radius r_{rel} at which ionization can take place.

From eq. (21.4.2) we have

$$v_{crit} = \left(\frac{2GM_c}{r_{ion}}\right)^{1/2} \tag{21.13.4}$$

Equating v_{crit} to v_{rel} we obtain

$$r_{rel} = \frac{4r_{ion}}{3} \qquad\qquad (21.13.5)$$

This relative velocity due to the corotation of the magnetized plasma attains the critical value v_{ion} at 4/3 the orbital radius at which ionization would occur if the plasma were not in a state of partial corotation with the central body.

There is yet another effect seen when the interacting plasma is in a state of partial corotation. Condensation and accretion of matter reduces the orbital radius by a factor 2/3 (as explained in ch. 17). Combining the effects of the tangential velocity and the condensation characteristic of a corotating plasma, we obtain the value for the effective ionization radius r'_{ion} for a gas falling through a corotating plasma:

$$r'_{ion} = \frac{2r_{rel}}{3} = \frac{2}{3}\frac{4r_{ion}}{3}$$

$$= 0.89 r_{ion} \qquad\qquad (21.13.6)$$

Therefore in fig. 21.11.2 the critical velocity scale should be displaced downward along the gravitational energy scale so that the value of r_{ion} is decreased to $0.89r_{ion}$ and corresponds to r'_{ion} for the case of corotation of the plasma.

Yet another correction may be of some importance. If the central body is accreting mass during a period of plasma accumulation, the angular momentum of the grains condensing in its environment will change during the accretion. Our present calculations are valid in the case that practically all the gas infall takes place when the central body is close to its final state of accretion. A refinement of the theory in this respect cannot be made before the variation of the gas content in the jet stream can be estimated. It should also be remembered that the formation of secondary bodies cannot start before the central body has grown sufficiently large to acquire a magnetic field which makes transfer of angular momentum possible.

METEORITES AND THEIR PRECURSOR STATES

22.1 INTERPRETATION OF THE EVOLUTIONARY RECORD IN METEORITES

In secs. 11.3 and 11.7 we analyzed the requirements of theories for the accretional process. The observed properties of many-body systems with collisional interaction, and resulting from net accretion, were discussed in ch. 4 (the asteroid populations) and in ch. 14 (the comet-meteor complex).

The meteorites are bodies that also belong to such systems; among objects with Earth-intersecting orbits they form a residue of material sufficiently cohesive to survive passage through the atmosphere. They are of particular interest since they can be studied in minute detail in the laboratory. Until we can sample well-defined small bodies in space, analysis of meteorites therefore provides the most direct evidence for the early evolution of primordial materials. The potential of these analytical data cannot however, be fully utilized until we understand the basic processes that have produced the meteorites. We are far from this today. The chemical and petrographical observations are mostly interpreted in terms of models that are in some essential respects divorced from modern knowledge of the behavior of matter in space and are in conflict with some laws of physics.

More specifically, the formation of the material now in meteorites is commonly attributed to the condensation of grains from a body of gas adjusting its temperature to that of the growing grains. Such a process can be realized in the laboratory but not in space. The reason is that under wall-free conditions the temperature of a condensing solid is different from the kinetic temperature of the surrounding gas in the optically thin surface region of the gas body where radiative cooling and, hence, condensation, is effective. This fact was recognized in space physics many years ago (Lindblad, 1935; Spitzer, 1968) and has been the subject of more recent analysis (Lehnert, 1970a; Arrhenius, 1972; Arrhenius and De, 1973); yet most interpretations of phenomena observed in meteorites still fail to take this into account (see, e.g., review by Grossman and Larimer, 1974).

Furthermore, the Laplacian concept of a homogeneous gas disc provides the general background for most current speculations. The advent of magnetohydrodynamics about 25 years ago and experimental and theoretical progress in solar and magnetospheric physics have made this concept obsolete (sec. 15.6), but this seems not yet to be fully understood.

By analogy with phenomena familiar from geology of the Earth, the properties of meteorites are often thought to be due to processes inside and on the surface of hypothetical planets which later have "exploded" and thrown out the meteorites as debris. Such bodies are assumed to have had gravitational fields large enough to produce gravitative differentiation and to retain an atmosphere; in other words, to be larger than the Moon. It is not generally realized that there are no known processes by which such large bodies can be blown apart, especially as this must be done in such a delicate way as not to destroy the fragile structure of some meteorite materials (sec. 22.4).

In short, the common current attempts to interpret meteorite data have led to contradictions that should be removed by a unified physical and chemical approach. The theories involved must not only account for the phenomena observed in meteorites, which are often ambiguous, but must at the same time be compatible with all other observed properties of the solar system and with modern experimental knowledge of the behavior of particles and fields in space.

22.2 SOURCES OF METEORITES

The information from meteorites differs substantially from knowledge about the materials making up planets and satellites which is discussed in ch. 20.

We do not know where the individual grains condensed, which after more or less extensive alteration provided the material for the meteorite precursor bodies. Nor can we reconstruct with certainty and in any detail the orbits in which these precursor bodies evolved. Several sources of meteorites have been proposed and mechanisms have been suggested for the transport of the meteoroids to Earth-crossing orbits without destruction of the material by sudden change in orbital energy. One such source consists of near-Earth objects such as the Apollo and Amor asteroids, or (which may be the same) comets which come close to or intersect the Earth's orbit (secs. 4.6.1 and 19.6).

Estimates of the chemical composition of Giacobinid and Perseid fluffy meteors from their emission spectra indicate a close similarity in their elemental composition to that of the much more compact chondritic meteorites (Millman, 1972). The Giacobinid showers are associated with Comet Giacobini-Zinner and the Perseids with Comet Swift-Tuttle (see ch. 14). This evidence would thus indicate that the composition of chondrites is not incompatible with their suggested cometary origin.

Measurement of the light emission from other comets, however, indicates considerable differences in chemical composition from any known type of meteorites. This is suggested particularly by the widely different intensities of sodium D emission in different comets at comparable solar distances. In several cases notable emission of sodium occurs at solar distances as large as 0.5–1.2 AU (e.g., Bobrovnikoff, 1942; Swings and Page, 1948; Greenstein and Arpigny, 1962). Hence if any groups of meteorites are of cometary origin, they would seem not to be representative of all common types of cometary materials.

Another possible source region suggested for meteorites is the asteroid belt. This has been investigated by Öpik (1963), Anders (1964), Arnold (1965), Wetherill and Williams (1968), and Zimmerman and Wetherill (1973), but conclusive arguments have yet to be produced demonstrating that this source can give rise to the observed flux of meteorites. Measurements of the reflection spectra of a number of different asteroids (McCord et al. 1970; Chapman, 1972a; Chapman and Salisbury, 1973; Johnson and Fanale, 1973) indicate varying types of surface materials, some similar and others dissimilar to known types of meteorites. Since this type of analysis does not yield very distinctive spectral signatures, it is difficult to decide whether there are genetic relationships between asteroids and meteorites or if those cases where similarities exist in the broad reflection features are coincidental and due to the fact that there are only a limited number of types of materials in the solar system. Some of the most common types of lunar rocks, for example, bear a close optical resemblance to a certain type of meteorite (basaltic achondrites), but these two materials are unlikely to be identical genetically.

In conclusion, it does not appear possible at the present time to identify individual meteorites or groups with specific source regions.

22.3 SELECTION EFFECTS

Most of the meteoroids approaching the Earth are destroyed in the atmosphere. It is estimated that, even of the big meteoroids entering the atmosphere, only one in several hundred has sufficient cohesive strength to reach the surface. From the retardation of meteors that burn up in the atmosphere, it has been concluded that they have a mean bulk density of about 0.8 g/cm³ (Verniani, 1973), indicating that they are fluffy aggregates (Verniani, 1969, 1973; McCrosky, 1970).

In some cases loosely coherent or fluffy vapor-grown crystal aggregates are preserved in pockets or cavities in meteorites (fig. 22.3.1). In general, the meteorites found on Earth are, at least by state of aggregation, representative only of a small fraction of the meteoroid material. To what extent

FIGURE 22.3.1.—Loose fiber aggregates of wollastonite
(CaSiO$_3$) in cavity from the meteorite Allende. Width
of field is 0.4 mm. (From Fuchs, 1971.)

there is also a chemical selection effect is uncertain; the meteor emission
spectra referred to in sec. 22.2 do not appear sufficiently distinctive to show
the differences characteristic of the various types of stone meteorites.

22.4 UPPER SIZE LIMITS OF METEORITE PRECURSOR BODIES

Most meteorites investigated are clearly fragments of larger bodies, generally referred to as meteorite parent bodies. Particularly by study of
nuclear transformations induced by cosmic rays, and of radiation damage
in the material, it has been possible to reveal facts bearing on geometry of
shielding and duration of exposure of the material. Such measurements,
which are discussed in more detail in sec. 22.9, confirm that the size of
some of the bodies in the chain of precursor stages of meteorites must have
exceeded the order of a few meters.

The largest possible size of any of the members in the sequence of meteorite precursor bodies can be estimated in different ways. One boundary is
set by the size at which fragments of such a body, if it could be fragmented,
would remain held together by gravitation. It is doubtful if a body larger

than about a thousand kilometers in size can ever be blown apart by collision with any other body in the solar system. It is also clear from the spin distribution of asteroids that they cannot originate by explosion of much bigger bodies. This is discussed in sec. 9.7–9.8.

A limit to precursor body mass is also imposed by the structural changes in the meteorite material accompanying instantaneous acceleration to escape velocity at collision. Meteorites with delicate, well-preserved structures and low cohesive strength, such as many carbonaceous and ordinary chondrites (see fig. 7.1.1), can hardly have been explosively accelerated to more than a few hundred meters per second and probably less. A body, for example, with $R = 0.01 R_\oplus = 67$ km and $M = 10^{-6} M_\oplus$ has an escape velocity $v = 0.01 v_\oplus = 110$ m/sec. To break up such a body requires an explosive event which on the Earth's surface would throw a large part of the debris up to a height of more than 600 m. It is questionable whether the fragile structures observed could tolerate such accelerations. If not, we may conclude that any one of the series of precursor bodies of such a meteorite must have been less than some 10 km in size.

Sizes of a hundred or a few hundred kilometers have been inferred from current interpretations of diffusion controlled crystal growth features in iron meteorites. These were believed to indicate cooling slow enough to require insulation thicknesses ranging up to the sizes quoted. However, the thermal history recorded in iron meteorites does not necessarily reflect a monotonic cooling from a high temperature state. It is more likely to have been a long series $(N \sim 10^6)$ of heating events due to gas friction in the nebular medium in the inner solar system (see sec. 21.12.2). Each such heating event could be of short duration (the inner solar-system fraction of elliptic orbits originally with aphelia in transplanetary space), and the amplitude of the maximum heating would decrease monotonically in time. Under these circumstances the objects could have been less than a hundred meters in size and still produce the observed features if they are a cooling phenomenon.

22.5 PRECURSOR STATES OF METEORITE PARENT BODIES

From the fact that parent bodies of meteorites must have existed, mostly considerably larger than the meteorites themselves, the question arises how these parent bodies were generated. This is in principle the same problem as the early growth of planetary embryos. We have seen in ch. 11 that the only physically acceptable mechanism so far specified for this is planetesimal accretion. This means that all composite bodies in the solar system must have formed by aggregation of smaller bodies and ultimately of small, condensed grains. Hence, in order to understand meteorite parent bodies we have to consider their accretion by a jet-stream mechanism.

As we have discussed earlier (secs. 6.6 and 12.2), "jet stream" is a convenient term for an assemblage of grains moving in similar Kepler orbits and interacting with each other either by collisions or with a gas as an intermediary. The reason why a jet stream keeps together can be described in a number of ways: by the focusing action of a gravitational field, by diffusion with a negative diffusion coefficient, or by the action of an "apparent attraction" or dynamic attraction between the grains.

Meteor streams and asteroidal jet streams are likely to be jet streams of this kind; they have been discussed in secs. 4.3.3 and 4.6.2. The profile of an asteroidal jet stream is shown in fig. 4.3.6. In the focal regions the relative velocities are found to be as low as 0.2–1.0 km/sec. This refers to visual asteroids with the size of 10 km or more. These are likely to be accompanied by a large number of small bodies which interact more frequently. Their relative velocities should therefore often be much smaller—less than 100 m/sec.

Hence, a jet stream should be depicted as a region where grains in similar orbits collide with a range of relative velocities. The average velocity is initially high, resulting in fragmentation, melting, and vaporization. As a result of the gradual dissipation of energy by collision or gas friction the average internal velocity decreases with time.

When a certain fraction of the population has attained relative velocities of the order of 10 m/sec, interparticle adhesion becomes effective (sec. 7.4) and accretion into larger bodies can begin. During this evolution the grains and grain aggregates, forming, breaking up, and regrouping while orbiting in space, are exposed to irradiation by cosmic rays. Gas molecules may be retained in a jet stream by means of the apparent attraction.

As in meteor streams, density waves may produce local concentrations (bunching) of particles, which may possibly sometimes result in the formation of comets (sec. 14.3). Much of the history of meteorites should be studied with the boundary conditions for formation and evolution of comets as background.

22.6 JET-STREAM EVOLUTION AND PROPERTIES OF METEORITES

We shall now discuss to what extent the properties of meteorites reflect the conditions in the particle streams from which they developed. Some types of meteorites, particularly the carbonaceous chondrites, have a high proportion of single crystals and crystal aggregates with high content of volatiles remaining occluded in the structure from the time of condensation, and with delicate growth and irradiation features perfectly preserved (see fig. 7.1.1). It is obvious that these particles have not undergone hyper-velocity collisions in the course of their aggregation into larger bodies. Hence it is likely that they have accreted in parent jet streams with suffi-ciently high gas content to achieve equalization of energy mainly by gas friction, and only to a limited extent by high-energy grain collision.

On the other hand, chondrules, the most abundant meteorite component, are rounded particles of silicate and other materials, with structure indicat-ing rapid quenching from melt or vapor. Meteoritic chondrules are probably a result of hypervelocity collision between single particles or small aggre-gates. Chondrules also form at impact on an aggregate of large dimensions such as the lunar soil, but in this case the proportion of chondrules and chondrule fragments is mostly small compared to fragmented debris and glass spashes, in contrast to conditions found in chondritic meteorites (Fredriksson et al., 1973).

The proportion of chondrules and chondrule fragments in a meteorite in relation to components unmodified by collision after their primordial condensation is thought to be a measure of the relative importance of colli-sion and gas friction as energy-equalizing processes, and hence of the gas content, in any specific meteorite parent jet stream. Carbonaceous chon-drites of Type I (Wiik, 1956), for example, have no chondrules or chondrule fragments, while in ordinary chondrites a large fraction of the mass con-sists of recognizable chondrule fragments and a varying amount of un-broken chondrules.

Other manifestations of high-velocity collisions in parent jet streams are (1) deformation, particularly noticeable in nickel-iron metal grains (Urey and Mayeda, 1959); (2) fragmentation; (3) shock phenomena (see, e.g., French and Short, 1968; Neuvonen et al., 1972); and (4) complete melting of sufficiently large volumes of material to form igneous rocks (Duke and Silver, 1967), which have been reduced to rubble in subsequent collisions (see fig. 22.8.1). A wide range of examples of such collision effects is also found in the lunar surface material, where, however, the relative extent of the various phenomena differs from the meteorites. This is likely to be due to direct and indirect effects of the substantial gravitational field of the Moon.

In these collision phenomena a high degree of inelasticity characterizes the encounter; i.e., the structure of the collision product shows that a substantial fraction of the kinetic energy of the colliding bodies has been converted into heat by fracturing, deformation, melting, and vaporization. This is of interest since the degree of inelasticity is a controlling parameter in the focusing of a jet stream (ch. 6).

The material in chondrites is found to be in various states of welding due to heating either at the time of its formation (Reid and Fredriksson, 1967) or at some later time (Van Schmus and Wood, 1967). A suggestive reason for such heating after aggregate formation is gas friction in the inner region of the solar system analogous to meteor heating in the Earth's upper atmosphere and discussed in sec. 21.12. Hence there is no need for ad hoc assumption of enhanced emission of corpuscular radiation from the Sun or other heat sources (sec. 22.9).

22.7 COHESIVE FORCES IN METEORITE MATERIAL

When the internal energy of a jet stream has decreased sufficiently, collisions on the average cease to be disruptive and statistical net growth of aggregate bodies (embryos) is in principle possible. For this to take place, however, a cohesive force must necessarily act between the particles; in view of the small masses involved, interparticle gravitation is ineffective as such a force.

The exploration of the Moon, particularly the investigation of the bonding forces in particle aggregates on the lunar surface, has pointed at two processes as being of importance for initiating cohesion in the space environment: electrostatic bonding and vapor deposition (sec. 7.4). Aggregates established by these processes can subsequently be compacted by shock. The fluffy state achieved by vapor deposition and by the persistent internal polarization in lunar dust particles exposed to the space environment has also been discussed in sec. 20.4(2). The cohesive force between the grains ranges between 10 and 170 dyn with dipole moments averaging a few hundred coulomb/cm. For such forces to cause adhesion at grazing incidence of orbiting grains, their relative velocities need to be lowered into the range of 10 m/sec from the order of magnitude of a few thousand m/sec characteristic of initial grains hitting each other in a jet stream.

Magnetic forces of a similar order of magnitude as the electret forces have led to clustering of magnetite (fig. 22.7.1) (Kerridge, 1970; Jedwab, 1967; Brecher, 1972a). This phenomenon probably is of subordinate importance in the main accretion process since it affects only ferromagnetic solids, but it is a spectacular manifestation of weak forces causing particle clustering in space and also illustrating the magnetic fields prevailing in the formative era (Brecher, 1971, 1972a,c; Bannerjee and Hargraves, 1971, 1972; Brecher and Arrhenius, 1974a,b; De, 1973). The hard component of the remanent magnetization and the magnetic alignment of the aggregates indicate that growth and/or aggregation took place in magnetic fields of the order of 0.1–1 G. The observed magnetization cannot derive from planetary fields (Brecher, 1971; Brecher and Arrhenius, 1974, 1975). To understand the origin and distribution of primordial fields and their effect on

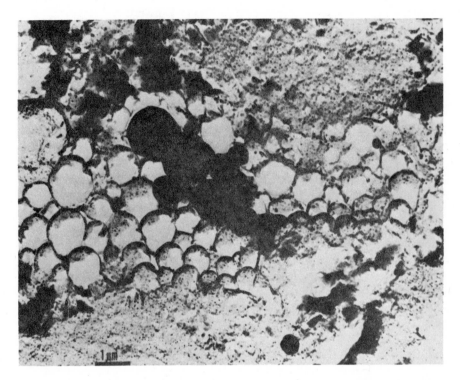

FIGURE 22.7.1.—Section through a cluster of spheroidal magnetite crystals in the carbonaceous chondrite Orgueil. (From Kerridge, 1970; replica electron micrograph.) Assuming that the cluster is as high as it is wide, it consists of at least a thousand spheroids. Each of these spheroids appears to be a single magnetite crystal with a faceted surface. The crystals are easily detachable from each other and are presumably held together magnetically. Loosely bonded clusters like these are likely to have accumulated at orbital relative velocities of the individual spheroids in the range below 10–100 m/sec.

the distribution of matter, it is necessary to consider the hydromagnetic processes active in space today and in the hetegonic era (see chs. 21 and 23).

The magnetite grains in carbonaceous meteorites such as those shown in fig. 22.7.1 crystallized and/or aggregated at grain temperatures below about 800K (Brecher, 1972c; Brecher and Arrhenius 1974, 1975) from a magnetized plasma at a temperature that was probably an order of magnitude higher (sec. 22.1). This magnetite is characterized by an exceptionally low nickel content (Boström and Fredriksson, 1966). The grains also lack the microscopic inclusions of metallic nickel which are characteristic of oxidized nickel-iron particles. Hence this magnetite could hardly be derived by oxidation of nickel-iron metal as is sometimes assumed.

22.8 EVOLUTIONARY SEQUENCE OF PRECURSOR
STATES OF METEORITES

The record in meteorites, discussed above, substantiates the self-evident but nonetheless commonly neglected fact that the immediate precursor bodies, from which the meteorites were derived, must themselves have been aggregated from smaller bodies in a chain of collision events extending over a considerable period of time. Above some critical energy, depending on the material properties of the colliding bodies (see secs. 22.6–22.7), the collisions must be disruptive; below this level, they would result in accretion.

From the fact that a population of large bodies now exists it is clear that accretional collisions for some time have prevailed over disruptive ones. In the early part of the history of the jet streams the reverse must have been the case in order for orbital energies to equalize and to account for the record of aggregate disruption, particle fragmentation, and extensive melt and vapor spray formation represented by some meteorite material. A schematic representation is given in fig. 22.8.1 of the processes involved and the products observed.

22.9 AGE RELATIONSHIPS IN THE EVOLUTION OF
METEORITE PARENT JET STREAMS

The discussion in ch. 12 shows that a satisfactory physical explanation of the accretion of the secondary bodies in the solar system requires continuous or intermittent emplacement of source gas and possibly also dust in the circumsolar region during a time period of the order of 10^8 yr. Recent innovations in radiochemical and mass spectrometric analysis of meteoritic materials have made it possible to resolve at an unprecedented level of precision the events that controlled the evolution of these materials in their formative era (Wasserburg et al., 1969; Papanastassiou and Wasserburg, 1969; Gopalan and Wetherill, 1969; Papanastassiou et al., 1973).

Other measurements permit conclusions regarding subsequent events in individual meteorite parent jet streams evolving into bodies, some of which yielded the meteorites by fragmentation. The observations of particular importance in this context are discussed in the following sections.

22.9.1 Closure of Reservoirs of Refractory Components

In this category belongs the establishment of relative proportions of elements forming refractory oxides such as aluminum, calcium, and other heavier elements in groups II, III, and IV of the periodic table. Reservoirs with different ratios between these elements are represented by different

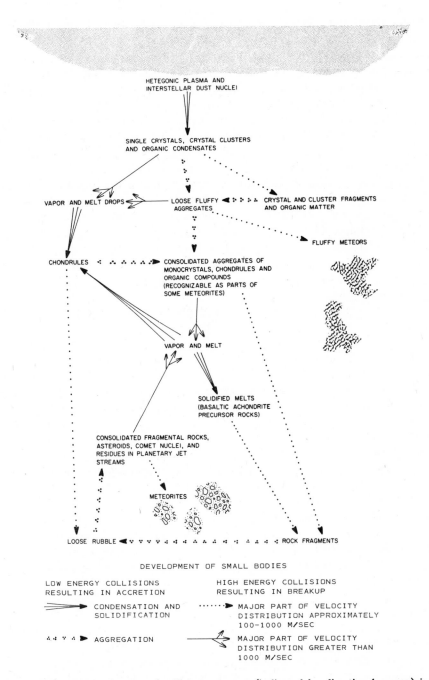

FIGURE 22.8.1.—Flow diagram of collision processes (indicated by directional arrows) in assemblages of particles and particle aggregates moving in Kepler orbits (jet streams).

meteorite groups; for example, the various groups of chondrites. The fact that these groups are chemically distinct with regard to proportions of different refractory elements suggests that the particular material from which the succession of meteorite precursor bodies must have been accreted existed as separate streams in space. These streams were maintained as largely separate reservoirs during the orbital evolution of meteorite material up to the most recent stage of formation of the meteorites in each stream.

Occasional exceptions to this rule are of equal interest, where an isolated chunk of material of one chemical type has been aggregated together with a major mass of material of another composition (see, e.g., Fodor and Keil, 1973). This indicates that separate jet-stream reservoirs existed close to each other in velocity space, so that material could occasionally although infrequently be scattered from one stream to another.

The establishment of the distinct chemical characteristics of the material in any jet stream could have taken place (a) in the generation of individual source clouds (sec. 21.11), (b) in the process of release of infalling matter from ionized source clouds by deionization (sec. 21.11), (c) as a result of the critical velocity phenomenon at emplacement (sec. 21.11), (d) in the process of condensation (Arrhenius and Alfvén, 1971), or (e) in the case of elements more volatile than those discussed here, by loss from the jet streams of a fraction of collision-generated vapor.

Hence we do not know very much about the establishment of the separate closed systems which are suggested by some groups of meteorites with different elemental and isotopic composition. Nonetheless, a fact of importance is that such groups exist and have been maintained as largely separate entities.

A particularly interesting case of refractory reservoir closure is that of strontium, since the subsequent generation of the isotope Sr^{87} by radioactive decay of Rb^{87} provides chronological information. From highly precise measurements of the present contents of Sr^{87} and Rb^{87} (normalized to Sr^{86}) Wasserburg and his collaborators (Papanastassiou et al., 1973) have demonstrated a range of initial Sr^{87}/Sr^{86} ratios in different meteorites and meteorite groups. They have shown that this range represents a time interval of at least 10^7 yr and chose to interpret it in terms of condensation events. However, in principle the concept can be expanded to refer to an interval of any of the events under (a) through (d) above.

22.9.2 Crystallization Ages

These are based on the accumulation of radioactive decay products inferred or measured in individual crystals. The system proven most practical and useful in space materials is that of Rb^{87}/Sr^{87}. The age defined is the latest event of crystallization. Petrological investigations sometimes make it possible to suggest whether the crystallization took place (a) from a low-density gas and hence marks a primordial condensation event, (b) from a dense gas or supercooled liquid suggesting crystallization from collisional melt and vapor spray, (c) from a comparatively slow-cooling melt generated by planetesimal collisions in the jet stream where the parent planetesimal of the meteorite ultimately developed, or (d) by the pericentric frictional heating mechanism (secs. 21.12, 22.4). Measured crystallization ages range over about 150 million yr from a maximum age of 4700 million yr (Wasserburg et al., 1969; Papanastassiou et al., 1973). Consequently, 150 million yr is the known range within which initial crystallization and recrystallization events took place and within which the meteorite parent jet streams underwent their early development, some of them dissipating their initially high internal energies by gas friction, others by collisions with sufficiently high relative velocities to cause melting and recrystallization.

22.9.3 Gas Retention Ages

In decay systems where the daughter nuclide is a gas, the amount of this relative to the parent nuclide (inferred or measured) marks the time when the host solid was generated by condensation at sufficiently low grain temperature or when hot solids had cooled enough to become capable of retaining the gas in their structure. The decay system I^{129}/Xe^{129} with a half-life of about 17 Myr is of particular interest since it is capable of measuring events on the time scale of the formative era, the order of 100 Myr (Hohenberg and Reynolds, 1969; Podosek, 1970). Since the parent nuclide in this case is also relatively volatile, high-energy grain collisions, such as in the development of the jet streams, are likely to largely remove both parent and daughter rather than just resetting the clock by selective removal of the daughter nuclide.

In contrast, condensing crystals, which by necessity must have been at a lower temperature than the surrounding gas (sec. 22.1), are bound to retain iodine and xenon from the outset. This is illustrated by the record high I^{129}-generated Xe^{129} contents in the alkali halogenide silicate condensates characteristic of some carbonaceous meteorites (Marti, 1973). Hence such iodine-xenon ages should approximate the condensation ages.

Since neither the original abundance of I^{129} is known, nor the time scales of source cloud evolution or of the emplacement process, the iodine-xenon measurements yield only relative age values. The range found in the comparatively few meteorites analyzed as yet amounts to a few tens of million years (Podosek, 1970). Additional measurements are likely to expand this range, since plasma emplacement and condensation would be expected to continue over a substantial fraction of 10^8 yr.

22.9.4 Degassing Ages

The proportion of gaseous decay products such as He^4 relative to the refractory parent elements uranium and thorium, or Ar^{40} in relation to K^{40} would in ideal cases give the age of crystallization. Gas losses are, however, almost always indicated. Collisional heating appears to be the main cause for such loss, and the U-Th/He and K/Ar ages can consequently give some approximate information on the timing of such events, particularly when structural features suggest that shock is the main loss mechanism (Heymann, 1967).

22.9.5 Particle Track and Plasma Implantation Records in Meteorites

Information on the aggregation history of the meteorite precursor material is provided at a microscopic level by the cosmic-ray particle track (fig. 22.9.1) and ion implantation record in the surface layer of exposed grains (Fleischer et al., 1967a,b; Lal, 1972a; Macdougall et al., 1974; Eberhardt et al., 1965; Wänke, 1965). A present-day counterpart of this phenomenon has been extensively studied in lunar surface materials, where the main source of the plasma is solar wind (1 keV range; penetration about 10–1000 Å in silicates) and solar flares (low MeV range; 0.1–100 μm penetration). In the formative era the solar and planetary plasma clouds are likely to have been the dominant sources of accelerated particles in these energy ranges (sec. 16.8), irradiating particles and aggregates in the meteorite parent jet streams. Hence these phenomena are not necessarily related or are only indirectly related to emission from the primeval Sun.

The bearing of some aspects of the particle track record on the embryology of meteorites is discussed in the next section.

22.9.6 Exposure Ages From High-Energy Cosmic Rays

Cosmic rays are largely absorbed in the surface 1-meter layer of meteorite material. Mainly due to spallation, a wide variety of radioactive and stable nuclides are formed in the absorber. Measurements of these have provided insight into the total dose that meteorite material has received at shallow depth below the surface of any of its precursor bodies. Detailed studies of the spatial distribution of different spallation products permit, in favorable cases, conclusions on gradients, distance to the surfaces existing during the periods of irradiation, and the shape of the body, if it remained unchanged during the period of irradiation (see, e.g., Fireman, 1958). The results also permit conclusions regarding the approximate constancy of cosmic radiation

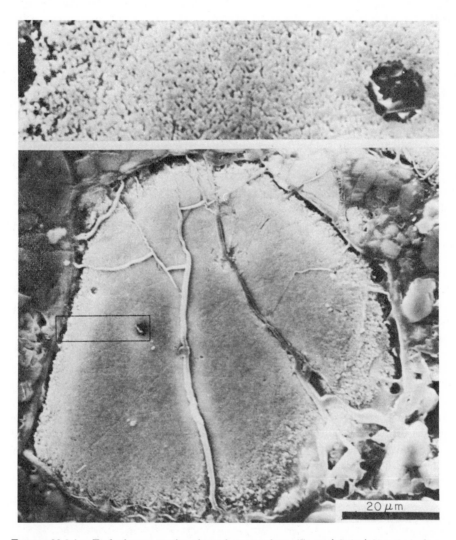

FIGURE 22.9.1.—Etched cross section through magnesium silicate (olivine) chondrule from the meteorite Fayetteville. The etching reveals a high concentration of cosmic-ray particle tracks at the surface, rapidly falling off toward the interior, reflecting the hardness spectrum of the radiation. The track distribution shows that the chondrule was turned around and irradiated from all sides before it was permanently embedded in the grain aggregate that now, in compacted form, constitutes the meteorite material. Before the preserved irradiation dose was received, the left part of the chondrule was broken off, presumably in a collision event. The area on the fracture edge, framed in the lower photograph, is shown in five times higher magnification in the upper photograph, illustrating the tracks and the radial track gradient in greater detail. The track density at the edge is 10^{10} cm^{-2}. (From Macdougall et al., 1974.)

on time scales of the order of 10^6–10^9 yr (Arnold et al., 1961); hence dosages can be interpreted in terms of duration of irradiation (comprehensive reviews are given by Honda and Arnold, 1967; Kirsten and Schaeffer, 1971; and Lal, 1972a).

The cosmic-ray induced radioactive nuclides used fall in two groups; the majority with half-lives less than the order of 10^6 yr and one (K^{40}) with half-life exceeding 10^9 yr. Measurable activities of nuclides in the former group thus place the related irradiation in the recent history of the solar system. The activity of long-lived species does not, however, provide any information on the period or periods when the irradiation was received.

Most exposure dosages are, however, for practical reasons, not based on measurements of radioactive nuclides, but of stable spallation products, such as He^3. Also in these cases, which form the basis for statistical conclusions, there is usually no evidence indicating when the irradiation was received, what part of the present meteoritic conglomerate was irradiated, or over how many separate intervals the exposure took place.

Nonetheless it is tacitly or explicitly assumed in most discussions of these matters, and indeed implied by the term "exposure age," that the material was brought into exposure by one single breakup event and that the total observed dose was accumulated in the time period immediately preceding the fall of the meteorite. This view again derives from the concept of meteorite parent bodies (which are equated with asteroids or cometary nuclei) as having been brought into existence as large bodies without a lineage of predecessors. After this unspecified creation they are supposed to inexorably undergo a one-way degradation process. Such a belief obviously ignores the need to build up the presently observed asteroidal and cometary bodies by a physically acceptable process, specifically by planetesimal accretion (secs. 11.3 and 12.1).

In contrast, then, it is necessary to assume that meteorite source material was already exposed to irradiation in the early history of the solar system and that a sequence of destructive and constructive collisions led to repeated shielding and exposure events of which the latest fragmentation, generating the meteorite, is only the last exposure. This is clearly reflected by the lower (MeV range) energy cosmic-ray particle track record (fig. 22.9.1) and by the distribution of keV range ions implanted in a surface layer of the order 10^3–10^4 Å.

Wänke (1966) has shown that material irradiated in this manner occurs much more commonly in some types of meteorites than in others (for example, in about 15 percent of all H-type chondrites investigated compared to only a few percent of L- and LL-type chondrites). This probably means that the planetesimals in the H-type parent jet stream spent a longer time in a relatively disseminated state, and that the L- and LL-type material was focused more rapidly, possibly due to an initially narrower spread in velocity space. Similar inferences are suggested by the variability in frequency of grains with particle track irradiation ranging, e.g., between 30 percent of all grains in the meteorite Fayetteville and $\sim$6 percent in Kapoeta (Macdougall et al., 1974; Wilkening et al., 1971).

In addition to irradiated single crystals or crystal fragments, similarly surface irradiated aggregates of various sizes have been found in meteorites (Pellas, 1972; Macdougall et al., 1972; Lal, 1972a). It is likely that such aggregates are more common than the number so far discovered would indicate since their identification in the lithified meteorite material becomes more difficult with increasing size. Such aggregates, which were certainly solidly compacted at irradiation, represent a stage in planetesimal evolution where some aggregates had been lithified, presumably by shock, fragmented again by collision, exposed to irradiation and reimmersed in fine-grained, noncohesive material, which later was also compacted. Among other observed phenomena which illustrate the hierarchical exposure evolution are probably the different exposure "ages" found in different parts of the same meteorite (Zähringer, 1966) and the systematic discrepancies in K^{40} and Cl^{36} exposure ages (Voshage and Hintenberger, 1963).

22.10 GENERAL REMARKS ON THE RECORD IN METEORITES

Meteorites provide tangible samples of solar-system materials that have not been extensively modified by the processes characteristic of bodies with substantial gravitational fields. From meteorite data alone it is not always possible to unravel the effects of these individual fractionation processes. However, seeing it in the general context of solar-system evolution we can state that the *variability in meteorite composition* must derive from differentiation (a) before or (b) during emplacement of matter around the Sun, (c) in the course of condensation, (d) during the evolution of the individual meteorite parent jet streams, or (e) during its residence on Earth.

The processes of emplacement of already fractionated matter in different regions of the solar system, and of interstellar transport of the source material, as well as other poorly known events further back in time, all introduce fractionation effects. Fractionation processes, taking place in the course of condensation and during subsequent collisional and frictional heating should be considered.

The *time relationships* of events recorded in meteorites need to be considered in the light of the fact that their precursor bodies must be products of both accretional and disruptive collisions. It is also necessary to take into account the circumstance that emplacement and condensation of matter in the circumsolar region cannot have been instantaneous, but must have continued over an extended period of time.

The *accretion, fragmentation and irradiation* record in meteorites clearly does not reflect processes taking place in the "regolith" of a planet-size parent body, miraculously created and later exploded. In contrast, this record should be understood as a result of the competing processes of accretion and fragmentation in assemblages of orbiting particles and particle aggregates in the meteorite parent jet streams.

In general our knowledge of phenomena relating to the history of the solar system becomes increasingly uncertain the further back we go in time. In studies of primordial solids this principle is to some extent reversed (Pellas, 1972) due to the fact that the decay, particularly of short-lived radionuclides, leaves an early record more accurate than the more recent one.

The main limitation of the record from meteorites is that their source regions cannot be identified. The yield from the powerful analytical methods developed for probing meteorites and lunar rocks is consequently likely to increase dramatically when they are also applied to samples from asteroids and comets (Alfvén and Arrhenius 1972b; Arrhenius et al, 1973).

For a complete picture of the range of materials in the solar system it is also necessary to obtain information about the entirely unknown structure and composition of solids from the C cloud (sec. 21.11). This includes the giant planets, but they cannot themselves provide samples of unaltered primordial solid material. Instead we need to draw on the small bodies originating from this region, such as the material in the Saturnian rings or in the Trojans (sec. 8.5.3). Exploration of the regular satellite systems of Jupiter, Saturn, and Uranus is also of basic importance for clarifying the chemistry of the hetegonic processes.

23

THE STRUCTURE OF THE GROUPS
OF SECONDARY BODIES

23.1 IONIZATION DURING THE EMPLACEMENT
OF PLASMA

In the preceding chapter we discussed the hypothesis that the location of the different groups of secondary bodies is determined by the critical velocity phenomenon. However, the internal structures of the groups differ in the respect that in some of them (e.g., the giant planets) the mass of the bodies decreases rapidly with increasing distance from the central body, whereas in other groups (e.g., the inner Saturnian satellites) the reverse is true. In this chapter we shall show that this difference in structure among the groups probably is related to the total energy dissipated in the process of emplacement of the plasma. This leads to the conclusion that the structure of a group depends on the ratio T/τ between the typical orbital period T of the secondary bodies of the group and the spin period τ of the central body. There is observational support of this dependence (see secs. 23.5–23.6). In fact the mass distribution in the groups is evidently a function of T/τ.

As in some of the earlier chapters we are obviously far from a detailed theory, and the aim of our discussion is essentially to call attention to what may be the basic phenomena determining the structure of the groups.

According to our model, a gas of mass m, originally at rest at "infinity," falls in to the ionization distance r_{ion} where it becomes partially ionized (fig. 23.2.1). By transfer of angular momentum from the central body this mass is brought into partial corotation (ch. 17). It condenses and through processes discussed in secs. 18.2 and 18.10 it is eventually placed in a circular orbit with the radius r. In sec. 17.6 we found that the total release of energy during this process is

$$W = \frac{GM_c m}{r}\left(\frac{\Omega}{\omega} + \frac{1}{2}\right) \qquad (23.1.1)$$

where $\omega = (GM_c/r^3)^{1/2}$ is the angular orbital velocity of m. As $r\omega \sim r^{-1/2}$ and as within a group r does not vary by more than a factor of 6 (see table 2.5.1),

we do not introduce a very large error if in our order-of-magnitude calculation we approximate eq. (23.1.1) by

$$W = \frac{GM_c m}{r_{ion}} \frac{T_{ion}}{\tau} \qquad (23.1.2)$$

where T_{ion} is the orbital period of a fictitious body orbiting at the ionization
distance r_{ion}, τ is the spin period of the central body, $\Omega\tau = 2\pi$, and $\omega T_{ion} = 2\pi$.

If we equate m to the mass of an atom m_a and let $r_{ion} = GM_c m_a/eV_{ion}$
(from eq. 21.10.2) we have

$$W = eV_{ion} \frac{T_{ion}}{\tau} \qquad (23.1.3)$$

Part of this energy will be dissipated in the central body or in its ionosphere and part of it in the plasma which is brought into partial corotation.
Without a detailed analysis it is reasonable to guess that these parts are
about equal. The energy is delivered to the plasma by the electric currents
which transfer the momentum and then primarily is converted to an increase in the electron temperature. When this has reached a certain value,
most of the energy is radiated, but a fraction ζ is used for ionization.

In laboratory studies of electric currents in gases it has been shown that
ζ seldom exceeds 5 percent. For example, in a glow discharge the minimum
voltage V_c between the electrodes (which actually equals the cathode potential drop) is usually 200–300 V (essentially only pure noble gases have
lower values). This holds, for example, for H_2, N_2, and air (V. Engel, 1955,
p. 202), for which the voltage needed to produce ionization is in the range
10–15 V. Hence this ratio $\zeta = V_{ion}/V_c$, which gives the fraction of the energy
which goes into ionization, is about 0.05. Even if the discharge in our case
differs in certain respects, we should not expect ζ to be drastically different.
Taking account of the fact that only a fraction of W is dissipated in the
plasma we should expect ζ to be less than 0.05.

Hence, even without making any detailed model of the process we may
conclude that if ζW denotes the energy that goes into ionization of the
plasma, ζ is not likely to exceed 0.05. This means that it is impossible to
produce a complete ionization of the plasma if T_{ion}/τ is of the order 10 or
less. A considerably higher value is probably needed for complete ionization
to occur.

We then conclude:

(1) Other things being equal, the degree of ionization during emplacement is a function of T_{ion}/τ.

(2) We may have complete ionization if T_{ion}/τ is, for example, 100 or more, but probably not if it is of the order of 10 or less.

In sec. 23.2 we shall treat the case

$$\frac{T_{ion}}{\tau} \gg \zeta^{-1} \qquad (23.1.4)$$

which indicates complete ionization, reserving the case of incomplete ionization

$$\frac{T_{ion}}{\tau} < \zeta^{-1} \qquad (23.1.5)$$

for sec. 23.3.

23.2 COMPLETE IONIZATION

We shall now discuss the extreme case $T_{ion}/\tau \gg \zeta^{-1}$, implying that the plasma is completely ionized. The gas which falls in is stopped at the critical velocity sphere, which is defined by $r_{ion} = 2GM_c/v_{crit}^2$, where it immediately becomes partially ionized (see fig. 23.2.1). The transfer of angular momentum gives it an azimuthal velocity which increases until partial corotation is achieved. The energy release associated with this process ionizes the plasma completely.

As stressed earlier, it is important to note that homogeneous models are obsolete in cosmic plasma physics. To reduce the speculative element which hetegonic theories necessarily include, it is essential to connect the models as far as possible with laboratory experiments and such cosmic phenomena as we observe today. For the discussion, references to magnetosphere and especially for solar phenomena are essential. The transfer of angular momentum through a set of "superprominences," as discussed in sec. 16.7 and by De (1973), is the background for our present treatment (see fig. 16.6.1).

Hence we should consider the infall of gas as taking place in a series of intermittent events with a finite extension and a finite lifetime. Several infalls could very well take place simultaneously. The gas which arrives at the critical velocity sphere r_{ion} and becomes partially ionized is rapidly incorporated in a superprominence which is almost completely ionized because $\int T_{ion}/\tau \gg 1$ guarantees that in the long run there is enough energy for ionization. The processes to which the infalling gas is subject at r_{ion} confine the gas to a magnetic flux tube. Its final destiny is either to fall along this flux tube to the central body or to attain an increasing angular momentum so that it is brought to the neighborhood of the equatorial plane. There are regions around the axis of the central body where the former process takes place, whereas the latter process occurs in a band near the equatorial plane.

Figure 23.2.1 is a projection on a meridional plane and should be interpreted with what is said above as a background.

As the average mass distribution is uniform over the surface of the sphere r_{ion}, the mass dM between the latitude circles at λ and $\lambda+d\lambda$ amounts to

$$dM = K \cos \lambda \, d\lambda \qquad (23.2.1)$$

K being a constant. The equation of the magnetic lines of force is

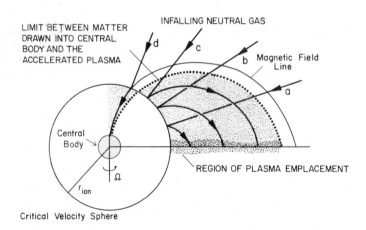

Critical Velocity Sphere

FIGURE 23.2.1.—Complete ionization of infalling gas. Gas falling in from infinity reaches the critical velocity at r_{ion} (the critical velocity sphere) and becomes partially ionized. It is rapidly included in "superprominences" which, if $\int T_{ion}/\tau \gg 1$, are almost completely ionized. Matter falling in at low latitudes (a, b, and c) will be emplaced near the equatorial plane and condense there. Matter arriving at the critical velocity sphere at high latitudes (d) will be drawn into the central body. Note that the processes a, b, and c do not necessarily interfere because they may occur at different times or even simultaneously at different longitudes.

$$r_B = r \cos^2 \lambda \qquad (23.2.2)$$

where r_B is the distance to the central body from a point on the line of force and r is the value of r_B at the equatorial plane. Putting $r_B = r_{ion}$ we obtain by differentiating eq. (23.2.2)

$$d\lambda = \frac{\cot \lambda}{2r} dr \qquad (23.2.3)$$

and

$$\frac{dM}{dr} = \frac{Kr_{ion}}{2} \frac{1}{r^2 \left(1 - \dfrac{r_{ion}}{r}\right)^{1/2}}. \qquad (23.2.4)$$

This function is plotted in fig. 23.2.2.

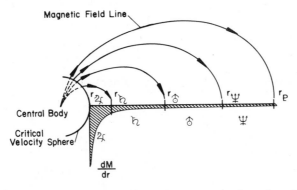

FIGURE 23.2.2.—Matter stopped at the critical velocity sphere is displaced outward along the magnetic field lines and condenses in the region of the equatorial plane. For a rough estimate it is assumed, rather arbitrarily, that all matter between the present orbits of Jupiter and Saturn is now included in Jupiter, etc. As shown by table 23.2.1, this gives roughly the observed mass distribution. The essence of the analysis is that the distributed density in the region of the giant planets is compatible with the model of sec. 23.2. (From Alfvén, 1962.)

Let us now see whether it is possible that the outer planets have originated from a gas having the mass distribution given by eq. (23.2.4).

We assume that r_{ion} coincides roughly with the present value of the orbital radius of Jupiter ($r_{\jupiter}$) and that all gas situated between $r_{\jupiter}$ and the
orbital radius of Saturn (r_b) is used to build up Jupiter. (The fact that,
according to ch. 17, all distances are likely to decrease by a factor of 2/3 is
not crucial in this respect.) In the same way we assume that all matter
between r_b and $r_{\saturn}$ (Uranus) is condensed to Saturn, etc. Thus we should
expect the following masses of the planets:

Jupiter:

$$M_{\jupiter} = A \int_{r_{\jupiter}}^{r_b} \frac{dr}{r^2 \left(1 - \frac{r_{ion}}{r}\right)^{1/2}} \qquad (23.2.5)$$

Neptune:

$$M_{\psi} = A \int_{r_{\psi}}^{r_P} \frac{dr}{r^2 \left(1 - \frac{r_{ion}}{r}\right)^{1/2}} \qquad (23.2.6)$$

where r_P is the orbital radius of Pluto and A is defined by

$$M_{total} = A \int_{r_{\jupiter}}^{r_P} \frac{dr}{r^2 \left(1 - \frac{r_{ion}}{r}\right)^{1/2}} \qquad (23.2.7)$$

The relative masses of the planets calculated from equations of the form
(23.2.7) and the observed masses are given in table 23.2.1. The calculated
values agree with observations within a factor of 2. (The integral from Pluto
to infinity is 32 units, but, as this mass has become ionized near the axial
region of the Sun, it is likely to have fallen directly into the Sun; note "d"
in fig. 23.2.1.)

TABLE 23.2.1

Mass Distribution Among Giant Planets Calculated for $\zeta T_{ion}/\tau \gg 1$

Planet	Mass (Earth = 1)	
	Calculated	Observed
Jupiter	320	317
Saturn	88	95
Uranus	26	15
Neptune	10	17

The assumption that the gas is divided exactly at the present distances of the planets is, of course, arbitrary, and a more refined calculation has been given elsewhere (Alfvén, 1954, ch. V). But if we go in the opposite direction, we can interpret the result as follows. Suppose that we distribute the masses of the outer planets so that we obtain a continuous mass distribution in the equatorial plane. A projection of this along the magnetic lines of force upon a sphere gives us an almost uniform mass distribution. Consequently, the mass distribution obtained in this way shows a reasonable agreement with the mass distribution among the giant planets.

We now turn our attention to the outer Saturnian satellites. This is a group which also has a very high value of T_{ion}/τ. The group is *irregular* (see sec. 23.8) and it is difficult to deduce the original mass distribution from the three existing bodies. However, it is evident that in this group also most of the mass is concentrated in the innermost body, Titan, which is situated somewhat below the ionization limit.

23.3 PARTIAL IONIZATION

It is only in two groups, the giant planets and the outer Saturnian satellites, that the innermost body is the biggest one. In all other groups there is a slow or rapid decrease in size inward. The reason for this is probably that the value of T_{ion}/τ is too small to satisfy eq. (23.1.4); this is discussed in detail in secs. 23.5–23.7.

A small value of T_{ion}/τ can be expected to have two different effects (see fig. 23.3.1):

(1) On the critical velocity sphere there is a limit between the region close to the axis from which the matter is drawn in to the central body and the region from which matter is brought to the equatorial plane. When T_{ion}/τ decreases, this limit is displaced away from the axis. The result of this is that

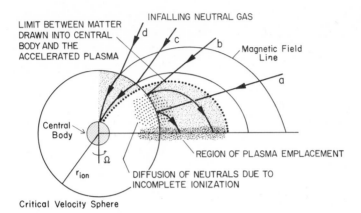

FIGURE 23.3.1.—Partial ionization of infalling gas. Small values of T_{ion}/τ (<20) imply an increase of the region near the axis of the central body from which matter is drawn into the central body. Incomplete ionization at r_{ion} is also implied and diffusion of neutral gas toward the central body will take place. The result is a displacement inward of the region of plasma emplacement and a change in the mass distribution within a group of secondary bodies.

no matter is brought down toward the equatorial plane at a large distance from the critical velocity sphere. Hence, in comparison with the case of very large T_{ion}/τ, the outer limit of the region where bodies are produced will be displaced inward.

(2) As all the gas is not ionized at the critical velocity sphere, part of it will fall closer to the central body, where sooner or later a considerable part of its condensates are collected in jet streams. Hence mass is collected even far inside the critical velocity sphere. These two effects are further discussed in sec. 23.7.

23.4 CHANGE OF SPIN DURING THE FORMATION OF SECONDARY BODIES

From this discussion we would expect the mass distribution within a group of bodies to depend on the value of T_{ion}/τ. However, the value of this quantity would not be the present value but the value at the time of formation. The angular momentum which Jupiter, Saturn, and Uranus have transferred to orbital momenta of their satellites is small (of the order of 1 percent; see table 2.1.2) compared with the spin momenta of these planets, and no other mechanism by which they can lose a large fraction of their momenta is known (see sec. 10.4). Hence, it is reasonable to suppose that they possessed about their present angular momenta at the time of formation of their satellite systems.

Their moments of inertia may have changed somewhat during the planetary evolution, but this change is likely to be rather small. Hence, it seems reasonable to state that the axial rotations of these planets had approximately their present angular velocity at the time when their satellite systems were formed.

This conclusion does not hold for the Sun. Its present angular momentum is only 0.6 percent of the total angular momentum of the solar system. Hence, if the Sun has lost angular momentum only through transfer to planets, it has transferred 99.4 percent of its original angular momentum to the orbital momenta of the giant planets. This effect would have made the value of T_{ion}/τ about 180 times larger at the beginning of the formation of the planetary system. However, the Sun may also have lost angular momentum to the solar wind. Whether this has been an appreciable amount or not is uncertain (see sec. 25.4), but it is possible that this factor of 180 should be still larger.

On the other hand, the moment of inertia of the Sun may have changed. If, at a very early stage, the Sun was burning its deuterium, its radius would be about 16 times larger than now (sec. 25.6). If the planets were formed around a deuterium-burning Sun, these two effects would approximately compensate each other, and the present values of T_{ion}/τ would be valid.

These considerations are not very important for the formation of the giant planets because this group would, for either extreme value of τ, have values of T_{ion}/τ which satisfy eq. (23.1.4). On the other hand, it does not seem legitimate to use the present values of T_{ion}/τ for the terrestrial planets. Hence we exclude them from our analysis.

23.5 OBSERVATIONAL VALUES OF T_K/τ

Before calculating theoretically the values of T_{ion}/τ for the different groups, we shall plot the observational values of the ratio T_K/τ between the Kepler period T_K of a secondary body and the period τ of the axial rotation of its central body. This gives us fig. 23.5.1.

It appears that for the giant planets the value of T_K/τ is of the order of several hundred and for the outer Saturnian satellites about one hundred. The Galilean satellites and the Uranian satellites have similar values, ranging from about 5 up to about 50. The inner Saturnian satellites have values between 2 and 10. (The values for the terrestrial planets, which should not be included in our analysis, lie between 3 and 30.)

To characterize each group by a certain value of T_K/τ we could take some sort of mean of the values for its members. From a theoretical point of view the least arbitrary way of doing so is to use the value T_{ion} of the Kepler motion of a mass moving at the ionization distance, as we have done in

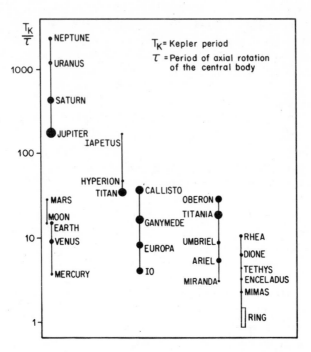

FIGURE 23.5.1.—Ratio between the orbital period T_K of secondary bodies and the spin period τ of the central body. The latter quantity may have changed for the Sun, but not for the planets. The secondaries are grouped according to the cloud in which they formed. From left to right are the terrestrial planets, the giant planets, outer Saturnian satellites, Galilean satellites of Jupiter, the Uranian satellites, and the inner satellites of Saturn. (From Alfvén, 1962.)

sec. 23.1. Referring to fig. 21.11.2 we see that each group falls into one of the clouds surrounding its central body. To analyze a group in terms of T_{ion}/τ we must choose the ionization distance r_{ion} for the group as a whole. In this treatment we shall use the r_{ion} which corresponds to the critical velocity v_{crit} of each cloud as denoted in fig. 21.11.2.

Setting $r = r_{ion}$, we have

$$T_{ion} = \frac{2\pi}{\omega} = 2\pi \left(\frac{r_{ion}^3}{GM_c} \right)^{1/2} \tag{23.5.1}$$

and from eq. (21.10.2),

$$\frac{GM_c}{r_{ion}} = \frac{v_{crit}^2}{2} \tag{23.5.2}$$

It follows that

$$T_{ion} = \frac{2^{3/2}\pi r_{ion}}{v_{crit}} = \frac{2^{5/2}\pi G M_c}{v_{crit}^3} \qquad (23.5.3)$$

where v_{crit} is the velocity characterizing the cloud.

23.6 MASS DISTRIBUTION AS A FUNCTION OF T_{ion}/τ

In fig. 23.6.1 the masses of the bodies are plotted as a function of the or-bital distances. The distances are normalized with the ionization distance r_{ion} as unit: $\delta = r/r_{ion}$. This value for each body is called the "normalized distance." The normalized distances for the planets and their satellites are given in table 23.6.1.

The values of the normalized distance are not rigorously obtained. As r_{ion} is a function of v_{crit} the uncertainty introduced in assigning a charac-teristic v_{crit} to a specific cloud (see sec. 21.11–21.12) also pertains to the values of the normalized distance. Further (see sec. 21.13), one ought to reduce the r_{ion} to $0.89 r_{ion}$ to take account of the 2/3 falldown process of condensation (see sec. 17.5) and the corotation of the plasma. However, we attempt only a general understanding of the relationship of T/τ to the mass distribution. Thus the inaccuracy introduced in choosing r_{ion}, and hence T_{ion}, for each group does not diminish the validity of the trends ob-served in each group.

For each group a straight line is drawn in fig. 23.6.1, and the slope of this line gives a picture of the variation of the average mass density of the gas from which the bodies condensed. Such a line can, in general, be drawn in such a way that the individual dots fall rather close to the line (mass differ-ence less that a factor of 2). An exception is found in the outer Saturnian group, where Hyperion falls very much below the line connecting Titan and Iapetus.

The figure shows that the mass distribution within the groups depends in a systematic way on the value of T_{ion}/τ. Among the giant planets ($T_{ion}/\tau = 520$) the masses decrease outward, as discussed in detail in sec. 23.2. The Jovian (Galilean) satellites with $T_{ion}/\tau = 29$ have almost equal masses. In the Uranian group ($T_{ion}/\tau = 12$) the masses increase outward, on the average, whereas the inner Saturnian satellites ($T_{ion}/\tau = 8$) show a rapid and mono-tonic increase outward. The outer Saturnian satellite group which has $T_{ion}/\tau = 80$ should be intermediate between the giant planets and the Jovian satellites. If a straight line is drawn between the dots representing Titan

TABLE 23.6.1

Normalized Distance for Secondary Bodies in the Solar System

Primary	Cloud	Secondary	Normalized distance r_{orb}/r_{ion}
Sun	B	Mercury	0.56
		Venus	1.05
		Earth	1.46
	A	Moon	0.67
		Mars	1.01
	C	Jupiter	0.49
		S..turn	0.89
		Uranus	1.79
		Neptune	2.81
	D	Triton	0.63
		Pluto	0.83
Jupiter	A	Amalthea	0.84
	C	Io	0.28
		Europa	0.44
		Ganymede	0.70
		Callisto	1.24
	D	Rudimentary	
Saturn	C	Mimas	0.41
		Enceladus	0.52
		Tethys	0.65
		Dione	0.83
		Rhea	1.16
	D	Titan	0.60
		Hyperion	0.73
		Iapetus	1.75
Uranus	D	Miranda	0.42
		Ariel	0.61
		Umbriel	0.85
		Titania	1.40
		Oberon	1.87

and Iapetus, the slope of this line is steeper than we would expect. However, Hyperion falls very far from this line, which hence does not represent the mass distribution within the group in a correct way. For reasons we shall discuss later, this group is not so regular as the other groups (see sec. 23.8). Furthermore, the T_{ion}/τ value for the giant planets is uncertain because we do not know the spin period of the primeval Sun, which indeed must have changed when it transferred most of its angular momentum to the giant

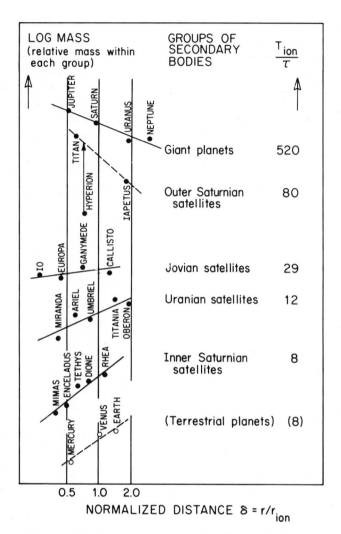

FIGURE 23.6.1.—Mass distribution within the groups of secondary bodies as a function of their normalized distances $\delta = r/r_{ion}$. The figure shows that within a group characterized by a large value of T_{ion}/τ, the mass decreases outward. For a value of T_{ion}/τ which is small, the mass decreases inward. (From Alfvén, 1962.)

planets. An evolution of the solar size and spin as suggested by Alfvén (1963) should give an average value of T_{ion}/τ for the giant planets which may be smaller than the value for the outer Saturnian satellites. This would eliminate the only exception to the systematic trend in fig. 23.6.1.

It was suggested above that the Mercury-Venus-Earth group should not be included in the analysis because we could not be sure that the Sun has the same angular velocity now as when this group was formed, which means that its T_{ion}/τ value may not be the correct one. The present value is $T_{ion}/\tau = 8.5$, close to the value of the inner Saturnian group. The mass distribution is also similar to the conditions in this Saturnian group (see fig. 23.6.1). Hence, if the present value of T_{ion}/τ for this group is used, the terrestrial planets fit, though probably coincidentally, in the sequence of fig. 23.6.1. Likewise, the Moon and Mars are deleted from the discussion because of the uncertainty of the Sun's spin period in the formative era.

23.7 DISCUSSION OF THE STRUCTURE OF THE GROUPS OF SECONDARY BODIES

In an earlier treatise (Alfvén, 1954) an attempt was made to develop a detailed theory of the variation of the mass distribution as a function of T_{ion}/τ. As this was done before experimental and theoretical investigations had clarified the properties of the critical velocity, the discussion must now be revised to some extent. We shall not try here to treat this problem quantitatively but confine ourselves to a qualitative discussion of the two effects which, according to sec. 23.3, should be important. These are best studied for the C cloud (sec. 21.11.1 and fig. 21.11.2) because this has produced three groups with very different values of T_{ion}/τ (giant planets with $T_{ion}/\tau =$ 520, Galilean satellites with $T_{ion}/\tau = 29$, and inner Saturnian satellites with $T_{ion}/\tau = 8$).

In the group of the giant planets the bodies have normalized distances $\delta = r/r_{ion}$, with a maximum of 2.81 (see fig. 23.6.1 and table 23.6.1). In the two other groups the maximum value of δ is 1.24 for the Galilean and almost the same (1.16) for the inner Saturnian satellites. The decrease in outward extension may be caused by the first effect discussed in sec. 23.3. Of the matter stopped at distance r_{ion}, that found in a larger region around the axis is drawn down to the central body (compare figs. 23.2.1 and 23.3.1). In this situation no matter is brought to the equatorial plane along those lines of force which intersect this plane at a large distance.

Further, the second effect discussed in sec. 23.3 allows matter to become ionized closer to the central body because not all the matter is ionized and stopped at the ionization distance r_{ion}. A result of this is that the innermost body of the Galilean group has a normalized distance of only $\delta = 0.28$, compared to 0.49 for the giant planets. In the inner Saturnian group this effect is even more pronounced because of the smaller value of T_{ion}/τ. Certainly, the innermost body (Mimas) of this group has a δ value of 0.41, but the satellite group continues inside the Roche limit in the form of the ring system. Here we find matter collected almost down to the surface of Saturn, corresponding to a δ value as low as 0.1.

TABLE 23.8.1

Values of T_{ion}/τ Where T_{ion} Is the Kepler Period of a Body at the Ionization Distance and τ Is the Period of Axial Rotation of the Central Body

Central body	τ	T_{ion}/τ for secondary bodies in cloud			
	10^5 sec	B	A	C	D
Sun	21.3	8.5 ♅–⊕	28 ☾–♂	520 ♃–♆	5000 P
Jupiter	0.354	0.50	1.6 Amalthea	29 Galilean satellites	286
Saturn	0.368		0.45	8.4 Inner satellites	80 Outer satellites
Uranus	0.389			1.3	12 Uranian satellites
Neptune	0.504			1.0	9.5
Earth (prior to capture of the Moon)	0.14(?)				2.2(?).

According to the theory, bodies are produced only in the groups above the line in the table.

A similar effect, although less pronounced, is indicated in the D cloud by the fact that the δ value of Miranda in the Uranian system is 0.42, and Titan, the innermost body of the outer Saturnian group, has $\delta = 0.60$. However, there is no similar difference between the outer limits.

23.8 COMPLETE LIST OF T_{ion}/τ FOR ALL BODIES

Table 23.8.1 presents all the T_{ion}/τ values above unity for the A, B, C, and D clouds captured around the largest bodies in the solar system (see fig. 21.11.2). Also some values slightly below unity are given for comparison.

The six groups represented in figs. 23.5.1 and 23.6.1 all have T_{ion}/τ values ≥ 8. As the process we have discussed has a general validity, we should expect similar groups to be produced in all cases where we find the same values of T_{ion}/τ, unless special phenomena occur which prevent their formation. In addition to these six groups, we also find high values of T_{ion}/τ in three more cases. This means that we would also expect groups of bodies in these cases:

(1) *D cloud around the Sun:* We would expect a group of planets outside the giant planets. Pluto and probably also Triton may belong to this group. (Like the Moon, Triton was initially a planet which later was captured; see McCord, 1966.) As the D cloud should contain heavy elements (see sec. 21.11), the high density of Pluto, and possibly Triton (see sec. 20.5), may be explained. According to ch. 19 the extremely large distance to the Sun has made the hydromagnetic transfer of momentum inefficient because the transplanetary magnetic field has interfered with the solar field. This group has only these two members. But there may also be as yet undiscovered members of this group.

(2) *D cloud around Jupiter:* The absence of regular D cloud satellites around Jupiter may appear surprising. However, as has been shown elsewhere (Alfvén, 1954, p. 161), the solar magnetic field, if it is strong enough, should prevent, or interfere with, the production of satellites. The region which is most sensitive to this interference is the D cloud region around Jupiter; next is the D cloud region around Saturn. Hence, the solar magnetic field may have prevented the D cloud satellites around Jupiter and at the same time made the outer Saturnian satellites as irregular as they are with regard to the sequence of masses and orbital radii.

Another possibility is that the D cloud region is too close to the Lagrangian points to allow the formation of a regular group.

(3) *D cloud around Neptune:* We should also expect a D cloud group around Neptune. If a group was once formed from such a cloud, it is likely to have been largely destroyed by the retrograde giant satellite Triton, when it was captured. The evolution of the Neptune-Triton system is likely to have been similar, in certain respects, to that of the Earth-Moon system (see ch. 24). This implies that Nereid is the only residual member of an initial group of satellites, most of which may have impacted on Triton in the same way as the Earth's original satellites presumably impacted on the Moon, forming the maria relatively late in lunar history.

It should be added that the A cloud around the Sun probably has produced Mars and also the Moon as an independent planet, which was later captured (ch. 24).

So far we have discussed all the cases in which T_{ion}/τ has a value in the same range as the six groups of fig. 23.6.1. It is of interest to see what happens if T_{ion}/τ is smaller than this. From table 23.8.1 we find that the next value ($T_{ion}/\tau = 1.6$) belongs to the A cloud around Jupiter. In the region where we expect this group, we find only one tiny satellite, the fifth satellite of Jupiter, which has a reduced distance $\delta = r/r_{ion} = 0.84$. This body may be identified as the only member of a group which is rudimentary because of its small T_{ion}/τ value. If we proceed to the next value, which is $T_{ion}/\tau = 1.3$ for the C cloud around Uranus, we find no satellites at all.

Hence, the theoretical prediction that no satellite formation is possible when T_{ion}/τ approaches unity is confirmed by the observational material. The transition from the groups of fig. 23.6.1 to the absence of satellites is represented by Jupiter's lone A cloud satellite, Amalthea.

23.9 COMPLETENESS

Summarizing the results of our analysis we may state that they justify our original assumption; namely, that it makes sense to plot the secondary bodies as a function of Γ. In fact, according to the diagram (fig. 21.2.1), a *necessary* condition for the existence of a group of secondary bodies is that the gravitational potential in those regions of space have specific values, and, whenever this condition is fulfilled, bodies are present.

All the known regular bodies (with a possible uncertainty in the iden- tification of Pluto and Triton) *fall within three horizontal bands*—with a possible addition of a fourth band for the Martian satellites. *Groups of bodies are found wherever a band falls within the natural limits of formation of secondary bodies.*

There is no obvious exception to this rule but there are three doubtful cases:

(1) The band producing the Uranian, the outer Saturnian, and outermost Jovian satellites may also have produced bodies in the planetary system. It is possible that Pluto and Triton, whose densities seem to be higher than those of the giant planets, are examples of such a group.

(2) From only looking at the observational diagram (fig. 21.2.1) we may expect a correspondence to Martian satellites in the outermost region of the Uranian system, and possibly also in the outskirts of the Saturnian system. However, we see from fig. 20.11.2 that no critical velocity is suffi- ciently small for infalling matter to be stopped in these regions; hence there is no theoretical reason to expect such bodies.

(3) It is likely that a group of natural satellites originally was formed around the primeval Earth but was destroyed during the capture of the Moon. Before the capture of the Moon the Earth had a much more rapid spin. A reasonable value for the spin period is 4 hr. With a D cloud around the Earth this gives $T/\tau = 2.2$. This value is intermediate between Amalthea and the inner Saturnian satellites. Hence we should expect that the Earth originally had a satellite system somewhat intermediate between Amalthea and the inner Saturnian satellites. The satellites were necessarily very small, and all were swallowed up or ejected by the much bigger Moon (see ch. 24).

23.9.1 Note on the Inner Limit of a Satellite System

As derived in sec. 17.3 the state of partial corotation is given by

$$v_\phi^2 = \frac{2GM_c}{3r} \qquad (23.9.1)$$

with

$$v_\phi = \omega r \cos \lambda \qquad (23.9.2)$$

As ω, the angular velocity of the orbiting body, cannot surpass the angular velocity Ω of the spinning central body, we cannot have equilibrium unless $r > r_0$ with r_0 defined by

$$r_0^3 \cos^2 \lambda \geq \frac{2GM_c}{3\Omega^2} \qquad (23.9.3)$$

Introducing the synchronous radius r_{syn} for a Kepler orbit when $\omega = \Omega$

$$r_{syn} \Omega^2 = \frac{GM_c}{r_{syn}^2} \qquad (23.9.4)$$

we find

$$\frac{r_0}{r_{syn}} = \left(\frac{2 \cos \lambda}{3}\right)^{1/3} \qquad (23.9.5)$$

The minimum distance r_{min} of condensed matter in circular orbit given by the 2/3 law (sec. 17.5) is

$$r_{min} = \frac{2r_0 \cos \lambda}{3} \qquad (23.9.6)$$

and

$$\frac{r_{min}}{r_{syn}} = \left(\frac{2}{3}\right)^{4/3} (\cos \lambda)^{5/3} = 0.58(\cos \lambda)^{5/3} \qquad (23.9.7)$$

446

Hence, within an order of magnitude, the synchronous orbit gives the inferior limit to the position of a satellite. Due to the nature of the condensation process (sec. 17.5), cos λ approaches unity.

There are only two cases known where matter is orbiting inside the synchronous orbit:

(1) *Phobos:* The orbital radius of Phobos is 0.44 of the synchronous orbit. Matter could be brought into circular orbit at this distance only if cos $\lambda = (0.44/0.58)^{3/5}$ or cos $\lambda < 0.85$ and $\lambda > 31°$. There is no apparent reason why condensation should have taken place exclusively so far from the equatorial plane of Mars. Possible explanations for the small orbital radius of Phobos are (a) Mars might have slowed down its spin after the generation of Phobos. This is compatible with the fact that according to the law of isochronism Mars should have had an initial spin period of the order of 5 hr (as with the Earth before the capture of the Moon). This would leave Phobos far outside the synchronous orbit. However, it is difficult to see how the required slowdown could have occurred. (b) Phobos might have been generated when Mars was much smaller than it is today. Even if the mass of a central body increases, the angular momentum of its orbiting body remains constant. Hence the mass must have increased at least in the proportion $(0.58/0.44)^3 = 2.29$. (c) It has sometimes been suggested that Phobos might be a captured satellite. Phobos' small eccentricity and inclination make this suggestion highly unlikely.

(2) *Saturnian rings:* The synchronous orbit is situated in the outer part of the B ring. The minimum value $0.58r_{syn}$ is very close to Saturn, being only 7 percent of Saturn's radius above the surface of the planet. The density in the C ring, which begins at 0.8 of the synchronous orbit, is very small, but this is due to the "ring's own shadow" (see sec. 18.6) and is not likely to be connected with the synchronous orbit. Hence in the Saturnian rings we see a confirmation that matter can also be accreted at some distance inside the synchronous orbit.

23.9.2 Slope of the Bands in the Gravitational Potential Energy Diagram

In ch. 21 we expected theoretically that the bands in which the secondary bodies are located should be horizontal; i.e., independent of the mass of the central body. In the diagram of fig. 21.2.1 we observe a slight slope of the bands. In fact, the gravitational energy at which the C groups are located is larger for Jupiter than for the Sun, and larger for Saturn than for Jupiter. From what has been discussed above, this slope is likely to be due to the fact that T_{ion}/τ values for these three groups differ. The similar difference between the D cloud groups of Saturn and Uranus may be attributed to the same effect.

23.9.3 Further Regularity of the Groups

Besides the regularity of the group structures as a function of T_{ion}/τ, the *total mass* of the secondary bodies depends in a regular way on the mass of the central body. This is shown in fig. 24.3.1.

Furthermore, it seems that the *number of satellites* is a unique function of T_{ion}/τ (fig. 24.3.2). These empirical regularities have not yet been analyzed theoretically. At present we must confine ourselves to stating that our way of analyzing the solar system leads to discoveries of a number of regularities that may be important for the formulation of future theories.

23.10 CONCLUSIONS ABOUT THE MODEL OF PLASMA EMPLACEMENT

The model of plasma emplacement which we have treated in chs. 21 and 23 must necessarily be more speculative than the theories in earlier chapters. The basic phenomenon, ionization at the critical velocity, although well established, is not yet so well understood in detail that we know the behavior of gas mixtures in this respect. Specifically it remains to be clarified what excess of a particular element is necessary to make the critical velocity of this element decisive for the stopping and ionization of the gas. Nor is the distribution of elements between molecular ions sufficiently known. In connection with what has been found in sec. 21.12, this means that we cannot predict the chemical composition of the bodies in a specific group.

Moreover, such predictions cannot yet be verified since the chemical composition of celestial bodies belonging to different clouds is not yet known. We are far from the days when it was claimed with certainty that Jupiter consisted almost entirely of pure solid hydrogen. It is now generally admitted that we do not know with certainty the bulk composition of the Earth and, still less, of any other body (see sec. 20.2–20.5). Hence, detailed, precise predictions will not be possible until the theory is refined under the influence of more adequate experimental and observational data.

The success of the model in giving a virtually complete and nonarbitrary classification of the bodies in the solar system qualifies it as a framework for future theories.

PART E

Special Problems

24

ORIGIN AND EVOLUTION OF THE EARTH-MOON SYSTEM

24.1 THE HETEGONIC ASPECT

There are a large number of theories of the origin of the Moon and of the evolution of the Earth-Moon system. A review is given by Kaula (1971). Neglecting those which obviously are dynamically impossible (unless a number of improbable ad hoc assumptions are introduced) we are left with two alternatives:

(1) The Moon accreted as a satellite of the Earth.

(2) The Moon was originally an independent planet that was later captured by the Earth.

If we confine our analysis to the Earth-Moon system a decision between these two alternatives is very difficult to make, indeed just as difficult as determining the origin of the planetary system from an analysis confined to the planetary system alone. As we have found, a clarification of the evolution of the planetary system is made possible only by comparing it with the satellite systems. This "hetegonic principle" is, indeed, what has made our analysis possible. Similarly, we can expect to understand the evolution of the Earth-Moon system only by comparing it with the other satellite systems.

We have found that accretion of secondary bodies around a primary body is a regular process, which can be described in detail and is summarized in the matrix of table 23.8.1. If these semiempirical laws are applied to the Earth, we see that satellites would be expected to form around this planet. Hence on a qualitative basis alternative (1) is reasonable. However, from a quantitative point of view we find that natural satellites of the Earth should have a mass three or four orders of magnitude smaller than the lunar mass (sec. 24.3). Hence it would, on this basis, seem highly unlikely that the Moon was accreted in the surrounding of the Earth. The fact that the Moon is definitely not a normal satellite has long been recognized.

The capture alternative brings the Moon into the same category as six other satellites (Jupiter 8, 9, 11, and 12, Saturn's Phoebe, and Neptune's Triton). The capture mechanism should be discussed with all these seven bodies in mind. Of these, five are very small and Triton is the only one which is comparable to the Moon in size. Hence the Earth-Moon system is to some extent analogous to the Neptune-Triton system. We can regard both systems as "double-planet" systems.

The reason why we find double planets in these two places in the solar system is obvious from our analysis of the emplacement of the A, B, C, and D clouds (Fig. 21.11.2). In both cases two adjacent clouds overlap, the A and B clouds because of the closeness of the corresponding critical velocities and the C and D clouds because the high T/τ value in the planetary system makes the C cloud extend further out than in the satellite systems. Hence we find that the A cloud is emplaced so close to the B cloud (which has produced Mercury, Venus, and the Earth) that the innermost member of the A cloud, the Moon, comes very close to the outermost member of the B cloud, the Earth. Similarly, the innermost member of the D cloud, Triton, was produced very close to Neptune, the outermost member of the C cloud.

24.2 COMPARISON WITH OTHER SATELLITE SYSTEMS

We know several examples of systems of secondary bodies encircling a primary body: The planetary system, the Jovian, Saturnian, and Uranian systems which are all well developed with five or more secondary bodies. The Martian system with only two satellites may perhaps also be included as a fifth system.

As discussed in previous chapters, the formation of secondary bodies encircling a primary body depends upon the critical velocity effect (ch. 21) and the transfer of angular momentum from a massive primary which rotates and possesses a magnetic dipole field (sec. 1.2, chs. 17 and 23). We have found (ch. 21, fig. 21.2.1) that the bodies in the solar system can be grouped as a function of gravitational energy. We see in fig. 21.2.1 three bands in which all the secondary bodies fall. Whether the tiny satellites of Mars indicate the existence of a fourth band is doubtful. We find further that whenever a band is located far enough above the surface of a central body (beyond the synchronous satellite orbit), we have a formation of secondary bodies in the region.

There are three exceptions to the general validity of the diagram: Venus has no satellites, probably because of its extremely slow rotation and lack of a magnetic field. Further, we find no satellite systems of the normal type around Neptune and the Earth. The reason for this seems to be straightforward. Both these bodies might very well have once produced normal satellite systems but they have been destroyed by the capture of Triton and of the Moon. Mercury has a very slow rotation, probably no magnetic field, and is probably also too small for satellite formation. Whether Pluto has any satellites is not known.

24.3 STRUCTURE OF A NORMAL SATELLITE SYSTEM OF THE EARTH

The regularity of the diagram (fig. 21.2.1) can be used as a basis for reconstructing the normal satellite systems of Neptune and Earth.

As Neptune has a mass which is only about 20 percent larger than that of Uranus, we expect its satellites to be rather similar to the Uranian satellites, but with orbital radii 20 percent larger (see eq. (21.10.2)). Such a system may have existed once, but when Triton was captured and slowly spiraled inward due to tidal interaction (McCord, 1966) it destroyed the original satellites which had masses of only a few percent of the mass of Triton. As McCord suggests, Nereid may be the only survivor (with a strongly perturbed orbit), the other satellites having collided with Triton.

The extrapolation from Uranus to the Earth (table 24.3.1) is more precarious because the mass ratio is as large as 14. The main effect should be a reduction of the orbital radii of the satellites by a factor 14. This would bring the counterpart of Oberon down to an orbital radius of 6.34 Earth radii, and that of Miranda to 1.37 Earth radii, the latter well inside the Roche limit of the Earth.

The accumulation of matter close to the surface of the Earth is likely to have been rather similar to the inner Saturnian satellite group (Rhea-Janus). In fact, the orbital radius of Rhea is 8.7 times the radius of Saturn. A reasonable guess would be that the Earth should have formed about half a dozen satellites (and perhaps also a ring).

TABLE 24.3.1

Earth Satellite Regions (Transposed From Uranian and Martian Systems)

	Orbital radius 10^9 cm	Radii of orbits with equal energy in Earth's gravitational field	
		10^9 cm	Earth radii
Martian satellites			
Deimos	2.35	21.8	34.2
Phobos	0.938	8.6	13.5
Uranian satellites			
Oberon	58.6	4.04	6.34
Titania	43.8	3.02	4.77
Umbriel	26.8	1.85	2.90
Ariel	19.1	(1.32)	(2.07)
Miranda	12.7	(0.87)	(1.37)

( ) Indicates orbits within the Roche limit of the Earth.
(From Alfvén and Arrhenius, 1972a.)

If the Martian system is extrapolated we should in addition expect a group of satellites at a distance of 13.5 to 34.2 Earth radii. The inferred normal satellites of the Earth would not be expected at the exact positions shown in table 24.3.1, but rather in the general regions indicated.

For an estimate of the masses of the Earth's satellites we plot the total mass of the secondary bodies as a function of the mass of the central body (fig. 24.3.1). We see that the total masses of the planets, and of the Jovian, the Saturnian, and the Uranian satellites all lie on a straight line; the extrapolation of this to the Earth gives 2×10^{23} g for the total mass of the Earth's normal satellites.

If we take the Martian system into consideration, the curve should bend downward and give a value of about 10^{22} g for the Earth. This means that the individual satellites may have had masses in the range 10^{21}–10^{22} g. Even

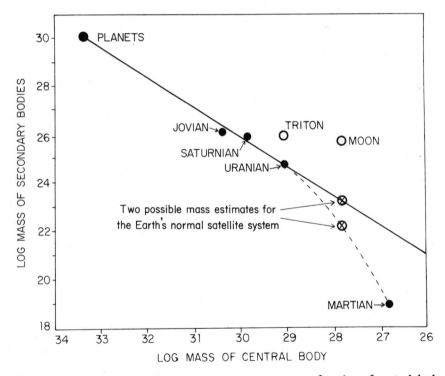

FIGURE 24.3.1.—Total mass of secondary body systems as a function of central body mass. Both Triton and the Moon have much larger masses than expected of normal satellites. Two possible mass estimates for a normal Earth satellite system are shown, one based on an extrapolation from the systems of Jupiter, Saturn, and Uranus, and the other, an interpolation also including the Martian satellite system. (From Alfvén and Arrhenius, 1972a.)

the highest value is only a small fraction of a percent of the lunar mass
$(0.73 \times 10^{26}$ g).

The structure of a system of secondary bodies depends not only on the
mass of the central body as indicated by fig. 21.2.1, but also on its axial
rotation. (This is the main reason why the bands in fig. 21.2.1 have a slope
(sec. 23.9.2) instead of being horizontal, as would be expected from an
extrapolation which assumes that the gravitational energy of a specific
cloud is constant for all central bodies.) Spin of the central body is essential
for the transfer of angular momentum to the surrounding plasma which
condenses and later accretes to secondary bodies.

The relevant parameter in this case is T_{ion}/τ, where τ is the spin period
of the central body and T_{ion} is a characteristic orbital period of the group
of secondary bodies defined in sec. 23.5. Figure 24.3.2 shows the number
of secondary bodies as a function of T_{ion}/τ for the different groups of satellites. Although the curve is purely empirical, theoretically we expect the

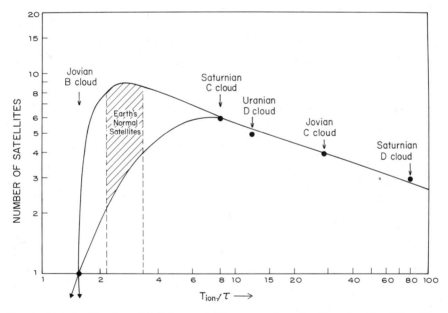

FIGURE 24.3.2.—Number of bodies in a satellite group is a function of T_{ion}/τ (where τ is
the spin period of the central body and T_{ion} is a characteristic orbital period of the bodies
in the group (sec. 23.5)). The groups of satellites are the outermost Saturnian satellites
(Saturnian D cloud), Galilean satellites (Jovian C cloud), Uranian satellites (Uranian D
cloud), inner Saturnian satellites (Saturnian C cloud), and innermost Jovian satellites
(Jovian B cloud). Assuming that the Earth's satellite system would fall into the pattern
established by these groups of satellites, the Earth may once have had just a few or as
many as 9 or 10 normal satellites. (From Alfvén and Arrhenius, 1972a.)

number of satellites to drop to zero as T_{ion}/τ approaches unity (ch. 23), and this is clearly indicated in fig. 24.3.2. As there are no observational points between $T_{ion}/\tau = 1.6$ and 8.4, the shape of the curve in this region remains uncertain. A lower limit to this part of the curve is obtained by placing the maximum of the curve at 8.4 (the point corresponding to inner Saturnian satellites), while an upper limit may be estimated by a freehand extrapolation with a maximum as high as 9 or 10 before the curve drops toward zero.

If we want to make a conjecture about the number of normal satellites of the Earth, we need to know the value of T/τ for the Earth. Using the present value of the Earth's spin period, which is 24 hr, we obtain $T/\tau = 0.36$. Obviously, we should use instead the spin period of the Earth before the Moon's capture resulted in tidal braking of the spin. There are various ways of estimating this period. Gerstenkorn (1955) found a precapture spin period for the Earth of about 2.6 hr. If we assume the Earth once had the entire angular momentum of the present Earth-Moon system, a value of about 4.1 hr is obtained.

Yet another way is to use the empirical observation that the quantity $\tau\Theta^{1/2}$ is constant for the planets, where Θ is the average density of a planet (see sec. 13.4). Applying this relation to the Earth and Jupiter we obtain a period of about 4.7 hr, while the value of 3.4 hr is indicated by applying it to the Earth and Saturn instead.

All these considerations indicate a value of the original spin period of the Earth somewhere in the range 3–5 hr, thus placing the value of T/τ in the range of about 2–3. Unfortunately, this falls in the uncertain interpolation region of the curve in fig. 24.3.2. We cannot be sure if the number of original satellites was 2 or 3 or as high as 8 or 9.

Furthermore, if the Martian satellites, which are excluded from the scheme of fig. 24.3.2, are included, we may expect another group of perhaps four or five more satellites for the Earth.

In conclusion we see that if we apply the principle that the Earth should be treated in the same way as the other planets, we arrive at a satellite system which, even if we cannot at present reconstruct it in detail, in any case is very different from the Earth-Moon system.

24.4 THE CAPTURE THEORY

According to Kaula (1971), the capture hypothesis (Alfvén, 1942, 1943a, 1946, 1954) "is an improbability, not an impossibility." However, he does not clarify why a lunar capture is improbable. In reality both observations and theoretical evidence indicate the contrary.

In the solar system there are six retrograde satellites (see table 2.1.3).

There is general agreement that all of them must have been captured. Figure 24.4.1 shows their orbital inclination and distance r_{sc}, with the radius R_c of the planet they encircle as unit. (If instead the distance to the closest Lagrangian point, which may be more relevant to the capture process, is chosen, a rather similar diagram is obtained.)

The diagram shows that the orbits of the small retrograde bodies are situated in the region $r_{sc}/R_c = 200–350$ and $i = 145°–175°$. We can well imagine that Triton originally was located in the same region but that tidal interaction has brought it closer to Neptune. The reason for this is that Triton is much larger than the other retrograde satellites, which are much too small to produce significant tidal effects. Hence observation indicates that a capture mechanism exists which results in wide capture orbits, subsequently contracting if the captured body is large enough to cause tides.

A body like the Moon may very well be captured in this manner. Furthermore, mechanisms exist (Gerstenkorn, 1955) by which the body can be transferred from such a shrinking capture orbit into a prograde orbit of the present lunar type. Therefore there could be no fundamental objection to the capture theory.

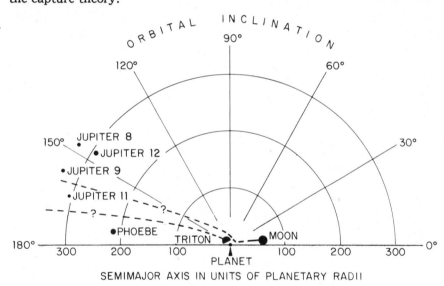

ORBITAL PARAMETERS OF CAPTURED SATELLITES AND POSSIBLE ORBITAL
EVOLUTION OF MOON AND TRITON

FIGURE 24.4.1.—Possible evolution (dashed lines) of the orbits of Triton and the Moon. These bodies are massive enough for tidal effects to modify their orbits from the typical large semimajor axis, retrograde orbit characteristic of the smaller, presumably captured satellites shown in the diagram. (From Alfvén and Arrhenius, 1972a.)

Capture requires that the body approach the planet in an orbit with parameters within rather narrow limits. Thus if a body approaches a planet in a random orbit, the chance that the approach will immediately lead to capture is very small. The most likely result of the encounter is that the body will leave the region of the planet with its orbit more or less changed. It is probably this fact which is behind objections to the capture theory.

However, we learn from Kepler that if the body leaves the neighborhood of the planet after an encounter, it will move in an ellipse which brings it back to the vicinity of the orbit of the planet, once or twice for every revolution. If the body is not in resonance, it will have innumerable new opportunities to encounter the planet (fig. 24.4.2). Hence even if at any specific encounter capture is "horrendously improbable" as Kaula puts it, subsequent encounters will occur a "horrendously" large number of times, so that the probability of a final capture becomes quite large, and may approach unity.

In fact, we can state as a general theorem (with specific exceptions) that *if two bodies move in crossing orbits and they are not in resonance, the eventual result will be either a collision or a capture.* (By "crossing" we mean that the projections of the orbits on the invariant plane intersect each other. There are some special cases where the theorem is not valid; e.g., if one of the bodies is ejected to infinity at an encounter.)

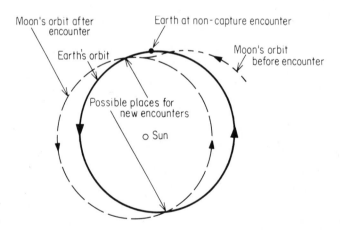

FIGURE 24.4.2.—If initially the orbits of the Earth and the planet Moon intersected, there would have been frequent encounters between the two bodies. Capture at any given encounter is unlikely. The most probable result is a deflection leading to a new orbit. However, this new orbit would also intersect the Earth's orbit so that a large number of new encounters would occur. The most probable final result is capture. (From Alfvén and Arrhenius, 1972a.)

Because celestial mechanics is time-reversible, a capture cannot be permanent unless orbital energy is dissipated. For small bodies the main sink of energy is likely to be viscous effects or collision with other bodies. For large bodies like the Moon or Triton, tidal interaction may make the capture permanent and will also produce drastic changes in the orbit after capture.

So far there is no detailed theory which explains the capture of the individual retrograde satellites. If a theory consistent with present-day conditions in the solar system is not forthcoming, it may be fruitful to turn to suggestions (e.g., Kaula, 1974; Kaula and Harris, 1973) that capture occurred during an accretionary phase of the hetegonic era. Satellite capture during accretion of a planet is indeed dynamically possible.

24.5 TIDAL EVOLUTION OF THE LUNAR ORBIT

Having discussed the Earth-Moon system by comparison with other satellite systems we shall now consider earlier studies of lunar orbital evolution which investigated tidal effects. To sum up the most important steps in this extensive discussion, Gerstenkorn (1955) concluded that the Moon was captured in an almost hyperbolic retrograde ellipse with an inclination $i = 150°$. It was shown by Goldreich (1968) that, because of a complicated transitional effect, the calculations were not altogether correct. This caused Gerstenkorn (1968; 1969) to make a new calculation which indicated a capture from a polar or even prograde orbit with a very small perigee. Independently Singer (1968; 1970) made calculations with similar results.

Furthermore, it was pointed out (Alfvén and Arrhenius, 1969) that the tidal theory which is used in all these calculations is highly unrealistic. Especially at close distances, a number of complicating effects are likely to arise so that calculations which are mathematically accurate do not represent reality. Resonance effects of the Allan type (Allan, 1967) may also interfere, preventing the Moon from ever coming close to the Roche limit and considerably prolonging the duration of the close approach. This would explain the long immersion of the Moon in the Earth's (possibly enhanced) magnetosphere, indicated by the natural remanent magnetization of lunar rocks in the age range 4–3 Gyr (e.g., Fuller, 1974; Alfvén and Arrhenius, 1972a; Alfvén and Lindberg, 1974).

All the possible schemes for the evolution of the lunar orbit discussed above should be taken with a grain of salt. They may describe the general type of evolution, but an exact treatment appears futile as long as the important secondary effects are not well understood. Hence the formal objections to Gerstenkorn's original model do not necessarily mean that this is less likely to describe the general type of orbital evolution.

Calculation of the time and duration of the close encounter also remains uncertain because of the poorly understood resonance and dissipation effects. For this reason the actual record in the Earth, meteorites, and the Moon would provide the most direct information on time and type of encounter.

In Gerstenkorn's original model the close approach would necessarily lead to large-scale heating, exceptional but possibly localized tidal effects, and possibly bombardment of both bodies with lunar debris if the Moon came within the Roche limit (Kopal, 1966). Combining amplitude indications from tidally controlled sediments and reef structures with the evidence for culminating breakup of meteorites at about 0.9 Gyr, we suggested as one of two likely alternatives that this may mark the time of closest approach if a development of this type actually occurred (Alfvén and Arrhenius, 1969). There is, however, some doubt about the preponderance of tidal sediments in this period and about the reliability of stromalites as tidal indicators when extended into the Precambrian. Nor does the high incidence of meteorite breakup in itself provide a compelling argument for a lunar interaction.

The second alternative (Alfvén and Arrhenius, 1969) (namely, an orbital evolution modified by resonance phenomena) would result in the Moon's residing in the Earth's environment for a considerable time and at a distance of the order 5–10 Earth radii (fig. 24.5.1); hence energy dissipation would take place at a more modest rate. This alternative is supported by the results subsequently obtained by exploration of the Moon.

Assuming that the generation of mare basalts on the Moon ranging from 3.7 to 3.3 Gyr (Papanastassiou and Wasserburg, 1971a) or perhaps as low as 3.0 Gyr (Murthy et al., 1971) was caused by collisions during the contraction of the Moon's capture orbit (see sec. 24.6), the closest approach to the Earth would have occurred in the range of 2.8–3.3 Gyr. The paucity of preserved sediments on the continents dating from this period and earlier could possibly be the result of the extensive and long-lasting tidal effects associated with this proposed lunar orbital evolution. However, it is difficult, given our present state of knowledge, to distinguish such an effect from the cumulative effects of damage incurred continually during geologic time.

24.6 DESTRUCTION OF A NORMAL SATELLITE
SYSTEM

In sec. 24.3 we discussed the possibility that the Earth originally had a satellite system with properties of other normal, prograde systems. If such a normal system existed, the only likely possibility for its destruction would be by the Moon as its orbit evolved after capture. With its orbit slowly contracting due to tidal dissipation, the Moon would sweep out the space

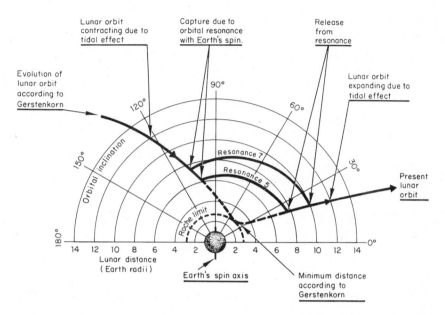

FIGURE 24.5.1.—Noncatastrophic alternative; spin-orbit resonance prevents the Moon from reaching the Roche limit. The retrograde lunar capture orbit contracts due to tidal dissipation until resonance between the lunar orbital period and the spin period of the Earth locks the Moon in a slowly expanding orbit. Since the Moon never comes very close, no breakup or autoejection of debris occurs and the tides do not reach catastrophic heights. When the orbital inclination has decreased below a critical angle (suggested in the diagram at about 25°), the resonance locking is broken and the Moon recedes to its present orbit at 60 Earth radii. The dotted curve represents the catastropic alternative (Moon reaching the Roche limit). (From Alfvén and Arrhenius, 1969.)

occupied by the normal satellites and either collide with them or eject them from their orbits; collision with the Earth or ejection to infinity could result from the latter type of perturbation. Such a development has already been proposed by McCord (1966) to explain the absence of a normal satellite system around Neptune; i.e., the satellites have been swept up by Triton after its capture by Neptune.

It is interesting to speculate about a development of this type for the Earth-Moon system since it implies that original Earth satellites now may be buried in the surface of the Moon where it might be possible to distinguish them on a chronological and perhaps compositional basis from the majority of planetesimals that impacted on the Moon during the much earlier terminal stage of accretion (as discussed in ch. 12). The late occurrence in time of the excavation of Mare Imbrium (Turner et al., 1971; Papanastassiou and Wasserburg, 1971b) and the low ages of the mare basalts have prompted several other authors to consider the possibility of a collision with a preexisting Earth satellite (Ganapathy et al., 1971; Kaula, 1971). It is, however, difficult to exclude entirely the possibility that some of the planetesimals in the Moon's or the Earth's formative jet streams survived as long as 0.5 to 1 Gyr after runaway accretion. In the latter case it is possible that such material, distributed in the Earth's orbit, caused collisional perturbation of the Moon's precapture orbit, thereby contributing to the capture of the Moon (Kaula and Harris, 1973; Kaula, 1974; Wood and Mittler, 1974; Öpik, 1972).

The low relative velocities suggested by some features of the near-circular basins on the Moon would also point at Earth satellite impact, as suggested by Kaula (1971). However, the accretion conditions in the parental jet stream would also lead to low relative velocities between accreting planetesimals (ch. 12).

The large near-circular basins on the Moon would seem to be features which could mark the resting places of original Earth satellites (or possibly of late, large lunar jet-stream members). Stuart-Alexander and Howard (1970) list nine such basins larger than 500 km, all located on the front

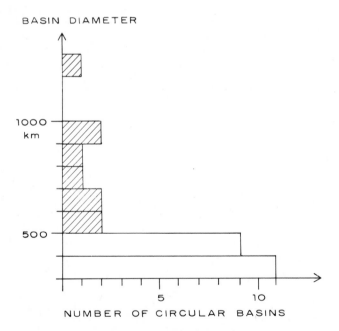

FIGURE 24.6.1.—Size distribution of circular basins on the Moon. The few large basins (indicated by diagonal stripes) may be the final resting places of either large lunar or terrestrial planetesimals or of the small "normal" satellites of the Earth. (From Stuart-Alexander and Howard, 1970.)

side of the Moon (fig. 24.6.1). Five or six of these basins contain positive mascons (Muller and Sjögren, 1969); their mass excesses are in the range 0.4–1.4×10²¹ g. By comparison, Earth's normal satellites would have had individual total masses in the range 10^{21}–10^{22} g (sec. 24.3). Urey and MacDonald (1971) have brought forward a number of arguments favoring the view that the mass excesses represent the projectile materials rather than the alternative possibility that they were formed by a sequence of basalt eruptions from an interior melt reservoir as proposed by Wood (1970).

A relatively large number of mascons has already been found (12 positive and 1 negative in the surveyed region bounded by latitude ±50° and longitude ±110°) and they extend into low mass ranges (present lower detection limit ∼10^{20} g). Hence it is unlikely that mascons are uniquely caused by impact of tellurian satellites. As has been pointed out above, however, low relative velocities must be a characteristic of planetesimals in a jet stream when t approaches $t_c/2$. Subsonic relative velocities, which appear necessary to prevent net loss from the impact crater (Urey and MacDonald, 1971), could thus be achieved both between the Moon and its planetesimals during accretion and between the Moon and normal Earth satellites during the contraction of the capture orbit.

Only about half the large basins which possibly could contain satellites have positive mascons. Hence the presumed projectiles in some cases did not have very high density relative to the lunar crust or they impacted with supersonic velocity. Only in the case of the Imbrian impact does enough information now exist to suggest the timing and other characteristics of the event.

24.7 ACCRETION AND THE HEAT STRUCTURE OF THE MOON

The magnitude of the accretion rate of a planet and the rate changes during the formative period are of particular interest since they would largely control the primary heat structure of the body. Secondary modifications of this structure may arise from buildup of radiogenic heat, from thermal conductivity, and from convection. The planetesimal accretion rate is determined by the gravitational cross section of a growing planetesimal and by the particle density in the surrounding region. This process is discussed in detail in secs. 12.9–12.11.

The accretion of the Moon was characterized by slow growth and a late runaway accretion phase (fig. 12.9.1). The greatest heating of the lunar surface due to impacting planetesimals occurred during this phase when the radius of the Moon had already attained 0.8 of its present size (fig. 12.11.1). During runaway accretion planetesimal velocity at impact is high

enough to melt the majority of accreting material, and transient temperatures at impact probably exceed 1800K.

The primordial heat profile of the Moon indicates that the interior of the
Moon was originally at a relatively low temperature and that the maximum
temperature and molten region would have been close to the surface. The
evidence available to date suggests that the deep interior of the Moon is
in the melting range, and hence that radiogenic heating of the interior has
altered the primary heat structure.

The sustained, average temperature over the surface of the embryonic
Moon is harder to predict since the rate of heat loss by radiation from, and
conduction through, the surface are controlled by a number of factors for
which we still lack sufficient scaling experience. Such factors are depth of
implantation and mode of dissipation of energy, size and velocity distribution of impacting planetesimals, and the properties of the impact-generated
atmosphere. Generalized knowledge of these parameters will hopefully be
derived from continued lunar exploration. Information on some related
parameters is provided by the impact waves recorded in the ringed maria
(Van Dorn, 1968, 1969) and from detailed analysis of the Imbrian impact
(Urey and MacDonald, 1971) in combination with direct study of returned
lunar samples and field relationships on the Moon.

Since the dominant fraction of mass and energy is contributed by the
larger planetesimals, the heating effects caused by them are of major
importance. During and after runaway accretion each major impact must
have resulted in implantation of a large fraction of the energy at considerable depth ($\sim 10^5$ cm). This would lead, particularly at subsonic impact, to
formation of molten pools insulated by the low-density fallout from the
explosion clouds. In each such magma chamber differentiation would be
expected to generate a sequence of heavy cumulates on the bottom and
light ones on the top. At each remelting event the low-density differentiates
would be transferred upward toward the new surface but with the previously settled heavy component remaining in place.

Regardless of the average sustained temperature in the outer layer of the
accreting embryo, which may be low or high depending on the accretion
rate, the integrated effect due to this phenomenon would be that of a heat
front sweeping low-density components from the interior to form a light
surface crust where the heat-generating radioactive nuclides would also
accumulate. In this way it is possible to understand both the interior
structure and the chemical composition and formation of the crust of the
Moon and other bodies in the solar system. (See detailed discussion in ch. 12.)

The maximum value of energy flux at the time of runaway accretion t_c
determines the maximum temperature reached and also the extent to which
simultaneous melting occurred over the entire surface. In a case like the
Moon (in contrast to the Earth) this parameter is sensitive to the value

chosen for the duration of infall of matter to the lunar jet stream t_{inf}, since t_c and t_{inf} here are of the same order of magnitude. For reasons discussed above we cannot yet quantitatively translate energy flux into surface temperature; hence we depend on direct observation for scaling. The most significant information now available comes from the distribution of the rubidium and strontium isotopes in lunar rocks (Papanastassiou and Wasserburg, 1971b). These results suggest that melting in the outer layer during terminal accretion was extensive enough to completely segregate Rb and Sr within individual reservoirs, but that the melt reservoirs did not equilibrate between each other.

Differentiation features on the Moon contrast in some significant respects with those we are used to seeing on Earth. For this reason it has been suggested (Arrhenius, 1969; Arrhenius et al., 1970; Gast, 1971) that the differentiation taking place before accretion could be responsible for the lunar surface composition. Similar proposals have been made to explain the layering of the Earth (Eucken, 1944b; Anders, 1968; Turekian and Clark, 1969) and could, in principle, be rationalized on the basis of partial overlap between the A and B clouds (sec. 24.8). However, it seems that the inescapable accretional heating may, in itself, satisfactorily account for currently known facts, including the loss of potassium and other volatile elements from the Moon.

Gast (1971, 1972), in an argument for the alternative of pre-accretionary differentiation, has suggested that volatile elements such as potassium could not be effectively removed from the Moon to the extent observed. The reason would be that the slowness of diffusion would prevent evaporative losses from occurring except from the most surficial layer of lunar magma basins. With the accretional heating considered here, however, violent convection must have been caused by planetesimal impact and gas release within the melt. The impacting projectiles could furnish one source of such escaping gas. Furthermore, because of the low lunar oxygen fugacity, magnesium silicates dissociate into gaseous MgO and SiO at an appreciable rate in the temperature range of 1400–1700K, leading to the extensive frothing observed in lunar lava (Arrhenius et al., 1970). Convection and gas scavenging hence would contribute to efficient transfer of volatiles from the melt into the temporary lunar atmosphere. Such an atmosphere would be rapidly ionized and removed, as seen from the prompt ionization of the clouds caused by artificial impact on the lunar surface and by gas eruptions (Freeman et al., 1972).

Hence it would seem that the separation and loss of volatile elements characteristic of the Moon (and to a lesser extent of the Earth) are a direct consequence of an accretional heat front, differentiating the outer 300–400-km layer of the Moon and the outer core and entire mantle in the case of the Earth.

24.8 COMPOSITION OF THE MOON

In Laplacian types of models all the source material for planets and satellites is assumed to be present at one time in the solar nebula and to be uniformly mixed to give a "cosmic composition." Striking differences in composition (see sec. 20.5) such as among the outer planets, the satellites of Jupiter, and in the Earth-Moon system are either left unexplained or ascribed to ad hoc processes without theoretical basis. In the present theory for emplacement of matter around the central bodies (sec. 21.11–21.12), controlled by the critical velocity phenomenon and ablation of trans-planetary material, the Moon and Mars would have formed from the A cloud, and the inner terrestrial planets from the B cloud, inheriting the specific and different chemical properties of these clouds. From these considerations the low density of the Moon and Mars compared to the inner terrestrial planets is understandable. The partial overlap of these two clouds may also provide an explanation for the possible inhomogeneous accretion of the Earth (sec. 24.9).

24.9 CONCLUSIONS

Our analysis, which is essentially a development of the planetesimal approach, leads to the following conclusions:

(1) The Moon originated as a planet ("Luna") which accreted in a jet stream in the vicinity of the Earth's jet stream. Together with Mars, it derived from the A cloud.

(2) The condensed material forming the Moon and the terrestrial planets would be derived (a) from condensable impurities in the infalling A cloud and B cloud (secs. 21.11–21.12), (b) by electromagnetic capture in the A and B clouds of transplanetary dust as described in sec. 21.12, (c) by ablation of transplanetary material in these plasma clouds (sec. 21.12), and (d) by capture of transplanetary material in the jet streams of the terrestrial planets (sec. 21.12).

The processes (a), (c), and (d) would contribute to making the jet streams of Moon and Earth chemically dissimilar. However, because of their closeness in space, temporary overlap of one or the other is possible in analogy with observations in meteorite streams (sec. 22.9.1). This could provide an explanation for layering (heterogeneous accretion) of either planet.

(3) We cannot decide at the present time whether the lunar jet stream was located outside or inside Earth's jet stream.

(4) Due to its smaller mass, the Moon accreted with a cool interior and reached a maximum temperature at about 80 percent of its present radius. In the surrounding mantle all material was processed through high transient

temperatures in the hot-spot front, but the entire present lunar crust was probably never all molten at the same time.

(5) The original lunar orbit intersected Earth's orbit (or was brought to intersection by some perturbation). This led to frequent Earth-Moon encounters which eventually resulted in capture.

(6) The Moon was probably captured in a retrograde orbit in the same way as the other six captured satellites were. Such a process may have taken place at a time when Earth still was accreting planetesimals. A capture by a very close encounter is less probable but cannot be excluded.

(7) From the regular distribution of secondary bodies in the solar system, one may conclude that Earth had an original satellite system. The structure of such a system depends on the mass of the central body. Extrapolation from the Uranian system to Earth suggests that Earth should have had a group of perhaps half a dozen small bodies. To this we should possibly add a group obtained by extrapolation of the Martian system to a larger central body mass. Hence Earth may originally have had a total of 5 to 10 normal satellites.

(8) During the tidal evolution of the lunar orbit the original satellite system was destroyed, as was that of Neptune. Most or all of the satellites may have been swept up by the Moon. It is possible that some of the near-circular basins and mascons on the Moon were produced in this way, but we cannot exclude the possibility that they are due to late planetesimals.

THE PROPERTIES OF THE
EARLY SUN

25.1 ON THE USE OF SOLAR-SYSTEM DATA TO STUDY THE EARLY SUN

Practically all other attempts to reconstruct the history of the solar system have been *based* on a more or less reasonable hypothesis about the properties of the early Sun. As has already been pointed out in the introduction, such a procedure is dangerous because in reality we know next to nothing about the early Sun. Theories about the formation of stars from interstellar clouds are speculative, and they seem to lack any observational confirmation. Such theories generally assume a basic process of gravitational collapse. This assumption is not necessarily correct; a "stellesimal" formation, in analogy with the "planetesimal" formation of planets and satellites, would be an interesting, and perhaps more attractive, alternative.

In the present study of the evolution of the solar system an attempt is made to avoid the uncertainties inherent in making assumptions about the early Sun. Our aim has not been to understand exclusively or preferentially the formation of planets around the Sun, but to develop a general theory of the formation of secondary bodies, planets or satellites, around a primary body, which may be either the Sun or a planet. The advantages of the method have been discussed in secs. 1.2 and 16.9, one of them being that the mechanism of formation of secondary bodies can be based largely on studies of the satellite systems *without necessarily making any hypothesis about the primeval Sun* (see fig. 16.9.1).

In this way it was possible to define the basic processes by which secondary bodies were formed. If we then make the plausible assumption that the planetary system has been formed by the same processes that have produced satellites, we are able to make important conclusions about the primeval Sun during the period the planets formed around it.

Using this method we shall here calculate the mass, magnetic field, and spin of the early Sun, and comment on its light and solar wind emission.

25.2 SOLAR MASS

As the empirical basis for our estimate we use:

(1) Diagram of the band structure of the secondary-body groups, fig. 21.2.1.

The diagram has been plotted with the mass of the planet-forming Sun assumed to be equal to the present mass. If this is incorrect we should expect a systematic displacement of the bands in the planetary system.

There is no doubt that such a displacement does exist. The bands are not horizontal as expected theoretically according to ch. 21 but are sloping. However, the bands in the different satellite systems also show a similar slope. An explanation of this phenomenon is given in sec. 23.9.2.

Hence to conclude that the mass of the planet-producing Sun was different from the present mass does not seem justified.

(2) Table of normalized distances (table 23.6.1). The values for the planets are larger by about a factor of two than the values for the Jovian and Saturnian satellites. In principle this may be due to a mass loss by the Sun of a factor $2^{1/2}$. However, the difference in the T_{ion}/τ values are probably a sufficient cause for the difference.

We conclude that there are no certain indications of a change in the solar mass since the formation of the planetary system, but changes of perhaps 25 percent in either direction cannot be excluded.

25.3 SOLAR MAGNETIC FIELD

The fact that the Sun has transferred angular momentum as far out as Neptune and Pluto makes it necessary to assume that, out to these distances, the solar magnetic field has been larger than the transplanetary field.

We do not know the strength of the transplanetary field, but it is not very likely that it was less than the present value of the "galactic field" which is believed to be of the order of 3×10^{-6} G. If a field deriving from a solar dipole $\mu_\odot$ should exceed 3×10^{-6} G at a distance of 6×10^{14} cm we find from

$$\mu = Br^3 \tag{25.3.1}$$

that

$$\mu_\odot > 3 \times 10^{-6}(6 \times 10^{14})^3 = 6.5 \times 10^{38} \text{ G cm}^3 \tag{25.3.2}$$

This is a very high value but it is difficult to see how it could be avoided in any theory involving hydromagnetic transfer of angular momentum; in order to transfer angular momentum to a region in space the solar magnetic field must dominate in that region. Fields of this magnitude or larger are suggested by the magnetization phenomena in meteorites (Brecher, 1971, 1972a,c; Brecher and Arrhenius, 1974, 1975).

If the Sun during the hetegonic era had its present radius, its surface field would have been 2×10^6 G. If the radius of the Sun when Pluto formed were 10^{12} cm (Brownlee and Cox, 1961), the surface field would be >650 G. This value is well within the range of observed stellar magnetic fields, whereas the value assuming the present radius of the Sun is higher than any observational value.

The solar magnetic field must also have been strong enough to bring the plasma around it into partial corotation and to support the plasma until this was achieved. The requirement for this is model-dependent and does not allow a very stringent derivation of the necessary magnetic field.

25.4 SOLAR SPIN PERIOD

As an introductory remark it should be pointed out that there are a number of papers claiming that the Sun has a swiftly rotating core. There seems to be no convincing observational support of these speculations. From a theoretical point of view, it has never been proven that such a situation is stable, and it seems indeed unlikely that it is. On the other hand, the angular velocity of the Sun is a function of latitude, and, as isorotation is likely to prevail in the interior of the Sun, the angular velocity in the solar interior will depend on the interior structure of the solar magnetic field. Reasonable models of this have been discussed by Alfvén and Fälthammar (1963). We shall not discuss these problems further here but only state that the differential rotation is a small effect that we need not consider in this context. In the following we assume that the whole Sun rotates with roughly the same angular velocity.

The slope of the curves in fig. 23.6.1 depends on the value of T_{ion}/τ. From this slope we can calculate the spin period of the Sun when the terrestrial planets and the giant planets were produced.

The slope of the curve for the terrestrial planets is intermediate between the curves for the Uranian satellites ($T_{ion}/\tau = 12$) and the inner Saturnian satellites ($T_{ion}/\tau = 8$) so we may use the value $T_{ion}/\tau = 10$. This implies that the Sun had a spin period of 20 days when the terrestrial planets were formed. This is close to the present value (25 days).

Concerning the giant planets, the slope of the curve is intermediate between those for the Jovian satellites ($T_{ion}/\tau = 29$) and the outer Saturnian satellites ($T_{ion}/\tau = 80$). However, the latter group is highly irregular, and should not be given much weight. Hence the only conclusion we could draw is that the T_{ion}/τ value should be *much* larger than 29, and hence that the solar spin period should be less than 1 yr. But we cannot exclude its having been very small, e.g., a few days, because the value of T_{ion}/τ may take on any value up to infinity.

25.5 SOLAR RADIATION, SOLAR WIND

Comparing the planetary system and the satellite systems, we have found no reason to introduce parameters of the central bodies other than mass, magnetic moment, and spin. *None of the observational facts we have analyzed here makes it necessary to conclude that the early Sun had any emission of light, ionizing radiation, heat, or solar wind.* The early irradiation recorded by particle tracks and by surface-implanted gases (sec. 22.9) could as well be due to accelerated particles in the super-prominences as to emission from the Sun. The former activity, associated with the angular momentum transfer, would presumably be large compared to the latter, which on the basis of preserved evidence could be negligible. A solar wind of the present type is excluded by the strong solar magnetic field and the high plasma densities in interplanetary space due to the infall of gas.

Whatever is the dominant source of the observed irradiation features, they may provide an upper limit for the solar source. Although the total dose can be fairly accurately measured, the flux cannot yet be estimated for lack of a value for the time interval (which would be of the order of 10^3–10^4 yr at a flux corresponding to the present solar wind and flare activity at 1 AU (Lal, 1972b)). However, the energy spectrum, which can be approximated from the irradiation profiles, would be expected to be permuted by major enhancement of solar activity due to a hypothetical Hayashi phase or a "solar gale."

In spite of the many thousand measurements of irradiated grains carried out on the various groups of meteorites and in lunar rocks, no noticeable deviation in the steepness spectrum has been observed (Macdougall et al., 1974). This suggests that during the time period covered by the irradiation record no such dramatic changes in the properties of the Sun took place. This does not exclude their occurrence prior to the hetegonic era.

Violent solar events have been introduced ad hoc in other theories in order to avoid specific difficulties in the late part of the hetegonic era or to remove records that conflict with present evidence (sec. 26.10.1). Such difficulties do not occur in the present treatment.

Although we consequently see no need for assumptions of strongly enhanced solar activity any time during or after the hetegonic era, no evidence seems to preclude a solar activity of the present kind throughout the development of the solar system. A solar thermal radiation of the same magnitude as the present one would, aside from the influence on condensation of volatiles, probably not produce very conspicuous effects. The high density of Mercury is sometimes attributed to its heating by the Sun. This may be correct, but does not necessarily follow. An analogous increase in density is found among the satellites of Jupiter (sec. 20.5.11) where it certainly has another cause.

25.6 EFFECTS PRODUCED BY A D-BURNING SUN

Some time ago, Brownlee and Cox (1961) concluded that before the Sun reached its present state it must have spent about 200 Myr in a deuterium-burning state. According to their model the Sun had a radius of 10^{12} cm during this stage (fig. 25.6.1).

This model did not receive much attention when it was first proposed, probably because at about the same time it became "generally accepted" that there could be no deuterium in the galactic medium from which the Sun supposedly formed (because the big bang could not produce deuterium!).

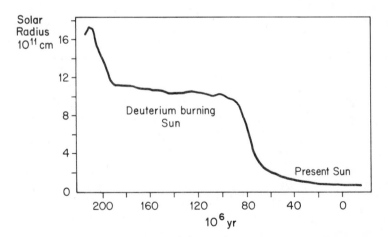

FIGURE 25.6.1.—The Brownlee-Cox model of solar evolution through a deuterium-burning stage. Under the assumptions that the initial content of deuterium corresponds to the deuterium/hydrogen ratio of the Earth and that the energy transport in the deuterium-burning Sun is nonconvective, the radius of the Sun would have remained at about 16 times the present value during the deuterium burning. This stage would last about 10^8 yr before contraction to the present size. A different initial content of deuterium (which is possible) would mainly change the duration of the deuterium-burning stage. (From Brownlee and Cox, 1961.)

Radio observations, however, have recently demonstrated that deuterium does exist in space (Solomon and Woolf, 1972), and Geiss and Reeves have suggested (1972) that the original deuterium content of the Sun can be reconstructed from the He³ content in the solar wind. Whether the Sun was produced by a gravitational collapse or by "stellesimal" accretion, it now seems unavoidable that the primeval Sun must have contained a reasonably large quantity of deuterium which must have been burned before the Sun could reach its present hydrogen-burning state.

It is beyond the scope of this treatise to analyze the evolution of the Sun in more detail. We shall only cite the results of a preliminary study (Alfvén, 1963) which indicate the following sequence of events:

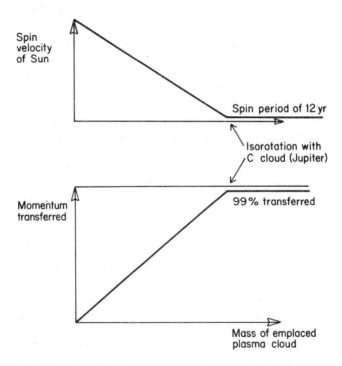

FIGURE 25.6.2.—Below: Angular momentum transferred to the C cloud as a function of the mass processed through this cloud. The transfer of momentum is proportional to the cumulative mass until a saturation is reached, when almost all the momentum is transferred. Above: Angular velocity of the Sun after the transfer. When saturation is reached, the solar angular velocity equals the Kepler velocity of Jupiter. If the transfer takes place when the Sun is in the deuterium-burning state with a moment of inertia 200 times the present value, the angular velocity increases by a factor of 200 as the Sun contracts, producing the present spin period (25 days) of the Sun when contraction is completed.

(1) The Sun was formed as a D-burning star with $R = 1.1 \times 10^{12}$ cm and $\tau = 20$ days.

(2) Terrestrial planets were formed. This required a rather small change in spin.

(3) Giant planets were formed. The Sun transferred 99.4 percent of its spin angular momentum and was brought into isorotation with Jupiter: $\tau = 12$ yr (fig. 25.6.2).

(4) After consuming its deuterium the Sun contracted to its present size, thereby increasing its spin to the present value which is determined by this process.

(5) There has probably been no large change in the mass or the spin of the Sun since the completion of process (4) (fig. 25.6.3).

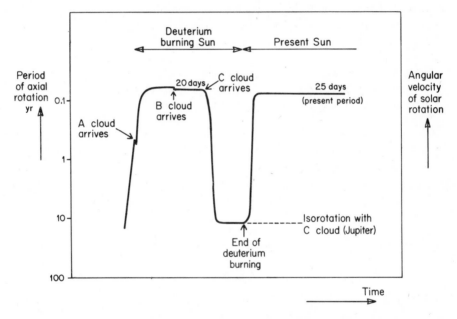

FIGURE 25.6.3.—Angular velocity of the Sun as a function of time. It is assumed that the solar system does not lose any angular momentum to infinity (angular momentum is conserved within the solar system). As the Sun contracts, its moment of inertia decreases, so that its angular velocity increases. The contraction during deuterium burning is small and the angular velocity remains constant. The B cloud (forming the Earth, Venus, and Mercury) forms during this period but does not change the solar angular momentum appreciably. (The A cloud may have formed earlier). When the C cloud (from which the giant planets accrete) forms, the Sun loses most of its angular momentum and is brought into isorotation with Jupiter (period 12 yr). When the deuterium is totally consumed, the Sun contracts to its present state, with the moment of inertia decreasing by a factor of 200. The angular velocity increases by the same factor, accounting for the present angular velocity of the Sun.

25.7 REMARKS ON THE FORMATION OF STARS

There is a general belief that stars are forming by gravitational collapse; in spite of vigorous efforts no one has yet found any observational indication of confirmation. Thus the "generally accepted" theory of stellar formation may be one of a hundred unsupported dogmas which constitute a large part of present-day astrophysics.

As was demonstrated in secs. 9.7–9.8, the isochronism of spins gives good support for the view that celestial bodies as different as asteroids of mass $\sim 10^{18}$ g and the giant planets of mass $\sim 10^{30}$ g are formed by the accretional process of ch. 12. We can completely rule out gravitational collapse.

Now the question arises: If a certain accretional process is effective over 12 orders of magnitude in mass, why should it not be valid over 3 orders of magnitude more, so as to include a star like the Sun with mass 2×10^{33} g?

There are good reasons to believe that stars are forming in dark clouds. The development of radio and infrared astronomy is now supplying us with a richness of data about their properties. As has been pointed out in sec. 15.1 there is clear evidence that hydromagnetic and plasma processes are of decisive importance. In the present analysis we have looked at the star-formation problem using solar-system data as the empirical basis.

The properties of the source cloud which we have derived seems to be reconcilable with the observed properties of dark clouds. A further study of these phenomena may lead to a new understanding of how stars are formed. A hydromagnetic treatment combining dark cloud observations and solar system data may lead to the solution of this important problem.

26

ORIGIN OF THE EARTH'S OCEAN AND ATMOSPHERE

26.1 EARTH'S OCEAN AND THE FORMATION OF
THE SOLAR SYSTEM

The problems of the origin and evolution of the ocean and the atmosphere cannot be resolved realistically without referring to the processes by which the Earth itself formed. The observational data from lunar and planetary exploration do not support the previously common but vague notion that the Earth had somehow already formed when differentiation took place and the ocean and atmosphere began to develop. On the contrary, the processes leading to the formation of the Earth must themselves play a decisive role in producing differentiation (secs. 12.12–12.13) and in giving rise to the precursors for the present ocean and atmosphere. The present properties of the ocean-atmosphere system furthermore place boundary conditions on the accretion history of the planet. They contribute to the implausibility of the planetary evolution, particularly the instantaneous formation of the planets, that follows from the Laplacian type of concept of solar-system formation. The major objections against such concepts, however, come from the modern knowledge of the behavior of matter in space (ch. 1).

In accordance with the models developed in the preceding chapters and with modern knowledge of plasma physics and hydromagnetics, we conclude that when the formation of our solar system began, neutral gas in the circumsolar region fell in toward the Sun and was ionized upon reaching the critical velocity for ionization. The same processes occurred around the magnetized protoplanets (Jupiter, Saturn, Uranus, and probably also Neptune and Earth) in the later stages of their formation. The plasma revolving around the Sun provided the source or the capturing medium (ch. 19) for the material that, in the form of small particles, aggregated to larger bodies which ultimately gave rise to the planets (chs. 12, 17, and 18).

26.2 THE REMOTE PRECURSOR STAGES

26.2.1 Occlusion of Volatiles in Solid Condensates

Vapor-grown crystals are abundant components of certain types of mete-orites which presumably form by the processes discussed in chs. 6 and 22 (also see fig. 7.7.1). This meteoritic material has chemical features indicative of the conditions of growth. Among these is the occurrence in some types of crystals of volatile components such as noble-gas atoms and halogen and hydroxyl ions. Because the inert gas atoms do not develop strong chemi-cal bonds with the host structure, they are particularly useful for studying modes of incorporation.

The noble gas fraction which is of particular interest to the problems of the Earth is observed to be strongly bound in the interior of the crystals and to require high activation energies for release when the meteorite mate-rial is heated for analysis. This indicates that the gas was incorporated in the crystals during growth from the vapor phase. In most crystal structures in meteorites the packing density is high and hence solid solubilities of inert gas atoms are virtually nil. The comparatively high concentrations of occluded noble gases must therefore be achieved by their incorporation in dislocations and other growth imperfections.

Besides the presumably growth-occluded component, meteorites also contain surface implanted and radiogenic noble-gas components which have distinct, characteristic signatures (Signer and Suess, 1963); these need not be further discussed here.

The fact that the occluded noble gases are strongly bound internally in the crystals shows that incorporation took place as a part of the crystal-lization process and not as a surface adsorption or other low-energy processes occurring after formation of the grains as is sometimes suggested. Further-more, it is well known from experiments that for noble-gas occlusion to be significant at crystal growth the temperature of the crystals has to be below the range 400–600K. The vapor phase temperature, however, must have been considerably higher. This follows from fundamental considerations of radiation from grain-gas systems in space (see, e.g., secs. 1.4 and 22.1; Lindblad, 1935; Lehnert, 1970a; Arrhenius and De, 1973).

Furthermore, as emphasized in secs. 1.4 and 15.6, any gas cloud in space with the dimensions visualized for a solar nebula must even at low tem-peratures be controlled by magnetohydrodynamic processes, and hence generate strong fields and electric currents and display a substantial degree of ionization. Therefore when considering the condensation and growth of solids in a primordial nebula we are concerned with a thermal state that must be common in gas-solid systems in space and where crystallizing grains at comparatively low temperature are immersed in, and exchange matter with, a hot, optically thin, partially ionized gas. This state is manifest in a wide variety of phenomena active in the solar system today or recorded during the early stage of formation. These phenomena are discussed in context throughout this work.

26.2.2 Primordial Grains As Carriers of Atmospheric and Oceanic Components

The composition of the occluded noble-gas component in primordial condensates should be compared to the composition of the atmosphere of the Earth and the formation of its ocean. Measurements on meteorites show that this component characteristically has a relative abundance distribution of primordial noble-gas species which is rather similar to that of the Earth's atmosphere (Signer and Suess, 1963). In contrast, the noble gas isotopic abundances derived by interpolation between isotopic abundances of neighboring elements in the periodic table (Suess and Urey, 1956) give an entirely different distribution with a much higher abundance of light noble gases.

These facts suggest that *the special noble-gas composition as found in meteorites and in the terrestrial atmosphere was established in the plasma from which the primordial condensates grew;* in the former case, in the region of space where the parent materials of meteorites formed, and, in the latter case, in the region where the parent materials of the Earth condensed. Several mechanisms may have contributed to the observed noble-gas fractionation in the circumsolar region (see review in Arrhenius, 1972).

The Earth would then have acquired its atmosphere and ocean as it grew from primordial grains and aggregates similar to, but not necessarily identifiable with, those found in meteorites. The release of the volatiles, mainly during the accretion process, would form a primordial atmosphere from which the present one has gradually developed.

Although the important discovery of the "planetary" component of noble gases in meteorites was made over a decade ago, the full implications of a genetic relationship were not realized until recently (Wasson, 1969; Fanale, 1971). Fanale aptly ascribes this delay to a climate of opinion which for a long time fostered a belief that the primordial atmosphere of the Earth must have been entirely removed by some ad hoc process. The present atmosphere would under these circumstances have evolved entirely by degassing of the interior of the planet, which somehow would have retained a sufficient mass of volatile components.

As demonstrated by Fanale, this is unlikely to have been the case; the primordial noble gases, with the possible exception of xenon, must at accretion by Earth have been largely transferred to the atmosphere where they still reside. They are not even noticeable as a group in the present gas flux from the Earth's interior, where the noble-gas component is dominated by radiogenic species; nor has a noble-gas group with these element proportions yet been found occluded in igneous rocks. Other chemically reactive volatiles show a complex partition between the atmosphere and the solid Earth as discussed below.

26.2.3 Extraterrestrial Sources of Water

In view of the small mass of the hydrosphere compared to the mantle (1:3000), concentrations as small as 300 parts per million of available hydroxyl in the accreting silicates that formed the Earth are sufficient to generate the total mass of the hydrosphere. Thus the material in meteorites fallen on the Earth and on the Moon (Gibson and Moore, 1973; Apollo 16 PET, 1973) would provide ample sources for both the ocean and the atmosphere; they have a content of hydroxyl and water ranging from a few hundred ppm to several percent.

The component of primordial solids of major importance as a source for terrestrial water is hydroxyl ion. This ion forms a regular structural component in magnesium and iron hydroxysilicates, which form the major mass of carbonaceous chondrites of Type I (Wiik, 1956). (Crystal hydrates of magnesium and sodium sulfates found in carbonaceous chondrites are probably not generated in space where they are unstable; they are likely to be forming by reaction with water vapor in terrestrial museums.)

It was previously believed (solely on the basis of geological intuition) that the hydroxysilicates in meteorites must be understood as a secondary reaction product between anhydrous silicates and water in vapor form or even as liquid water in rivers and swamps on a planet from which the sediments would subsequently have been removed as meteorites when the planet exploded. Apart from the prohibitive physical difficulties that meet such exploded-planet theories (sec. 22.2), it is now known from experiment (Meyer, 1969, 1971) that magnesium hydroxysilicates, analogous to those in meteorites, can crystallize directly at grain temperatures below about 500K from plasmas containing magnesium, silicon, hydrogen, and oxygen species. Furthermore, minor substitution with hydroxyl also occurs in terrestrial silicates common in space, such as olivine and pyroxene (Martin and Donnay, 1972). Such partial hydroxylation is also likely to occur during the growth of these silicates in free space, particularly in vapor crystallization at high relative pressure of atomic and ionic species of oxygen and hydrogen.

The fact that meteorite materials carry sufficient hydroxyl to account for the entire hydrosphere on Earth should not be taken to mean that the Earth formed from any of these specific materials, which probably represent different condensation events and regions in space. But the observations imply that primordial condensates in different parts of the solar system, although varying markedly in chemical composition (ch. 20), have incorporated substantial amounts of volatiles, which were subsequently released in the accretional hot-spot front during the formation of the planets (sec. 26.3.2).

26.2.4 Reservoir of Inert and Reactive Volatiles

An important related question concerns the chemical composition of the Earth's total store of primordial volatiles, determined by the average composition of the planetesimals from which the Earth was built and modified by the loss processes discussed below. In the case of the primordial noble gases thus accreted, the observations mentioned above indicate relative elemental and isotopic proportions similar to those found in the occluded noble-gas component in meteorites.

In contrast, the content and proportions of reactive volatiles in the Earth's source material (primarily species of H, C, N, O, S, and the halogens) are obscured by the fact that it is totally unknown how much of these elements is hidden in the Earth's interior. Analyses of crustal rocks and extrusions from the upper mantle are not informative on this point since they are likely to be contaminated by the oceanic and atmospheric reservoirs. Extraterrestrial materials do not, at the present state of knowledge, provide much quantitative guidance on this point either, since their absolute and relative contents of reactive volatiles are extremely variable (Bogard et al., 1973; Gibson and Johnson, 1971, 1972; Collins et al., 1974).

26.3 THE IMMEDIATE PRECURSOR STAGES

26.3.1 Evolution of the Earth's Precursor Planetesimals

As shown above, we can, with some assurance, trace the Earth's ocean and atmosphere back in time to the plasma phase which preceded the formation of solid grains in circumsolar and transplanetary space. The evolutionary stages of grain formation in eccentric Kepler orbits around the magnetized gravitating central body have been discussed in chs. 16–18, 21, and 23. Once jet streams have formed (ch. 6), accretional processes can become active (chs. 7 and 12).

In the case of the Earth the runaway accretion of the protoplanet and the exhaustion of the parent jet stream at time t_c occurred very early during formation of the solar system; according to sec. 12.8, 3.5×10^7 yr after the onset of condensation in the terrestrial region of space. The mass present at that time sufficed to give rise to a protoplanet with about half Earth's present radius (fig. 26.3.1). During the remaining part of the time period of infall of gas, assumed to last approximately 3×10^8 yr, growth was maintained at a low and steady rate, determined by the rate of injection of newly condensed material into the jet stream and hence by the rate of inflow of gas into the B cloud (sec. 21.11.1). At the end of the infall time t_{inf} the jet stream was rapidly exhausted and the accretion of the planet terminated, as shown in fig. 26.3.1.

26.3.2 Temperature Distribution in the Growing Protoplanet

When an impacting planetesimal is brought to rest on the surface of the embryo its kinetic energy is almost entirely converted to heat energy, part of it locally and part of it in other regions of the embryo. The discussion in secs. 12.10–12.11 established that the temperature profile of a growing protoplanet is a function of the number and mass of impacting planetesimals, which reach a maximum during runaway accretion. We concluded, therefore, that the inner core of the Earth accreted cold, the accretion temperature rose to a maximum when the outer core formed, and the accretion temperature then fell abruptly and remained low (averaged over the entire surface of the Earth) during the accretion of the mantle, as depicted in fig. 26.3.1.

It is tempting to see in this primeval heat distribution of the Earth an explanation of the fact that, in its present state, our planet is known to have a solid inner core and mantle and a liquid outer core. Acceptance of this explanation requires that since the formative era the heat distribution has not changed very much due to thermal conduction. Further, radioactive heating would add another component to the heat profile in a manner depending on the largely unknown distribution of uranium, thorium, and potassium.

26.3.3 The Core of the Earth

It should be noted that the above interpretation of the Earth's internal structure presupposes that the core of the Earth is a primary feature. Still, 10 years ago there was no compelling evidence against the ingenious and widely accepted suggestion by Elsasser (1963) that the Earth's core formed at a relatively late time in geological history when radioactive heating of an originally homogeneous Earth had proceeded far enough to cause melting of iron (or iron sulfide) in an outer zone of the planet. Gravitational settling of the molten metal toward the center of the planet would release large amounts of gravitational energy and lead to a thermal runaway process, completely melting the Earth.

The following observations place such a development in doubt:

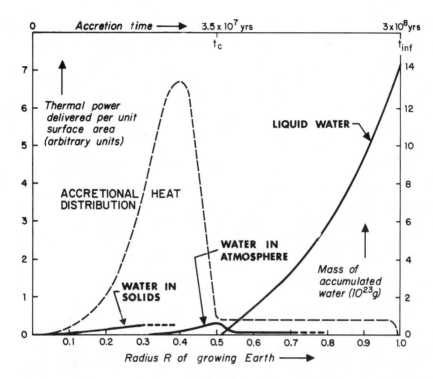

FIGURE 26.3.1.—The dashed curve and the left-hand ordinate show the thermal power (in arbitrary units) delivered per unit surface area of the growing Earth by impacting planetesimals (ch. 12). The lower abscissa shows the radius of the growing Earth in fractions of the present radius. The upper (nonlinear) abscissa scale shows the time elapsed from inception of accretion. The three solid curves show the accumulation of water on Earth. The left curve represents the amount retained in the cooly accreted inner core (arbitrary units). The middle curve shows the accumulated water in the atmosphere and the right-hand curve shows the accumulated liquid water; both in units of 10^{23} g. The final mass of accumulated water has been adjusted to equal the present ocean mass. (From Arrhenius et al., 1974.)

(1) Preserved crustal segments have been found to extend as far back in time as 3.7 Gyr (Black et al., 1971). This is difficult to reconcile with the necessary rate of cooling, particularly if the total store of volatiles, with the exception of a small fraction in solution in the melt, was transferred into a thick insulating atmosphere. The example from Venus further suggests that such a situation may be irreversible.

(2) Rocks derived from the upper mantle characteristically have high concentrations of nickel and platinum; nickel concentrations are mostly of the order of 10^{-3}. It has been pointed out by Ringwood (1966) that the concentrations of these noble metals in the silicates would be brought to

much lower levels if they had been in contact with and approached equilibrium with molten iron or iron sulfide. That such extraction of nickel and platinum into the metallic phase actually takes place under similar kinetic conditions is indicated by the composition of lunar rocks, where most metallic iron and iron sulfides from the source planetesimals have been drained away from the surface layer in the accretional front of hot spots. As a result lunar silicates have nickel and platinum contents which are an order of magnitude lower than their counterparts in terrestrial mantle rocks.

To satisfy the need for a core formed concurrently with, rather than subsequent to, the formation of the Earth, we need to assume either that the material accumulating in the region of the terrestrial planets during the first approximately 4×10^7 yr ($0 < t \leq t_{inf}$; fig. 26.3.1) was particularly rich in iron or that the core, as suggested by Ramsey (1948, 1949), consists of a compressed metallic material with chemical composition similar to that of the mantle. These alternatives are discussed in sec. 20.5.

26.3.4 Heat Release and Volatilization of Water During Accretion

Sections 12.6–12.9 have treated the mass and time relationships for accretion of planets in detail. The heating of the accreted material, carrying in it the volatile sources of the ocean and the atmosphere, is of crucial importance for fractionation of the volatiles and their ultimate disposition. The major amount of heat in the accretion process derived from the conversion into thermal energy of the kinetic energy of the impacting bodies (planetesimals).

When a planetesimal hits an embryo (protoplanet), its impact velocity is

$$v_{imp} = (v_{es}^2 + u^2)^{1/2} \qquad (26.3.1)$$

where v_{es} is the escape velocity for the embryo and u is the original velocity of the planetesimal relative to the embryo. In the later stage of accretion, u becomes small compared to v_{es}. Hence, the amount of kinetic energy released at each impact is slightly above $\frac{1}{2}mv_{es}^2$, where m is the mass of the impacting planetesimal. A fraction γ of this energy will be converted to thermal energy of fusion within the planetesimal, melting the mass-fraction α, given by

$$\alpha = \frac{\gamma v_{es}^2}{2L} \qquad (26.3.2)$$

L being the latent heat of fusion for the projectile material. If we take iron-magnesium silicates to be representative of the solid material in the planetesimals, the latent heat of fusion (Fe_2SiO_4: 295 J/g, $MgSiO_3$: 616 J/g, Mg_2SiO_4: 455 J/g) may be taken to be of the order of 500 J/g.

As an example, when the embryo has grown to half the present size of the Earth, we find on putting $R = 0.5 R_\oplus$, $\Theta = 5.5$ g/cm^3, and $L = 500$ J/g that

$$\alpha = 25\gamma \qquad (26.3.3)$$

The factor γ depends on the structure of the planetesimals. If these are hard solids some of the energy will be transmitted as shock waves which are dissipated at depth in the embryo (Levin, 1972). If they are fluffy aggregates a large fraction will be dissipated locally. Even if γ were as low as 4 percent, there is energy enough for the whole planetesimal to be melted. It is likely that the target material will be heated at the same time. Hence it is possible that a considerable fraction, if not all of the planetesimal, will be melted and/or heated to sufficiently high temperatures for the major part of its volatile components to be released in the form of gas.

The extent to which water vapor and other volatile compounds will be retained as an atmosphere around the protoplanet is determined by the balance between thermal escape of the molecules and the increasing gravitational retention by the protoplanet as its mass grows. Thus there will be a gradual accumulation of water vapor with time, and, under suitable conditions, this may condense to form liquid water.

These conditions are largely determined by the temperature of the surface of the growing protoplanet, which in turn depends on the planetesimal impact rate and the heat release at each impact. Before we proceed in sec. 26.4.3 to outline the process of the accumulation of water, we shall therefore briefly review the characteristics of the accretional heat distribution.

26.4 ACCUMULATION OF WATER DURING THE ACCRETION OF THE EARTH

26.4.1 Simple Model

The rate of increase of mass with radius for an embryo of uniform density is (see sec. 7.3)

$$\frac{dM_{em}}{dR} = 4\pi R^2 \Theta \qquad (26.4.1)$$

Let us suppose that each mass unit of impacting matter releases β mass units of water. Then the rate of increase of water content in the environment of the embryo is

$$\frac{dM_{H_2O}}{dR} = \beta \frac{dM_{em}}{dR} = 4\pi\Theta\beta R^2 \qquad (26.4.2)$$

where M_{H_2O} is the mass of the water released.

The water vapor thus accumulated will form a part of the atmosphere around the embryo. At the top of this atmosphere the water molecules will approach a Maxwellian velocity distribution and a corresponding equilibrium temperature. The molecules which have thermal velocity in excess of the escape velocity for the embryo can escape eventually from the neighborhood of the embryo. As shown by Jeans, if the root mean square velocity of a gas is only of the order of 20 percent of the escape velocity, the gas can escape entirely in the course of a billion years or so. Hence we can make a crude model by assuming that prior to the Earth's being large enough to have an escape velocity greater than five times the thermal velocity no vapor is gravitationally retained by the embryo. Once the escape velocity equals or exceeds five times the thermal velocity, all the vapor is retained. The relevant temperature of the water vapor that will determine its rate of gravitational escape is the temperature characteristic of the atmosphere that is formed by the release of the occluded gases. This temperature is not related to the accretionally heated surface temperature of the embryo but is determined by the radiation fields of the Sun and of the plasma in the primordial magnetosphere surrounding the Earth (De, 1973).

The thermal conditions at the top of this proto-atmosphere may be comparable to those in the Earth's exosphere today, possibly having a characteristic temperature of about 1000K corresponding to a thermal velocity of about 1 km/sec for the main constituents of the atmosphere. If the escape velocity must be 5 times this we find that the Earth must have reached a size of about half its present value in order to retain the atmospheric gases and water vapor. This is about the present size of Mars and is reconcilable with the fact that Mars seems to be close to the limit where its gravitation is large enough to keep an atmosphere.

Figure 26.3.1 shows the primeval heat structure of the Earth resulting from accretion as discussed in sec. 26.3.2. The ordinate (left) for this curve is proportional to the temperature. We note that, after the low temperature accretion of the inner core, the temperature of the surface layer of the embryonic Earth continues to rise and culminates at $R{\sim}0.4R_\oplus$. Hence water vapor cannot condense during this period and must remain in the atmosphere. However, the gravitational retention of water vapor at this stage is negligible. As accretion proceeds, now at a low rate determined by the injection of source material into the terrestrial region, the surface temperature of the protoplanet falls to a low average value which is probably close to the present surface temperature of the Earth. This would allow the water vapor to condense and begin the formation of a proto-ocean.

Figure 26.3.1 also shows the accumulation of water with increasing radius of the protoplanet calculated under the assumption that all the atmosphere is lost if $R<0.4R\oplus$, but retained if $R>0.4R\oplus$. The total accumulation when the radius reaches the present value has been matched to equal the present ocean mass.

Meteorite materials of the type discussed in sec. 26.2.3 have sufficient hydroxyl contents to account for the present hydrosphere. Hence if the primordial grains had the same water content they would be an ample source for the present ocean.

26.4.2 Accretional Hot-Spot Front and State of Water

As was shown in secs. 12.10–12.11 above and in fig. 26.3.1 for the case of the Earth, heat delivery to the surface layer of the protoplanet first reached a maximum and then declined to a low mean value when the size of the present outer core was reached. After this culmination, the accretion of the outer regions of the Earth proceeded at a low rate, controlled by the continued injection rate of matter (assumed here to be constant) into the terrestrial region of space and terminating at the time t_{inf} when this injection ceased. During the era between t_c and t_{inf} the average rate of heating of the surface of the protoplanet hence must have been low. At the same time, however, local heating at each individual impact site continued to be high and actually increased due to the increase of v_{es}. The transformation of kinetic energy of the infalling bodies to thermal energy has been discussed in sec. 26.3.4. Since the major fraction of mass, and hence potential thermal energy, is concentrated in the largest embryos impacting on the growing Earth (Safronov, 1969; Ip, 1974a), it is these large projectiles that control the thermal evolution.

Assuming that the size distribution of accreting planetesimals was such as to place the major fraction of mass in bodies sufficiently large to penetrate the atmosphere and the ocean, the major fraction of heat was delivered in large impacts repeated relatively rarely at any given location (once every ten to a few hundred years in any impact area) during the era of mantle and crust formation. As pointed out in secs. 12.12–12.13, each major impact is likely to have created a deep subsurface region of molten rock which, in contrast to secondary ejecta and a thin surface crust, would cool slowly. In such melt reservoirs differentiation of magma could take place with the heavy components sinking to the bottom and the light materials accumulating at the top. Although the average surface temperature of the Earth during this era would have remained low, each individual impact region would, in the course of time, be remelted and differentiated several times over. Radial progression of this accretional front of hot spots, discontinuous in space and time, resulted in the selective removal toward the surface of light differentiates forming the Earth's crust and of volatiles forming the atmosphere and the ocean.

The water vapor released at individual impacts after time t_c would condense and contribute to the growing proto-ocean due to the low average surface temperature during this era.

26.4.3 Details of the Model

The development discussed in secs. 26.3–26.4 above has purposely been made simplistic to reiterate in principle the energetics of growth of the planet and to illustrate the course of retention of oceanic and atmospheric components with time. There are several complicating factors, some of which can be discussed qualitatively with some certainty at the present time; for others observational basis is still lacking. Some of the resulting modifications and uncertainties are discussed in the following sections.

26.4.3.1 Atmospheric loss mechanism. In sec. 26.4, it was assumed that water vapor was lost from the exosphere by molecular evaporation during the embryonic growth stage of the planet. After achieving such a size that water molecules cannot escape the gravitational field, other mechanisms of water loss must predominate. If one assumes solar energy flux of at least the present magnitude during the major fraction of Earth's history (see sec. 25.5), water vapor in the upper atmosphere will be dissociated and form a number of species including atomic and molecular hydrogen, hydroxyl, and oxygen ions; of these the hydrogen species have a high escape rate and are preferentially lost to space. The escape rate is probably controlled by the water-vapor transfer rate from the troposphere across the stratospheric cold trap (Harteck and Jensen, 1948; Urey, 1952, 1959).

It is thus generally believed that a part of the terrestrial oxygen is the residue of water from which the hydrogen component has escaped. An estimate of the relative importance of this selective loss can be obtained from the budget shown in table 26.4.1.

The table shows that, if we make the extreme assumption that the oxygen now present in limestone derives entirely from dissociated water by reaction of such oxygen with primoridial carbon compounds, then limestone would be a major store of such oxygen. However, the limestone may partly or entirely have formed by other reactions instead; carbon dioxide may have been one of the primordial gas components of planetesimals (Gibson and

TABLE 26.4.1

Distribution of Terrestrial Oxygen

Oxygen reservoirs	Mass of stored oxygen $(10^{23}$ g)
Hydrosphere (including sediment pore water)	16.7
Limestone ($CaCO_3$)	4
Excess in oxidized iron compounds	0.2
Atmosphere	0.05
Sulfates	0.04

Moore, 1973), it may have been produced by reaction of planetesimal carbon with oxygen in iron silicate in the accretional heat front (Ringwood, 1959), or carbonates could have formed by reaction of methane and water with silicates (Urey, 1952). Hence the largest conceivable loss of water by escape of hydrogen would amount to about 25 percent of the present mass of water; the actual amount is probably much smaller.

The amount of atmospheric oxygen used up by oxidation of transition-element compounds, primarily those of iron, has been estimated on the basis of the extreme assumptions: (1) of an original oxygen-iron average oxidation state corresponding to FeO; and (2) that all iron in present-day sediments occurs as Fe_2O_3 and forms on the average 3.5 percent of shale and deep-sea sediments. The total thus obtained is only a small fraction of the oxygen in the present ocean. However, this calculation ignores the unknown amount of water-derived oxygen bound to divalent or trivalent iron in the mantle and in crustal igneous rocks (see Holland, 1964). Particularly the amount in the mantle constitutes a substantial uncertainty.

The rate of removal of gas from bodies in space is also affected by inter-action with corpuscular radiation from the Sun. It is sometimes assumed that a "solar gale" arose after the planets had formed, removing all planetary atmospheres in the inner part of the solar system.

The need for such an ad hoc mechanism was rooted in the belief that the primordial components were missing from the Earth's atmosphere. As discussed in sec. 26.2, it is now realized that on the contrary our present atmosphere can only be understood as a product of the primordial accretion modified by loss of hydrogen and helium, by photochemical and biological processes, by reaction with the solid Earth, and by the radiogenic gas flux from the Earth's interior. The records from the Moon and from meteorites also have failed to give evidence of any major enhancement of solar corpuscular radiation during or after the formative era. For a discussion of the corpuscular radiation effects during this era, see secs. 16.8 and 25.5.

26.4.3.2 Effect of atmosphere and ocean on accretional heating. In principle the developing hydrosphere and atmosphere could alter the distribution of accretional heat. The atmosphere and ocean would dissipate projectile energy by frictional heating and would decrease the radiative cooling efficiency of the collision-heated spots on the surface. The latter effect would become important if a large fraction of accumulated water were evaporated into a hot atmosphere. This is, however, not likely to have taken place since such a runaway greenhouse effect (Rasool and De Bergh, 1970) might be irreversible, whereas the geological record shows existence of sediments and organic life of Earth already at the −3 Gyr level (Engel et al., 1968). The lack of development of a hot atmosphere can be understood since the calculated size distribution of accumulating planetesimals places the major amount of mass in large projectiles (sec. 26.4.2). This would concentrate the accretional heat in limited regions, and, with sufficient intervening time available between major impact events, efficient reradiation of surficial heat into space would take place.

At a large projectile mass/surface ratio, energy dissipation in the atmosphere and the ocean would also become small compared to the energy release after penetration to the solid surface, even in the case of objects with the assumed properties of comets (Lin, 1966).

26.4.3.3 Effect of planetesimal impact. Terrestrial experience gives little guidance concerning the nature of impact processes of the magnitude involved in planetary accretion. In the projectile mass range studied in controlled experiments on Earth with massive projectiles, the mass of ejecta exceeds that of the projectile for hypersonic impacts (sec. 7.4).

At projectile masses far beyond this range, however, the fraction of projectile material retained in the target would be expected to increase particularly at impact speeds several times the velocity of sound in the projectile material. This is indicated by the effects of the largest impacts on the lunar surface. Hence local implantation of kinetic energy converted to heat is likely to have been an important process during the accretion of the Earth.

26.5 INTRODUCTION OF WATER IN THE LITHOSPHERE

26.5.1 The Assumption of Primordial Impregnation

Crustal igneous rocks on Earth have a low but persistent content of water and occasionally very high contents of carbon dioxide (von Eckermann, 1948, 1958; Tuttle and Gittens, 1966). Because of the unknown extent of these components at greater depth in the Earth, the total store of volatiles in the solid Earth is highly uncertain. The questions of how and when these volatiles became buried are important to the problem of the formation of the ocean and atmosphere. One commonly made, intuitively based suggestion is that an excess over the present amount was somehow introduced into the interior of the Earth during its early history. This situation would be or would become metastable, causing a net transport of water from the lithosphere to the ocean during a substantial fraction of geological time and possibly still today. No observational basis has been found for this assumption, which was originally made to secure a storage place for the present ocean and atmosphere while the original atmosphere was supposed to be destroyed. As discussed above, such a catastrophe is counterindicated by the noble-gas distribution in the atmosphere; hence the need for any such temporary ocean storage has disappeared.

To explain the present content of reactive volatiles (primarily water and carbon dioxide) in igneous rocks, Fanale (1971), on the basis of a proposal that the Earth became completely melted (Hanks and Anderson, 1969), suggested that the volatiles were partitioned in equilibrium between the melted Earth and a hot, high-pressure atmosphere in contact with it. This would seem excluded on the basis of quantitative considerations of the accretion process (ch. 12). These indicate early exhaustion of the Earth's jet stream and slow subsequent growth during the major part of the approximately 10^8-yr accretion period (fig. 26.3.1). Under these circumstances, the average temperature of the Earth's surface must have been low during accumulation of the mantle and the crust. The thorough outgassing of the noble gases recognized by Fanale is, as demonstrated by the late bombardment effects on the Moon, the natural consequence of local heating at each individual impact and does not in itself require or suggest simultaneous heating of the whole surface layer of the Earth.

It is furthermore doubtful that a thoroughly melted Earth would have had time to cool enough to yield a still preserved crust 0.7 Gyr after formation, particularly with a hot atmosphere containing a major part of the present ocean and of the carbon dioxide reservoir. Finally, the spotty occurrence of deep-seated igneous rocks rich in carbon dioxide suggests that this was introduced locally by a mechanism such as described below, rather than by equilibration of a molten Earth with a hot, massive atmosphere.

26.5.2 Steady-State Impregnation and Release

There is indeed a straightforward and observationally supported way in which the igneous rocks of the crust and upper mantle would be continuously impregnated with reactive volatiles from the atmosphere and the ocean. The evidence for convection-driven lateral movement of large plates of the Earth's crust suggests strongly that water and carbonate containing sediments and hydrated submarine eruptives are sinking and assimilating into the upper mantle in subduction zones, compensating for the rise of magma and generation of new crust in the seafloor spreading zones. This vertical mixing is sufficiently fast (approximately 5 cm/year) to have drowned all

ocean sediments appreciably older than a few percent of the Earth's estimated age; so all reactive volatiles now found in igneous rocks can be understood as contamination mainly from the ocean, introduced into the solid
Earth much later than the time of formation of the Earth's primordial crust.

Thus an efficient mechanism for circulation of volatiles between the ocean-
atmosphere system and the upper mantle has been operating through the
geological eras recorded on the ocean floor and presumably during the entire
history of the Earth after its formation. This does not exclude the possibility that some (probably small) fraction of the primordial volatiles was
left behind in the growing lithosphere as a result of incomplete outgassing
during accretion of the Earth.

26.5.3 Possible Remains of Planetesimal Volatiles in Earth's Crust and Mantle

At atmospheric pressure most gases are practically insoluble in silicate
melts. However, considerable excess amounts of gas can be incorporated
during shock melting of porous materials and can, at solidification, be
retained in disequilibrium in such melts when they solidify due to the
inefficiency of diffusion-limited removal processes (Fredriksson and De Carli,
1964). On the other hand, convection in such melts, and stripping by
boiling of components such as hydrocarbons and monoxides of carbon,
silicon, and potassium, contribute toward relieving such disequilibria. These
retention and removal phenomena are exemplified in the lunar igneous
rocks where frothing due to gas escaping from the melts is common.

Conditions in the lunar crust also indicate that, in the culminating stage
of accretional heating (which on Earth probably occurred at the outer
core and on the Moon near or at the present surface; see fig. 12.11.1), the
removal of any water vapor possibly associated with the molten and vaporized projectile material was highly efficient, resulting in oxygen partial
pressures less than 10^{-14} b. The sporadic occurrences of volatiles in lunar
materials are considered to derive from postformative impact of volatile-
rich projectiles on the cold lunar surface and in some instances perhaps to
be due to vapor transport through crustal fractures from the coldly accreted
inner core (which could be considerably warmer today due to radioactive
heating).

During the accretion of the Earth's mantle and crust, large impacts
could well have implanted hydroxyl-containing material sufficiently deep
so that the (pressure dependent) solubility in the melt remained comparatively high, and removal was not complete before solidification, in spite of
repeated remelting by new impacts and the gravitational upward removal of
light components which produced the crust. Because of the complexity of
these processes and our lack of knowledge of large-scale impact effects, it is

difficult now to estimate the ultimate efficiency of material separation by the accretional hot-spot front.

A continued systematic search for primordial gas components such as radiogenic Xe^{129} from the Earth's crust and mantle could narrow the limits of uncertainty (Boulos and Manuel, 1971). Primordial ratios of appropriate neon and argon isotopes associated with He^3 found in terrestrial materials (Clarke et al., 1969) would also serve as indicators of the possible importance of residual primordial gases.

Improved knowledge of the temperature distribution in the mantle would also contribute to the vertical transport efficiency problem since at least at moderate pressures the large cations of the elements contributing to radioactive heating are concentrated in the light component migrating toward the surface in the accretional heat front.

26.6 THE OCEAN AND THE EARTH-MOON SYSTEM

The evolution of the ocean must have been markedly affected by the fact that an abnormally massive body causing significant tidal effects exists in the vicinity of the Earth. A similar case is that of Neptune and its captured satellite Triton which has an orbit which decidedly is tidally modified (sec. 24.4) (McCord, 1966).

Tidal forces in the early evolution of the Earth-Moon system should be of considerable importance, and the question arises of the relative role of the ocean in tidal dissipation. Since dissipation in the solid Earth is considered insignificant (Munk, 1968), the ocean would provide the most important medium for tidal energy exchange.

It was believed earlier that capture of the Moon (ch. 24) must have had catastrophic tidal effects on Earth leading to complete evaporation of the ocean to form a hot atmosphere. However, the long duration of the high magnetic field immersion, indicated by the magnetization of lunar rocks in the time interval -4 to -3 Gyr (Strangway et al., 1972; Alfvén and Lindberg, 1974) suggests that the capture and the subsequent approach and recession of the Moon to its present orbit were associated with resonance effects (fig. 24.5.1). Such resonance effects could limit the closest approach of the Moon to distances much larger than the Roche limit.

All these questions concerning the history of the Moon need to be answered before we can have a detailed picture of the evolution of the Earth's ocean-atmosphere system.

26.7 SUMMARY AND CONCLUSIONS

(1) Physically acceptable models for accretion of planets and their source planetesimals are limited by the dynamic laws for motion of the primordial

solid condensate grains and by the boundary conditions for kinetic evolution of assemblages of particles in Kepler orbits.

(2) Analysis of the preplanetary conditions indicates a slow and cold accretion of the inner core of the Earth which temporarily changed into a rapid and hot accretion when Earth had reached approximately half of its present radius and about 10 percent of its present mass.

(3) In the subsequent phase, during which 90 percent of the Earth formed, accretion was slow and controlled by the influx of source material in the terrestrial region of space. During this period, extending over the order of 10^8 yr, each impacting planetesimal must have produced intense local heating, so that every part of the Earth became melted several times, but this heating was discontinuous in time and place so that the average temperature of the surface of the growing protoplanet remained low. During this period most of the gas, with the exception of hydrogen and helium, was retained.

(4) Due to the low average temperature of the Earth's surface, water vapor released in individual local impacts would during the slow, major phase of accretion condense to form a growing hydrosphere.

(5) The noble-gas composition of the present atmosphere indicates that it is directly inherited from the source planetesimals. The present atmosphere must consequently be considered as original. It differs from its primordial state only by escape of H and He, change in molecular composition due to photosynthesis, and removal of carbon into the crust, mainly as calcium carbonate.

(6) There is no need for the assumption of a solar gale removing the primitive atmosphere. Such an assumption also lacks support in the meteorite irradiation record.

(7) The observed present-day flux of volatiles from the crust into the ocean-atmosphere system must largely represent the return of volatiles which have been recycled from the ocean and atmosphere through the crust and upper mantle several times during geological history. The removal branch in this cycle is the dragging down of water and carbonate-containing sediments into the crust and upper mantle in the subduction zones, resulting from or driving the observed lateral motion of crustal plates.

(8) There is, consequently, no longer any basis for the earlier notion that the ocean and atmosphere have gradually emerged at the surface of the Earth during geological history. Instead, available evidence indicates that the ocean and the atmosphere have essentially been in place not only during the entire history of the Earth as an adult planet, but also during the major phase of accretion beginning at the stage that the proto-Earth was roughly of the size of Mars.

CONCLUDING REMARKS

Having completed our analysis of the origin and evolution of the solar system, we can summarize the general results as follows:

Our analysis is based on the following principles:

(1) We aim at a *general theory of the formation of secondary bodies* around a primary body. This hetegonic theory should be equally applicable to the formation of planets around the Sun and the formation of satellites around a planet.

The results confirm that this approach is sensible. In fact it is shown that the properties of a system of secondary bodies is a unique function of the mass (sec. 21) and the spin (sec. 23) of the central body. No special assumption needs to be introduced concerning the Sun.

(2) To avoid the uncertainty concerning the state of the primeval Sun and its environment, the analysis should *start from the present state* of the solar system and *systematically reconstruct increasingly older states*. Hence, part A is a critical review of those initial facts which are considered to be relevant for a reconstruction of the origin and evolution of the system.

(3) Before an analysis of the evolution of the solar system can be made, it is essential to *clarify what physical laws govern its evolution*. A lack of clarity in this respect has been disastrous to many other attempts at such analysis. More specifically the following mistakes have been made:

(a) Based on the prehydromagnetic Laplacian concepts, the importance of electromagnetic effects has been neglected. Studies have been made without any knowledge at all of plasma physics or with erroneous concepts of its laws ("frozen-in" field lines, etc.) (ch. 15).

(b) Reliance upon such Laplacian concepts has also led to pictures of the solar nebula as a vapor disc containing all the present matter now in the solar system (or more) together with a complement of light gases, all of which condense in a short time. This has given rise to very high estimates of the instantaneous gas density in the system, unreasonable both in terms of the length of the formation interval and the conditions for angular momentum transfer.

(c) Condensation of solids has been thought to occur in a state of temperature equilibrium between grains and gas, and it has not been realized that in space the solid grain temperature normally is an order of magnitude lower than the plasma or gas temperature under such conditions where condensation can take place during cooling of the medium. This has lead to chemical interpretations which are clearly unrealistic.

(d) The nature of collisions between grains has not been understood. It has been assumed that these result only in fragmentation, and the accretional processes which necessarily are more important have been neglected. Studies of electrostatic attraction and of collision involving fluffy aggregates are essential.

(e) The orbital evolution of a population of grains, although of obvious importance, has not been properly considered. It is necessary to introduce the concept of jet streams as an intermediate stage in the accretional process.

(4) It seems that *the origin and evolution of the solar system can be reconstructed as a result of the following processes:*

(a) Emplacement of plasma in specific regions around the central bodies. The critical-velocity phenomenon is essential for this process. The resulting chemical differentiation produces substantial differences in the composition of the bodies (chs. 20–21).

(b) The transfer of angular momentum from the central body to the surrounding plasma: A partial corotation is established as demonstrated by the structure of the Saturnian rings and the asteroid belt (ch. 18).

(c) The condensation from this state results in populations of grains which are focused into jet streams in which the accretion of planets or satellites takes place (ch. 9).

(d) Whereas all these processes took place during a period of some hundred million years, there was a slow evolution during 4–5 Gyr to attain the present state.

Following the actualistic principle (2), (d) is analyzed in Part A; (c), in Part B; (b), in Part C; and (a), in Part D.

The general conclusion is that with the empirical material now available *it is already possible to reconstruct the basic events leading to the present structure of the solar system.* With the expected flow of data from space research the evolution of the solar system may eventually be described with a confidence and accuracy comparable to that of the geological evolution of the Earth.

REFERENCES

Alexander, A. F. O'D., 1953. Saturn's rings—minor divisions and Kirkwood's gaps, *Brit. Astron. Assoc. J.* **64**: 26.

Alexander, A. F. O'D., 1962. *The Planet Saturn: A History of Observation, Theory and Discovery* (Macmillan, New York).

Alfvén, H., 1942. On the cosmogony of the solar system, *Stockholms Observatorium Ann.* **14**(2): 3.

Alfvén, H., 1943a. On the cosmogony of the solar system, *Stockholms Observatorium Ann.* **14**(5): 3.

Alfvén, H., 1943b. On the effect of a vertical magnetic field in a conducting atmosphere, *Ark. Mat. Astro. Fysik* **29A**(11): 1.

Alfvén, H., 1946. On the cosmogony of the solar system, *Stockholms Observatorium Ann.* **14**(9): 3.

Alfvén, H., 1954. *On the Origin of the Solar System* (Oxford Univ. Press, London).

Alfvén, H., 1961. On the origin of cosmic magnetic fields, *Astrophys. J.* **133**: 1049.

Alfvén, H., 1962. On the mass distribution in the solar system, *Astrophys. J.* **136**: 1005.

Alfvén, H., 1963. On the early history of the Sun and the formation of the solar system, *Astrophys. J.* **137**: 981.

Alfvén, H., 1964. On the origin of the asteroids, *Icarus* **3**: 52.

Alfvén, H., 1968, Second approach to cosmical electrodynamics, *Ann. Géophysique* **24**: 1.

Alfvén, H., 1969. Asteroidal jet streams, *Astrophys. Space Sci.* **4**: 84.

Alfvén, H., 1971. Apples in a spacecraft, *Science* **173**: 522.

Alfvén, H., 1975. *Electric Current Structure of the Magnetosphere,* Report No. 75-03 (Division of Plasma Physics, Roy. Instit. Tech., Stockholm) to published in *Proceedings of the Nobel Symposium on Physics of Hot Plasma in the Magnetosphere.*

Alfvén, H., and G. Arrhenius, 1969. Two alternatives for the history of the moon, *Science* **165**: 11.

Alfvén, H., and G. Arrhenius, 1970a. Structure and evolutionary history of the solar system, I, *Astrophys. Space Sci.* **8**: 338. Note: Numerous illustrations and tables in the text are adapted from those appearing in this paper.

Alfvén, H., and G. Arrhenius, 1970b. Origin and evolution of the solar system, II, *Astrophys. Space Sci.* **9**: 3. Note: Numerous illustrations and tables in the text are adapted from those appearing in this paper.

Alfvén, H., and G. Arrhenius, 1972a. Origin and evolution of the Earth-Moon system, *The Moon* **5**: 210.

Alfvén, H., and G. Arrhenius, 1972b. Exploring the origin of the solar system by space missions to asteroids, *Naturwiss.* **59**: 183.

Alfvén, H., and G. Arrhenius, 1973. Structure and evolutionary history of the solar system, III, *Astrophys. Space Sci.* **21**: 117. Note: Numerous illustrations and tables in the text are adapted from those appearing in this paper.

Alfvén, H., and G. Arrhenius, 1974. Structure and evolutionary history of the solar system, IV, *Astrophys. Space Sci.* **29**: 63. Note: Numerous illustrations and tables in the text are adapted from those appearing in this paper.

Alfvén, H., and C.-G. Fälthammar, 1963. *Cosmical Electrodynamics, Fundamental Principles,* 2nd edit. (Oxford Univ. Press, London).

Alfvén, H., and L. Lindberg, 1975. Magnetization of celestial bodies with special application to the primeval Earth and Moon, *The Moon* **10**: 323.

Alfvén, H., and A. Mendis, 1973. The nature and origin of comets, *Nature* **246**: 410.

Alfvén, H., M. Burkenroad and W.-H. Ip, 1974. Cosmogony of the asteroidal belt, *Nature* **250**: 634.

Allan, R. R., 1967. Resonance effects due to the longitudinal dependence of the gravitational field of a rotating body, *Planet. Space. Sci.* **15**: 53.

Allen, C. W., 1963. *Astrophysical Quantities,* 2nd edit. (The Athlone Press, Univ. of London, London).

Aller, L. H., 1967. Earth, chemical composition of and its comparison with that of the Sun, Moon and planets, in *Int. Dictionary of Geophysics, Vol. 1,* S. K. Runcorn, ed. (Pergamon Press, New York): 285.

Anders, E., 1964. Origin, age and composition of meteorites, *Space Sci. Rev.* **3**: 583.

Anders, E., 1965. Fragmentation history of asteroids, *Icarus* **4**: 399.

Anders, E., 1968. Chemical processes in the early solar system as inferred from meteorites, *Accounts Chem. Res.* **1**: 289.

Anders, E., and M. E. Lipschutz, 1966. Critique of paper by N. L. Carter and G. C. Kennedy, Origin of diamonds in the Canyon Diablo and Novo Urei meteorites, *J. Geophys. Res.* **71**: 643.

Anderson, J. D., G. W. Null and S. K. Wong, 1974. Gravity results from Pioneer 10 Doppler data, *J. Geophys. Res.* **79**: 3661.

Angerth, B., L. Block, U. Fahleson and K. Soop, 1962. Experiments with partly ionized rotating plasmas, *Nucl. Fusion* **Suppl. Part I**: 39.

Angus, J. C., H. A. Will and W. S. Stanko, 1968. Growth of diamond seed crystals by vapor deposition, *J. Appl. Phys.* **39**: 2915.

Apollo 16 Preliminary Examination Team, 1973. The Apollo 16 lunar samples: petrographic and chemical description, *Science* **179**: 23.

Arnold, J. R., 1965. The origin of meteorites as small bodies: II—The model, *Astrophys. J.* **141**: 1536. The origin of meteorites as small bodies: III—General considerations, *Astrophys. J.* **141**: 1548.

Arnold, J. R., 1969. Asteroid families and "jet streams," *Astron. J.* **74**: 1235.

Arnold, J. R., M. Honda and D. Lal, 1961. Record of cosmic ray intensity in the meteorites, *J. Geophys. Res.* **66**: 3519.

Arrhenius, G., 1969. Kosmologisk revolution från månen, *Forskning och Framsteg* **7**: 2.

Arrhenius, G., 1972. Chemical effects in plasma condensation, in *From Plasma to Planet,* A. Elvius, ed. (Wiley, New York): 117.

Arrhenius, G., and H. Alfvén, 1971. Fractionation and condensation in space, *Earth Planet. Sci. Lett.* **10**: 253.

Arrhenius, G., and C. Andersen, 1973. Unpublished experimental data.

Arrhenius, G., and S. K. Asunmaa, 1973. Aggregation of grains in space, *The Moon* **8**: 368.

Arrhenius, G., and S. K. Asunmaa, 1974. Adhesion and clustering of dielectric particles in the space environment 1. Electric dipole character of lunar soil grains, in *Lunar Science V* (The Lunar Science Institute, Houston, Tx.): 22.

Arrhenius, G., and B. R. De, 1973. Equilibrium condensation in a solar nebula, *Meteoritics* **8**: 297.

Arrhenius, G., S. Asunmaa, J. I. Drever, J. Everson, R. W. Fitzgerald, J. Z. Frazer, H. Fujita, J. S. Hanor, D. Lal, S. S. Liang, D. Macdougall, A. M. Reid, J. Sinkankas and L. Wilkening, 1970. Phase chemistry, structure and radiation effects in lunar samples, *Science* **167**: 659.

Arrhenius, G., S. K. Asunmaa and R. W. Fitzgerald, 1972. Electrostatic properties of lunar regolith, in *Lunar Science III*, C. Watkins, ed. (The Lunar Science Institute, Houston, Tx.): 30.

Arrhenius, G., H. Alfvén and R. Fitzgerald, 1973. *Asteroid and Comet Exploration,* NASA CR–2291, (Govt. Printing Office, Washington, D.C.).

Arrhenius, G., B. R. De and H. Alfvén, 1974. Origin of the ocean, in *The Sea, Vol. 5,* E. D. Goldberg, ed. (Wiley, New York): 839.

Asunmaa, S. K., and G. Arrhenius, 1974. Adhesion and clustering of dielectric particles in the space environment 2. The electric dipole moments of lunar soil grains, in *Lunar Science V* (The Lunar Science Institute, Houston, Tx.): 25.

Asunmaa, S. K., S. S. Liang and G. Arrhenius, 1970. Primordial accretion; inference from the lunar surface, in *Proc. Apollo 11 Lunar Science Conf. Vol. 3,* A. A. Levinson, ed. (Pergamon, New York): 1975.

Axford, I., 1973. Personal communication.

Babic, M., S. Sandahl and S. Torvén, 1971. The stability of a strongly ionized positive column in a low pressure mercury arc, in *Proc. Xth Internat. Conf. on Phenomena in Ionized Gases,* P. A. Davenport and R. N. Franklin, eds. (Oxford, Parsons, Henley-on-Thames, England): 120.

Banerjee, S. K., 1967. Fractionation of iron in the solar system, *Nature* **216:** 781.

Banerjee, S. K., and R. B. Hargraves, 1971. Natural remanent magnetization of carbonaceous chondrites, *Earth Planet. Sci. Lett.* **10:** 392.

Banerjee, S. K., and R. B. Hargraves, 1972. Natural remanent magnetizations of carbonaceous chondrites and the magnetic field in the early solar system, *Earth Planet. Sci. Lett.* **17:** 110.

Baxter, D., and W. B. Thompson, 1971. Jetstream formation through inelastic collisions, in *Physical Studies of Minor Planets,* NASA SP–267, T. Gehrels, ed. (Govt. Printing Office, Washington, D.C.): 319.

Baxter, D., and W. B. Thompson, 1973. Elastic and inelastic scattering in orbital clustering, *Astrophys. J.* **183:** 323.

Berlage, H. P., 1930. On the electrostatic field of the sun as a factor in the evolution of the planets, *Proc. Koninkl. Ned. Acad. Wet. Amsterdam* **33:** 719.

Berlage, H. P., 1932. On the structure and internal motion of the gaseous disc constituting the original state of the planetary system, *Proc. Koninkl. Ned. Acad. Wet. Amsterdam* **35:** 553.

Berlage, H. P., 1940. Spontaneous development of a gaseous disc revolving round the sun into rings and planets, *Proc. Koninkl. Ned. Acad. Wet. Amsterdam* **43:** 532.

Berlage, H. P., 1948a. The disc theory of the origin of the solar system, *Proc. Koninkl. Ned. Acad. Wet. Amsterdam* **51:** 796.

Berlage, H. P., 1948b. Types of satellite systems and the disc theory of the origin of the planetary system, *Proc. Koninkl. Ned. Acad. Wet. Amsterdam* **51:** 965.

Birch, F., 1964. Density and composition of mantle and core. *J. Geophys. Res.* **69:** 4377.

Birch, F., 1965. Energetics of core formation, *J. Geophys. Res.* **70:** 6217.

Birkeland, K., 1908. *The Norwegian Polaris Expedition,* 1902–1903 (Aschehoug and Co., Christiania, Norway).

Bishop, E. V., and W. C. DeMarcus, 1970. Thermal histories of Jupiter models, *Icarus* **12:** 317.

Black, L. P., N. H. Gale, S. Moorbath, R. J. Pankhurst, and V. R. Mc-
Gregor, 1971. Isotopic dating of very early Precambrian amphibolite
facies gneisses from the Godthaab District, West Greenland, *Earth
Planet. Sci. Lett.* **12**: 245.

Block, L. P., 1955. Model experiments on aurorae and magnetic storms,
Tellus **7**: 65.

Block, L. P., 1956. On the scale of auroral model experiments, *Tellus* **8**: 234.

Block, L. P., 1967. Scaling considerations for magnetospheric model experiments, *Planet. Space Sci.* **15**: 1479.

Block, L. P., 1972. Potential double layers in the ionosphere, *Cosmic
Electrodyn.* **3**: 349.

Bobrovnikoff, N. T., 1942. Physical theory of comets in light of spectroscopic
data, *Rev. Mod. Phys.* **14**: 168.

Bogard, D. D., E. K. Gibson, Jr., D. R. Moore, N. L. Turner and R. B.
Wilkin, 1973. Noble gas and carbon abundances of the Haverö, Dingo
Pup Donga and North Haig ureilites, *Geochim. Cosmochim. Acta*
37: 547.

Boström, R., 1968. Currents in the ionosphere and magnetosphere, *Ann.
Géophysique* **24**: 681

Boström, R., 1974. Ionosphere-magnetosphere coupling, in *Magnetospheric Physics,* B. M. McCormac, ed. (D. Reidel, Dordrecht, Holland):
45.

Boström, K., and K. Fredriksson, 1966. Surface conditions of the Orgueil
meteorite parent body as indicated by mineral associations, *Smithsonian
Miscellaneous Collections* **151**(3): 1.

Boulos, M. S., and O. K. Manuel, 1971. Xenon record of extinct radio-
activities in the earth, *Science* **174**: 1334.

Brandt, J. C., 1970. *Introduction to the Solar Wind* (W. H. Freeman
and Co., San Francisco, Calif.).

Bratenahl, A., and G. M. Yeates, 1970. Experimental study of magnetic
flux transfer at the hyperbolic neutral point, *Phys. Fluids* **13**: 2696.

Brecher, A., 1971. On the primordial condensation and accretion environment and the remanent magnetization of meteorites, in *The Evolutionary and Physical Problems of Meteoroids,* NASA SP–319, C. L.
Hemmenway, A. F. Cook and P. M. Millman, eds. (Govt. Printing Office,
Washington, D.C.): 311.

Brecher, A., 1972a. Memory of early magnetic fields in carbonaceous chondrites, in *On the Origin of the Solar System,* H. Reeves, ed. (Centre
Nationale de la Recherche Scientifique, Paris): 260.

Brecher, A., 1972b. *Vapor Condensation of Ni-Fe Phases and Related
Problems,* Part I of Ph.D. Thesis, Univ. of Calif., San Diego, California.

Brecher, A., 1972c. *The Paleomagnetic Record in Carbonaceous Chondrites,* Part II of Ph.D. Thesis, Univ. of Calif., San Diego, California.

Brecher, A., and G. Arrhenius, 1974. The paleomagnetic record in carbonaceous chondrites: natural remanence and magnetic properties, *J. Geophys. Res.* **79**: 2081.

Brecher, A., and G. Arrhenius, 1975. The paleomagnetic record in carbonaceous chondrites: modeling of natural remanence and paleofield intensities, *J. Geophys. Res.*, in press.

Brouwer, D., 1951, Secular variations of the orbital elements of minor planets, *Astron. J.* **56**: 9.

Brouwer, D., 1963. The problem of the Kirkwood gaps in the asteroid belt, *Astron. J.* **68**(3): 152.

Brouwer, D., and G. M. Clemence, 1961a. Orbits and masses of planets and satellites, in *The Solar System, Vol. III, Planets and Satellites,* B. M. Middlehurst and G. P. Kuiper eds. (Univ. Chicago Press, Chicago, Ill.): 31.

Brouwer, D., and G. M. Clemence, 1961b. *Methods of Celestial Mechanics* (Academic Press, New York).

Brouwer, D., and A. J. J. van Woerkom, 1950. The secular variations of the orbital elements of the principal planets, *Astron. Papers Am. Ephemeris* **13**: 81.

Brown, E. W., and C. A. Shook, 1964. *Planetary Theory* (Dover, New York).

Brown, H., I. Goddard and J. Kane, 1967. Qualitative aspects of asteroid statistics, *Astrophys. J. Suppl. Ser.* **14**(125): 57.

Brownlee, R. R., and A. N. Cox, 1961. Early solar evolution, *Sky and Tel.* **21**: 252.

Cameron, A. G. W., 1962. The formation of the sun and planets, *Icarus* **1**: 13.

Cameron, A. G. W., 1963. Formation of the solar nebula, *Icarus* **1**: 339.

Cameron, A. G. W., 1973. Accumulation processes in the primitive solar nebula, *Icarus* **18**: 407.

Carlqvist, P., 1969. Current limitations and solar flares, *Solar Phys.* **7**: 377.

Carpenter, R. L., 1970. A radar determination of the rotation of Venus, *Astron. J.* **75**: 61.

Chamberlin, T. C., 1905. Fundamental problems in geology, in *Carnegie Institution Yearbook No. 4* (Carnegie Inst. Tech., Pittsburgh, Penn.): 171.

Chapman, C. R., 1972a. *Surface Properties of Asteroids,* Ph.D. Thesis, Massachusetts Institute of Technology, Cambridge, Massachusetts.

Chapman, C. R., 1972b. Paper presented at the Colloquium on Toro, Tucson, Arizona, Dec. 1972.

Chapman, C. R., and I. W. Salisbury, 1973. Comparison of meteorite and asteroid spectral reflectivities, *Icarus* **19**: 507.

Chapman, C., T. V. Johnson and T. B. McCord, 1971. A review of spectro-photometric studies of asteroids, in *Physical Studies of Minor Planets,* NASA SP–267, T. Gehrels, ed. (Govt. Printing Office, Washington, D.C.): 51.

Chebotarev, G. A., 1967. *Analytical and Numerical Methods of Celestial Mechanics* (Elsevier, New York).

Clarke, W. B., M. A. Beg and H. Craig, 1969. Excess He^3 in the sea: evidence for terrestrial primordial helium, *Earth Planet. Sci. Lett.* **6:** 213.

Cloutier, P. A., 1971. Ionospheric effects of Birkeland currents, *Rev. Geophys. Space Phys.* **9:** 987.

Cloutier, P. A., H. R. Anderson, R. J. Park, R. R. Vondrak, R. J. Spiger and B. R. Sandel, 1970. Detection of geomagnetically aligned currents associated with an auroral arc, *J. Geophys. Res.* **75:** 2595.

Cohen, C. J., and E. C. Hubbard, 1965. Libration of the close approaches of Pluto to Neptune, *Astron. J.* **70:** 10.

Cohen, C. J., E. C. Hubbard and C. Oesterminter, 1967. New orbit for Pluto, *Astron. J.* **72:** 973.

Collins, L. W., E. K. Gibson and W. W. Wendlandt, 1974. The composition of the evolved gases from the thermal decomposition of certain metal sulfates, *Thermochim. Acta* **9:** 15.

Cook, A. F., F. A. Franklin and F. D. Palluconi, 1973. Saturn's rings—a survey, *Icarus* **18:** 317.

Danielsson, L., 1969a. Statistical arguments for asteroidal jet streams, *Astrophys. Space Sci.* **5:** 53.

Danielsson, L., 1969b. *On the Interaction Between a Plasma and a Neutral Gas,* Report No. 69–17 (Division of Plasma Physics, Roy. Instit. of Tech., Stockholm).

Danielsson, L., 1970. Experiment on the interaction between a plasma and a neutral gas, *Phys. Fluids* **13:** 2288.

Danielsson, L., 1971. The profile of a jetstream, in *Physical Studies of Minor Planets,* NASA SP–267, T. Gehrels, ed. (Govt. Printing Office, Washington, D.C.): 353.

Danielsson, L., 1973. Review of the critical velocity of gas-plasma interaction, part I: experimental observations, *Astrophys. Space Sci.* **24:** 459.

Danielsson, L. and N. Brenning, 1975. Experiment on the interaction between a plasma and a neutral gas II, *Phys. Fluids* **18:** 661.

Danielsson, L., and W.-H. Ip, 1972. Capture resonance of the asteroid 1685 Toro by the Earth, *Science* **176:** 906.

Danielsson, L., and L. Lindberg, 1964. Plasma flow through a magnetic dipole field, *Phys. Fluids* **7:** 1878.

Danielsson, L., and L. Lindberg, 1965. Experimental study of the flow of a magnetized plasma through a magnetic dipole field, *Ark. Fysik* **28:** 1.

Danielsson, L., and R. Mehra, 1973. The Orbital Resonances between the Asteroid Toro and the Earth and Venus, Report (Division of Plasma Physics, Roy. Instit. of Tech., Stockholm).

De, Bibhas, 1973. On the mechanism of formation of loop prominences, *Solar Physics* **31**: 437.

Defant, A., 1961. *Physical Oceanography 1* (Pergamon, New York).

Delsemme, A., 1972. Vaporization theory and non-gravitational forces in comets, in *On the Origin of the Solar System*, H. Reeves, ed. (Centre Nationale de la Recherche Scientifique, Paris): 305.

Delsemme, A. H., 1973. Origin of short period comets, *Astron. Astrophys.* **29**: 377.

DeMarcus, W. C., 1958. The constitution of Jupiter and Saturn, *Astron. J.* **63**: 2.

DeMarcus, W. C., and R. T. Reynolds, 1963. The Constitution of Uranus and Neptune, *Mémoires Soc. R. Sc. Liège, 5ᵉ sér.* **VII**: 51.

Dermott, S. F., and A. P. Lenham, 1972. Stability of the solar system: evidence from the asteroids, *The Moon* **5**: 294.

Dessler, A. J., 1968. Solar wind interactions, *Ann. Geophysique* **24**: 333.

Dohnanyi, J. S., 1969. Collisional model of asteroids and their debris, *J. Geophys. Res.* **74**: 2531.

Dole, S. H., 1962. The gravitational concentration of particles in space near the Earth, *Planetary Space Sci.* **9**: 541.

Dollfus, A., 1961. Visual and photographic studies of planets at the Pic du Midi, in *The Solar System, Vol. III, Planets and Satellites*, G. P. Kuiper and B. M. Middlehurst, eds. (Univ. Chicago Press, Chicago, Ill.): 568.

Dollfus, A., 1971a. Diameter measurements of asteroids, in *Physical Studies of Minor Planets*, NASA SP–267, T. Gehrels, ed. (Govt. Printing Office, Washington, D.C.): 25.

Dollfus, A., 1971b. Physical studies of asteroids by polarization of the light, in *Physical Studies of Minor Planets*, NASA SP–267, T. Gehrels, ed. (Govt. Printing Office, Washington, D.C.): 95.

Drickamer, H. G., 1965. The effect of high pressure on the electronic structure of solids, in *Solid State Physics, Vol. 17*, F. Seitz and D. Turnbull, eds. (Academic Press, New York): 1.

Drobyshevskii, E. M., 1964. The volt-ampere characteristics of a homopolar cell, *Soviet Physics—Technical Physics* **8**: 903.

Duke, M. B., and L. T. Silver, 1967. Petrology of eucrites, howardites and mesosiderites, *Geochim. et Cosmochim. Acta* **31**: 1637.

Dyce, R. B., and G. H. Pettengill, 1967. Radar determination of the rotations of Venus and Mercury, *Astron. J.* **72**: 351.

Eberhardt, P., J. Geiss and N. Grögler, 1965. Über die Verteilung der Uredelgase im Meteoriten Khor Temiki, *Tschermaks Min. Petr. Mitt.* **10**: 535.

von Eckermann, H., 1948. The alkaline district of Alnö Island, *Sverig. Geol. Undersök. Ser. Ca.* **36**.

von Eckermann, H., 1958. The alkaline and carbonatitic dikes of the Alnö formation on the mainland northwest of Alnö Island, *Kungl. Vetenskaps Akademiens Handl., Fjärde serien* **7**(2).

Elsasser, W. M., 1963. Early history of the Earth, in *Earth Science and Meteoritics*, J. Geiss and E. D. Goldberg, eds. (North-Holland Publ. Co., Amsterdam, Holland): 1.

von Engel, A., 1955. *Ionized Gases* (Oxford Univ. Press, London).

Engel, A. E. J., B. Nagy, L. A. Nagy, C. G. Engel, G. O. W. Kremp and C. M. Drew, 1968. Alga-like forms in Onverwacht Series, South Africa: oldest recognized lifelike forms on Earth, *Science* **161**: 1005.

Ephemerides of Minor Planets for 1969 (Institute of Theoretical Astronomy, Acad. Sci. USSR. Publication "Nauka" Leningrad Department, Leningrad, 1968), published annually.

Epstein, S. and H. P. Taylor, Jr., 1970. The concentration and isotopic composition of hydrogen, carbon and silicon in Apollo 11 lunar rocks and minerals, in *Proc. Apollo 11 Lunar Science Conf., Vol. 2*, A. A. Levinson, ed. (Pergamon Press, New York): 1085.

Epstein, S., and H. P. Taylor, Jr., 1972. O^{18}/O^{16}, Si^{30}/Si^{28}, C^{13}/C^{12}, and D/H studies of Apollo 14 and 15 samples, in *Lunar Science III*, C. Watkins, ed. (The Lunar Science Institute, Houston, Tx.): 236.

Eucken, A., 1944a. Über den Zustand des Erdinnern, *Naturwiss* **Heft 14/26**: 112.

Eucken, A., 1944b. Physikalisch-chemische Betrachtungen über die früheste Entwicklungsgeschichte der Erde, *Nachr. Akad. Wiss. in Gottingen, Math.-Phys. Kl.,* **Heft 1**: 1.

Everhart, E., 1969. Close encounters of comets and planets, *Astron. J.* **74**: 735.

Everhart, E., 1972. The origin of short-period comets, *Astrophys. Lett.* **10**: 131.

Everhart, E., 1974. Paper presented at IAU Coll. No. 25, Goddard Space Flight Center, Greenbelt, Md., in Oct. 1974.

Fahleson, U., 1973. Plasma-vehicle interactions in space. Some aspects on present knowledge and future developments, in *Photon and Particle Interactions with Surfaces in Space*, R. J. L. Grard, ed. (Reidel, Dordrecht, Holland): 563.

Fälthammar, C.-G., 1974. Laboratory experiments of magnetospheric interest, *Space Sci. Rev.* **15**(6): 803.

Fanale, F. P., 1971. A case for catastrophic early degassing of the Earth, *Chem. Geol.* **8:** 79.

Fireman, E. L., 1958. Distribution of helium-3 in the Carbo meteorite, *Nature* **181:** 1725.

Fleischer, R. L., P. B. Price, R. M. Walker, M. Maurette and G. Morgan, 1967a. Tracks of heavy primary cosmic rays in meteorites, *J. Geophys. Res.* **72:** 355.

Fleischer, R. L., P. B. Price, R. M. Walker and M. Maurette, 1967b. Origins of fossil charged-particle tracks in meteorites, *J. Geophys. Res.* **72:** 331.

Fodor, R. V., and K. Keil, 1973. Composition and origin of lithic fragments in L- and H-group chondrites, *Meteoritics* **8:** 366.

Fowler, W. A., 1972. What cooks with solar neutrinos?, *Nature* **238:** 24.

Franklin, F. A., and G. Colombo, 1970. A dynamical model for the radical structure of Saturn's rings, *Icarus* **12:** 338.

Fredriksson, K., and P. De Carli, 1964. Shock emplaced argon in a stony meteorite, *J. Geophys. Res.* **69:** 1403.

Fredriksson, K., A. Noonan and J. Nelen, 1973. Meteoritic, lunar and Lonar impact chondrules, *The Moon* **7:** 475.

Freeman, J. W., Jr., M. A. Fenner, R. A. Lindeman, R. Medrano and J. Meister, 1972. Suprathermal ions near the Moon, *Icarus* **16:** 328.

French, B., and N. Short, 1968. *Shock Metamorphism of Natural Meteorites* (Mono Book Corp., Baltimore, Md.).

Fuchs, L. H., 1971. Occurrence of wollastonite, rhönite and andradite in the Allende meteorite, *Amer. Miner* **56:** 2053.

Fuller, M., 1974. Lunar magnetism, *Rev. Geophys. Space Phys.* **12:** 23.

Ganapathy, R., J. C. Laul, J. W. Morgan and E. Anders, 1971. Glazed lunar rocks: origin by impact, *Science* **172:** 556.

Gast, P. W., 1971. The chemical composition of the Earth, the Moon, and chondritic meteorites, in *The Nature of the Solid Earth*, E. C. Robertson, ed. (McGraw-Hill, New York): 19.

Gast, P. W., 1972. The chemical composition and structure of the Moon, *The Moon* **5:** 121.

Gault, D. E., and E. D. Heitowit, 1963. The partition of energy for hypervelocity impact craters formed in rock, in *Sixth Symposium on Hypervelocity Impact, Vol. 2:* 419.

Gault, D. E., E. M. Shoemaker and H. J. Moore, 1963. *Spray Ejected from the Lunar Surface by Meteoroid Impact*, NASA Tech. Note No. D–1767 (Govt. Printing Office, Washington, D.C.).

Gault, D. E., W. L. Quaide and V. R. Oberbeck, 1968. Impact cratering mechanics and structures, in *Shock Metamorphism of Natural Materials*, B. M. French and N. M. Short, eds. (Mono Book Corp., Baltimore, Md.): 87.

Gehrels, T., ed., 1971. *Physical Studies of Minor Planets*, NASA SP–267 (Govt. Printing Office, Washington, D.C.).

Gehrels, T., 1972a. Physical parameters of asteroids and interrelations with comets, in *From Plasma to Planet*, A. Elvius, ed. (Wiley, New York): 169.

Gehrels, T., 1972b. Paper presented at the Coll. on Toro, Tucson, Arizona, Dec., 1972.

Geiss, J., and H. Reeves, 1972. Cosmic and solar system abundances of deuterium and helium-3, *Astron. Astrophys.* **18**: 126.

Gerstenkorn, H., 1955. Über Gezeitenreibung beim Zweikörperproblem, *Z. Astrophys.* **36**: 245.

Gerstenkorn, H., 1968. A reply to Goldreich, *Icarus* **9**: 394.

Gerstenkorn, H., 1969. The earliest past of the Earth-Moon system, *Icarus* **11**: 189.

Gibson, E. K., and S. M. Johnson, 1971. Thermal analysis—inorganic gas release studies of lunar samples, in *Proc. Second Lunar Science Conf., Vol. 2*, A. A. Levinson, ed. (MIT Press, Cambridge, Mass.), 1351.

Gibson, E. K., and S. M. Johnson, 1972. Thermogravimetric-quadrupole mass-spectrometric analysis of geochemical samples, *Thermochim. Acta* **4**: 49.

Gibson, E. K., and G. W. Moore, 1973. Volatile-rich lunar soil: evidence of possible cometary impact, *Science* **179**: 69.

Giuli, R. T., 1968a. On the rotation of the Earth produced by gravitational accretion of particles, *Icarus* **8**: 301.

Giuli, R. T., 1968b. Gravitational accretion of small masses attracted from large distances as a mechanism for planetary rotation, *Icarus* **9**: 186.

Goldreich, P., 1965. An explanation of the frequent occurrence of commensurable motions in the solar system. *Mon. Not. Roy. Astron. Soc.* **130**(3): 159.

Goldreich, P., 1968. On the controversy over the effect of tidal friction upon the history of the Earth-Moon system. A reply to comments by H. Gerstenkorn, *Icarus* **9**: 391.

Goldreich, P., and S. Peale, 1966. Spin-orbit coupling in the solar system, *Astron. J.* **71**: 425.

Goldreich, P., and S. Peale, 1967. Spin-orbit coupling in the solar system II. The resonant rotation of Venus, *Astron. J.* **72**: 662.

Goldreich, P., and S. J. Peale, 1968. The dynamics of planetary rotations, *Ann. Rev. Astron. Astrophys.* **6**: 287.

Goldreich, P., and S. Soter, 1966. Q in the solar system, *Icarus* **5**: 375.

Gollnow, H., 1962. A search for magnetic stars, *Publ. Astron. Soc. Pac.* **74**: 163.

Gopalan, K., and G. W. Wetherill, 1969. Rubidium-strontium age of amphoterite (LL) chondrites, *J. Geophys. Res.* **74**: 4349.

Greenstein, J. L., and C. Arpigny, 1962. The visual region of the spectrum of comet Mrkos (1957d) at high resolution, *Astrophys. J.* **135**: 892.

Grevesse, N., G. Blanquet and A. Boury, 1968. Abondances solaires de quelques éléments représentatifs au point de vue de la nucléo-synthese, in *Origin and Distribution of the Elements*, L. H. Ahrens, ed. (Pergamon, New York): 177.

Grossman, L., and J. Larimer, 1974. Early chemical history of the solar system, *Rev. Geophys. Space Phys.* **12**: 71.

ter Haar, D., 1948. Studies on the origin of the solar system, *Det Kgl. Danske Videnskabs Selskab Mat.-Fys. Meddelelser, København* **25**(3).

ter Haar, D., 1949. Stellar rotation and age, *Astrophys. J.* **110**: 321.

ter Haar, D., 1967. On the origin of the solar system, *Ann. Rev. Astron. Astrophys.* **5**: 267.

Haerendel, G., and R. Lüst, 1970. Electric fields in the ionosphere and magnetosphere. in *Particles and Fields in the Magnetosphere*, B. M. McCormac, ed. (D. Reidel Publ. Co., Dordrecht, Holland): 213.

Hagihara, T., 1961, The stability of the solar system, in *The Solar System, Vol. III, Planets and Satellites*, B. M. Middlehurst and G. P. Kuiper, eds. (Univ. Chicago Press, Chicago, Ill.): 95.

Halliday, I., 1969. Comments on the mean density of Pluto, *Pub. Astron. Soc. Pac.* **81**: 285.

Hamid, S., B. G. Marsden and F. L. Whipple, 1968. Influence of a comet belt beyond Neptune on the motions of periodic comets, *Astron. J.* **73**: 727.

Hanks, T. C., and D. L. Anderson, 1969. The early thermal history of the Earth, *Phys. Earth Planet. Inter.* **2**(1): 19.

Hapke, B. W., A. J. Cohen, W. A. Cassidy and E. N. Wells, 1970. Solar radiation effects on the optical properties of Apollo 11 samples, in *Proc. Apollo 11 Lunar Science Conf., Vol. 3*, A. A. Levinson, ed. (Pergamon Press, New York): 2199.

Harris, P. G., and D. C. Tozer, 1967. Fractionation of iron in the solar system, *Nature* **215**: 1449.

Harteck, P., and J. H. D. Jensen, 1948. Über den Sauerstoffgehalt der Atmosphäre, *Z. Naturforsch.* **3a**: 591.

Hassan, H. A., 1966. Characteristics of a rotating plasma, *Phys. Fluids* **9**: 2077.

Herczeg, T., 1968. Planetary cosmogonics, in *Vistas in Astronomy, Vol. 11*, A. Beer, ed. (Pergamon Press, London): 175.

Heymann, D., 1967. On the origin of hypersthene chondrites: ages and shock effects of black chondrites, *Icarus* **6**: 189.

Hirayama, K., 1918. Researches on the distribution of the mean motion of asteroids, *J. Coll. Sci. Imp. Univ. Tokyo* **41**: article 3.

Hirschberg, J., 1973. Helium abundance of the Sun, *Rev. Geophys. Space Phys.* **11:** 115.

Hohenberg, C. M., and J. H. Reynolds, 1969. Preservation of the iodine-xenon record in meteorites, *J. Geophys. Res.* **74:** 6679.

Holland, H. O., 1964. On the chemical evolution of the terrestrial and cytherean atmospheres, in *The Origin and Evolution of Atmospheres and Oceans,* P. J. Brancazio and A. G. W. Cameron, eds. (Wiley, New York): 86.

Honda, M., and J. R. Arnold, 1967. Effects of cosmic rays on meteorites, in *Handb. Physik, Vol. 46/2,* (Springer-Verlag, Berlin-Heidelberg): 613.

van Houten, C. J., I. van Houten-Groeneveld, P. Herget and T. Gehrels, 1970. The Palomar-Leiden survey of faint minor planets, *Astron. Astrophys. Supp. Ser.* **2:** 339.

Howard, H. T., G. L. Tyler, G. Fjeldbo, A. J. Kliore, G. S. Levy, D. L. Brunn, R. Dickinson, R. E. Edelson, W. L. Martin, R. B. Postal, B. Seidel, T. T. Sesplaukis, D. L. Shirley, C. T. Stelzried, D. N. Sweetnam, A. I. Zygielbaum, P. B. Esposito, J. D. Anderson, I. I. Shapiro and R. D. Reasenberg, 1974. Venus: Mass, gravity, field, atmosphere and ionosphere as measured by the Mariner 10 dual-frequency radio system, *Science* **183:** 1297.

Hoyle, F., 1960. On the origin of the solar nebula, *Quart. J. Roy. Astron. Soc.* **1:** 28.

Hoyle, F., 1963. Formation of the planets, in *Origin of the Solar System,* R. Jastrow and A. G. W. Cameron, eds. (Academic Press, New York): 63.

Hoyle, F., and N. C. Wickramasinghe, 1968. Condensation of the planets, *Nature* **217:** 415.

Hubbard, W. B., 1969. Thermal models of Jupiter and Saturn, *Astrophys. J.* **155:** 333.

Ip, W.-H., 1974a. Studies of Small Bodies in the Solar System, Ph.D. Thesis, Univ. of Calif., San Diego, California.

Ip, W.-H., 1974b. Personal communication.

Ip, W.-H., 1974c. Planetary accretions in jet streams, *Astrophys. Space Sci.* **31:** 57.

Ip, W.-H., and R. Mehra, 1973. Resonances and librations of some Apollo and Amor asteroids with the Earth, *Astron. J.* **78:** 142.

Ip, W., and A. Mendis, 1974. On the effect of accretion and fragmentation in interplanetary matter streams, *Astrophys. Space Sci.* **30:** 233.

Janiczek, P. M., P. K. Seidelmann and R. L. Duncombe, 1972. Resonances and encounters in the inner solar system, *Astron. J.* **77:** 764.

Jedwab, J., 1967. La magnetite en plaquettes des meteorites carbonées d'Alais, Ivuna et Orgueil, *Earth Planet. Sci. Lett.* **2:** 440.

Jefferys, W. H., 1967. Nongravitational forces and resonances in the solar system, *Astron. J.* **72:** 872.

Jeffreys, H., 1962. *The Earth; Its Origin, History and Physical Constitution,* 4th ed. (Cambridge Univ. Press, Cambridge, England).

Johnson, T. V., and F. P. Fanale, 1973. Optical properties of carbonaceous chondrites and their relationship to asteroids, *J. Geophys. Res.* **78:** 8507.

Jokipii, J. R., 1964. The distribution of gases in the protoplanetary nebula, *Icarus* **3:** 248.

Joss, P. C., 1972. Unpublished preprint.

Kaula, W. M., 1968. *An Introduction to Planetary Physics; The Terrestrial Planets* (Wiley, New York).

Kaula, W. M., 1971. Dynamical aspects of lunar origin, *Rev. Geophys. Space Phys.* **9:** 217.

Kaula, W. M., 1974. Mechanical processes affecting differentiation of proto-lunar material, in *The Soviet-American Conference on Cosmochemistry of the Moon and Planets,* NASA SP–370 (U.S. Govt. Printing Office, Washington, D.C.). To be published 1976.

Kaula, W. M., and A. W. Harris, 1973. Dynamically plausible hypotheses of lunar origin, *Nature* **245:** 367.

Kelley, M. C., F. S. Mozer and U. V. Fahleson, 1971. Electric fields in nighttime and daytime auroral zone, *J. Geophys. Res.* **76:** 6054.

Kerridge, J. F., 1970. Some observations on the nature of magnetite in the Orgueil meteorite, *Earth Planet. Sci. Lett.* **9:** 299.

Kerridge, J. F., and J. F. Vedder, 1972. Accretionary processes in the early solar system: an experimental approach, *Science* **177:** 161.

Kiang, T., 1966. Bias-free statistics of orbital elements of asteroids, *Icarus* **5:** 437.

Kinard, W. H., R. L. O'Neal, J. M. Alvarez and D. H. Humes, 1974. Interplanetary and near-Jupiter meteoroid environments: preliminary results from the meteoroid detection experiment, *Science* **183:** 321.

Kirsten, T. A., and O. A. Schaeffer, 1971. High energy interactions in space, in *Elementary Particles Science Technology and Society,* L. C. L. Yuan, ed. (Academic Press, New York): 76.

Kopal, Z., 1966. On the possible origin of the lunar maria, *Nature* **210:** 188.

Kopal, Z., 1973. *The Solar System* (Oxford Univ. Press, New York).

Kresák, Ľ., 1968. Structure and evolution of meteor streams, in *Physics and Dynamics of Meteors,* Ľ. Kresák and P. Millman, eds. (D. Reidel, Dordrecht, Holland): 391.

Kuiper, G. P., 1951. On the origin of the solar system, in *Astrophysics,* J. A. Hynek, ed. (McGraw-Hill, New York): 404.

Kuiper, G. P., 1957. Further studies on the origin of Pluto, *Astrophys. J.* **125:** 287.

Kumar, S. S., 1972. On the formation of Jupiter, *Astrophys. Space Sci.* **16:** 52.

Lal, D., 1972a. Accretion processes leading to formation of meteorite parent bodies, in *From Plasma to Planet,* A. Elvius, ed. (Wiley, New York): 49.

Lal, D., 1972b. A "cometary" suggestion, in *From Plasma to Planet,* A. Elvius, ed. (Wiley, New York): 349.

Lehnert, B., 1966. Ionization process of a plasma, *Phys. Fluids* **9**: 774.

Lehnert, B., 1967a. Experimental evidence of plasma instabilities, *Plasma Phys.* **9**: 301.

Lehnert, B., 1967b. Space-charge effects by nonthermal ions in a magnetized plasma, *Phys. Fluids* **10**: 2216.

Lehnert, B., 1970a. On the conditions for cosmic grain formation, *Cosmic Electrodyn.* **1**: 219.

Lehnert, B., 1970b. Minimum temperature and power effect of cosmical plasmas interacting with neutral gas, *Cosmic Electrodyn.* **1**: 397.

Lehnert, B., 1971. Rotating plasmas, *Nucl. Fus.* **11**: 485.

Levin, B. J., 1972. Origin of the Earth, in *The Upper Mantle,* A. R. Ritsema, ed., *Tectonophysics* **13**: 7.

Levin, B. J., and V. S. Safronov, 1960. Some statistical problems concerning the accumulation of planets, *Theor. Probab. Appl.* **5**: 220.

Lewis, J. S., 1971a. Consequences of the presence of sulfur in the core of the Earth, *Earth Planet. Sci. Lett.* **11**: 130.

Lewis, J. S., 1971b. Satellites of the outer planets: their physical and chemical nature, *Icarus* **15**: 174.

Lin, S.-C., 1961. Limiting velocity for a rotating plasma, *Phys. Fluids* **4**: 1277.

Lin, S.-C., 1966. Cometary impact and the origin of tektites, *J. Geophys. Res.* **71**: 2427.

Lindberg, L., and C. T. Jacobsen, 1964. Studies of plasma expelled from a coaxial plasma gun, *Phys. Fluids Supp.* S44: 844.

Lindberg, L., and L. Kristoferson, 1971. Reverse deflection and contraction of a plasma beam moving along curved magnetic field lines, *Cosmic Electrodyn.* **2**: 305.

Lindberg, L., E. Witalis and C. T. Jacobsen, 1960. Experiments with plasma rings, *Nature* **185**: 452.

Lindblad, B. A., 1935. A condensation theory of meteoritic matter and its cosmological significance, *Nature* **135**: 133.

Lindblad, B. A., and R. B. Southworth, 1971. A study of asteroid families and streams by computer techniques, in *Physical Studies of Minor Planets,* NASA SP–267, T. Gehrels, ed. (Govt. Printing Office, Washington, D.C.): 337.

Lodochnikov, V. N., 1939. Some general problems connected with magma producing basaltic rocks, *Zap. Mineral. O-va* **64**: 207.

Lovell, A. C. B., 1954. *Meteor Astronomy* (Oxford Univ. Press, London).

Lundquist, S., 1951. On the stability of magneto-hydrostatic fields. *Phys. Rev.* **83**: 307.

Lüst, R., and A. Schlüter, 1955. Angular momentum transport by magnetic fields and the braking of rotating stars, *Z. Astrophys.* **38**: 190.

Lyttleton, R. A., 1936. On the possible results of an encounter of Pluto with the Neptunian system, *Mon. Not. Roy. Astron. Soc.* **97**: 108.

Lyttleton, R. A., 1953. *The Comets and Their Origin* (Cambridge Univ. Press, Cambridge, England).

Lyttleton, R. A., 1968. On the distribution of major axes of long-period comets, *Mon. Not. Roy. Astron. Soc.* **139**: 225.

Lyttleton, R. A., 1969. On the internal structures of Mercury and Venus, *Astrophys. Space Sci.* **5**: 18.

Maas, R. W., E. P. Ney and N. J. Woolf, 1970. The 10 micron emission peak of Comet Bennett 1969i, *Astrophys. J., Part 2* **161**: L101.

McCord, T. B., 1966. Dynamical evolution of the Neptunian system, *Astron. J.* **71**: 585.

McCord, T. B., J. B. Adams and T. V. Johnson, 1970. Asteroid Vesta: spectral reflectivity and compositional implications, *Science* **168**: 1445.

McCrea, W. H., 1960. The origin of the solar system, *Proc. Roy. Soc. London* **256**: 245.

McCrosky, R. E., 1970. Fireballs and the physical theory of meteors, *Bull. Astron. Inst. Czechosl.* **21**: 271.

MacDonald, G. J. F., 1966. Origin of the Moon; dynamical considerations, in *The Earth-Moon System,* B. G. Marsden and A. G. W. Cameron, eds. (Plenum Press, New York): 165.

Macdougall, D., B. Martinek and G. Arrhenius, 1972. Regolith dynamics, in *Lunar Science III,* C. Watkins, ed. (The Lunar Science Institute, Houston, Tx.): 498.

Macdougall, D., R. S. Rajan and P. B. Price, 1974. Gas-rich meteorites: possible evidence for origin on a regolith, *Science* **183**: 73.

McQueen, R. L., and S. P. Marsh, 1960. Equations of state for nineteen metallic elements from shock-wave measurements to two megabars, *J. Appl. Phys.* **31**: 1253.

Majeva, S. V., 1971. Thermal history of the Earth with iron core, *Izv. Akad. Nauk SSSR, Fiz. Zemli,* No. 1:3. Eng. trans., *Physics Solid Earth* **1971**: 1.

Malmfors, K. G., 1945. Determination of orbits in the field of a magnetic dipole with applications to the theory of the diurnal variation of cosmic radiation, *Ark. f. Mat. Astr. Fys.* **32A**(8)

Manka, R. H., F. C. Michel, J. W. Freeman, P. Dyal, C. W. Parkin, D. S. Colburn and C. P. Sonett, 1972. Evidence for acceleration of lunar ions, in *Lunar Science III,* C. Watkins, ed., (The Lunar Science Institute, Houston, Tx.): 504.

Marcus, A. H., 1967. Formation of the planets by the accretion of plane-tesimals: some statistical problems, *Icarus* **7**: 283.

Marsden, B. G., 1968. Comets and non-gravitational forces, *Astron. J.* **73**: 367.

Marsden, B. G., 1970. On the relationship between comets and minor planets, *Astron. J.* **75**: 206.

Marti, K., 1973. Ages of the Allende chondrules and inclusions, *Meteoritics* **8**: 55.

Martin, R. F., and G. Donnay, 1972. Hydroxyl in the mantle, *Amer. Mineralogist* **57**: 554.

Mason, B., ed., 1971. *Handbook of Elemental Abundances in Meteorites* (Gordon and Breach Sci. Publ., New York).

Mendis, A., 1973. Comet-meteor stream complex, *Astrophys. Space Sci.* **20**: 165.

Meyer, C., Jr., 1969. *Sputter Condensation of Silicates.* Ph.D. thesis, Scripps Institution of Oceanography, Univ. of Calif., San Diego, California.

Meyer, C., Jr., 1971. An experimental approach to circumstellar condensation, *Geochim. Cosmochim. Acta* **35**: 551.

Millman, P. M., 1972. Cometary meteoroids, in *From Plasma to Planet,* A. Elvius, ed. (Wiley, New York): 157.

Morrison, D., 1973. New techniques for determining sizes of satellites and asteroids, *Comments on Astrophys. Space Phys.* **5**: 51.

Morrison, D., 1974. Albedos and densities of the inner satellites of Saturn, *Icarus* **22**: 51.

Moulton, F. R., 1905. Report of F. R. Moulton, Carnegie Institution Yearbook No. 4 (Carnegie Inst., Tech., Pittsburgh, Penn.): 186.

Mozer, F. S., and U. V. Fahleson, 1970. Parallel and perpendicular electric fields in an aurora, *Planet. Space Sci.* **18**: 1563.

Mrkos, A., 1972. Observation and feature variations of comet 1969e before and during the perihelion passage, in *From Planet to Plasma,* A. Elvius, ed. (Wiley, New York): 261.

Müller, E. A., 1968. The solar abundances, in *Origin and Distribution of the Elements,* L. H. Ahrens, ed., (Pergamon, New York): 155.

Muller, P. M., and W. L. Sjögren, 1969. Lunar gravimetry and mascons, *Appl. Mech. Rev.* **22**: 955.

Munk, W. H., 1968. Once again-tidal friction, *Quart. J. Roy. Astron. Soc.* **9**: 352.

Munk, W., and G. J. F. MacDonald, 1960. *The Rotation of the Earth; a Geophysical Discussion* (Cambridge Univ. Press, Cambridge, England).

Murphy, R. E., D. P. Cruikshank and D. Morrison, 1972. Radii, albedos, and 20-micron brightness temperatures of Iapetus and Rhea, *Astrophys. J., Part 2* **177**: L93.

Murthy, V. R., and H. T. Hall, 1970. On the possible presence of sulfur in the Earth's core, *Phys. Earth Planet. Inter.* **2**: 276.

Murthy, V. R., N. M. Evensen, B. Jahn and M. R. Coscio, Jr., 1971. Rb-Sr ages and elemental abundances of K, Rb, Sr and Ba in samples from the Ocean of Storms, *Geochim. Cosmochim. Acta* **35**: 1139.

The Nautical Almanac, issued annually by the Nautical Almanac Office (Govt. Printing Office, Washington, D.C.).

Neugebauer, G., E. Becklin and A. R. Hyland, 1971. Infrared sources of radiation, *Ann. Rev. Astron. Astrophys.* **9**: 67.

Neukum, G., A. Mehl, H. Fechtig and J. Zahringer, 1970. Impact phenomena of micrometeorites on lunar surface material, *Earth Planet. Sci. Lett.* **8**: 31.

Neuvonen, K. J., B. Ohlson, H. Papunen, T. A. Häkli and P. Ramdohr, 1972. The Haverö ureilite, *Meteoritics* **7**: 515 and subsequent articles.

Newburn, R. L., Jr., and S. Gulkis, 1973. A survey of the outer planets Jupiter, Saturn, Uranus, Neptune, Pluto, and their satellites, *Space Sci. Rev.* **3**: 179.

Newton, H. A., 1891. On the capture of comets by planets, especially their capture by Jupiter, *Mem. Nat. Acad. Sci.* **6**: 7.

Nieto, M. M., 1972. *The Titius-Bode Law of Planetary Distances* (Pergamon Press, New York).

Nordenskiöld, A. E., 1883. *Studier och Forskningar* (Centraltryckeriet, Stockholm).

Ohyabu, N., and N. Kawashima, 1972. Neutral point discharge experiment, *J. Phys. Soc. Japan* **33**: 496.

Oort, J. H., 1963. Empirical data on the origin of comets, in *The Solar System, Vol. IV, The Moon, Meteorites and Comets,* B. M. Middlehurst and G. P. Kuiper, eds. (Univ. Chicago Press, Chicago, Ill.): 665.

Öpik, E. J., 1961. The survival of comets and cometary material, *Astron. J.* **66**: 381.

Öpik, E. J., 1962. Jupiter: chemical composition, structure and origin of a giant planet, *Icarus* **1**: 200.

Öpik, E. J., 1963. The stray bodies in the solar system. Part I, Survival of cometary nuclei and the asteroids, *Advan. Astron. Astrophys.* **2**: 219.

Öpik, E. J., 1966. The dynamical aspects of the origin of comets, in *Nature et Origine des Comètes, Mem. Soc. R. Sci. Liège* **12**: 523.

Öpik, E. J., 1972. Comments on lunar origin, *Irish Astron. J.* **10**: 190.

Orowan, E., 1969. Density of the Moon and nucleation of planets, *Nature* **222**: 867.

Papanastassiou, D. A., and G. J. Wasserburg, 1969. Initial strontium isotopic abundances and the resolution of small time differences in the formation of planetary objects, *Earth Planet. Sci. Lett.* **5**: 361.

Papanastassiou, D. A., and G. J. Wasserburg, 1971a. Lunar chronology and evolution from Rb-Sr studies of Apollo 11 and 12 samples, *Earth Planet. Sci. Lett.* **11**: 37.

Papanastassiou, D. A., and G. J. Wasserburg, 1971b. Rb-Sr ages of igneous rocks from the Apollo 14 mission and the age of the Fra Mauro formation, *Earth Planet. Sci. Lett.* **12**: 36.

Papanastassiou, D. A., C. M. Gray and G. J. Wasserburg, 1973. The identification of early solar condensates in the Allende meteorite, *Meteoritics* **8**: 417.

Pellas, P., 1972. Irradiation history of grain aggregates in ordinary chondrites. Possible clues to the advanced stages of accretion, in *From Plasma to Planet,* A. Elvius, ed. (Wiley, New York): 65.

Persson, H., 1963. Electric field along a magnetic line of force in a low-density plasma, *Phys. Fluids* **6**: 1756.

Persson, H., 1966. Electric field parallel to the magnetic field in a low-density plasma, *Phys. Fluids* **9**: 1090.

Petschek, H. E., 1960. Comment following Alfvén, H., Collision between a nonionized gas and a magnetized plasma, *Rev. Mod. Phys.* **32**: 710.

Piotrowski, S., 1953. The collisions of asteroids, *Acta Astron.* Ser. A5: 115.

Podgorny, I. M., and R. Z. Sagdeev, 1970. Physics of interplanetary plasma and laboratory experiments, *Soviet Phys. Usp.* **12**: 445.

Podosek, F. A., 1970. Dating of meteorites by the high-temperature release of iodine-correlated Xe^{129}, *Geochim. Cosmochim. Acta* **34**: 341.

Porter, J. G., 1961. Catalogue of cometary orbits, *Mem. Brit. Astron. Ass.* **39**(3): 1.

Porter, J. G., 1963. The statistics of comet orbits, in *The Solar System, Vol. IV, The Moon, Meteorites and Comets,* B. M. Middlehurst and G. P. Kuiper, eds. (Univ. Chicago Press, Chicago, Ill.): 550.

Price, P. B., 1973. A cosmochemical view of cosmic rays and solar particles, *Space Sci. Rev.* **15**: 69.

Price, P. B., R. S. Rajan, I. D. Hutcheon, D. Macdougall and E. K. Shirk, 1973. Solar flares, past and present (abst.), in *Lunar Science IV,* J. W. Chamberlain and C. Watkins, eds. (The Lunar Science Institute, Houston, Tx.): 600.

Rabe, E., 1957a. On the origin of Pluto and the masses of the protoplanets, *Astrophys. J.* **125**: 290.

Rabe, E., 1957b. Further studies on the orbital development of Pluto, *Astrophys. J.* **126**: 240.

Ramsey, W. H., 1948. On the constitution of the terrestrial planets, *Mon. Not. Roy. Astron. Soc.* **108**: 406.

Ramsey, W. H., 1949. On the nature of the Earth's core, *Mon. Not. Roy. Astron. Soc., Geophys. Suppl.* **5**: 409.

Rasool, S. I., and C. De Bergh, 1970. The runaway greenhouse and the accumulation of CO_2 in the Venus atmosphere, *Nature* **226**: 1037.

Reid, A. M., and K. Fredriksson, 1967. Chondrules and chondrites, in *Researches in Geochemistry, Vol. 2*, P. H. Abelson, ed. (John Wiley, New York), 170.

Reynolds, R. T., and A. L. Summers, 1965. Models of Uranus and Neptune, *J. Geophys. Res.* **70**: 199.

Richter, N. B., 1963. *The Nature of Comets* (Metheun, London).

Ringwood, A. E., 1959. On the chemical evolution and densities of the planets, *Geochim. Cosmochim. Acta* **15**: 257.

Ringwood, A. E., 1966. Chemical evolution of the terrestrial planets, *Geochim. Cosmochim. Acta* **30**: 41.

Roach, J. R., 1975. Counterglow from the Earth-Moon libration points, *Planet. Space Sci.* **23**: 173.

Roy, A. E., and M. W. Ovenden, 1954. On the occurrence of commensurable mean motions in the solar system, *Mon. Not. Roy. Astron. Soc.* **114**: 232.

Safronov, V. S., 1954. On the growth of planets in the protoplanetary cloud, *Astron. Zh.* **31**: 499.

Safronov, V. S., 1958, The growth of terrestrial planets, *Vopr. Kosmog.* **6**: 63.

Safronov, V. S., 1960. Accumulation of planets of the earth's group, *Vopr. Kosmog. Akad. Nauk SSSR* **7**: 59.

Safronov, V. S., 1969. *Evolution of the preplanetary cloud and the formation of the earth and planets* (Nauka, Moscow) (in Russian).

Safronov, V. S., and E. V. Zvjagina, 1969. Relative sizes of the largest bodies during the accumulation of planets, *Icarus* **10**: 109.

Samara, G. A., 1967. Insulator-to-metal transition at high pressure, *J. Geophys. Res.* **72**: 671.

Schindler, K., 1969. Laboratory experiments related to the solar wind and the magnetosphere, *Rev. Geophys.* **7**: 51.

Schmidt, O. Yu, 1944. Meteoritic theory of the origin of the Earth and planets, *Dokl. Akad. Nauk SSSR* **45**(6): 245.

Schmidt, O. Yu, 1945. Astronomical age of the Earth, *Dokl. Akad. Nauk SSSR* **46**(9): 392.

Schmidt, O. Yu, 1946a. On the law of planetary distances, *Comptes Rendus (Doklady) de l'Academie des Sciences de l'USSR* **52**: 8.

Schmidt, O. Yu, 1946b. A new theory on the origin of the Earth, *Priroda* No. 7: 6.

Schmidt, O. Yu, 1947. A new theory on the origin of the Earth and planets, *Trans. All-Union Geog. Soc.* No. 3: 265.

Schmidt, O. Yu, 1959. *A Theory of the Origin of the Earth; Four Lectures,* G. H. Hanna, trans. (Lawrence and Wishart, London): 139.

Schubart, J., 1968. Long-period effects in the motion of Hilda-type planets, *Astron. J.* **73**: 99.

Schubart, J., 1971. Asteroid masses and densities, in *Physical Studies of Minor Planets*, NASA SP–267, T. Gehrels, ed. (Govt. Printing Office, Washington, D.C.): 33.

Schweizer, F., 1969. Resonant asteroids in the Kirkwood gaps and statistical explanations of the gaps, *Astron. J.* **74**: 779.

Seidelmann, P. K., W. J. Klepczynski, R. L. Duncombe and E. S. Jackson, 1971. Determination of the mass of Pluto, *Astron. J.* **76**: 488.

Sherman, J. C., 1969. *Some Theoretical Aspects of the Interaction between a Plasma Stream and a Neutral Gas in a Magnetic Field*, Report No. 69–29 (Division of Plasma Physics, Roy. Instit. of Tech., Stockholm).

Sherman, J. C. 1972. The critical velocity of gas-plasma interaction and its possible hetegonic relevance, in *From Plasma to Planet*, A. Elvius, ed. (Wiley, New York): 315.

Sherman, J. C., 1973. Review of the critical velocity gas-plasma interaction, part II: theory, *Astrophys. Space Sci.* **24**: 487.

Signer, P., and H. E. Suess, 1963. Rare gases in the sun, in the atmosphere, and in meteorites, in *Earth Science and Meteoritics*, J. Geiss and E. D. Goldberg, eds. (North-Holland Publ. Co., Amsterdam, Holland): 241.

Simakov, G. V., M. A. Podurets and R. F. Trunin, 1973. Novye Dannye o Szhimaemosti Okislov i Ftoridov i Gipoteza ob Odnorodnom Sostave Zmeli, *Dokl. Akad. Nauk SSSR* **211**: 1330.

Sinclair, A. T., 1969. The motions of minor planets close to commensurabilities with Jupiter, *Mon. Not. Roy. Astr. Soc.* **142**: 289.

Singer, S. F., 1968. The origin of the moon and geophysical consequences, *Geophys. J.* **15**: 205.

Singer, S. F., 1970. Origin of the moon by capture and its consequences, *Trans. Am. Geophys. Union* **51**: 637.

Soberman, R. K., S. L. Neste and K. Lichtenfeld, 1974. Particle concentration in the asteroid belt from Pioneer 10, *Science* **183**: 320.

Sockol, P. M., 1968. Analysis of a rotating plasma experiment, *Phys. Fluids* **11**: 637.

Solomon, P., and N. Woolf, 1972. *Interstellar Deuterium: Chemical Fractionation*, Report No. 14 (School of Phys. and Astron., Univ. Minnesota, Minneapolis, Minnesota).

Spitzer, L., 1968. *Diffuse Matter in Space* (Interscience, New York).

Stein, W., 1972. Circumstellar infrared emission—theoretical overview, *Pub. Astron. Soc. Pac.* **84**: 627.

Stenflo, J. O., 1969. A mechanism for the build-up of flare energy, *Solar Phys.* **8**: 115.

Strangway, D. W., W. A. Gose, G. W. Pearce and J. G. Carnes, 1972. Magnetism and the history of the Moon, in *American Institute of Physics Conference Proceedings of Magnetism and Magnetic Materials, No 10:* 1178.

Stuart-Alexander, D. E., and K. A. Howard, 1970. Lunar maria and circular basins—a review, *Icarus* **12:** 440.

Suess, H. E., and H. C. Urey, 1956. Abundances of the elements, *Rev. of Mod. Phys.* **28:** 53.

Swings, P., and T. Page, 1948. The spectrum of Comet 1947n, *Astrophys. J.* **108:** 526.

Takenouchi, T., 1962. On the characteristic motion and the critical argument of asteroid (279) Thule, *Ann. Tokyo Astron. Obser.* **7:** 191.

Taylor, R. C., 1971. Photometric observations and reductions of lightcurves of asteroids, in *Physical Studies of Minor Planets,* NASA SP–267, T. Gehrels, ed. (Govt. Printing Office, Washington, D.C.): 117.

Toksöz, M. N., S. C. Solomon, J. W. Minear and D. H. Johnston, 1972. Thermal evolution of the Moon, *The Moon* **4:** 190.

Torvén, S., 1972. Personal communication.

Trulsen, J., 1971. Collisional focusing of particles in space causing jet streams, in *Physical Studies of Minor Planets,* NASA SP–267, T. Gehrels, ed. (Govt. Printing Office, Washington, D.C.): 327.

Trulsen, J., 1972a. Formation of comets in meteor streams, in *The Motion, Evolution of Orbits and Origin of Comets,* G. A. Chebotarev, et al., eds. (D. Reidel, Dordrecht, Holland): 487.

Trulsen, J., 1972b. Theory of jet streams, in *From Plasma to Planet,* A. Elvius, ed. (Wiley, New York): 179.

Turekian, K. K., and S. P. Clark, Jr., 1969. Inhomogeneous accumulation of the Earth from the primitive solar nebula, *Earth Planet. Sci. Lett.* **6:** 346.

Turner, G., J. C. Huneke, F. A. Podosek and G. J. Wasserburg, 1971. ^{40}Ar–^{39}Ar ages and cosmic ray exposure ages of Apollo 14 samples, *Earth Planet. Sci. Lett.* **12:** 19.

Tuttle, O. F., and J. Gittens, eds., 1966. *Carbonatites* (Interscience, New York).

Urey, H. C., 1952. *The Planets: Their Origin and Development* (Yale Univ. Press, New Haven, Conn.).

Urey, H. C., 1959. The atmosphere of the planets, in *Handbuch der Physik, Vol. 52* (Springer-Verlag, Berlin): 363.

Urey, H. C., 1972. Abundances of the elements, Part IV: Abundances of interstellar molecules and laboratory spectroscopy, *Ann. N. Y. Acad. Sci.* **194:** 35.

Urey, H. C., and G. J. F. Macdonald, 1971. Origin and history of the Moon, in *Physics and Astronomy of the Moon*, Z. Kopal, ed. (Academic Press, New York): 213.

Urey, H. C., and T. Mayeda, 1959. The metallic particles of some chondrites, *Geochim. Cosmochim. Acta* **17**: 113.

Urey, H. C., K. Marti, J. W. Hawkins and M. K. Liu, 1971. Model history of the lunar surface, in *Proc. Second Lunar Science Conf.*, A. A. Levinson, ed. (MIT Press, Cambridge, Mass.): 987.

Van Dorn, W. G., 1968. Tsunamis on the moon? *Nature* **220**: 1102.

Van Dorn, W. G., 1969. Lunar maria: structure and evolution, *Science* **165**: 693.

Van Schmus, W. R., and J. A. Wood, 1967. A chemical-petrological classification for the chondritic meteorites, *Geochim. Cosmochim. Acta* **31**: 747.

Vedder, J. F., 1972. Craters formed in mineral dust by hypervelocity microparticles, *J. Geophys. Res.* **77**: 4304.

Verniani, F., 1967. Meteor masses and luminosity, *Smithsonian Contrib. Astrophys.* **10**: 181.

Verniani, F., 1969. Structure and fragmentation of meteorites, *Space Sci. Rev.* **10**: 230.

Verniani, F., 1973. An analysis of the physical parameters of 5759 faint radio meteors, *J. Geophys. Res.* **78**: 8429.

Vinogradov, A. P., 1962. Origin of the Earth's shells, *Izv. Akad. Nauk SSSR, Ser. Geol.* **11**: 3.

Vinogradov, A. P., A. A. Yaroshevskii and N. P. Il'in, 1971. Physicochemical model of element separation in the differentiation of mantle material, *Phil. Trans. Roy. Soc. London, Ser. A* **268**: 409.

Voshage, H., and H. Hintenberg, 1963. The cosmic-ray exposure ages of iron meteorites as derived from the isotopic composition of potassium and production rates of cosmogenic nuclides in the past, in *Radioactive Dating* (Int. Atomic Energy Agency, Vienna): 367.

Vsekhsvyatsky, S. K., 1958. *Physical Characteristics of Comets* (Nauka, Moscow) (U. S. NASA Tech. Translation F80, 1964).

Wänke, H., 1965. Der Sonnenwind als Quelle der Uredelgase in Steinmeteoriten, *Z. Naturforsch.* **20A**: 946.

Wänke, H., 1966. Meteoritenalter und verwandte Probleme der Kosmochemie, *Fortschr. Chem. Forsch.* **7**: 332.

Wasserburg, G. J., D. A. Papanastassiou and H. G. Sanz, 1969. Initial strontium for a chondrite and the determination of a metamorphism or formation interval, *Earth Planet. Sci. Lett.* **7**: 33.

Wasson, J. T., 1969. Primordial rare gases in the atmosphere of the Earth, *Nature* **223**: 163.

Wasson, J. T., 1972. Formation of ordinary chondrites, *Rev. Geophys. Space Phys.* **10**: 711.

von Weizsäcker, C. F., 1944. Über die Entstehung des Planetsystems, *Z. Astrophys.* **22**: 319.

Wetherill, G. W., 1968. Lunar interior: constraint on basaltic composition, *Science* **160**: 1256.

Wetherill, G. W., and J. G. Williams, 1968. Evaluation of the Apollo asteroids as sources of stone meteorites, *J. Geophys. Res.* **73**: 635.

Whipple, F. L., 1964. Evidence for a comet belt beyond Neptune, *Proc. Nat. Acad. Sci.* **51**: 711.

Whipple, F. L., 1968. Origins of meteoritic matter, in *Physics and Dynamics of Meteors*, L. Kresák and P. Millman, eds. (D. Reidel, Dordrecht, Holland): 481.

Whipple, F. L., 1972. Cometary nuclei—models, in *Comets Scientific Data and Missions*, G. P. Kuiper and E. Roemer, eds. (Lunar and Planetary Laboratory, Univ. Arizona, Tucson, Arizona): 4.

Wiik, H. B., 1956. The chemical composition of some stony meteorites, *Geochim. Cosmochim. Acta* **9**: 279.

Wilcox, J. M., 1972. Why does the Sun sometimes look like a magnetic monopole? in *Comments on Modern Physics, Part C—Comments on Astrophysics and Space Physics* **4**: 141.

Wilkening, L., D. Lal, and A. M. Reid, 1971. The evolution of the Kapoeta howardite based on fossil track studies. *Earth Planet Sci. Lett.* **10**: 334.

Williams, J. G., and G. S. Benson, 1971. Resonances in the Neptune-Pluto System, *Astron. J.* **76**: 167.

Williams, J. G., and G. W. Wetherill, 1973. Minor planets and related objects XIII. Long-term orbital evolution of (1685) Toro, *Astron. J.* **78**(6): 510.

Wood, J. A., 1964. The cooling rates and parent planets of several iron meteorites, *Icarus* **3**: 429.

Wood, J. A., 1967. The early thermal history of planets: evidence from meteorites, in *Mantles of the Earth and Terrestrial Planets*, S. Runcorn, ed. (Interscience, New York): 3.

Wood, J. A., 1970. Petrology of the lunar soil and geophysical implications, *J. Geophys. Res.* **75**: 6497.

Wood, J. A., and H. E. Mitler, 1974. Origin of the Moon by a modified capture mechanism, *or* half a loaf is better than a whole one, in *Lunar Science V* (The Lunar Science Institute, Houston, Tx.): 851.

Worrall, G., and A. M. Wilson, 1972. Can astrophysical abundances be taken seriously?, *Nature* **236**: 15.

Zähringer, J., 1966. Die Chronologie der Chondriten auf Grund von Edelgasisotopen-Analysen, *Meteoritika* **XXVII**: 25.

Zimmerman, P. D., and G. W. Wetherill, 1973. Asteroidal sources of meteorites, *Science* **182:** 51.

Zmuda, A. J., F. T. Heuring and J. H. Martin, 1967. Dayside magnetic disturbances at 1100 kilometers in the auroral oval, *J. Geophys. Res.* **72:** 1115.

SYMBOLS

The symbol index is arranged alphabetically, giving English and then Greek symbols. Astrological symbols appear immediately following the English alphabet. The final portion of the index consists of the most commonly used subscripts. The section and equation numbers appearing in the central column refer to the first use of that symbol. Where one symbol has several distinct usages, each meaning is given with a section reference. For subscripted symbols that do not appear in the main body of the symbol index, the meaning may be determined by looking up the symbol and subscript in the separate portions of the index.

A	Sec. 8.3	Apocenter
A	Sec. 6.4 Eq. (6.4.13)	Variable of substitution
a	Sec. 2.1 Sec. 6.4 Sec. 7.2	Length of semimajor axis Point label Variable of substitution
B	Sec. 5.3	Magnetic field
B_{Tp}	Sec. 19.2	The transplanetary magnetic field (the magnetic field strength in the region of space outside Pluto)
B	Sec. 6.4 Eq. (6.4.14)	Variable of substitution
b	Sec. 4.3 Sec. 7.2	Point label Variable of substitution
C	Sec. 2.1 Eqs. (2.1.1)–(2.1.3)	Orbital angular momentum per unit mass

C_M	Sec. 2.1	Orbital angular momentum
C_r	Sec. 13.1 Eq. (13.1.1)	Spin angular momentum
c	Sec. 5.3 Sec. 6.4 Sec. 7.2	Velocity of light Point label Variable of substitution
D	Sec. 6.7 Eq. (6.7.4)	Net transport of guiding centers
d	Sec. 8.3 Sec. 21.8	Point label Distance between electrodes
E	Sec. 4.3 Eqs. (4.3.4)–(4.3.5) Sec. 5.3 Sec. 9.3	Proper eccentricity Electric field East
E_{ion}	Sec. 21.4.3 Eq. (21.4.4)	The value of the electric field at which discharge and ionization of gas become possible
$E_{||}$	Sec. 15.3	Electric field parallel to the magnetic field
e	Sec. 2.1 Sec. 5.5 Sec. 15.3	Eccentricity 2.718 (the base of the natural logarithms) Charge on the electron
F	Sec. 17.2 Eq. (17.2.4)	Sum of the gravitational, centrifugal, and electromagnetic forces per unit mass
f	Sec. 3.2	Force per unit mass
f_{ap}	Sec. 6.4 Eq. (6.4.3)	Force per unit mass due to apparent attraction to the guiding center of motion
f_B	Sec. 17.2	Electromagnetic force per unit mass
f_c	Sec. 3.2 Eq. (3.2.2)	Centrifugal force per unit mass
f_G	Sec. 3.2	Force per unit mass due to gravitation
f_{per}	Sec. 6.4 Eq. (6.4.4)	Force per unit mass due to a gravitational perturbation
f_q	Sec. 5.3	Electromagnetic force per unit mass

f_t	Sec. 18.3 Eq. (18.3.2)	Tidal force per unit mass
f_Ψ	Sec. 5.5	Force per unit mass due to impinging energy flux; radiation pressure
G	Sec. 2.1	Universal gravitational constant
$\mathcal{g}$	Sec. 4.3 Sec. 8.2	Absolute visual magnitude Acceleration due to Earth's gravitational field
h	Sec. 2.2 Sec. 9.2	Height above a specified surface Height of tides on a celestial body
I	Sec. 4.3 Eqs. (4.3.6)–(4.3.7) Sec. 15.4	Proper inclination Electric current
i	Sec. 2.1	Orbital inclination to the ecliptic plane
i_{eq}	Sec. 2.2	Inclination of equator to the orbital plane
i_τ	Sec. 13.6	Inclination of spin axis to the orbital plane
K	Sec. 11.2 Eq. (11.2.3) Sec. 23.2	Constant, in cm/g Constant, in units of mass
K_r	Sec. 3.3 Eq. (3.3.9)	Constant, in radians
K_z	Sec. 3.3 Eq. (3.3.17)	Constant, in radians
k	Sec. 6.8	Boltzmann's constant
L	Sec. 1.4 Eq. (15.1.1) Sec. 8.5 Sec. 16.3 Fig. 16.3.1 Sec. 26.3 Eq. (26.3.2)	Critical hydromagnetic parameter Lagrangian points one and two Electrostatic double layer Latent heat of fusion
L_4, L_5	Sec. 20.5	Lagrangian points four and five
l	Sec. 8.2	Length of a simple pendulum or the radial distance of a secondary body describing

	Sec. 15.1	circular motion about a primary body
		Length (linear extent of medium)
M	Sec. 4.1	Mass of a macroscopic body
M_B	Sec. 16.4	Total mass of plasma suspended by the magnetic field at any one given time
M_{H_2O}	Sec. 26.4	Mass of water released by impacting
	Eq. (26.4.2)	planetesimals
M_j	Sec. 12.5	Mass of a jet stream
m	Sec. 5.4	Mass of a small particle or grain
m_a	Sec. 11.2	Mass of an atom
m_e	Sec. 21.9	Mass of the electron
m_H	Sec. 11.2	Mass of the hydrogen atom
m_{per}	Sec. 6.4	Small mass introducing a perturbative
	Eq. (6.4.4)	gravitational force
N	Sec. 4.3	Number function
	Sec. 9.3	North
N	Sec. 6.7	Number density
n	Sec. 2.2	Index of numeration
	Sec. 3.3	The integers
	Eq. (3.3.15)	
O	Sec. 4.3	The center or origin of motion
P	Sec. 8.3	Pericenter
P_B	Sec. 15.1	Magnetic permeability
P_0	Sec. 4.3	Forced oscillation
	Eq. (4.3.6)	
p	Sec. 4.3	Albedo
p_0	Sec. 4.3	Forced oscillation
	Eq. (4.3.4)	
Q	Sec. 9.2	An inverse function of the angle which a tidal bulge makes with respect to the tide-producing body
	Sec. 16.3	Charge passing through a circuit during a given interval of time

534

$\mathcal{Q}_0$	Sec. 4.3 Eq. (4.3.7)	Forced oscillation
q	Sec. 2.5	Ratio of the orbital distances of the innermost and outermost orbiting bodies in one group of secondary bodies
	Sec. 5.3	Electric charge
q_n	Sec. 2.2	Ratio of the orbital distances of adjacent secondary bodies
q_0	Sec. 4.3 Eq. (4.3.5)	Forced oscillation
R	Sec. 2.2	Radius of a solid body
R_G	Sec. 12.3 Eq. (12.3.4)	Radius of growing embryo at transition point between nongravitational accretion and gravitational accretion
R_{Ξ}	Sec. 2.2	Radius of gyration; inertial radius
r	Sec. 2.4 Sec. 3.2	Orbital radius Radial direction
r_B	Sec. 23.2 Eq. (23.2.2)	Distance from the central body to a point on a magnetic field line from the dipole magnetic field of that body
r_{ion}	Sec. 21.4 Eq. (21.4.1)	Ionization distance (radial distance at which infalling matter can become ionized)
r_L	Sec. 11.2 Eq. (11.2.4)	Distance from a secondary body to its interior or exterior Lagrangian points one and two
r_{min}	Sec. 23.9 Eq. (23.9.6)	Minimum value of orbital radius of condensed matter which is in orbit around the primary body
r_{MR}	Sec. 18.3	The Modified Roche Limit (the radial distance at which matter orbiting a primary body cannot accrete to form a secondary body due to the tidal force of the primary)
r_{orb}	Sec. 2.1	Radial distance from primary body to orbiting secondary body

r_{per}	Sec. 6.4 Eq. (6.4.4)	Radial distance of the perturbing mass m_{per} from the guiding center of motion of another mass.
r_R	Sec. 18.3	The Roche limit (the radial distance at which the tidal force of the primary exceeds the self-gravitational force of the secondary)
r_{rel}	Sec. 21.13.3	Orbital distance at which ionization can take place for matter falling through a corotating plasma
r_s	Sec. 17.2 Eq. (17.2.13)	Radius of the surface which is the demarcation for plasma falling in toward the central body or falling into the equatorial plane
r_{syn}	Sec. 23.9	Orbital radius of a synchronous satellite; i.e., a satellite revolving with orbital velocity equal to the rotational velocity of its primary
r_{Tp}	Sec. 19.2 Eq. (19.2.2)	The maximum radial distance at which angular momentum transfer from the Sun has ever occurred; furthest extension of the transplanetary magnetic field.
S	Sec. 6.4 Eq. (6.4.3) Sec. 9.3	Displacement from the guiding center of motion of the particle executing that motion South
s	Sec. 16.3	Arc length
T	Sec. 2.1	Sidereal period of revolution
T_e	Sec. 5.5 Eq. (5.5.10)	e-folding time (the time in which the value of a given parameter changes by a factor of e (2.718))
T_{gy}	Sec. 5.4	Period of gyration
T_{gz}	Sec. 2.2	Sidereal period of revolution of a grazing satellite; i.e., a secondary body having an orbit of semimajor axis equal to the radius of the primary body
T_{ion}	Sec. 23.1	Orbital period of a body orbiting at the ionization distance r_{ion}

T_Φ	Sec. 4.3	Period of variation in the proper elements of asteroid orbital motion
T	Sec. 6.8	Temperature
T_e	Sec. 17.3	Electron temperature
T_i	Sec. 17.3	Ion temperature
t	Sec. 3.3	Time
t_a	Sec. 12.3	Time of accretion (time at which an accreting embryo would attain an infinite radius)
t_c	Sec. 12.6 Eq. (12.6.6)	Time of catastrophic increase of an accreting embryo
t_{es}	Sec. 2.2 Eq. (2.2.3)	"Time of escape" (the ratio of the radius of a body to its escape velocity)
t_I	Sec. 16.3 Eq. (16.3.5)	Duration of a current flow
t_{inf}	Sec. 12.4	Infall time (duration of infall of matter into the solar system)
t_j	Sec. 12.5 Eq. (12.5.8)	Time at which the small radius of a contracting jet stream would reach zero
t_{res}	Sec. 16.5	Residence time (the interval in which matter resides in the plasma state)
t_ν	Sec. 6.8	Time between occurrence of collisions; inverse of collision frequency
U	Sec. 12.2 Eq. (12.2.3)	Volume of a toroidal jet stream
u	Sec. 6.8	Relative velocity; "internal velocity" of a jet stream
V	Sec. 5.4	Electrostatic potential; voltage
V_b	Sec. 21.8	Burning voltage
V_{Ion}	Sec. 15.3	Ionization voltage
v	Sec. 5.5	Velocity
v_{crit}	Sec. 15.3 Eq. (15.3.1)	Critical velocity at which an infalling atom can become ionized

	Sec. 21.8	The experimental value of relative velocity of a plasma and a gas at which increased ionization occurs.
v_{es}	Sec. 2.2 Eq. (2.2.2)	Escape velocity
v_{imp}	Sec. 12.10 Eq. (12.10.1)	Impact velocity
v_{ion}	Sec. 21.4 Eq. (21.4.1)	The value of infall velocity at which ionization of infalling matter can take place
v_m	Sec. 12.12 Eq. (12.12.1)	Velocity capable of imparting sufficient kinetic energy to melt a specified mass
v_{orb}	Sec. 2.1	Orbital velocity of secondary body
v_{rel}	Sec. 21.13 Eq. (21.13.3)	Relative velocity
W	Sec. 8.2 Sec. 9.3	Energy (potential and/or kinetic) West
W_m	Sec. 12.12	Energy needed to melt a specified mass
W_T	Sec. 17.3	Thermal energy
w	Sec. 9.2	Energy dissipation; power
w_T	Sec. 12.10 Eq. (12.10.2)	Thermal power per unit surface area delivered by impacting mass
X	Sec. 13.4 Eq. (13.4.3)	Variable of substitution
x	Sec. 3.2 Sec. 12.2	Rectilinear coordinate lying in the horizontal plane Small radius of a toroidal jet stream
x_0	Sec. 6.4	Magnitude of the x axis of the epicycle described about a guiding center
Y	Sec. 13.4 Eq. (13.4.4)	Variable of substitution
y	Sec. 3.2	Rectilinear coordinate lying in the horizontal plane
Z	Sec. 13.3 Eq. (13.3.4)	Variable of substitution

z	Sec. 3.2	Rectilinear coordinate in the axial direction
☉	Sec. 2.3 Fig. 2.3.1	Sun
☿	Sec. 2.1 Table 2.1.1	Mercury
♀	Sec. 2.1 Table 2.1.1	Venus
⊕	Sec. 2.1 Table 2.1.1	Earth
☽	Sec. 2.1 Table 2.1.1	Moon
♂	Sec. 2.1 Table 2.1.1	Mars
♃	Sec. 2.1 Table 2.1.1	Jupiter
♄	Sec. 2.1 Table 2.1.1	Saturn
♅	Sec. 2.1 Table 2.1.1	Uranus
♆	Sec. 2.1 Table 2.1.1	Neptune
♇	Sec. 2.1 Table 2.1.1	Pluto
☊	Sec. 17.5	Ascending node
☋	Sec. 17.5	Descending node
α	Sec. 6.8 Sec. 7.2 Eq. (7.2.4)	Dimensionless proportionality factor Dimensionless constant
α_z	Sec. 2.2	Ratio of radius of gyration to equatorial radius of body
α_z^2	Sec. 2.2	Normalized moment of inertia (moment of inertia per unit mass and unit radius squared)

539

β	Sec. 7.2	Dimensionless constant
	Eq. (7.2.5)	
	Sec. 11.2	Dimensionless proportionality factor
Γ	Sec. 21.2	Specific gravitational potential of second-
	Eq. (21.2.1)	ary body with respect to the primary body
Γ_{ion}	Sec. 21.4	Value of gravitational potential at which
	Eq. (21.4.2)	infalling matter can become ionized
γ	Sec. 5.5	Dimensionless proportionality factor
	Eq. (5.5.4)	
	Sec. 7.2	Dimensionless constant
	Eq. (7.2.6)	
γ_B	Sec. 16.5	Dimensionless proportionality factor
	Eq. (16.5.1)	
Δ	Sec. 3.3	Indicating incremental change
δ	Sec. 6.7	Geometrical factor
	Eq. (6.7.1)	
	Sec. 12.10	Dimensionless proportionality factor in-
	Eq. (12.10.6)	dicating maximum in temperature profile of an accreting embryo
	Sec. 17.3	Degree of ionization
	Sec. 23.5	Dimensionless proportionality factor; the normalized distance (the ratio of the or- bital radius of a body to the ionization distance for its primary body)
ϵ	Sec. 9.2	An angle
ζ	Sec. 23.1	Dimensionless proportionality factor in-
	Eqs. (23.1.4)–(23.1.5)	dicating degree of ionization of infalling matter
η	Sec. 9.3	Viscosity
Θ	Sec. 2.2	Mean density of a body
θ	Sec. 8.3	An angle
κ	Sec. 8.2	Constant of integration
	Eq. (8.2.3)	
Λ	Sec. 3.6	Dimensionless constant
	Eq. (3.6.1)	

λ	Sec. 3.2	Meridional angle or latitude
μ	Sec. 16.3	Magnetic dipole moment
μ_{lm}	Sec. 16.4	Lower limit of the magnetic dipole moment such that the tangential component of the magnetic field is equal to the magnitude of the total magnetic field strength
ν	Sec. 6.8	Collision frequency; number of collisions per unit time
Ξ	Sec. 13.1	Moment of inertia
ξ	Sec. 8.4 Eq. (8.4.1)	Libration angle
π	Sec. 2.1	3.1415 . . . . . (ratio of the circumference to the diameter of a circle)
ρ	Sec. 6.8	Density of dispersed matter
ρ_{dst}	Sec. 2.4 Eqs. (2.4.1)–(2.4.2)	Distributed density (density of a secondary body's mass when distributed along the orbit of that secondary)
Σ	Sec. 2.1	Indicating summation
σ	Sec. 5.5 Sec. 6.8 Sec. 12.3 Eq. (12.3.1)	Cross section Collision cross section Capture cross section
σ_E	Sec. 15.1	Electrical conductivity
σ_j	Sec. 12.7	Cross section of a jet stream
τ	Sec. 2.2	Spin period of a body
Υ	Sec. 9.2 Eq. (9.2.1)	Oblateness or ellipticity of a body
Φ	Sec. 15.3	Magnetic flux
Φ_p	Sec. 15.3	Poloidal magnetic flux
Φ_P	Sec. 4.3 Eqs. (4.3.4)–(4.3.5)	Longitude of proper perihelion
Φ_Ω	Sec. 4.3 Eqs. (4.6)–(4.7)	Longitude of proper node

ϕ	Sec. 3.2	Azimuthal angle or longitude
χ	Sec. 6.7 Eq. (6.7.5) Sec. 11.2 Eq. (11.2.2)	Constant, in number/cm³ Constant, in cm K/g
χ_m	Sec. 7.2 Eq. (7.2.6)	Constant, in units of number times a variable power of mass
χ_R	Sec. 7.2 Eq. (7.2.4)	Constant, in units of number times a variable power of radius
χ_σ	Sec. 7.2 Eq. (7.2.5)	Constant, in units of number times a variable power of cross section
Ψ	Sec. 5.5	Energy flux
ψ	Sec. 8.2	An angle
Ω	Sec. 9.3	Rotational angular velocity
Ω_{es}	Sec. 13.3 Eq. (13.3.3)	Rotational escape velocity
ω	Sec. 6.4	Orbital angular velocity

Subscripts

c	Central or primary body
sc	Secondary body
em	Embryo
gn	Grain
Lm	Limiting value
0	Initial value or parameter values for the guiding center or circular motion
K	Denoting orbital parameters for a body describing Kepler (circular) motion
A	Apocenter, aphelion, apogee, etc.
P	Pericenter, perihelion, perigee, etc.
Ω	Ascending (and descending) node
x, y, z	Components in the x, y, and z directions
r, ϕ, λ	Components in the r, ϕ, and λ directions

☉, ☿, ♀, ⊕, ☽, ♂,   Sun, Mercury, Venus, Earth, Moon, Mars,

♃, ♄, ♅, ♆, ♇   Jupiter, Saturn, Uranus, Neptune, Pluto

INDEX

☆ U.S. GOVERNMENT PRINTING OFFICE: 1976 O—575—780